ASPEN PUBLISHERS

CONTRACTS

7TH EDITION

D1232777

NEIL C. BLOND

LOUIS PETRILLO

Seventh Edition Revised By

David Gruning

William L. Crowe Sr. Distinguished Professor of Law
Loyola University
New Orleans College of Law

 Wolters Kluwer

Law & Business

AUSTIN   BOSTON   CHICAGO   NEW YORK   THE NETHERLANDS

To contact Customer Care, e-mail customer.care@aspenpublishers.com, call 1-800-234-1660, fax 1-800-901-9075, or mail correspondence to:

Aspen Publishers
Attn: Order Department
PO Box 990
Frederick, MD 21705

Printed in the United States of America.
1 2 3 4 5 6 7 8 9 0

ISBN 978-0-7355-8613-0

About Wolters Kluwer Law & Business

Wolters Kluwer Law & Business is a leading provider of research information and workflow solutions in key specialty areas. The strengths of the individual brands of Aspen Publishers, CCH, Kluwer Law International and Loislaw are aligned within Wolters Kluwer Law & Business to provide comprehensive, in-depth solutions and expert-authored content for the legal, professional and education markets.

CCH was founded in 1913 and has served more than four generations of business professionals and their clients. The CCH products in the Wolters Kluwer Law & Business group are highly regarded electronic and print resources for legal, securities, antitrust and trade regulation, government contracting, banking, pension, payroll, employment and labor, and healthcare reimbursement and compliance professionals.

Aspen Publishers is a leading information provider for attorneys, business professionals and law students. Written by preeminent authorities, Aspen products offer analytical and practical information in a range of specialty practice areas from securities law and intellectual property to mergers and acquisitions and pension/benefits. Aspen's trusted legal education resources provide professors and students with high-quality, up-to-date and effective resources for successful instruction and study in all areas of the law.

Kluwer Law International supplies the global business community with comprehensive English-language international legal information. Legal practitioners, corporate counsel and business executives around the world rely on the Kluwer Law International journals, loose-leafs, books and electronic products for authoritative information in many areas of international legal practice.

Loislaw is a premier provider of digitized legal content to small law firm practitioners of various specializations. Loislaw provides attorneys with the ability to quickly and efficiently find the necessary legal information they need, when and where they need it, by facilitating access to primary law as well as state-specific law, records, forms and treatises.

Wolters Kluwer Law & Business, a unit of Wolters Kluwer, is headquartered in New York and Riverwoods, Illinois. Wolters Kluwer is a leading multinational publisher and information services company.

Check Out These Other Great Titles:

BLOND'S LAW GUIDES

Comprehensive, Yet Concise . . . JUST RIGHT!

Each Blond's Law Guide book contains: Black Letter Law Outline · EasyFlow™ Charts · Case Clips · Mnemonics

Available titles in this series include:

Blond's Civil Procedure

Blond's Constitutional Law

Blond's Contracts

Blond's Criminal Law

Blond's Criminal Procedure

Blond's Evidence

Blond's Property

Blond's Torts

ASK FOR THEM AT YOUR LOCAL BOOKSTORE
IF UNAVAILABLE, PURCHASE ONLINE AT http://lawschool.aspenpublishers.com

Law school is very different from your previous educational experiences. In the past, course material was presented in a straightforward manner both in lectures and texts. You did well by memorizing and regurgitating. In law school, your fat casebooks are stuffed with material, most of which will be useless when finals arrive. Your professors ask a lot of questions but don't seem to be teaching you either the law or how to think. Sifting through voluminous material seeking out the important concepts is a hard, time-consuming chore. We've done that job for you. This book will help you study effectively. We hope to teach you the law and how to think.

Preparing for Class

Most students start their first year by reading and briefing all their cases. They spend too much time copying unimportant details. After finals they realize they wasted time on facts that were useless on the exam.

Case Clips

Case Clips help you focus on what your professor wants you to get out of your cases. Facts, Issues, and Rules are carefully and succinctly stated. Left out are details irrelevant to what you need to learn from the case. In general, we skip procedural matters in lower courts. We don't care which party is the appellant or petitioner because the trivia is not relevant to the law. Case Clips should be read before you read the actual case. You will have a good idea what to look for in the case, and appreciate the significance of what you are reading. Inevitably you will not have time to read all your cases before class. Case Clips allow you to prepare for class in about five minutes. You will be able to follow the discussion and listen without fear of being called upon.

"Should I read all the cases even if they aren't from my casebook?"

Yes, if you feel you have the time. Most major cases from other texts will be covered at least as a note case in your book. The principles of these cases are universal and the fact patterns should help your understanding. The Case Clips are written in a way that should provide a tremendous amount of understanding in a relatively short period of time.

EasyFlow™ Charts

A very common complaint among law students is that they "can't put it all together." When you are reading 400 pages a week it is difficult to remember how the last case relates to the first and how November's readings relate to September's. It's hard to understand the relationship between different torts topics when you have read cases for three or four other classes in between. Our EasyFlow™ Charts will help you put the whole course together. They are designed to help you memorize fundamentals. They reinforce your learning by showing you the material from another perspective.

Outlines

More than one hundred lawyers and law students were interviewed as part of the development of this series. Most complained that their casebooks did not teach them the law and were far too voluminous to be useful before an exam. They also told us that the commercial outlines they purchased were excellent when used as hornbooks to explain the law, but were too wordy and redundant to be effective during the weeks before finals. Few students can read four 500-page outlines during the last month of classes. It is virtually impossible to memorize that much material and even harder to decide what is important. Almost every student interviewed said he or she studied from homemade outlines. We've written the outline you should use to study.

"But writing my own outline will be a learning experience."

True, but unfortunately many students spend so much time outlining they don't leave time to learn and memorize. Many students told us they spent six weeks outlining, and only one day studying before each final!

Mnemonics

Most law students spend too much time reading, and not enough time memorizing. Mnemonics are included to help you organize your essays and spot issues. They highlight what is important and which areas deserve your time.

CONTENTS

EASYFLOW™ CHARTS

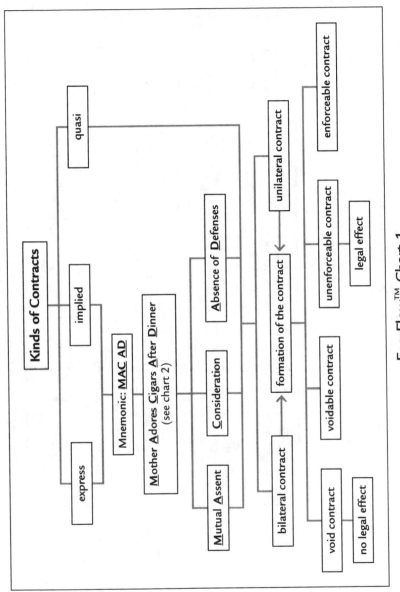

EasyFlow™ Chart 1

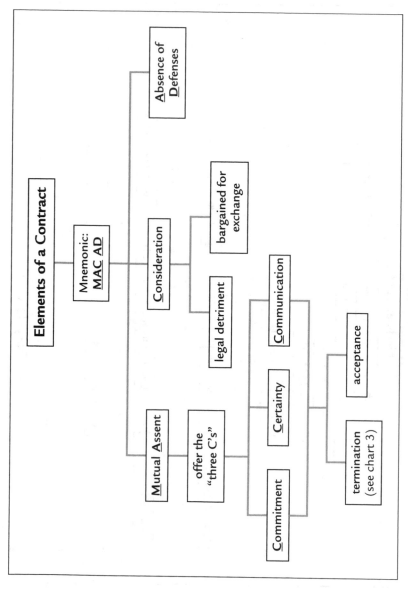

EasyFlow™ Chart 2

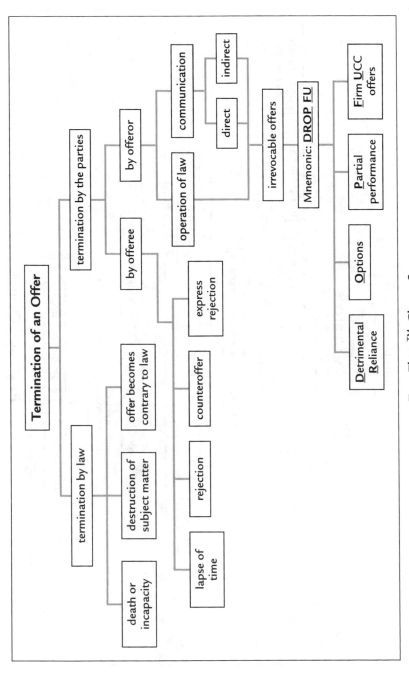

EasyFlow™ Chart 3

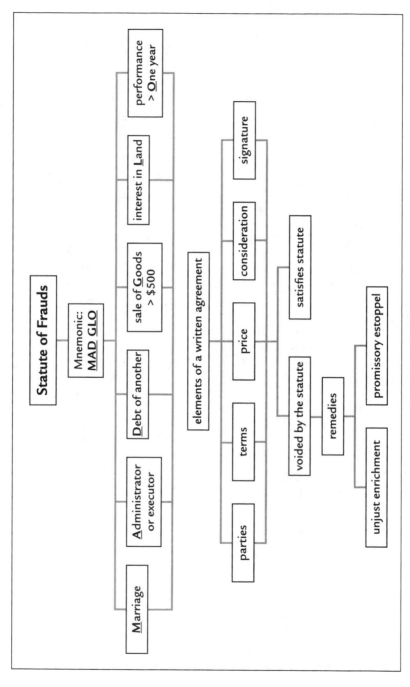

EasyFlow™ Chart 4

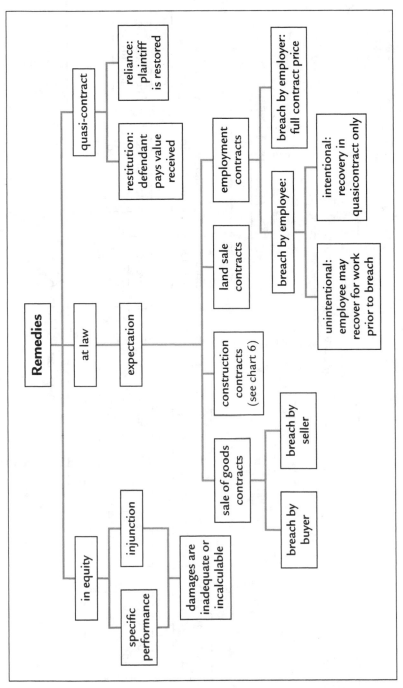

EasyFlow™ Chart 5

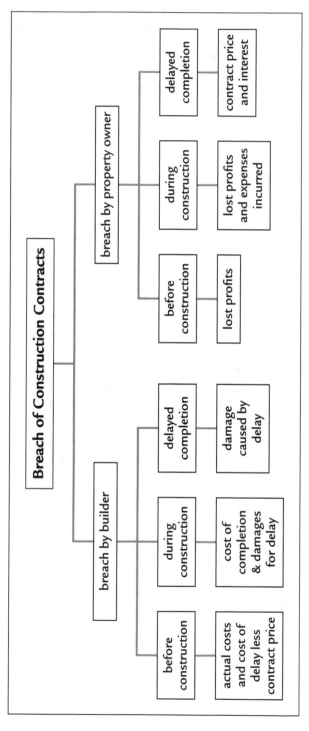

Breach of Construction Contracts

breach by builder

breach by property owner

before construction — actual costs and cost of delay less contract price

during construction — cost of completion & damages for delay

delayed completion — damage caused by delay

before construction — lost profits

during construction — lost profits and expenses incurred

delayed completion — contract price and interest

EasyFlow™ Chart 6

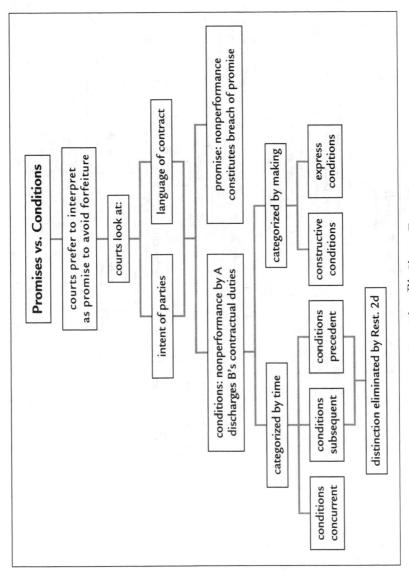

Promises vs. Conditions

courts prefer to interpret as promise to avoid forfeiture

courts look at:

- intent of parties
- language of contract

conditions: nonperformance by A discharges B's contractual duties

promise: nonperformance constitutes breach of promise

categorized by time

- conditions concurrent
- conditions subsequent
- conditions precedent

distinction eliminated by Rest. 2d

categorized by making

- constructive conditions
- express conditions

EasyFlow™ Chart 7

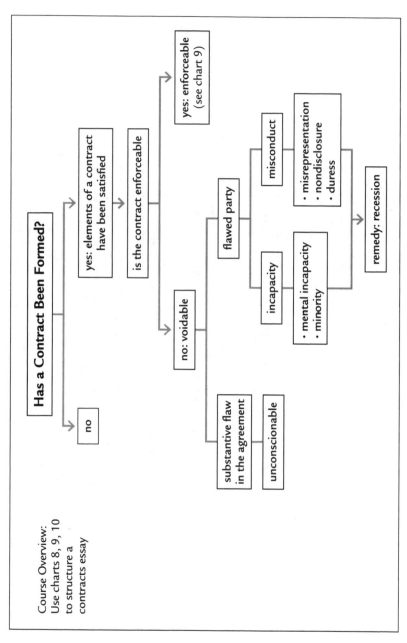

Course Overview:
Use charts 8, 9, 10
to structure a
contracts essay

Has a Contract Been Formed?

no

yes: elements of a contract
have been satisfied

is the contract enforceable

yes: enforceable
(see chart 9)

no: voidable

substantive flaw
in the agreement

unconscionable

flawed party

incapacity

misconduct

· mental incapacity
· minority

· misrepresentation
· nondisclosure
· duress

remedy: recession

EasyFlow™ Chart 8

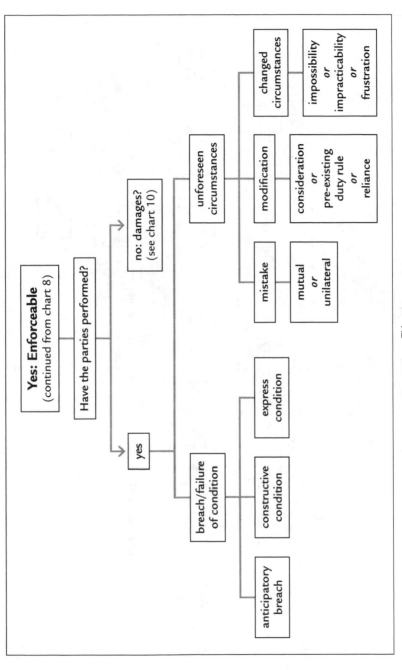

EasyFlow™ Chart 9

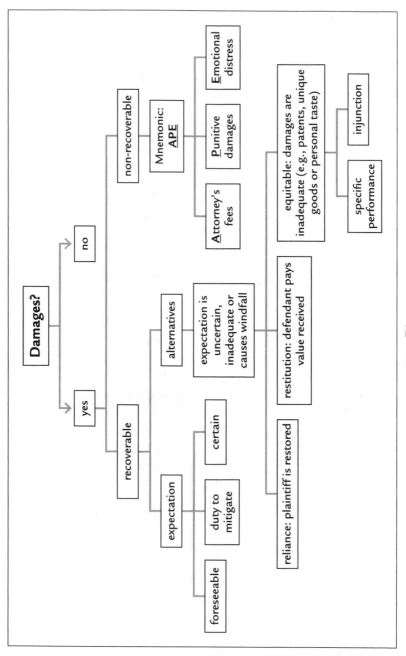

EasyFlow™ Chart 10

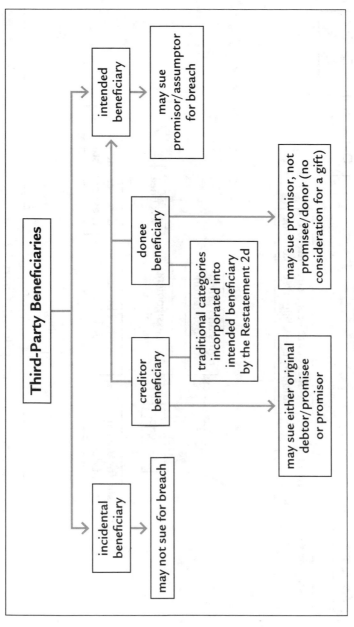

EasyFlow™ Chart 11

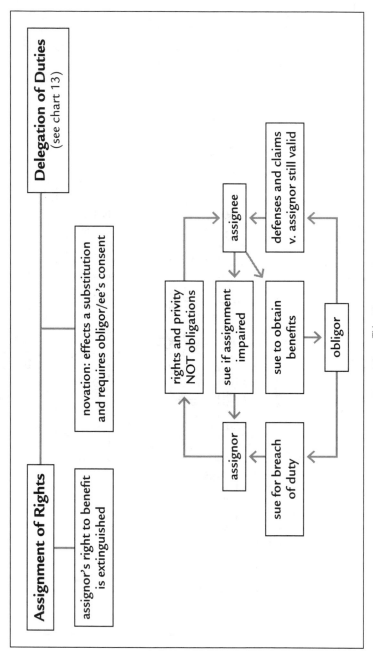

Delegation of Duties
(see chart 13)

novation: effects a substitution
and requires obligor/ee's consent

Assignment of Rights

assignor's right to benefit
is extinguished

rights and privity
NOT obligations

assignee

defenses and claims
v. assignor still valid

sue if assignment
impaired

sue to obtain
benefits

obligor

assignor

sue for breach
of duty

EasyFlow™ Chart 12

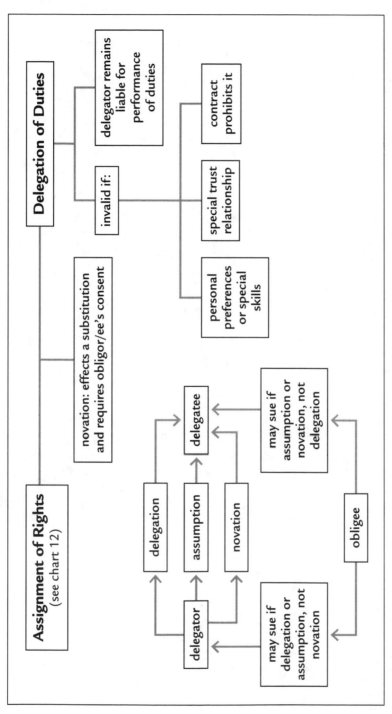

EasyFlow™ Chart 13

Introduction to Contracts

I. CONTRACT DEFINED

A contract is a promise that the law enforces. By enforcement we typically understand some action in court producing an order that compels a promisor either to pay damages for failing to perform his promise or for failing to perform it properly or that compels the promisor to produce the very result the promise held forth to the promisee. There are also other ways in which the law may recognize the enforceability of a promise, but this is the essential core of the idea. And in most contracts you study in your contracts course, there the promise of one party is matched with the promise of the other party. But at any moment, the law will focus on the particular promise whose enforcement must be decided.

II. KINDS OF CONTRACTS

A. Express Contracts

A contract is express when the promisor makes the promise at issue expressly, that is, in words. Sometimes the promisor states "I promise to do X" or "I promise to pay Y dollars" or "I promise to deliver 100 widgets tomorrow" or "I promise not to do Z for 12 months." In each case, there is a promise — an express commitment in words by the promisor. The words may be written or oral; either way, the promise is express. Likewise, without using the particular word "promise" other words are used to express the same idea: the communication of a commitment by the speaker, which also shows an intent to be bound by that commitment. In express contracts we read or hear the words of a party and decide whether they are a promise.

B. Contracts Implied in Fact

A contract is said to be implied in fact when words are not used to express the commitment of the promisor, but some action does so. This occurs in some cases in which the parties agree that a certain action by one of them indicates that he is making a commitment to perform, making a promise. In ancient example, the parties may agree to a contract of exchange, even if they don't speak the same language: each one shows the other what item she wants to exchange for some item the other has, making basic gestures of disapproval and, finally, approval. In several cases, courts found the parties had agreed that beginning to perform would indicate a commitment by one of the parties. As with express contracts, in contracts that are implied in fact, we are "reading" not the words of a party but his action or actions to decide whether a promise exists.

C. Contracts Implied in Law (Quasi-Contracts)

Contracts may also be implied in law. This is quite distinct from a contract implied in fact, despite the similarity of the label. With express and implied-in-fact contracts, we can say that there is a promise, based on the words or actions of the promisor. With a contract implied in law, however, we know that in fact there is no promise at all. Still, the law provides a remedy as if there were an enforceable promise. Hence, implied-in-law contracts are also known as quasi-contracts, the Latin word "quasi" meaning "as if." It's helpful to remember that quasi-contracts are not truly contracts at all; they are not promises that the law enforces. Quasi-contracts are best understood instead as a remedy that tracks the remedy that would properly be granted if the party against whom the remedy is sought had in fact made a promise. **Example:** A man is injured by a streetcar and rendered unconscious; a doctor renders medical assistance competently, but the accident victim dies without regaining consciousness. The doctor's remedy against the victim's estate for payment of his fee is not in contract (the victim never made a promise, either express or implied), but in quasi-contract for the fee the doctor ordinarily charges for such services.

D. Unilateral-Bilateral Distinction

1. Bilateral Contract: Promise for Promise

If each party makes a promise to the other, and if each promise is made in exchange for the other promise, the contract is **bilateral**. Each party is bargaining, so to speak, for the promise of the other party.

Example: A promises B that he will sell B ten baseball cards, and B promises to pay A one dollar.

2. Unilateral Contract: Promise for Performance

In a unilateral contract, one party makes a promise in exchange for a performance by the other party. The promisor is bargaining for the performance, and does not want a promise for his promise.

Example: A promises to pay B $100 if B paints A's home. A is not bargaining for B's promise to paint the house, but for the painting of the house by B.

3. Distinguishing Unilateral and Bilateral Contracts

Bilateral and unilateral contracts impose different obligations on the parties. In a bilateral contract, both parties are bound once they make their promises. In a unilateral contract, in principle neither party is bound until the promisee finishes the performance that the promisor bargained for. Likewise, if the promisee in a unilateral contract starts to perform and then stops, the promisor has no action against him for breach. And the promisor may withdraw his promise before the promisee finishes the performance, since strictly speaking there is no contract until the performance is complete.

Example: A promises B he will pay him $100 if B walks across the Brooklyn Bridge. When B is halfway across, A may still withdraw his promise because he is not bound to pay the $100 until B completes the performance.

The result in the example is the classic view, but it is clearly unsatisfactory. The current view is that the start of performance by the promisee renders the promisor's offer irrevocable.

The difference between unilateral and bilateral contracts is not as important today as in the past. One significant difference, however, is the extent of the obligations they impose. Once parties exchange promises in bilateral contracts, they are obligated to perform their promises. In a unilateral contract, the nonpromising party is not obligated to perform and the promisor's obligation does not arise until the requested act is completed.

III. VALIDITY OF CONTRACTS

A. Enforceable

An enforceable contract is one that the law recognizes and therefore enforces in some way.

Enforcement may occur through a decree of specific performance — making the promisor perform his promise. Or it may occur through an award of damages that is intended to compensate the promisee for the loss of the promised performance.

B. Void
A void contract is one that the law refuses to recognize at all and therefore has no legal effect.
Example: A promises B that he will pay her $100 for throwing a cream pie in the face of a candidate running for political office. B throws the pie (and connects), but the law will not enforce A's promise to pay the $100 to B.

C. Voidable
A contract that is voidable is enforceable, but one party may void it for a reason the law recognizes, such as fraud or minority, while the other party may not use that reason to void the contract.
Example: A, who is a minor, promises B to buy B's house. If B seeks to enforce A's promise, A may avoid her contract to buy the house based on her minority. But if A wants to go through with the contract, B cannot use A's minority as a basis to avoid his promise to sell her the house.

D. Unenforceable
An enforceable contract may become unenforceable for reasons provided by law. The major examples are the running of a statute of limitations and bankruptcy. In both, the promisee cannot enforce the contract.
An unenforceable contract sometimes has effect. **For example,** if a promisor voluntarily pays a debt on which the statute of limitations has run, generally the law will not help the promisor recover the payment.

IV. SOURCES OF CONTRACT LAW

A. Judicial Decisions as Common Law
The common law of contract law was first shaped primarily by the royal and local courts in England through the decisions of judges in cases, usually on appeal. American courts continued that process. Now the phrase "common law" is a synonym for judge-made law, as opposed to legislation. A rule recognized in judicial decisions serves as precedent that binds a court that later deals with the same issue.
Term of art: *Stare decisis* is short for *stare decisis et quieta non movere,* meaning stand by matters decided and do not disturb matters that are settled.

B. Legislation: The Uniform Commercial Code
Legislation has always played a role in the law of contract, so much so that the Statute of Frauds (see Chapter 11) is considered part of the common law of contract. Today, comprehensive statutes, like the Uniform Commercial Code (the UCC), have adopted and

modified rules of the common law of contract. Article 2 of the UCC on Sales, for example, adopts several rules on offer and acceptance studied in most basic contracts courses.

Thus, legislation is a more powerful source of contract law than judicial decision.

C. Restatements

Restatements are a persuasive but not binding source of contract law. They attempt to summarize and make clear the law of contract in both legislation and judicial decision, sometimes recommending a majority rule or a better rule. Courts are therefore not bound to follow the Restatements, but they are bound to follow legislation or precedent.

Legislation and judicial decisions may be called **primary** sources of contract law, and a Restatement is a **secondary** source. Restatements are therefore a source of law on the same level with treatises on contract by noted authors (e.g., Farnsworth, Murray, Corbin, Williston). Restatements are the product of the American Law Institute (the ALI). The ALI issued the first Restatement of Contracts in 1932 and replaced it with the Restatement (Second) of Contracts. The ALI is a private organization with no formal connection with any state or the federal government.

CHAPTER 2

Formation of Agreement

FORMATION OF AGREEMENT

To create a valid contract, three general requirements must be met.

First, the parties must reach an **agreement**. The whole agreement will often contain promises on both sides, although cases typically focus on the breach and enforcement of just one promise. Agreement is broken down into the elements of offer and acceptance.

Second, not all promises are enforceable as contracts. To mark a promise as enforceable, the common law requires **consideration** or a **substitute** for consideration, either **promissory estoppel** or a written **covenant** (now quite rare).

Third, the contract must survive any **defenses** that the promisor might raise against the promisee who seeks to enforce the contract.

Mnemonic: **M**other **A**dores **C**igars **A**fter **D**inner

1.   **M**utual **A**ssent

2.   **C**onsideration

3.   **A**bsence of **D**efenses

This chapter deals with the first requirement of an enforceable contract, an agreement. Agreements are formed through mutual assent, that is, each party "agrees" to the contract: the promisor agrees to be bound and the promisee agrees to take the promisor's commitment. Contracts generally contain more than one commitment by and to each party to the contract. The law of contract typically analyzes only one agreement by itself. In isolation, an agreement is the combination of an offer by one party and an acceptance of that offer by the other party. This scheme works best for simple contracts such as a one-time sale of goods, where the parties only have to agree on basic elements, such as price, quantity, or date of delivery. Such contracts can easily be phrased in terms of a distinct offer and a distinct acceptance. For complex contracts, where the parties negotiate a long-term relationship, such as a partnership, the parties may haggle over numerous items, producing a final document to which both consent. Nevertheless, the offer and acceptance model still dominates the analysis of the agreement process.

I. OFFER

An offer is a manifestation of willingness to enter into a bargain or an agreement that invites another person's acceptance. (Rest. 2d §24.) So an offer that is accepted becomes an agreement. One who makes an offer is the offeror, and the person to whom it is made is the offeree. To be a valid offer (i.e., to constitute an offer), a manifestation of intent to enter a bargain must have the "3 Cs":

> **Commitment** or promise by the offeror with intent to be bound
>
> **Certainty** and definitiveness of terms of the promise
>
> **Communication** of the offer to the offeree

A. Commitment or Promise

The first requirement for an offer is that it embody a promise or commitment, as opposed to a statement of present intention or preliminary negotiation. Statements such as "I intend to sell you my car" or "come talk to me about buying my car" are not offers. Saying "if you pay me $100, I will sell you my car" is a valid offer.

1. Objective Test

Whether a statement is an offer depends on whether a reasonable person would believe it to be an offer, regardless of the party's subjective belief. For example, given the trade customs of an industry, would a reasonable person think that an offer was made? The courts consider several factors:

Mnemonic: **LIMPS**

a. Language

Have the words "offer" or "promise" been used? Courts also consider the definitiveness of the terms and language of a proposal to help decide whether it is an offer. "First come, first served" may indicate an offer because it provides buyers with a clear means of accepting by buying first.

      b. **Industry Customs**
         Courts determine whether the type of language and manner of the proposal is usually considered to be an offer in a specific industry.

      c. **Method of Communication**
         Communications made by mass media (i.e., TV, newspaper, billboard) are often held to be invitations for offers, not offers themselves. For example, a TV ad announces that a dealer has 100 cars for sale for $1,000 each. The dealer did not make an offer to the entire TV audience (which could be millions) to buy his cars for $1,000. Rather, he "invited" members of the audience to offer to buy his cars.

      d. **Prior Practices Between the Parties**
         If the parties had prior transactions, the courts will consider the significance of the questioned statements in light of statements made in previous dealings.

      e. **Surrounding Circumstances**
         Courts also consider the manner and context in which a statement was made (e.g., in jest, in anger, etc.), and whether it was reasonable to construe the statement as an offer under those circumstances.

  2. Commitments and promises are distinguished from opinions.
     All statements made leading up to an agreement are not necessarily commitments. For example, A hired B to pick A's crops, only partly because B told A that the task would take approximately two or three weeks. B has not made an offer to pick the crops in two to three weeks, unless he in fact promises that he will do it in that time.

  3. Price Quotations
     A price quotation is not an offer to sell unless:
     a. The seller who names or quotes the price specifies the quantity he is willing to sell, not merely the per-unit cost, and
     b. The quote is made to a specific person, not the general public.

  4. Auctions
     An auctioneer solicits bids, which are offers; he does not make offers.

B. **Certainty of Terms**
  The subject matter of a proposal must be definite and certain; otherwise, a court would be unable to determine the terms if the offer evolves into an enforceable contract. Some consequences of missing or vague terms are as follows:

  1. Time of Payment and Performance
     The absence of these terms is not fatal because the court can imply that performance is due within a reasonable time (UCC §2-309).

2. Identity of the Parties and Subject Matter
   These must be certain.
3. Quantity Must Be Specified
   Quantity is a required term except for output and requirement contracts (see below).
4. Price
   Under the common law, parties had to agree to a price. Under the Uniform Commercial Code, price and some other missing terms can be implied. (UCC §2-305.) If the parties only intend to be bound if they set a price, price will not be implied, and there will be no contract.
5. Part Performance or Acceptance
   Vagueness and uncertainty of terms can also be overcome if there is part performance or acceptance.
   a. Part Performance
      If the parties have already begun performing the contract, the manner in which they acted upon vague terms can be determinative of their meaning.
   b. Acceptance
      If the contract terms are uncertain or ambiguous, proof of one possible interpretation will establish the terms.
   c. Terms to Be Agreed Upon
      Offers that include some of the terms and state that other terms will be agreed upon in the future are too vague if the omitted terms are material to the agreement (e.g., quantity), and a contract will not be formed even if this "offer" is "accepted."
6. Output and Requirements Contracts
   Output and requirements contracts are valid despite an absence of definite terms, so long as both parties act in good faith.
   a. Requirements Contract
      Airline contracts with Refinery to supply it with "all the jet fuel it needs." There is no definite quantity, but if Airline makes a good faith effort to buy a certain amount of fuel and Refinery makes a good faith effort to provide it, the contract is valid.
   b. Output Contract
      A cereal company contracts with Farmer to buy "all wheat grown in year X." Neither knows how much wheat will be sold, but the absence of a specific quantity is not fatal in such a contract to buy all of the seller's output.
C. Communication to the Offeree
   The offeree must have knowledge of the offer.

II. TERMINATION OF AN OFFER

When an offer is made, it creates a power of acceptance in the offeree; if he accepts the offer, the offeror is bound. Termination of the offer extinguishes this power. An offer can only be terminated before the offeree accepts it. Termination can occur by an act of either party or by operation of law.

A. Revocation by the Offeror

An offeror may revoke his offer so long as it has not been accepted by the offeree. An offer can be revoked in various ways:

1. Communication to the Offeree

Communication of termination of an offer can be direct or indirect. Indirect communication may involve a third party who notifies the offeree of the offeror's revocation. The indirect communication must be correct, given by a reliable source and understandable to a "reasonable person." **Example:** A makes an offer to B then sells the item to C before B accepts. The act of selling to another is a reasonable indication of revocation if B is aware of the sale. However, if B is not *notified* of A's revocation — either directly or indirectly — before he accepts, then the acceptance is valid and A is contractually bound to sell to B.

2. By Publication

Offers that are made by publication can be revoked by publication. Unlike direct and indirect communications, the revocation is effective when published, not when it is received by the offeree.

B. Irrevocable Offers

In general, an offeror may terminate his offer, even if he promised not to do so, unless the offer is irrevocable. An offer becomes irrevocable in several ways.

Mnemonic: **DROP FU**

1. Detrimental Reliance

Offers are irrevocable for a reasonable time period if the offeree relied to his detriment on the offer being held open, and it is reasonably foreseeable to the offeror that the offeree would so rely. **Example:** A general contractor relies on a sub-contractor's offer in determining the costs of the overall job.

2. Options

If the offeree gives consideration to the offeror in return for the offeror's promise to keep the offer open and not to revoke it, then the offeror is bound to do so. This forms a contract known as an option, because the offeree now has the option to accept or to reject the offer.

Example: A gives B $20 not to revoke his offer for two weeks. The Restatement holds an option contract valid even if there is no actual consideration, so long as consideration is recited in a written and signed document. Rest. 2d §87.

3. **P**artial Performance of a Unilateral Contract

Traditionally, a unilateral contract was revocable at any time prior to completion of the requested performance. For example, A promises to pay B $100 if B crosses a bridge. B may only "accept" by performing the act that A desires, namely, crossing the bridge. It used to be thought that A could revoke at any time before B reached the other side. Now most jurisdictions hold the view that when B begins performance an option contract is formed and A may not revoke the offer. Rest. 2d §45. The offeree may discontinue his performance at any time. Mere preparation to begin performance, however, is not considered to be partial performance (e.g., when B puts on his bridge-crossing shoes and says his pre-crossing mantra).

4. **F**irm Offers (**UCC §2-205**)

A signed writing by a merchant to buy or sell goods that has firm terms and assures that the offer will be held open is enforceable, even without consideration. Duration:

a. Period Stated

If the period is actually stated, the offer will remain open for the stated period or three months, whichever is less.

b. Period Not Stated

If the period is not stated, the offer remains open for a "reasonable time," not to exceed three months.

C. Termination by the Offeree

An offeree can terminate an offer in three ways:

1. Express Rejection

2. Counteroffer

A counteroffer occurs when an offeree tries to add or change terms in the original offer. This is considered a rejection of the original offer, as well as a new offer. **Example:** A offers to sell his car to B. B makes a counteroffer to buy the car if A repaints it. A's original offer to sell has been rejected, and B's offer to buy with additional conditions is the new offer. A is actually the offeree now.

a. Mere Inquiry

A "mere inquiry" is not a counteroffer. As long as the offeree suggests that he is still considering the original offer, a counteroffer has not been made. **Example:** B tells A, "I'm still thinking about buying your car, but I would like to know how you feel about lowering the price."

b. Irrevocable Offer

A counteroffer does not revoke an irrevocable offer.

      c. Date Effective

        A rejection is effective when it is received by the offeror, who then can extend a new offer to another party.

      d. "Battle of the Forms" Exception

        See Acceptance, below.

   3. Passage of Time

     If an offer specifies a time within which it must be accepted, failure to accept within that time period will constitute a rejection. If no time period is specified, a reasonable time period is given for response. In either case, the time period starts when the offeree actually gets the offer.

D. Termination by Law

   1. Death or Incapacity

     The death or incapacity (e.g., insanity) of either party before the offer is accepted will terminate the offer. The death or incapacity does not have to be communicated to the other party. Irrevocable offers are not terminated by death or incapacity. (Rest. 2d §48.)

   2. If the subject of the offer, such as the goods offered for sale, is destroyed prior to acceptance, the offer is terminated. (Rest. 2d §35.)

   3. If the contract becomes contrary to law prior to acceptance, the offer will be terminated. (Rest. 2d §35.) **Example:** A offers to sell liquor to B. While the offer is open, Congress outlaws alcohol consumption. A's offer is terminated. Had B already accepted, the contract would become void.

III. ACCEPTANCE

An acceptance is a manifestation of assent to the terms of an offer in the manner required by the offer. A contract is created once an acceptance is communicated. To be valid an acceptance must meet the following requirements:

A. Acceptor

   Only the specific person to whom the offer was made can accept. The power of acceptance cannot be assigned. Exception: An option can be assigned.

B. Communication

   Acceptance of an offer for a bilateral contract is not effective until it is communicated to the offeror.

   1. Objective Manifestation of Assent Required

     The offeree's subjective state of mind is irrelevant. However, the offeree must realize that an offer was made. Absent such knowledge, his acceptance is invalid.

   2. Acceptance Received by the Offeror

The obvious situation is where the offeree conveys acceptance to the offeror, either by telephone communication or in person. But problems can develop if there is a delay between the time the offeree accepts and the time the offeror receives the communication, such as when the offeree accepts by mail.

a. Mailbox Rule (Majority)

An acceptance is effective (and a contract is thus formed) upon the dispatch, not the actual receipt, of the acceptance. Exceptions:

i. The offer explicitly states that acceptance is not effective until actually received.

ii. Options

Exercise (i.e., acceptance) of an option contract is only effective upon receipt by the offeror.

b. Means of Acceptance Stipulated

An offeror can specify the means of acceptance of his offer (e.g., only upon actual receipt or in a specified place).

c. Reasonable Means of Acceptance

If offeror does not specify the method of conveying acceptance then any reasonable means is valid. Even if a specific method is given, an acceptance that is conveyed in a different way is valid if it is actually received by the offeror before he revokes the offer.

d. Acceptance Lost in Transmission

An acceptance that is lost in transmission is valid if it was properly sent, but may be excused if it will cause hardship to the offeror, such as if the offeror already sold the property.

e. Restatement (Second) §40 Exception

In general, a rejection becomes effective upon receipt, and an offer is effective upon dispatch. However, where an offeree dispatches a rejection and then dispatches an acceptance, the acceptance is only effective if received before the rejection.

Examples:

i. Rejection Before Acceptance

An offeree mails a rejection on Monday and an acceptance on Tuesday. Both letters are delivered on Wednesday. The acceptance is effective only if the offeror gets it before he receives the rejection.

ii. Acceptance Before Rejection

Offeree mails acceptance on Monday and it is delivered on Thursday. Offeree also mails a rejection on Tuesday and it arrives on Wednesday.

(1) Majority Rule

Under the mailbox rule, acceptance is effective as of Monday unless the offeror limited the manner of conveying the acceptance. However, the offeror may be able to prevent the contract under the theory of estoppel by showing that he relied on the rejection to his detriment.

(2) Minority Rule

Some courts rule that if an offeror actually receives the rejection first, no contract can be created.

f. "Crossing" Offers

If two parties send identical offers to each other, neither one knowing of the other's offer, a contract is not formed when the offers "cross in the mail." There must be knowledge of an offer before a contract can be formed.

g. Mistake in Transmission

If an offer is mistakenly changed *during* the process of transmission to the offeree (e.g., teletype or clerical error) and the offeree does not know and could not reasonably have been expected to know of the error, then the offer can be accepted on its mistaken terms (majority view).

3. Exceptions to the Requirement of Communication of Acceptance

Mnemonic: **S**earch **A**nd **W**ill **D**estroy

a. **S**ilence

If an offeree does not respond to an offer but accepts the benefits of the offer, and prior dealings or custom would lead a reasonable person to believe that this is the way in which an acceptance is made, then silence can constitute acceptance.

b. **A**ct

If an offeror specifies that performance of a certain act will constitute acceptance, performing the requisite act will form a contract. Note: This is not a unilateral contract—an act in return for a promise; rather, the act here is used to symbolize the promise.

c. **W**aiver Expressly Contained in the Offer

The offeror may expressly waive communication of acceptance.

d. **D**ominion

In general, if an "offeree" accepts unsolicited goods and exercises dominion over them, he has accepted an offer (to purchase the goods) and formed a contract. However, some states have statutes that classify unsolicited goods as gifts to the recipient.

4. Unilateral Contracts

In the context of unilateral contracts, performance of an act (as opposed to making a promise for bilateral contracts) constitutes acceptance of the offer. The offeree's act must be consummated:

a. Knowingly

With the **knowledge** of the offeree and motivation from the offer. Rest. 2d §51, comment a.

b. Completely

The offeree must **completely** perform the requisite act. Partial performance merely creates an option for the offeree to complete the performance and form a contract.

c. Notification

The offeree must notify the offeror, even after completing performance, if the offeree's performance would not otherwise come to the offeror's attention. (Majority rule.)

C. The Acceptance Changes the Terms of the Offer

1. Last Shot Rule

Under the common law, if the acceptance does not match the offer because it tries to change one or more of the offer's terms, no contract is formed. The offer and acceptance have to reflect each other. This is known as the "mirror image" rule for formation of an agreement.

Any variation in the acceptance constitutes a rejection of the offer and an extension of a counteroffer. This was sometimes called the "last shot rule" because contracting parties often varied their acceptances in an effort to get the "last shot." By sending a counteroffer instead of an acceptance, the most recent offeree at any stage would be able to set the terms of the final agreement to its favor.

2. First Shot Rule

A written acceptance of an offer for the "sale of goods" is valid, notwithstanding terms that vary from the offer, unless acceptance is expressly conditioned on assent to the additional or different terms. This has been referred to as the "first shot rule": there is some incentive to send out the first form, against which the consistency of future terms is to be judged. UCC §2-207(1).

3. Battle of the Forms and Related Problems

In routine business transactions, most parties use standardized printed forms. However, one company's standard forms rarely match the other's. A "battle of the forms" results when courts have to decide whose forms govern. UCC §2-207.

a. Conditional Acceptance

If a party sends an acceptance that is conditional upon the offeror's assent to new or conflicting terms that are included in the acceptance, there is no contract until and unless the original offeror manifests his acceptance.

b. Acceptance Contains Additional Terms

i. Neither party is a merchant —

The contract terms are those of the original offer.

ii. One party is not a merchant —

The additional terms become part of the contract if the offeror explicitly assents.

iii. All parties are merchants —

The additional term becomes part of the contract unless the offeror objects or the term is a material alteration.

c. Offer and Acceptance Differ on a Particular Issue (Varying But Not Additional Terms)

i. Knockout Rule (Majority)

The disputed terms are "knocked out" of both the offer and acceptance, and UCC standard "gap fillers" (e.g., implied time of performance) control.

ii. Minority Rule

Offeror's clause overrides ("first shot").

d. Written Confirmation of Oral Agreement

i. Under UCC §2-207, additional terms contained in a written confirmation are treated the same as additional terms contained in an acceptance (see above).

ii. When the confirmation contains terms that differ from the oral agreement, the terms of the oral agreement usually control.

e. If an acceptance materially deviates from the offer, it will not be effective.

i. Material deviations usually involve price, quality, quantity, or delivery terms.

ii. Although the writings of the parties do not establish a contract, conduct by both parties recognizing the existence of a contract is sufficient to establish a contract. The terms consist of those terms on which the writings agree, together with gap fillers from the UCC. UCC §2-207(3).

f. Custom Forms

If the parties use custom-written offer and acceptance forms, as opposed to standardized contract forms, then the traditional offer and acceptance rules apply without variation.

CASE CLIPS

Embry v. Hargadine-McKittrick Dry Goods Co. (1907)

Facts: Embry, toward the end of his yearly contract, was nervous that it would not be renewed, and asked his employer McKittrick for reassurance. McKittrick said, "Go ahead, get your men out, you're all right." McKittrick denied that he intended a promise to renew Embry's contract by that statement, and Embry's written contract was not renewed. Instructions to the jury stated that unless both parties subjectively intend to form an employment contract, no contract exists.

Issue: Is a party's assent to be determined by his actual or subjective state of mind or by the outward manifestation of assent as reasonably understood by the promisee?

Rule: If a party outwardly manifests assent to the contract by a promise and the other party reasonably understands that manifestation to be a promise, there is a contract. Here, Embry in fact believed McKittick's statement to be a promise to renew the employment contract, and Embry's belief was reasonable.

Kabil Dev. Corp. v. Mignot (1977)

Facts: Kabil conducted oral negotiations with the Mignots regarding the provision of helicopter services. Kabil sued for breach of contract when such service was not provided. Kabil's vice-president was allowed to testify that he "felt" an agreement had been reached.

Issue: Can a party's personal perceptions be introduced as evidence of whether a contract was formed?

Rule: Whether a contract was formed is to be determined by objective manifestations of the parties. Subjective opinions not misleading to the jury may be admissible when illustrative of the behavior and perceptions of the parties and whether such behavior gave reasonable notice of intent to the other party.

McDonald v. Mobil Coal Producing, Inc. (1991)

Facts: McDonald left his employ at Mobil when rumors linking him to the sexual harassment of a co-worker surfaced. It was disputed whether he resigned or was fired. At the beginning of his employment at Mobil, McDonald signed a contract that described his job status as terminable at will. He was later given an employee manual that contained a disclaimer against its use as an employment contract. The manual included information on employee procedure and policies. McDonald challenged his dismissal on the ground that the manual modified his initial at-will contract to one of termination only for cause.

Issue 1: What is necessary to create a legally effective disclaimer?

Rule 1: For a disclaimer to be effective it must be conspicuous (e.g., set off from other text, placed under a specific sub-heading, written in a different font, and capitalized).

Issue 2: Can an employee manual modify an at-will employment contract?

Rule 2: In the absence of a conspicuous disclaimer, the objective theory of contract formation allows for the modification of an at-will employment contract if the employer's actions create a reasonable reliance by the employee. Subjective intent to contract is irrelevant. In this case, the court found that the manual modified the contract, since there was no conspicuous disclaimer.

Moulton v. Kershaw (1884)

Facts: The defendant, a salt dealer, sent a letter to another dealer, offering to sell him salt in shipments of 80 to 95 barrels at the price of $0.85 per barrel. The plaintiff ordered 2,000 barrels, but the defendant refused to fill the order.

Issue: Is a letter that solicits the sale of goods considered to be an offer?

Rule: A general letter or circular is not construed to be a firm offer to sell. The absence of a specific quantity in the letter prevents it from being an offer.

Note: The defendant had stated the size and cost of a shipment, but had not offered to provide a certain number of shipments. Thus, it is unfair to construe the letter as an offer.

Joseph Martin Jr. Delicatessen v. Schumacher (1981)

Facts: A clause in the lease agreement stated that "the tenant may renew this lease for an additional period of five years at annual rentals to be agreed upon." When the tenant sought to exercise the option, the landlord doubled the rent. The tenant sued for specific performance at a reasonable rent, and the landlord brought an action for eviction.

Issue: Is a clause in a realty lease that specifies "rent will be agreed upon" too vague to be enforced?

Rule: A lease renewal clause that does not specify the rent to be paid, or some specific manner of calculating the rent, is merely an "agreement to agree" and is not enforceable.

Empro Manufacturing Co., Inc. v. Ball-Co Manufacturing, Inc. (1989)

Facts: Empro was negotiating for the purchase of Ball-Co's assets. Empro sent Ball-Co a three-page letter of intent that contained detailed terms, including the price and payment schedule. The letter also contained "general terms and conditions" and stated that a definitive agreement was "subject to" a variety of conditions, including shareholder approval. Upon learning that Ball-Co was negotiating with another party, Empro contended that the parties intended to be bound by the letter of intent.

Issue: May parties be bound to a document that memorializes essential terms of an agreement, but anticipates future negotiation?

Rule: Because intent in contract law is objective, parties who make their pact "subject to" a later definitive agreement manifest an intent not to be bound, which under the parol evidence rule becomes the definitive intent, even if one party later says otherwise.

Wheeler v. White (1965)

Facts: White contracted to finance construction on Wheeler's property. White later encouraged Wheeler to demolish the buildings existing on the property, which he did. White then backed out, claiming that the contract terms were too indefinite.

Issue: Can a promise be enforced even if a valid contract was not formed?

Rule: Where a promisee acts to his detriment in reasonable reliance upon an otherwise unenforceable promise, he may be entitled to recover damages incurred by the reliance if necessary to avoid injustice.

Raffles v. Wichelhaus (1864)

Facts: The defendant contracted to buy Indian cotton from the plaintiff that was to arrive on a ship called the *Peerless*. Unknown to both parties there were two ships named *Peerless* that delivered cotton from India. The ship the defendant was expecting arrived in October. The ship the plaintiff sent the cotton aboard arrived in December. The defendant refused the later shipment.

Issue: If parties to a contract are unaware of an ambiguity, is the contract void because there was no "meeting of the minds"?

Rule: When parties to a contract are unaware that they have different understandings of a material ambiguity, the agreement is unenforceable because there was no "meeting of the minds."

Cobaugh v. Klick-Lewis, Inc. (1989)

Facts: Cobaugh arrived at the ninth tee of a golf course to find a 1988 Chevrolet Beretta on display, as well as signs purporting to award the car to anyone who could make a hole-in-one. Cobaugh subsequently shot a hole-in-one and attempted to claim his prize. The signs had originally been put up for a charity event that had been played two days previously, and had been mistakenly left standing.

Issue: Can a court enforce a unilateral promise that was not intended to be offered to the eventual claimant?

Rule: The apparent intent of the offeror, not his subjective intent, determines the power of acceptance. The promoter of a contest is bound to perform his promise if a person acts on it before the offer is withdrawn. In this case, the act of shooting for the hole-in-one constituted acceptance of the offer.

Allied Steel and Conveyors, Inc. v. Ford Motor Co. (1960)

Facts: Ford ordered machinery from Allied with its own order form, which stated that the order was not binding until accepted and "acceptance should be executed on acknowledgment copy which should be returned to the buyer." A clause in the purchase order provided that Allied was to be liable for all injuries resulting from negligence in the installation of the machinery. It began installing the machinery without sending the acknowledgment copy as formal acceptance. An Allied employee was injured as a result of the negligence of Ford's employees in connection with Allied's work. Allied claimed it was not liable, because it did not formally accept the offer.

Issue: Can the beginning of performance act as an acceptance to an offer that provides a specific means of communicating acceptance?

Rule: Beginning performance with the knowledge, consent, and agreement of the offeror is a valid means of accepting an offer. "Acceptance should be executed on acknowledgment copy" is merely a suggestion.

Note: Although this case seems to contradict *White v. Corlies and Tift*, both courts were actually looking to whether the offeror knew of the acceptance.

Davis v. Jacoby (1934)

Facts: Whitehead wrote to his niece, Davis, that if she and her husband came to care for his sick wife and help with the business, they would "inherit everything." Davis immediately accepted the proposition, but Whitehead committed suicide before Davis and her husband arrived. Davis cared for Mrs. Whitehead until her death a week later. When Whitehead's will was opened it revealed that he had left everything to his nephews. Davis argued that she was entitled to the property based on the contract made prior to Whitehead's death.

Issue: Is an offer presumed to be bilateral or unilateral in the absence of any indication by the offeror?

Rule: When there is doubt as to whether an offer is for a unilateral or bilateral contract, the law will presume the offer was for a bilateral contract. An offer requesting a response by mail is more likely an offer for a bilateral contract than a unilateral contract.

Note: If the contract had been unilateral and thus accepted by performance, Davis would not have recovered, since the death of Whitehead would have acted as revocation before acceptance.

Petterson v. Pattberg (1928)

Facts: Pattberg offered Petterson the chance to pay the balance of his mortgage at a discount by a certain date. When Petterson attempted to pay the balance before the deadline (and thus to accept Pattberg's offer), Petterson told him that he had already sold the mortgage to a third party who was unwilling to reduce the payment.

Issue: Can an offer for a unilateral contract be withdrawn?

Rule: An offer for a unilateral contract can be withdrawn until the moment the requested act is performed.

Brackenbury v. Hodgkin (1917)

Facts: Hodgkin promised her daughter and son-in-law, the Brackenburys, that she would bequeath her farm to them if they would move in and take care of her. The Brackenburys moved in and cared for Hodgkin until disputes arose, and Hodgkin ordered them to leave.

Issue: Can an offer of a unilateral contract be withdrawn after the offeree has performed part of the requested act?

Rule: A unilateral contract is accepted by performance. The offer is no longer revocable once the offeree has begun performance of the requested act. Completion of the act obligates the offeror to perform its promise.

Thomason v. Bescher (1918)

Facts: Bescher executed a writing, under seal, that created an option for Thomason to purchase a tract of Bescher's land. The writing stated that payment of $1 was given as consideration, although in actuality the payment was never made. To complete the sale, Thomason was required to demand the deed and tender the contract price before a specified date. Before tender was made, Bescher notified Thomason that the offer was withdrawn. Thomason sued for specific performance.

Issue: May an offer creating an option contract be revoked before tender is made?

Rule: An option contract is a binding agreement, and irrevocable within the time designated, as long as the terms of the contract are fair and equitable.

Note: The use of the seal has been abolished in most states (as well as under UCC §2-203), but under traditional usage no consideration was required to support a contract under seal. The Restatement (Second) requires that an option contract be a signed writing, but does not require consideration to be actually delivered.

James Baird Co. v. Gimbel Bros., Inc. (1933)

Facts: The defendant sent a "sub-bid" for the cost of installing linoleum to the plaintiff, a general contractor, who used the sub-bid in calculating its costs for the overall project. The sub-bid expressly stated that acceptance should be conveyed only after (and if) the contractor was awarded the project. The defendant later realized that its bid was incorrect and notified the plaintiff that it was withdrawing it. The plaintiff had already sent in its bid. When the plaintiff won the project, it accepted the offer of the defendant who refused to perform.
Issue: Can an offer, for which no consideration was received, be revoked prior to acceptance even if the offeree relied on it?
Rule: If no consideration is received for an offer that was clearly not intended to be a binding promise, it is revocable even if the offeree relied on it to his detriment.

Drennan v. Star Paving Co. (1958)

Facts: Drennan, a contractor, used a bid from Star Paving, a subcontractor, to calculate the costs of a larger bid it was submitting to a third party. After Drennan was awarded the job, Star Paving claimed that its "sub-bid" was erroneously low and refused to work at that price. Although it had not formally accepted the offer, Drennan had relied on the price, as is customary in the construction industry. It sued to recover the difference between the Star bid and the amount paid to another subcontractor.
Issue: May a party be required to perform by the terms of an offer that was never actually accepted?
Rule: If an offeror should reasonably expect that his offer will induce justifiable reliance by the offeree of a substantial and definite nature, the offer is enforceable even if the reliance occurs prior to a formal acceptance of the offer.

Hoffman v. Red Owl Stores (1965)

Facts: Relying on Red Owl's repeated advice and promises that he would be able to obtain a Red Owl supermarket franchise, Hoffman sold his existing business, moved to a new town, bought and sold a small grocery, and took out a loan. Red Owl later informed Hoffman that there would be no deal. Hoffman sued to recover lost income and expenses he incurred in reliance on Red Owl's promise. Red Owl claimed it was not liable because there was no contract, as it had never made Hoffman an offer.

Issue: Can a party be liable under the theory of promissory estoppel for breaking a promise, even though the terms of the promise were too vague and indefinite to constitute an offer?

Rule: A party will be liable for a promise made during preliminary negotiations if the promisor should reasonably expect to induce an action or forbearance of a definite and substantial nature by the promisee, the promise does induce such action or forbearance, and injustice would result if relief were not granted.

Livingstone v. Evans (1925)

Facts: Evans offered to sell his Sand to Livingstone for $1,800. Livingstone sent a counteroffer to buy at a lower price. Evans rejected Livingstone's offer, saying, "cannot reduce price." When Livingstone agreed to pay $1,800, Evans refused to sell.

Issue: Does an offeree who has made a counteroffer still have the power to accept the original offer?

Rule: A counteroffer is a rejection of the offer and it cannot be accepted at a later date. The original offer can only be accepted if it is renewed.

Note: The court held that Evans' statement that he "cannot reduce price" was itself a reaffirmation of his earlier offer, which Livingstone validly accepted.

Idaho Power Co. v. Westinghouse Elec. Corp. (1979)

Facts: Westinghouse sent Idaho Power its standardized list of product, which also contained certain conditions, including a disclaimer of liability for damages resulting from defective products. Idaho ordered a voltage regulator with its standardized order form (acceptance), which stated that it "superseded all previous agreements" but was silent as to liability. The regulator was defective.

Issue: What is the legal effect of an agreement when the terms of the offer and acceptance vary?

Rule: Under UCC §2-207, a contract between merchants is valid even if the terms of the offer and acceptance are not identical, unless acceptance is conditioned upon assent to the different terms.

Note: Thus Idaho's acceptance was not a counteroffer and, because it was silent as to liability, Westinghouse's disclaimer applies.

Morrison v. Thoelke (1963)

Facts: The plaintiff mailed an acceptance to the defendant. Before the acceptance was received, the plaintiff called to revoke acceptance.
Issue: When does an acceptance become effective?
Rule: According to the mailbox rule, acceptance becomes effective at the time it is posted. Therefore subsequent revocations are not effective even if received before the acceptance.
Note: Some courts hold that acceptance becomes effective upon receipt.

Hobbs v. Massasoit Whip Co. (1898)

Facts: Massasoit had bought eel skins from Hobbs on four or five prior occasions. On this occasion, Hobbs sent skins that Massasoit did not want. Massasoit neither notified Hobbs nor returned the skins, and eventually destroyed them.
Issue: May a party's conduct serve as an acceptance regardless of that party's state of mind?
Rule: When the silence or inaction of an offeree warrants the offeror's belief that the goods were accepted, that conduct serves as an acceptance regardless of intent.

Morone v. Morone (1980)

Facts: The parties were an unmarried couple who lived together for 20 years, holding themselves out to the community as husband and wife. Together they had two children. After they separated, the plaintiff sued under implied contract to get her share of the couple's earnings and assets. She also claimed that the defendant had expressly promised that he would support her in return for her domestic services.
Issue 1: May a contract regarding earnings and assets be implied from a relationship of an unmarried couple?
Rule 1: An implied contract between an unmarried couple living together is too indefinite to be enforced as well as contrary to statutes that have abolished common law marriage.
Issue 2: Is an express contract between such a couple enforceable?
Rule 2: An express contract is enforceable so long as illicit sexual relations were not part of the consideration of the contract.

Continental Forest Products, Inc. v. Chandler Supply Co. (1974)

Facts: Chandler placed an order for two carloads of plywood with North America Millwork. Unbeknownst to Chandler, the North America employee who took the order left his position and gave the order to his new employer, Continental. When Continental's shipment arrived, Chandler sought to deduct from the purchase price a trade debt owed to it by North America.

Issue: May courts fashion equitable remedies without regard to the express or implied terms of an agreement?

Rule: Justice and equity may sometimes require courts to impose an obligation without reference to the intent or agreement of the parties.

Note: In the instant case, justice requires that Chandler only pay the amount that it would have paid had the transaction gone the way the company had intended.

Balfour v. Balfour (1919)

Facts: The plaintiff lived in a different country from her husband for health-related reasons. He had agreed to pay her a living allowance to support her. Their relationship deteriorated, and they eventually separated. The plaintiff sought to enforce their agreement.

Issue: Is any agreement between a husband and wife enforceable in a court of law?

Rule: Agreements between family members are usually unenforceable because, at the time they are made, the parties to the agreements usually do not have the "intent" to enter into an enforceable contract. However, if the requisite intent was present, then the agreement would be enforceable.

Davis v. General Foods Corp. (1937)

Facts: Davis offered to reveal to General Foods a new idea for creating fruit flavors for ice cream. When General Foods agreed to review the idea it did so on the condition that any compensation to Davis would be at its discretion. It used the product and never paid Davis.

Issue: Is a promise reserving discretion over compensation too indefinite to be enforced?

Rule: If a promisor retains an unlimited right to control the nature and extent of his performance, the promise is too indefinite to be legally enforceable. This is an "illusory promise," i.e., the promisor seems to have promised something but really has reserved the right to give nothing.

Sullivan v. O'Connor (1973)

Facts: Sullivan sued her surgeon for breach of contract after the plastic surgery performed on her nose failed to "enhance her beauty and improve her appearance" as expressly promised.

Issue: Does a doctor breach a contract if a medical procedure does not produce the desired results?

Rule: If a doctor expressly promises that a procedure will produce certain results, a patient may recover damages if that promise is not fulfilled.

Note: Because of the fear that patients will elevate a doctor's opinion to a promise, some courts require written proof of the promise. Other courts completely deny recovery in such cases.

Shaheen v. Knight (1957)

Facts: Shaheen underwent an operation to be sterilized after which his wife had a baby. The doctor, Knight, had specifically promised that the procedure would be effective.

Issue: Can a contract for specified results exist between doctor and patient?

Rule: While courts are reluctant to require a doctor to guarantee success, a contract that specifies a particular result will be enforced.

Note: The court refused to grant Shaheen damages for the birth of the child on the grounds that it contravenes public policy to assess "damages" for the "fun, joy and affection" of raising a child.

Hewitt v. Hewitt (1974)

Facts: The parties agreed to live together and share assets and earnings as a husband and wife would. The "wife" worked hard to support her husband's education, business and social interests. Common law marriage was not recognized in this jurisdiction. The wife sued to recover half the assets at separation.

Issue: Can two unmarried persons be required to share equally in income and assets if they agreed to such a plan, even though both were aware they were not legally married?

Rule: Courts can determine that the conduct of unmarried persons living together demonstrates an implied contract or an agreement of partnership or joint venture. A nonmarital partner can recover in quantum meruit for the reasonable value of services rendered, less the reasonable value of support received, if they can show that services were rendered with the expectation of monetary reward.

Cotnam v. Wisdom (1907)

Facts: Cotnam's decedent was fatally injured after being thrown from a streetcar. Wisdom and another physician were summoned but were unable to save the patient. The physicians sued to recover the value of the services rendered. The trial judge instructed the jury that the size of the decedent's estate was relevant to the issue of the amount of recovery.

Issue 1: Can a physician recover for the value of services rendered when no express contract was made with the patient?

Rule 1: A physician may recover under the theory of quasi-contract for the reasonable value of services provided during an emergency.

Issue 2: What amount can a physician recover for emergency services provided under quasi-contract?

Rule 2: The physician should be granted reasonable compensation for services rendered. The financial standing of the victim is not relevant.

Lefkowitz v. Great Minneapolis Surplus Store, Inc. (1957)

Facts: Great Minneapolis advertised in a newspaper that it would sell one lapin stole for $1 on a "first come, first served" basis. It refused to sell to Lefkowitz, who arrived first, claiming that the sale was for women only.

Issue: When is a newspaper advertisement considered an offer?

Rule: A newspaper advertisement that is clear, definite, explicit, and leaves nothing open for negotiation is considered to be an offer. While the offer may be modified, new and arbitrary conditions not in print may not be imposed after acceptance.

Note: UCC §2-204 recognizes offers even when some issues are left for future negotiations.

Fairmount Glass Works v. Crunden-Martin Woodemvare Co. (1899)

Facts: Crunden-Martin asked Fairmount to quote the "lowest price" at which it would sell certain goods. Fairmount provided a price quote sheet with terms and conditions "for immediate acceptance." Crunden-Martin sent in an order, but Fairmount refused to fill it.

Issue: Is a price quote an offer?

Rule: Use of the phrase "for immediate acceptance" in a price quote has the legal effect of making the quote an offer.

Note: Price quotations are generally not considered offers, especially if they are unsolicited.

The Sun Printing and Publishing Ass'n v. Remington Paper and Power Co., Inc. (1923)

Facts: Sun agreed to buy from Remington 1,000 tons of newsprint per month for 16 months. The price for the first four months was specified, but the price for the remainder of the contract was to be "reasonably agreed upon" with a limitation that it could not rise above the price the Canadian

Export Paper Company (an unrelated party) charged its large customers. When prices rose sharply, Remington refused to sell after the fourth month, claiming that the contract was indefinite.

Issue: Is a contract void for indefiniteness when the price term is left open to be determined by the parties at a later date?

Rule: A contract is void for indefiniteness if a material term such as price has been omitted.

Note: The modern view, as expressed in UCC §2-305, allows enforcement of contracts with open price terms.

Itek Corp. v. Chicago Aerial Indus. Inc. (1968)

Facts: Itek and CAI signed a "letter of intent" providing that they "shall make every reasonable effort to agree upon" a contract. CAI later broke off negotiations when it received an offer from another company.

Issue: Is a party liable for failure to honor its promise to attempt to reach a contract?

Rule: A party that breaks off negotiations after signing a letter of intent to make every reasonable effort to reach an agreement is liable if it fails to act in good faith.

Cole-McIntyre-Norfleet Co. v. Holloway (1919)

Facts: The defendant's salesman took an order for barrels of meal from Holloway and gave him four months within which to exercise the order (i.e., ask that the meal be shipped). The order contract provided that it was not binding until approved at the home office and that the company could not be bound by its salesperson. When Holloway asked for delivery of the meal, he was told that the home office rejected his order. Holloway suffered monetary loss because the price of meal had sharply risen in the meantime.

Issue: Does an unreasonable delay in rejecting an offer constitute an acceptance?

Rule: When the subject of a contract, either by its nature or by virtue of market conditions, will become unmarketable by delay, a delay in notifying the other party of its decision will amount to an acceptance by the offeree.

United States v. Braunstein (1947)

Facts: The United States solicited bids for 9,599 25-pound boxes of raisins. Braunstein offered ten cents a pound. The United States accepted Braunstein's offer, but a clerk erred in cabling the response, which stated that the United States "accepts" 10 cents per 25-pound box. Braunstein did not reply to the acceptance, the United States discovered the error and notified Braunstein who again made no response. The United States sold the raisins elsewhere and sued for the loss on the sale.

Issue: If the language accepting an offer leads the other party to believe that the offeree does not intend what he says, is the acceptance effective?

Rule: If either party to a contract knows that the other has made an error and therefore does not intend to be bound by its words, the words or acts do not operate as an offer or acceptance.

Roto-Lith, Ltd. v. F.P. Bartlett & Co. (1962)

Facts: Roto-Lith ordered emulsifier from Bartlett. Bartlett accepted Roto-Lith's offer by sending an "acknowledgment" form and an invoice, both of which disclaimed all warranties in conspicuous type on the front. Roto-Lith accepted the emulsifier, which later turned out to be defective. Roto-Lith claimed that the disclaimer of warranties on Bartlett's acceptance form was a material addition to the terms of the offer and was therefore a rejectable proposal under UCC §2-207(2).

Issue: Does an additional term on an acceptance that is solely to the offeree's advantage become a part of a binding contract?

Rule: An acceptance that includes an additional term made solely for the offeree's advantage is an acceptance that is expressly conditioned upon the offeror's assent to the additional terms.

Note: Roto-Lith assented to the additional terms by its actions in accepting delivery of the goods with knowledge of the conditions specified in the acknowledgment.

Woodburn v. Northwestern Bell Tel. Co. (1979)

Facts: Woodburn, a physician, sued Northwestern for failing to list him in the Yellow Pages. Northwestern asserted that it had filed an express limitation of damages with the state commerce commission and a similar limitation was printed on the back of the form Woodburn used to place his order.

Issue: When does a clause that limits liability for damages become part of a contract?

Rule: A contractual limitation of liability is enforceable if there was mutual assent to it. A party is allowed to introduce evidence on whether the other party reasonably was or should have been aware of the contract term.

Air Products & Chem., Inc. v. Fairbanks Morse, Inc. (1973)

Facts: Air Products ordered several electric motors from Fairbanks. Fairbanks returned Air Product's order form with a copy of its acknowledgment form, which contained an additional term that limited Fairbanks' liability in case of defect.

Issue: Can a limitation of liability that is contained in a seller's acknowledgment form become part of the contract of sale when the buyer's purchase order contained no such term and the buyer never expressly agreed to such terms?

Rule: A disclaimer for consequential loss is sufficiently material to require express conversation between parties over its exclusion or inclusion in a contract under UCC §2-207(2)(b).

Capital Sav. & Loan Ass'n v. Przybylowicz (1978)

Facts: Capital S & L granted and drew up the terms of a $34,500 residential mortgage loan to the Przybylowiczs, which stated that the Przybylowiczs were required to repay the loan in 300 monthly payments of $251.76. Unknown to both, Capital had miscalculated the terms. The payments should have been $289.53 per month. In reliance upon the loan, the Przybylowiczs sold their home and contracted to build a new one. Capital sought to reform the contract.

Issue: Can a written contract be reformed because of an error by one of the parties?

Rule: When a party relies on an erroneous statement made by the other party to a contract, and the first party could not have been expected to discover the error, the contract will be enforced if the other party is a professional who regularly engages in the activity involved.

Feinberg v. Pfeiffer Co. (1959)

Facts: Pfeiffer agreed to pay Feinberg $200 per month for life when she retired. Feinberg worked for a few more years and retired. Her pension was terminated after several years when she refused to have it reduced to $100 per month.

Issue: Can a promisor withdraw a promise that was given without consideration?

Rule: Past employment is considered past consideration, which does not constitute adequate legal consideration. However, if one acts to her detriment by quitting lucrative employment in justifiable reliance on a promise, the promise will be enforced if an injustice would result otherwise.

Dickinson v. Dodds (1876)

Facts: On June 10, Dodds offered to sell Dickinson a parcel of land and promised to keep the offer open until June 12. On June 11, Dickinson learned that Dodds intended to sell the land to another person. That afternoon Dickinson left a note accepting the offer.

Issue: What is the effect of an offer upon notice to the offeree that the offeror has made an offer to another party?

Rule: Information that leads an offeree to reasonably conclude that an offer has been withdrawn voids the offer.

Southern California Acoustics Co. v. C.V. Holder, Inc. (1969)

Facts: Southern, a subcontractor, submitted a bid to Holder, a contractor, who submitted its overall bid along with a list of subcontractors that included Southern. After Holder was awarded the project, a local trade newspaper published the names of all the subcontractors. When it saw its name in the trade paper, Southern assumed it was part of the project and did not seek other jobs. Holder received approval to replace Southern with another subcontractor.

Issue: Can a contractor substitute subcontractors after the contractor's bid has been accepted?

Rule: A contractor cannot substitute a listed subcontractor, absent a proper reason such as the subcontractor's insolvency, failure or refusal to perform, or failure or refusal to meet bonding requirements.

Note: This rule is based on the Subletting and Subcontracting Fair Practices Act. Today a subcontractor that is listed due to a clerical error can be substituted.

Cushing v. Thomson (1978)

Facts: Cushing's mailed acceptance was postmarked April 5 but dated April 3. Thomson withdrew the offer on April 4. Cushing represented that it was customary office procedure for letters to be sent out the same day that they were placed in the outbox, April 3, in this case. The court found for Cushing.

Issue: Can a party introduce evidence beyond the postmark as to the date an acceptance was mailed?

Rule: A party is allowed to introduce evidence as to when an acceptance was mailed if the postmark is insufficient.

Rhode Island Tool Co. v. United States (1955)

Facts: After the United States mailed an acceptance of Rhode Island's bid, but before Rhode Island received it, Rhode Island notified the defendant of an error in the bid.

Issue: May an erroneous bid be withdrawn after acceptance is posted?

Rule: When one has the right to withdraw a bid because it is erroneous, a binding contract will not result from posting of an acceptance.

Note: This court is in the minority that rejects the "mailbox" rule.

Palo Alto Town & Country Village, Inc. v. BBTC Co. (1974)

Facts: The defendant's lease contained an option to renew, to be exercised five months before the end of the term of lease. The defendant sent a properly stamped, addressed notice of exercise of the option six months before the lease expired, but the plaintiff never received the notice.

Issue: Is notice by an optionee of his exercise of an option effective upon its deposit in the mail or upon its receipt by the optionor?

Rule: Absent any provisions in the option contract to the contrary, the exercise of an option becomes effective at the time written notice of acceptance is deposited in the mail.

Carlill v. Carbolic Smoke Ball Co. (1893)

Facts: Carbolic offered a cash reward to anyone who contracted influenza after using its medical product. Carlill followed the product's usage instructions, but contracted the flu anyhow.

Issue: When a company advertises a reward if its product performs unsatisfactorily, must the consumer notify the company that he is accepting the offer before he uses the product?

Rule: If the advertisement is sufficiently specific as to the requirements for getting the reward (i.e., what the plaintiff can or cannot do) then its "offer" can be "accepted" by any person who fulfills the conditions of the advertisement, and there is no requirement to notify the company before using its product.

Strong v. Sheffield (1895)

Facts: Sheffield guaranteed her husband's debt to Strong on the condition that he would forbear from demanding payment for an unspecified period of time. Strong forbore for two years before presenting the note for collection. Sheffield claimed her guarantee was unenforceable for lack of consideration, because Strong's promise was illusory. Payment could have been demanded at any time without violating the letter of his promise to ask for the money when he wanted it.

Issue: Does a promise to forbear from collection of a debt for an unspecified period of time constitute valid consideration?

Rule: Forbearance to collect on a note is illusory and insufficient consideration if the forbearer had the option of demanding payment at any time.

Crook v. Cowan (1870)

Facts: Cowan sent a carpet dealer, Crook, a detailed, unconditional order for carpets. Crook accepted the order and shipped the carpets without notice to Cowan. Cowan had made other arrangements, thinking that Crook had not accepted.

Issue: Must one offering property for sale convey a formal acceptance?

Rule: A party who holds its property out for sale is not required to send a formal acceptance if it receives a detailed and unconditional order (offer).

Note: The dissent viewed this as a unilateral contract and required formal notice.

Bishop v. Eaton (1894)

Facts: Eaton promised that he would guarantee any loans that Bishop made to Eaton's brother. Bishop repaid a debt of Eaton's brother and sent properly addressed and stamped notification to Eaton, who resided in a distant land. Eaton claimed that he never received the letter.

Issue: What constitutes acceptance of an offer for a unilateral contract where it is unlikely the offeror will find out whether the offeree performed?

Rule: Where one performs in response to an offer for a unilateral contract, and the offeror is unlikely to know whether the offeree has performed, the offeror will be bound if the offeree makes a reasonable and seasonable effort to notify the offeror of his performance. The offeror need not actually receive the notification.

White v. Corlies and Tift (1871)

Facts: White submitted an estimate to perform work for Corlies and Tift. Corlies and Tift then sent White an offer to do the work. White began work without formally communicating acceptance of the offer. Corlies and Tift changed its mind and revoked the offer.

Issue: Can an offer be accepted by beginning performance without giving any other indication of assent?

Rule: Acceptance of an offer must be actually communicated to the offeror.

Note: The resolution of this case turned on whether Corlies and Tift required return performance or a return promise in response. The court ruled that this was not a unilateral contract and therefore a return "promise" was required.

Lucy v. Zehmer (1954)

Facts: Zehmer signed a memorandum agreeing to sell his family farm to Lucy. Zehmer claimed that it was part of a joke he was playing on Lucy.

Issue: Can a contract be avoided if one party claims that the "whole matter was a joke"?

Rule: The intention of a party to a contract is judged by his words and acts (objective standard), not by his unexpressed state of mind (subjective standard).

Frigaliment Importing Co. v. B.N.S. Int'l Sales Corp. (1960)

Facts: B.N.S. agreed to supply Frigaliment with 100,000 lbs. of chicken. While Frigaliment interpreted "chicken" to mean only young chickens suitable for broiling and frying, B.N.S understood it to mean any bird of that genus that met the contractual specifications of weight and quality.

Issue: How does a court resolve conflicting interpretations of a key word in the contract?

Rule: If a party seeks to introduce a narrower definition of a word in the contract, it bears the burden of proving that its definition was accepted by the other party or that it is the acceptable trade use of the term.

Spaulding v. Morse (1947)

Facts: As part of his divorce settlement, Morse was required to pay $1,200 per year to a trust fund for the education and maintenance of his son. The amount was to rise to $2,200 for the four years the son spent in college. The son was drafted when he graduated from school. Morse refused to pay the $1,200 during the son's tenure in the Army, claiming he was not required to do so by the agreement.

Issue: In interpreting the meaning of a contract, can a court look at the circumstances surrounding its formulation in addition to its express terms?

Rule: A written contract is to be interpreted with a view to the circumstances of the parties at the time of its making. If the purpose was to provide support for the son, who is now being maintained and educated by the Army, the promisor's duties are relieved.

Lonergan v. Scolnick (1954)

Facts: The defendant advertised his property for sale and responded to the plaintiff's inquiries by describing the location of the property and stating his lowest price. The defendant's reply carried the caption "this is a form letter." The plaintiff made a second inquiry, but received the defendant's response only after the property was sold.

Issue: Is a form letter an offer?

Rule: A contract is not formed when the minds of the parties have not met and mutually agreed upon some specific thing. A contract does not exist if it is clear that the parties do not intend to bind themselves without further negotiations.

Akers v. J.B. Sedberry, Inc. (1955)

Facts: Sedberry did not respond when Akers and another employee offered to resign during a meeting. Several days later, Sedberry accepted the offer to resign.
Issue: Does an offer made during a conversation end with the conversation?
Rule: Ordinarily, an offer made by one to another in a face-to-face conversation is deemed to continue only to the close of the conversation and cannot be accepted thereafter. If there is no express provision, an offer must be accepted within a reasonable time, which depends on the circumstances surrounding the offer, business usage, or nature of the contract.

Ardente v. Horan (1976)

Facts: The Horans accepted Ardente's bid for their home. In signing the contract, Ardente added a condition that some of the furniture be left in the home.
Issue: Is a conditional acceptance of an offer valid to create a contract?
Rule: A contract is not formed by a conditional acceptance unless the original offeror assents to the additional conditions (Rest. 2d §39).

Shuey v. United States (1875)

Facts: The United States used newspapers to publicize a reward for the arrest of an accomplice in the murder of President Lincoln. The offer was later revoked in the same manner. Shuey, unaware of the revocation, gave information that led to the arrest of the accomplice. She was given a smaller reward.
Issue: How may a general offer that is made to unknown persons via the mass media be revoked?
Rule: An offer of a reward made by means of a published proclamation can be revoked in the manner in which it was made or through similar publicity. There is no legal duty to satisfy an acceptor who does not know of the revocation.

Marchiondo v. Scheck (1967)

Facts: The defendant offered to pay the plaintiff, a broker, a certain commission if the plaintiff succeeded in selling the defendant's property to a specified buyer within six days. The defendant revoked the offer on the sixth day. The plaintiff obtained the buyer's agreement on that same day.

Issue: Can an offer to enter a unilateral contract be revoked at any time?
Rule: When an offer specifies acceptance by performance, the offer is for a unilateral contract and cannot be revoked once the offeree begins performance (e.g., by beginning to solicit the buyer).

Adams v. Lindsell (1818)

Facts: The defendant's offer was delayed in the mail because he addressed it incorrectly. The plaintiff sent out an acceptance immediately. The defendant sold the goods to a third party after the acceptance was mailed but before he received it.
Issue: When does an acceptance sent by mail become effective?
Rule: An acceptance sent by mail becomes effective as of the moment it leaves the offeree's control, i.e., when it is mailed.

Klockner v. Green (1969)

Facts: Klockner's stepmother orally promised Klockner and his daughter that they would receive her estate if they cared for her during her lifetime. Klockner provided care as his stepmother had asked but claimed he would have cared for her even if no promise was made. The stepmother twice drew up a will but never signed it because of superstition. After her death, Klockner sued to recover on the oral promise.
Issue: What is the intent required to accept an offer?
Rule: A valid enforceable contract can be made, obligating one to bequeath her property, even if the services given in exchange for the bequest would have been provided absent the promise.

Holman Erection Co. v. Orville E. Madsen & Sons, Inc. (1983)

Facts: Madsen incorporated Holman's bid for a subcontract in its bid for a general contract. Madsen received the general contract but subcontracted the work to someone else.
Issue: Does a general contractor accept a subcontractor's offer if that subcontractor's offer is used in preparing an offer for a general contract that is later obtained?
Rule: The use of a subcontractor's bid in preparing the general bid does not constitute acceptance of the subcontractor's offer.

Phillips v. Moor (1880)

Facts: The defendant contracted to buy the plaintiff's hay. Before delivery or payment, the hay was destroyed.

Issue: With whom lies the risk of loss of goods that are sold but not yet delivered?

Rule: After the terms of sale are agreed upon and the bargain is struck, the property and risk of accident to the goods vest in the buyer.

Note: Under UCC §2-509, "the risk of loss passes to the buyer on his receipt of the goods if the seller is a merchant; otherwise the risk passes to the buyer on tender of delivery."

Day v. Caton (1876)

Facts: The plaintiff claimed that the defendant expressly agreed to pay for half the value of a wall between their properties. The defendant, who had silently watched the work in progress, denied any such agreement.

Issue: Does a party's silence when witnessing beneficial services rendered on his property obligate him to pay for those services?

Rule: A promise to pay for valuable beneficial services will be inferred if a party voluntarily accepted them, knowing that they were rendered with an expectation of compensation.

Bastian v. Gafford (1977)

Facts: Gafford inquired whether Bastian would be interested in building on Gafford's property. Bastian orally agreed and prepared the plans but was denied the job because his payment schedule was unsatisfactory to the bank financing the construction. Bastian sued to recover the cost of drafting his unused plans, claiming that the parties had an implied-in-fact contract.

Issue: When can a party recover for services rendered in preparation for a contract?

Rule: To recover for services rendered in preparation for a contract, a party must show that the circumstances suggest an implied agreement to pay, or an implied-in-fact agreement.

Note: The case was remanded to determine the existence of an implied-in-fact contract, or agreement to pay for the services; the court below applied the standard of unjust enrichment, which is relevant only in the context of quasi-contract, not implied-in-fact contract.

Pine River State Bank v. Mettille (1983)

Facts: Pine River fired Mettille, an at-will employee. Pine River had given Mettille an employee handbook that contained disciplinary procedures.

Issue: Do disciplinary procedures in an employee handbook, distributed after employment begins, become part of an employee's contract of employment?

Rule: Where an employment contract is for an indefinite duration, continued employment acts as acceptance of new terms of a unilateral contract as embodied in a personnel manual.

Channel Home Centers v. Grossman (1986)

Facts: Channel Home Centers and Grossman signed a letter of intent providing that they would negotiate in good faith for Channel to lease premises in a mall that was being purchased by Grossman, and that Grossman would withdraw the premises from the market. Grossman used the letter to obtain credit and then rented the premises to Channel Home's competitor.

Issue: Is a letter of intent in which the parties promise to bargain in good faith enforceable?

Rule: An agreement to negotiate in good faith is enforceable if the parties intended to be bound, and there are definite terms and consideration.

Note: In the instant case, the letter was enforceable because it was evidence of an intent to be bound, the terms were detailed in the letter, and the credit obtained by use of the letter was consideration.

Dorton v. Collins & Aikman Corp. (1972)

Facts: The Carpet Mart made an oral offer to Collins & Aikman to buy carpeting. Collins & Aikman sent its standard acceptance form, which included an arbitration clause to settle disputes. When a dispute arose, it sought to settle by arbitration. The lower court ruled that since the acceptance included new terms, a contract was formed by the conduct of the parties, and inconsistent terms should be "knocked out" as per UCC §2-207.

Issue: Are parties bound by an arbitration clause included on the back of an acceptance form?

Rule: Under the "battle of the forms" rule of UCC §2-207, a document can be an acceptance even if it is not a "mirror image" of the offer, provided that the conflicting term is not a material alteration.

Note: Some courts hold arbitration clauses to be material alterations.

C. Itoh (America) Inc. v. Jordan Int'l Co. (1977)

Facts: Itoh submitted a purchase order that was accepted by Jordan, subject to conditions printed on the reverse of the acceptance. The reverse contained an arbitration clause, which Jordan sought to enforce when a dispute subsequently arose. Itoh was unaware of the provision.

Issue: Does performance of a defective agreement give rise to a contract?

Rule: When two parties acted under the belief that they had formed a contract, and the parties were unaware that the contract was defective, they have formed a contract based only on the terms to which they had actually agreed.

Daitom, Inc. v. Pennwalt Corp. (1984)

Facts: Pennwalt issued a preprinted purchase order for machinery with standard conditions. Daitom issued a standard preprinted sales form with a different warranty.

Issue: Where a vendor and a vendee issue different preprinted forms stating different terms for service and warranty, what provisions are given effect?

Rule: In a battle of the forms, differing terms knock each other out and the UCC supplies standard provisions.

Cohen v. Cowles Media Co. (1990)

Facts: Cohen offered politically inflammatory documents to reporters on the condition that his identity be kept anonymous. The reporters intended to fulfill the promise, but their editors insisted on printing his name. Cohen received negative media coverage for his disclosure and lost his job.

Issue 1: May one recover on the grounds of fraudulent misrepresentation if a party fails to keep a promise?

Rule 1: For fraud, there must be a misrepresentation of a past or present fact. Thus, a representation as to a future act only supports an action for fraud if the promisor had no intention of performing at the time the promise was made, not merely because the represented act did not occur.

Issue 2: Is an enforceable contract formed where information is given to a reporter in exchange for confidentiality?

Rule 2: An enforceable contract is not formed where information is given to a reporter in exchange for confidentiality, because in the special milieu of news gathering, a source and a reporter do not ordinarily believe that they are making a legally binding contract.

Issue 3: May a political news source recover in estoppel if a promise of anonymity is broken?

Rule 3: A political news source may not recover in estoppel if a promise of anonymity is broken, because the potential for civil damages in this context would violate the First Amendment by interfering with editorial judgment and chilling public debate.

Southworth v. Oliver (1978)

Facts: Southworth entered into preliminary talks with Oliver for the sale of Oliver's land. Southworth claimed the parties agreed to give the matter further consideration. Soon afterward Oliver sent Southworth and three other ranchers a written document stating a price and terms for the sale of the land. Southworth accepted, but problems arose when another rancher also wanted part of the parcel. Oliver claimed that no offer was made to Southworth, so the acceptance was invalid.

Issue: By what standard does a court determine whether statements constitute an offer?

Rule: Whether an offer exists depends on what a reasonable person in the position of the offeree would have believed. While a price quotation is usually not an offer, it can be under certain circumstances. A court will also look at the language used, the definiteness of the terms, and whether the offeree is named.

La Salle Nat'l Bank v. Vega (1988)

Facts: La Salle sued Vega for specific performance and damages resulting from breach of a real estate contract. As a defense, Vega denied the existence of the contract. The document in question provided that the "attached rider is part of this contract." The attached rider provided that "upon execution of this contract by seller, this contract shall be presented to the trust for full execution." The seller signed the document, but a trustee did not.

Issue: May an offeror require written acceptance of an offer by a third party?

Rule: An offeror has complete control over an offer and may condition acceptance to the terms of the offer.

Ever-Tite Roofing Corp. v. Green (1955)

Facts: Green's request to have Ever-Tite re-roof his house stated that acceptance could be given in writing or by commencing work. As Green requested that the entire job be done on credit, Ever-Tite had to verify his creditworthiness, which took eight days. Ever-Tite's workmen arrived to start work the next day and found that Green had revoked the offer and hired another company two days earlier. Green claimed that Ever-Tite waited too long to accept.

Issue: In the absence of an express provision, what is the time limit within which an offer must be accepted?

Rule: The power to create a contract by acceptance of an offer terminates at the time specified in the offer or, if no time is specified, at the end of a reasonable time. Where the offeror should be aware of the source of delay in the offeree's acceptance (e.g., to get credit approval), it is reasonable to allot more time for acceptance.

Corinthian Pharmaceutical Sys., Inc. v. Lederle Laboratories (1989)

Facts: Lederle periodically issued price lists to customers stating that all orders were subject to acceptance at the home office, prices were subject to change without notice, and unfilled current orders would be invoiced at the price in effect at the time of shipment. Aware that Lederle was going to drastically increase the price of DTP vaccine in the near future, Corinthian ordered 1,000 vials. Lederle acknowledged receipt of the order, shipped 50 vials at the lower price, and sent a letter stating that the remaining 950 vials would be invoiced at the increased price if Corinthian still wanted them.

Issue 1: Does acknowledgment of a receipt of a sales order constitute acceptance?

Rule 1: An offer to make a contract invites acceptance in any manner and by any medium that is reasonable in the circumstances, but the offeree must do some act that manifests the intention to accept the offer and make a contract. An automated and ministerial acknowledgment that an order has been received is not a communication or act that is sufficient to constitute an acceptance.

Note: The court here found that under the circumstances, acceptance occurred when the goods were shipped.

Issue 2: If a buyer makes an offer and the seller ships nonconforming goods without otherwise manifesting acceptance, what are the consequences?

Rule 2: An order to buy goods is accepted by a prompt shipment of goods, even if they are nonconforming goods. However, when a shipment of nonconforming goods is accompanied by seasonable notice that the shipment is not an acceptance but an accommodation to the buyer, the shipment is a counteroffer.

Note: The court in this case found that a shipment of 50 vials did not conform with an order for 1,000 vials, and that the letter was seasonable notification that the shipment was not an acceptance of the original order. Thus, the defendant did not have to sell the remaining 950 vials at the lower price.

Hendricks v. Behee (1990)

Facts: On March 3, Behee's agent mailed an offer to the Smiths to purchase real estate. On March 4, the Smiths signed the proposed agreement. Before Behee was notified of the acceptance (ca. March 6), he notified the real estate agent that the offer was withdrawn.

Issue: Does an offeree accept an offer for a bilateral contract by communicating acceptance to his agent?

Rule: An offer for a bilateral contract that is not supported by consideration may be withdrawn if acceptance has not been communicated to the offeror, even if the offeree has already communicated an intent to accept to its own agent.

Glover v. Jewish War Veterans of United States (1949)

Facts: Jewish War Veterans offered a reward for information leading to the arrest of a murderer. Glover, unaware of the reward, provided the information during a police interrogation.

Issue: Is a person who accepts an offer without knowledge of the existence of the offer legally entitled to the benefits of the offer?

Rule: There can be no contract unless an acceptance is made with knowledge of an offer and an intention to accept it.

"Industrial America," Inc. v. Fulton Indus. Inc. (1971)

Facts: Industrial, a broker specializing in mergers and acquisitions, responded to Fulton's advertisement to acquire other companies by introducing one of its clients to Fulton. The client and Fulton agreed to a merger without the use of Industrial's services or payment of a commission. Fulton's advertisement had proclaimed that "brokers [were] fully protected."

Issue: If an offer states that acceptance can be made by performance, must the offeree also show an intention to accept?

Rule: When acceptance can be accomplished by performance of an act (e.g., finding a company that wants to merge), such performance alone will constitute an acceptance unless there is a manifestation to the contrary.

Russell v. Texas Co. (1956)

Facts: Russell was the surface owner of a parcel of land to which Texas Co. had underground rights. Texas also made use of the surface area, which prompted Russell to offer a revocable permit that would be "accepted" if Texas continued to use the roadway, water, or materials on the land. Texas did not stop using the land, but claimed that no contract was formed because it had not intended to accept Russell's offer.

Issue: Does the use of the benefits of an offer constitute an acceptance?

Rule: If an offeree exercises dominion over things that were offered to him, such exercise of dominion, in the absence of other circumstances showing a contrary intention, is an acceptance. The test is not the offeree's subjective intent, but rather what the offeror could reasonably conclude from the offeree's actions.

Ammons v. Wilson & Co. (1936)

Facts: Ammons placed an order (offer) with Wilson's salesman subject to approval by Wilson's home office. In past dealings, Ammons received a response from the defendant within a week. Wilson rejected the offer after 12 days of silence.

Issue: Can acceptance be implied from silence?

Rule: Where previous dealings or other circumstances give an offeror reason to believe that silence or inaction is intended by the offeree as a manifestation of assent, silence and inaction operate as an acceptance.

Harris v. Time, Inc. (1987)

Facts: Harris' son opened an envelope that indicated that Time would give him a free watch simply for opening the envelope. The contents revealed that he would also have to subscribe to a magazine to obtain the watch. Harris, a prominent public-interest lawyer, sued Time for $15 million on theories of breach of contract, promissory estoppel, as well as several tort claims.

Issue: Do junk-mail envelopes create unilateral contract offers?

Rule: Although a misleading promise on an envelope may technically support a breach of contract action, where the only detriment suffered is the act of opening the envelope, the action will be dismissed as *de minimis.*

Minneapolis & St. Louis Ry. Co. v. Columbus Rolling-Mill Co. (1886)

Facts: In response to a query, Columbus provided the Minneapolis & St. Louis Railroad with a price quote for the purchase of 2,000 to 5,000 tons of iron rails. The railroad was given 12 days to accept. It ordered only 1,200 tons at the quoted price, and Columbus refused to fill the order. Before the 12 days were up, the railroad made a second order for 2,000 tons, and Columbus again refused.

Issue: Is an "acceptance" that changes the terms of the offer, such as quantity, a rejection of the offer and a counteroffer?

Rule: Responding to an offer with an "acceptance" that changes a material term has the legal effect of being a rejection of the offer and a counteroffer. The original offeror now has the power to reject or accept.

Leonard Pevar Co. v. Evans Prods. Co. (1981)

Facts: Pevar called Evans for a price quotation. Pevar claims it ordered plywood and entered into an oral contract for sale. Evans admits there was a phone call but denies that it accepted an order. Two days later, Pevar sent a written purchase order to Evans specifying price, quantity and shipping instructions but making no reference to warranties. Evans sent an acknowledgment to Pevar, which stated in boilerplate fashion that the sales contract would be expressly contingent upon Pevar accepting all terms in the document including a disclaimer of all warranties.

Issue: How should courts resolve the "battle of the forms"?

Rule: If a court determines that an oral agreement has been reached and the parties send each other additional terms that do not materially alter the oral agreement, then the terms will be incorporated into the agreement. If the terms materially alter the agreement, they will not be incorporated, and standardized "gap filler" provisions of the UCC will provide the terms of the contract. If a court determines that in the absence of an oral contract the parties have exchanged writings that do not contain identical terms and there is a clause conditioning acceptance on assent to the additional or different terms, there is no contract and either party may walk away from the deal. If the writings of the parties do not establish a contract but the conduct of both parties indicates they recognize the existence of a contract, a court will imply a contract. The terms will include those on which the parties' writings agree, and the remainder will be provided by UCC "gap fillers."

Note: The court remanded the case to determine which of the above rules was applicable to the facts.

Humble Oil & Refining Co. v. Westside Investment Corp. (1968)

Facts: Westside granted Humble an exclusive and irrevocable option to purchase land in exchange for consideration of $35,000. Humble suggested amending the terms of the sales contract but later tried to exercise the option on its original terms.

Issue: Does the rule that a qualified acceptance acts as a rejection also void an option secured in exchange for consideration?

Rule: An option secured in exchange for valuable consideration will remain in effect, even after its holder makes a counteroffer.

Varney v. Ditmars (1916)

Facts: In February 1911, the plaintiff, an architect, was told that he would receive a raise immediately and a bonus if he stayed through the year and completed certain projects. Upon falling sick in November, the plaintiff was discharged. He sued for wages to the end of the year and for his bonus.

Issue: Is an executory contract enforceable if it is silent as to the price term?

Rule: An executory contract that is silent as to the price term is too indefinite to be binding.

Note: The court only considers the issue of the bonus. Cardozo, in dissent, argues that the court ignored that the employment contract was to run to the end of the year and that the plaintiff should have been compensated accordingly.

Community Design Corp. v. Antonell (1984)

Facts: Antonell was employed by CDC as an architect. The president of CDC promised a bonus to any employee still working at Christmas time. The amount of the bonus was to be determined by the vice-president of CDC, who had also promised Antonell a one-week paid vacation if drawings were completed on time. Antonell received neither. CDC argued that the agreement was too indefinite to be enforced because the amount of the bonus and the degree of completion were indefinite.

Issue: Is an oral employment agreement too vague to be enforceable if the exact job requirements and compensation rate are missing?

Rule: Where one party has received the benefit of the other's performance and the existence of a contract is clear, the benefited party must act in good faith to fulfill its promises. Reasonable compensation is to be determined by the jury.

Metro-Goldwyn-Mayer, Inc. v. Scheider (1976)

Facts: MGM made an initial oral contract to hire Scheider to act in a television series. In the weeks that followed, most of the essential terms were settled. Scheider acted in and was compensated for the pilot film, but refused to act in the series to follow. Scheider claimed that the contract was never set, as the starting date for filming the TV series was not specified.

Issue: Is an employment contract unenforceable if it is missing an essential term?

Rule: If the parties have agreed to what they regard as the essential elements of an agreement, and performance has begun on the good faith understanding that agreement on the unsettled matters will follow, courts will find and enforce a contract even though the parties have expressly left certain elements for future negotiation, provided the elements can be objectively determined.

Oglebay Norton Co. v. Armco, Inc. (1990)

Facts: For many years, Oglebay shipped iron ore for Armco. Armco relied upon Oglebay to ship its goods, and Oglebay made expensive capital improvements to accommodate Armco's shipping needs. The contract had a pricing mechanism whereunder Armco would pay the shipping rates recognized by leading ore shippers for that season. If there was no recognized rate, the parties were to agree upon a rate, based upon the rate being charged for similar transportation by leading independent shippers. The parties could not agree upon a rate.

Issue: May a court fill in a price term when a contractual pricing mechanism fails to establish a price?

Rule: Where parties clearly intended to be bound by a contract, but the price term was to be fixed by some agreed market mechanism that fails to do so, a court may set a reasonable price based on market conditions at the time of performance.

Konic Int'l Corp. v. Spokane Computer Servs., Inc. (1985)

Facts: Spokane was searching for a surge protector. It had found several units priced between $50 and $200, but none served its needs. Konic had an appropriate unit, which it offered for sale for the price of "fifty-six, twenty." The defendant accepted. The unit was delivered, installed, and used for a short period, until the parties realized that Konic had meant $5,620, and Spokane had understood $56.20.

Issue: What is the status of a contract when the parties have different, reasonable understandings of a price term?

Rule: When parties have different understandings of a material contract term (such as a hundred fold discrepancy in price), and the term is expressed in an ambiguous form to which both meanings could apply, there is no meeting of the minds and therefore no contract.

Beachcomber Coins, Inc. v. Boskett (1979)

Facts: Beachcomber, a coin dealer, sought rescission of a coin purchased by him from Boskett. At the time of purchase neither party knew that the coin was actually counterfeit. Beachcomber had inspected the coin prior to buying.

Issue: Is a contract voidable for a mutual mistake of fact?

Rule: A contract is voidable by either party when both parties are under a misapprehension regarding a fact assumed by both as the basis of their transaction. Moreover, negligent failure of a party to know or discover the erroneous fact does not preclude rescission.

Lenawee County Bd. of Health v. Messerly (1982)

Facts: Unknown to the Messerlys, a previous owner of their land had installed an illegal underground septic tank. The Messerlys then sold the property, which included a three-unit apartment building, to Pickles.

The contract had an "as is" clause, which shifted the risk of unknown defects to Pickles. Six days after the sale, sewage from the tank oozed up to the surface of the property, and the county condemned the property until the sewage system could conform to the sanitation code. The Pickles sought rescission of the sales contract.

Issue: Is a hidden defect sufficient grounds for rescission of a contract on the basis of mutual mistake?

Rule: A rescission on the grounds of mutual mistake may be granted when the mistake relates to a basic assumption of the parties upon which the contract is made and which materially affects the agreed performances of the parties. However, where both parties are equally innocent and have allocated the risk of loss, rescission will not be granted.

Note: Courts are divided on the effectiveness of "as is" clauses. (Rest. 2d §124.)

Ayer v. Western Union Tel. Co. (1887)

Facts: Western Union made an error while transmitting Ayer's offer. Ayer complied with the erroneous offer and sued to recover its loss from Western Union.

Issue: Is an offeror obligated to comply with an offer whose terms are incorrectly transmitted?

Rule: The party that selects the means of communication of its offer bears the risk of loss caused by errors in transmission (i.e., must comply with the mistaken terms). However, it can recover its loss from the negligent transmitter of the message.

K.D. v. Educational Testing Service (1976)

Facts: While registering to take the LSAT, K.D. signed a stipulation stating that the Educational Testing Service (ETS) "reserve[d] the right to cancel any test score if . . . there is adequate reason to question its validity." Finding a suspiciously high correlation between K.D. and a nearby student, ETS offered a free retest as an alternative to canceling K.D.'s score. In seeking to enjoin the ETS from canceling his score (he refused the retest), he claimed it was a contract of adhesion, as he was unable to negotiate its terms or contract elsewhere.

Issue: When may a contract be voided on the grounds that it was an adhesion contract?

Rule: An offending clause of a contract of adhesion may be voided if it is found to be unfair and unreasonable.

Note: Here, the court found that ETS had taken a reasonable measure to protect its reputation for accurate aptitude forecasting.

Hoffman v. Horton (1972)

Facts: The auctioneer at a land sale closed on Hoffman's initial bid of $177,000. Prior to or simultaneously with the auctioneer's act of closing the bidding, a higher bid was placed by another party. The auctioneer reopened the bidding; Hoffman finally bought the land at a higher price and sued to recover the difference.

Issue: May an auctioneer reopen bidding for land when a higher bid is made just prior to or simultaneously with the falling of the hammer?

Rule: UCC §2-328 provides auctioneers with discretion to reopen the bidding when it is apparent to them that a higher bid has been made "prior to or simultaneously with" the failing of the hammer.

Note: Although the UCC is technically applicable only to the sale of goods, it is considered guiding in the sale of land.

United States v. Briggs Manufacturing Co. (1972)

Facts: Briggs quoted shipping prices to Toombs to induce Toombs to purchase housing.

Issue: May an estimated price be regarded as a term of an offer?

Rule: When both parties anticipate that an estimated price is reasonably accurate and will be relied upon, the doctrine of equitable estoppel may preclude one party from passing on damages not foreseen from the offer. Briggs was estopped from claiming damages not listed as potential costs.

Texaco, Inc. v. Pennzoil Co. (1987)

Facts: Pennzoil sought to recover damages from Texaco for tortious interference with a contract between Pennzoil and the "Getty entities" (Getty Oil Co., the Sarah C. Getty Trust and the J. Paul Getty Museum). The jury found that the Getty entities intended to bind themselves to an agreement providing for the purchase and division of their assets by Pennzoil. On appeal, Texaco claimed that as a matter of law the agreement's language reflected an intent to be bound only at a later point upon execution of a formal, final agreement.

Issue: Is the determination of whether an informal agreement is binding a matter of fact for the jury or one of law for the court to decide?

Rule: When a question of the parties' intent to be bound is not clear from their writings, the matter is left to the jury.

Note: Four factors are used to determine whether a party intended to be bound only by a formal, signed agreement: express stipulation of binding conditions, partial performance, remaining negotiable terms and the complexity and magnitude of the agreement as requiring a final, formal writing.

Haines v. City of New York (1977)

Facts: In 1924, the City of New York agreed with the Town of Hunter and Village of Theater that the City would provide and maintain sewage treatment plants in order to prevent the release of untreated sewage into the City's reservoir, while the Town and Village would maintain the appropriate easements. In addition, the agreement provided that the City would extend sewage lines as growth required. Haines, a developer, brought this action to compel the City to extend its lines to new properties, and if necessary, to expand or rebuild the facilities to meet the new capacity requirements.

Issue: In the absence of a clause designating duration, how long are parties bound by a contract?

Rule: Where the parties have not expressly provided for the duration of an agreement, the court shall imply that the parties intended performance to continue for a reasonable time.

Note: This rule does not apply to employment, exclusive agency, distributorship or requirements contracts.

Wagenseller v. Scottsdale Memorial Hospital (1985)

Facts: Catherine Wagenseller enjoyed a good relationship with her manager, Kay Smith, and her employer, Scottsdale Hospital. Wagenseller and Smith took a trip together during which Wagenseller refused to join in the lewd behavior, such as public excretion and "mooning," of Smith and their other companions. Following the trip, the relationship between Wagenseller and Smith deteriorated until Wagenseller was terminated by Smith. Wagenseller brought this action for reinstatement and other remedies.

Issue: Are there any limitations on the employment-at-will doctrine, which provides that an employer may fire an employee for any reason, including one unrelated to job performance?

Rule: An employee whose contract does not specify duration is terminable for good cause or no cause, but not for "bad" cause. Terminations for refusal to violate public policy, such as statutes banning indecent exposure, are bad causes.

Southwest Engineering Co. v. Martin Tractor Co. (1970)

Facts: Martin agreed to supply Southwest with a generator and other equipment. A memorandum of the agreement made on Martin stationery specified most of the terms besides the manner of payment. Martin later refused to perform, claiming that the contract was too indefinite, and that it violated the Statute of Frauds.

Issue 1: Is an agreement that is recorded in a memorandum valid?

Rule 1: A written memorandum that is signed contains terms for a contract for the sale of goods, and specifies the quantity involved will satisfy the writing requirement of the Statute of Frauds.

Issue 2: Does a valid agreement that lacks some terms fail as being too vague?

Rule 2: A court can enforce a contract that has some missing terms if the essential terms are present and the parties intended to enter into a contract. Missing terms can be implied by the court (UCC §2-310, 2-204(3)).

Note: "Signed" includes any symbol or printing that is intended to authenticate the writing.

Eckles v. Sharman (1977)

Facts: The owner of the Utah Stars, a professional basketball team, brought this action for breach of contract against the team's former coach, Sharman. The contract stated generally that Sharman would receive a pension plan and an option to buy 5 percent of the Stars and that failure to resolve one portion of the contract would not void the rest. The specifics of the option and pension were negotiated but never resolved during the year that Sharman coached the Stars. Sharman then left to coach another team, claiming the contract was invalid.

Issue: When does failure to agree on terms of a contract render the contract invalid?

Rule: Failure to agree on terms will invalidate a contract if the terms are essential. Essence depends on the intent of the parties.

Broadnax v. Ledbetter (1907)

Facts: Having recaptured a criminal without knowledge of any reward for doing so, the plaintiff brought this action to compel delivery of the reward.

Issue: Must a party have knowledge of an offer before acting in order to satisfy the meeting of the minds requirement and bind the offeror?

Rule: An offeror is only bound by a promise if such promise induced action in another party. If a party acted without knowledge, there is no meeting of the minds and that action cannot serve as acceptance of the offer.

Wilhoite v. Beck (1967)

Facts: Ruth Beck, a cousin of Lawrence, brought this action against Lawrence's estate for room, board, care and companionship rendered during the 20 years Lawrence lived in Beck's home.

Issue: May an implied contract to pay for valuable services be inferred between relatives?

Rule: An implied contract to pay for services will be found where there is evidence that the parties intended to arrange for payment.

Note: Blood relationships do not in and of themselves raise a presumption of gratuity. However, a blood relationship between parties living together as a family may raise a rebuttable presumption of gratuity. In this case, the evidence suggested that Lawrence intended to compensate Beck for services, that she did not do so in her will, and that the relationship between them did not raise a presumption of gratuity.

Fujimoto v. Rio Grande Pickle Co. (1969)

Facts: Jose Bravo and George Fujimoto were hired by Rio Grande Pickle Co. to perform jobs with significant managerial authority. In order to encourage Bravo and Fujimoto to work hard and to stay with the company, the president of Rio Grande offered each a written contract containing a promise of a bonus of 10 percent of company profits. After receiving the offers, the two continued to work for 14 months. Rio Grande refused to deliver the bonuses, claiming that Bravo and Fujimoto never accepted the offers.

Issue: How may an offer be accepted if no provision for acceptance has been specified?

Rule: The mode of expressing assent is inconsequential so long as it effectively makes known to the offeror that the offer has been accepted.

Note: In this case, the employees' assent by continuing to work should have been unmistakable to Rio Grande.

Swift & Co. v. Smigel (1971)

Facts: Smigel promised Swift & Co. that he would make good any bills for provisions incurred by Pine Haven, the corporation of which he possessed a one-half stock interest. During the period Swift was delivering merchandise to Pine Haven, Smigel was found by a court to be incompetent.

Issue: Does an offer terminate upon adjudication of an offeror's incompetence?

Rule: An offer accepted in good faith without knowledge of the offeror's incompetence is valid until notice is given.

Diamond Fruit Growers, Inc. v. Krack Corp. (1986)

Facts: When sued by the Diamond Fruit Growers, Inc. for the value of fruit lost when a Krack cooling system failed, the Krack Corp. sued Metal-Matic, its tubing supplier. Metal-Matic had expressly conditioned its tubing sales on a clause limiting liability to refunds, replacements or costs of repairs to defective tubing. Although a discussion of the liability clause ended in Metal-Matic's refusal to change its terms, the two continued to do business together.

Issue: When disagreements over terms remain after the bargaining process has ended, which terms govern?

Rule: All agreed upon terms constitute the contract, and the gaps are to be filled by the UCC, unless the disputed terms are so material as to void the contract.

Note: In this case, the evidence was sufficient to support the imposition of third-party damage liability on Metal-Matic. This case is a sound rejection of the common law last-shot rule in favor of the neutrality of UCC §2-207(3).

Plantation Key Developers, Inc. v. Colonial Mortgage Co. of Indiana, Inc. (1979)

Facts: Colonial Mortgage agreed to make permanent mortgages available for one year for purchasers of Plantation Key Developers condominiums for a $60,000 fee. The contract provided Plantation with an option to extend the arrangement at rates to be adjusted by Colonial only as market conditions demanded. The terms of the extension were to be secured with an additional $30,000 upon renewal. Plantation sued for breach of the option contract when Colonial nearly tripled the loan service fee for the six-month extension without market impetus.

Issue: In an option contract, what responsibility does the offeror have to maintain the terms promised to the offeree?

Rule: If the offeree has secured the contract with consideration (here, $60,000), the offeror is required to keep the option open on the terms originally specified.

Normile v. Miller (1985)

Facts: Normile made an offer to purchase real estate from Miller. The offer contained a time limit for acceptance. Miller rejected the offer and made a counteroffer with no time provision. Before Normile answered the counteroffer, Miller contracted to sell the land to a third party. After Normile found out that Miller had revoked her counteroffer by selling to the third party, Normile signed the counteroffer and returned it to Miller within the time limit stated in the original offer.

Issue: Does a time limit provision from an original offer apply to a counteroffer that does not expressly adopt it?

Rule: A time limit provision in an original offer is not incorporated into a counteroffer if it is not expressly adopted, because the counteroffer serves as a rejection of the original offer.

Mid-South Packers, Inc. v. Shoney's, Inc. (1985)

Facts: Mid-South negotiated to sell pork products to Shoney's and wrote a "proposal." The proposal stated the pork price and required that 45 days' notice be given prior to any price adjustment. Without accepting or rejecting the proposal, Shoney's purchased pork from Mid-South. Subsequently, Mid-South raised the price of pork and Shoney's paid the increased price, but withheld money on their final order. Shoney's claimed that according to the terms of the original contract, it did not have to pay the higher price until 45 days after notice of the increase. Mid-South claimed these transactions were not covered by the original proposal.

Issue: Does a proposal become a binding contract when the parties begin transacting before the proposal is accepted or rejected?

Rule: A proposal is considered at most a firm offer, which will only be binding for three months according to UCC §2-205. After three months, the parties can alter the contract.

Brown Machine, Inc. v. Hercules, Inc. (1989)

Facts: Brown sent Hercules a proposal containing a price quote for the sale of a press. This proposal contained a clause stating that Hercules would indemnify Brown if Brown was held liable for any claims arising from the operation or misuse of the press. Hercules responded with a purchase order with no indemnification clause rejecting all additional terms proposed by Brown. Brown sent back an order acknowledgment that contained the same indemnity clause as the original proposal. Brown delivered the press. A Hercules employee was injured while using the press, and recovered against Brown. Brown sued Hercules for indemnification, claiming that its original proposal containing the indemnity clause was an offer that Hercules accepted. Hercules claimed that it never accepted Brown's proposal. Rather Hercules' purchase order without the indemnity clause was the offer that Brown accepted.

Issue 1: Is a proposal containing a price quotation an offer, or an invitation to make an offer?

Rule 1: A price quotation is not an offer, but rather an invitation to enter into negotiations, unless it is sufficiently detailed to be construed as an offer creating the power of acceptance.

Issue 2: Do additional terms in an acceptance constitute a counteroffer?

Rule 2: An acceptance with additional terms will be considered a counteroffer only if the acceptance is expressly made conditional on assent to the additional terms. The additional terms will be incorporated into the contract only if they do not materially alter it.

Walker v. Keith (1964)

Facts: Plaintiff leased a lot from Defendant. The lease contained a renewal option that stated the rent for the additional term would be agreed upon if the option was exercised. The option failed to provide a method as to how future rent should be fixed. The parties were unable to agree upon the new rent.

Issue: Is a provision stating that the parties will agree upon future rent, which lacks a method as to how the rent should be fixed, so indefinite that it is not binding?

Rule: A renewal option that fails to specify either an agreed rent, or an agreed method by which to fix the rent, is unenforceable because it is too indefinite.

Favrot v. Barnes (1976)

Facts: Favrot and Barnes signed a prenuptial agreement stipulating they would limit sexual intercourse to once a week. Favrot filed for divorce because his wife demanded intercourse more than three times a day.

Issue: Is a contract term that attempts to modify marital obligations enforceable?

Rule: The law does not authorize contractual modifications of marriage obligations. Marriage obliges each spouse to fulfill certain obligations, including sex, which cannot be altered by a pre-marital agreement.

Morone v. Morone (1980)

Facts: The parties were an unmarried couple who lived together for 20 years, holding themselves out to the community as husband and wife. Together they had two children. After they separated, the plaintiff sued under implied contract to get her share of the couple's earnings and assets. She also claimed that the defendant had expressly promised that he would support her in return for her domestic services.

Issue 1: May a contract regarding earnings and assets be implied from a relationship of an unmarried couple?

Rule 1: An implied contract between an unmarried couple living together is too indefinite to be enforced as well as contrary to statutes that have abolished common law marriage.

Issue 2: Is an express contract between such a couple enforceable?

Rule 2: An express contract is enforceable so long as illicit sexual relations were not part of the consideration of the contract.

Nebraska Seed Co. v. Harsh (1915)

Facts: Nebraska Seed alleged that a seed-purchase contract was formed when it accepted an offer it received in a letter from Harsh. Harsh denied that the letter was an offer.

Issue: Does a letter to a dealer discussing price and quantity constitute a binding offer by the seller?

Rule: A letter is not an offer if the language used is general and not intended to be an offer. The court ruled that the letter was not an offer.

Arcadian Phosphates, Inc. v. Arcadian Corp. (1989)

Facts: Plaintiff claimed that a memorandum describing the sale of Defendant's fertilizer business was a binding contract. The memorandum documented a number of terms, but some terms remained to be negotiated. Plaintiff sued based on breach of contract and promissory estoppel.

Issue: Is a preliminary agreement binding when the parties have not yet committed to all of the terms?

Rule: A preliminary agreement is binding if the language of the agreement manifests an intent to be bound. Other indications of intent are the context of negotiations, the existence of open terms, partial performance, and the necessity of putting the agreement in final form. Promissory estoppel may also be used to enforce a commitment to a preliminary agreement by showing a clear and unambiguous promise, a reasonable and foreseeable reliance by the promisee, and an injury sustained by the promisee.

Giant Food, Inc. v. Ice King, Inc. (1988)

Facts: Giant negotiated to have Ice King supply it with ice. Ice King argued that it was led to believe that they were negotiating to supply Giant with ice regularly, but Giant only considered Ice King to be a safety valve, to be used only if its own plant was not operational.

Issue: Is there a cause of action for the tort of negligent misrepresentation when a party issues statements that induce reliance?

Rule: There is a duty to furnish correct information when a relationship gives one party the right to rely upon the other. When information is negligently misrepresented, and reliance is justified, a party has a right to relief.

Marsh v. Lott (1908)

Facts: Marsh sought specific performance for the sale of real estate. Marsh claimed that he gave consideration of 25 cents in exchange for the option to purchase land for $100,000.

Issue: What constitutes sufficient consideration for an option to purchase real estate?

Rule: Any money consideration, however small, paid in exchange for an option to purchase property at its adequate value, is binding upon the seller for the time specified.

Beard Implement Co., Inc. v. Krusa (1991)

Facts: Beard alleged a breach of contract by Krusa for the purchase of a combine, claiming that Krusa had signed a purchase order and issued a check as a down payment. The purchase order, however, was not signed by Beard's representative.

Issue: Is there an acceptance if a purchase order is signed by the buyer but not by the seller?

Rule: If a purchase order clearly requires the signature of the seller's authorized representative, no contract exists.

American Parts Co., Inc. v. American Arbitration Assoc. (1967)

Facts: Deering Milliken orally agreed to sell fabric to American Parts. Deering sent American Parts two "confirmation of order" forms that contained a price term and an arbitration provision. American Parts claimed that the price term was incorrect but accepted shipment from Deering and paid the incorrect price. American Parts eventually stopped purchasing from Deering, and Deering tried to invoke the arbitration provision in the "confirmation of order." However, American Parts claimed that each shipment was a separate transaction and denied that the "confirmation of order" was a contract. American Parts sued for a stay of arbitration proceedings.

Issue: Does a written "confirmation of order" that contains an additional term operate as a modification to a prior oral contract?

Rule: If the seller and purchaser are both merchants, and a firm oral agreement is reached, the seller's written confirmation of order acts as a modification of the contract if the confirmation's changes are immaterial to the contract, and the seller performs the contract as written.

Owen v. Tunison (1932)

Facts: Owen wrote Tunison to ask if he would sell his store property for $6,000. Tunison replied "It would not be possible for me to sell it unless I received $16,000 cash." Owen then wrote back accepting this term but Tunison refused to sell.

Issue: Is a price quote in response to an inquiry an offer to sell?

Rule: A seller's minimum acceptable price is not an offer to sell, but rather an invitation to negotiate.

Harvey v. Facey (1893)

Facts: Harvey was interested in a piece of property owned by Facey. He sent Facey a telegram asking him the minimum price for which he would sell the property. Facey quoted a price and Harvey sent a telegram stating that he would pay it. Harvey sued for specific performance.

Issue: Does a statement of the minimum price at which a vendor will sell constitute an offer?

Rule: A mere statement of the lowest price at which a vendor will sell is not an offer to sell at that price to the person making the inquiry.

International Filter Co. v. Conroe Gin, Ice & Light Co. (1925)

Facts: International Filter sold its products through traveling salesmen who carried order forms. The forms stated that a contract would be formed once a buyer "accepted" the offer by ordering the product, and an executive officer at International Filter's home office approved the order ("accepted" the acceptance). Conroe sent an order that was approved, but he later sought to cancel the order.

Issue: Must "acceptance of an acceptance" of an offer be directly and formally communicated?

Rule: A valid contract can be formed without communication of approval of acceptance if the offer indicates that such communication is not required.

Ragosta v. Wilder (1991)

Facts: Defendant offered to sell "The Fork Shop" as long as the plaintiff met him at a bank with the purchase price at any time until November 1, provided the property had not been sold yet. Plaintiff met all these conditions, but the defendant refused to sell "The Fork Shop." Plaintiff sued for specific performance, claiming that his obtaining financing for the sale was both consideration to support the option contract and performance that served as acceptance of the option.

Issue 1: Will a detriment to the promisee constitute consideration to keep an option open?

Rule 1: A detriment to the promisee will constitute consideration only if it was bargained for by the other party.

Issue 2: Will performance under an otherwise unenforceable option provision keep the option open?

Rule 2: Performance under an otherwise unenforceable option provision will keep the option open only if it is performance invited by the option, not mere preparation for performance.

Step-Saver Data Systems, Inc. v. Wyse Technology (1991)

Facts: Step-Saver purchased computer programs from the defendant, TSL. Step-Saver would order the programs by telephone, and TSL would accept the order and promise prompt delivery. Printed on the packaging of each copy of the program was a "box-top" license, which disclaimed all warranties and instructed the purchaser to return the program if he did not accept these terms. Step-Saver experienced problems with the programs and sued for breach of warranty. TSL argued that it was not liable because the box-top warranty disclaimer was incorporated into the contract.

Issue: Will a box-top disclaimer be incorporated into the terms of a contract if a contract existed before delivery?

Rule: An additional term detailed in a box-top license will not be incorporated into the parties' contract if addition of the term would materially alter the parties' agreement (UCC §2-207).

Toys, Inc. v. F.M. Burlington Co. (1990)

Facts: Toys leased space in Burlington's mall. The lease granted Toys an option to renew the lease for another term, with rent to be based upon the prevailing rate at the time of renewal. Burlington claimed that the option was unenforceable because of an indefinite rent term.

Issue: Is an option contract in a lease that does not fix a specific rent unenforceable for lack of definiteness?

Rule: Option contracts in leases may be enforceable, even if they do not fix a specific rent. The test is whether the option agreement contains all material and essential terms to be incorporated in the subsequent document. It is not necessary that the option agreement contain all the terms of the contract as long as it contains a practicable, objective method of determining the essential terms.

Commerce & Industry Ins. Co. v. Bayer Corp. (2001)

Facts: Seller Bayer sold nylon tow to Buyer Malden Mills. Buyer's form contained an arbitration clause. Seller's form had no clause on dispute resolution but did impose its standard terms as a condition of contract. Fire destroyed Buyer's building; Buyer and its property insurer blamed Seller's nylon tow.

Issue: Is an arbitration clause in the buyer's form only enforceable if the seller's form conditions the contract on accepting its standard terms?

Rule: If the seller's invoice conditions the contract on agreement to its terms, the buyer's arbitration clause is not enforceable. The contract is formed by the parties' conduct under UCC §2-207(3). Terms common to the forms of buyer and seller are in the contract; terms not in both are not.

Izadi v. Machado (Gus) Ford, Inc. (1989)

Facts: A Ford dealer's newspaper advertisement made an offer in prominent text that very small print at the bottom severely qualified. Izadi tried to accept the offer without the qualifications, and the dealer refused, relying on the small print.

Issue: May an advertisement be treated as an offer to enter a contract?

Rule: If a reasonable person would read an advertisement as an offer, it may be accepted and form a contract even if the advertiser did not subjectively intend to make an offer.

Cook v. Coldwell Banker/Frank Laiben Realty Co. (1998)

Facts: Coldwell Banker offered its at-will employees a bonus based on commissions earned, which would be paid at the end of the year. Coldwell Banker announced in September that the year-end bonus would be paid the following March. Cook remained an employee until the end of the year, earning a bonus. She joined another firm in January. Coldwell Banker refused to pay her the bonus.

Issue: May the offeror of a bonus whose purpose is to retain employees revoke the offer if an employee quits?

Rule: The offeror of a bonus based on commissions earned may not revoke it once the bonus has been earned. An employee's continued employment binds the offeror not to revoke it while the employee is earning the right to a bonus.

Harlow & Jones, Inc. v. Advance Steel Co. (1976)

Facts: Buyer Advance agreed on the telephone with Broker VanAs to buy 1,000 tons of steel from Seller Harlow, with shipment in "Sept.-Oct. 1974." Seller and Buyer each confirmed the sale in writing but never acknowledged the other's form in writing. The parties did not set firm delivery dates. Buyer rejected a shipment in November as late. Seller resold it at a loss.

Issue: May a contract for the sale of goods be formed orally?

Rule: A contract for the sale of goods may be formed orally under the UCC and may be confirmed by the parties' conduct. The provisions of the forms the parties send after the contract is formed are memoranda that confirm the sale, and provisions in the forms that agree become part of the sale contract. Buyer may only reject a shipment for material delay, especially in an international sale.

Maglica v. Maglica (1998)

Facts: Anthony, divorced, met and began living with Claire. They both worked in and for Anthony's business, and both were paid a salary. Anthony alone owned it. They held themselves out as married, but state law did not recognize common law marriage. They broke up, and Claire demanded compensation on theories of a contract implied in fact to share the value of the business and of quantum meruit based on her work for the business. The trial court instructed the jury it could not use their cohabitation, their holding themselves out as man and wife, or services as companion and confidant as evidence of an implied contract. For quantum meruit, the trial court also instructed the jury it could measure the value of the services Claire provided by the value they produced for Anthony's business. The jury awarded Claire $84 million.

Issue: In a case by a former cohabitant for compensation, (1) may the jury consider all factors in their relationship in determining whether there was an implied contract to share the increase in value of assets, and (2) in determining the amount of an award in quantum meruit, may the jury consider the impact of the services provided on the value of the assets at issue?

Rule: Contracts implied in fact between cohabitants to share property built up during the relationship can be proved based on a variety of factors, including cohabitation, holding themselves out as married, or companionship. The Court remanded for a new trial on this issue. Quantum meruit claims are measured by the value of services from the view of the service provider, not the impact on the service recipient's business. Including the impact on the business risks giving the service provider a windfall; businesses prosper for all sorts of reasons and causes, and it is impossible to be certain that the services are responsible for any increase in value. Thus, the Court remanded for retrial on that issue also.

Note: Claire accepted a $29 million settlement before the retrial.

ProCD v. Zeidenberg (1996)

Facts: ProCD compiled information, put it in a database, and sold it on a CD-ROM. ProCD sells the product to commercial users for a high price and to non-commercial users at a lower price. It includes a license on paper within each box and on the program itself when the CD-ROM is used, which provides that use of the program by a non-commercial buyer indicates a promise to limit use to non-commercial purposes. Zeidenberg bought the product at the consumer price and created his own business selling the information. Zeidenberg claimed the sale was complete when he bought the item at the store and ProCD could not add new contract terms when Zeidenberg later opened and used the product.

Issue: May a seller bind the buyer to limitations on use of the thing bought that the buyer only becomes aware of after he has paid for and taken possession of the item, and that the buyer agrees to by continuing to use the thing?

Rule: Yes. When, after purchase and delivery, the seller informs the buyer of limitations on use that will bind the buyer if he uses the item (a "shrinkwrap license"), then the buyer must make a choice. He either must accept those limitations, or he must reject the goods under UCC §2-602, which enables the buyer to reject goods after inspection.

Register.com v. Verio (2004)

Facts: Applicants registered internet domain names with Register.com. Verio got information about those applicants from Register's systems by using multiple queries (WHOIS). After each WHOIS query, Register displayed restrictions on the use of the data obtained. For example, the data could be used to send mass unsolicited advertisements (spam). Verio violated those limitations, arguing that it was not bound by the limitations because the restriction on use only appeared after each query.

Issue: May a domain name registrar bind a user by contract not to use information gained from the registrar by computerized queries?

Rule: Yes. While Verio might argue it was not bound by the restrictions if it had made only one query, here it made multiple queries and thus knew of the restrictions that conditioned use of Register's query system and was therefore bound by them.

Shoemaker v. Commonwealth Bay (1997)

Facts: Mortgagors were obligated to maintain insurance on the mortgaged property as term of the mortgage contract. Mortgagors were notified their policy would not be renewed. They alleged that mortgagee made a promise on the telephone to maintain insurance but failed to do so. Mortgagee alleged that notices that the home would be uninsured as of a certain date were sent, which Mortgagors denied receiving. Fire destroyed the house.

Issue: May a claim of promissory estoppel be made in this case?

Rule: Yes. A claim of promissory estoppel requires three elements: (1) the maker of the promise should have reasonably expected to induce action or forbearance by the promise; (2) the promisee must in fact rely on the promise; and (3) injustice can only be avoided by enforcing the promise. Issues of material fact were present for each element.

Specht v. Netscape Communications Corp. (2002)

Facts: When users downloaded Netscape's free SmartDownload plug-in, to see the license terms applicable to that program they had to scroll down below the download button, click on an invitation to review SmartDownload's terms, continue to another webpage called "License and Support Agreements," read through introductory text, finally to find the terms of the license to which they were agreeing by downloading the plug-in.

Those terms included an agreement to arbitrate any dispute between the user and Netscape.

Issue: Is one who downloads software bound by terms of a license that are not spelled out, including an arbitration clause, provided they can be found on the website?

Rule: No. A provider of a free product must provide reasonably conspicuous notice that use will bind the recipient to contract terms. Here, the screens appeared so as to conceal that they acted as express acceptance of Netscape's terms.

Copeland v. Baskin Robbins (2002)

Facts: Baskin Robbins planned to shut down a plant. Copeland wanted to buy the plant, if the seller promised to buy seven million gallons of product from Copeland over three years. Baskin Robbins agreed to do so, and Copeland paid a deposit of $3,000. Thereafter, they could not agree on price and quality of the product that Copeland would sell to Baskin Robbins. So Baskin Robbins returned Copeland's deposit, calling off the sale of the plant. Copeland sued Baskin Robbins for refusing to agree on those terms.

Issue: Is a promise to negotiate an agreement enforceable as a contract?

Rule: Yes, a contract to negotiate requires parties to negotiate in good faith, and is unlike an unenforceable agreement to agree. Damages for breach are limited to the reliance interest.

Hill v. Gateway 2000, Inc. (1997)

Facts: Hill bought computer via telephone. Gateway delivered the computer in a box that also contained a document stating terms of the sales contract that would bind Hill unless he returned the computer at his expense within 30 days. The terms included an arbitration clause. Hill kept the computer for 30 days, and eventually sued based on defects and insufficiency of Gateway service. Gateway moved to dismiss under the arbitration clause; the trial court ruled for Hill.

Issue: May a seller enforce contract terms that the seller communicates and the buyer learns of at delivery of the thing sold?

Rule: The final contract here includes the terms seller includes in the box. The buyer cannot read and ignore them, nor ignore them altogether without reading them. Reading aloud all terms during the initial telephone order is impractical, and approval-or-return is better for buyers as a group.

Note: The case's rolling contract view of formation has been criticized because it permits the seller to use the buyer's silence as acceptance of the seller's new terms in the contract.

Klocek v. Gateway Inc. (2000)

Facts: Klocek bought a computer from Gateway. Gateway delivered the computer in a box that also contained a document stating its standard terms of the sales contract that would bind Klocek if he kept the computer more than five days. The terms included an arbitration clause. Klocek kept the computer for more than five days, and eventually sued based on defects and poor Gateway service. Gateway moved to dismiss under the arbitration clause; the trial court ruled for Klocek.

Issue: May a seller enforce contract terms that the seller communicates and the buyer learns of at delivery of the thing sold?

Rule: No. When the buyer is in the position of offeror and vendor of offeree, when vendor encloses additional terms with the item sold he makes either an expression of acceptance or a written confirmation under UCC §2-207, and such terms are proposals for additions to the contract that the buyer must accept for them to become part of the contract and to bind the buyer. Thus, the arbitration clause cannot be enforced.

Note: This court disapproves of the U.S. Seventh Circuit's decisions for the seller in ProCD v. Zeidenberg and Hill v. Gateway 2000, Inc.

Leonard v. Pepsico Inc. (1999)

Facts: Pepsico created a marketing campaign based on consumers acquiring points by buying its product that consumers could use to redeem products (Pepsi promotional items). In a television commercial, Pepsico showed a character redeeming a military jet through the program. Leonard attempted to redeem the jet by using a combination of points and cash, worth about $700,000. The jet was worth about $23 million. Leonard claimed that he had accepted Pepsico's offer to convey the jet to him for that consideration.

Issue: Can an offeree accept an offer that a reasonable person would understand was a joke and not seriously intended as an offer?

Rule: No. If no reasonable person could understand the commercial as an offer, Leonard cannot accept it and enforce a contract based on it. The court refused to order discovery that might reveal Pepsico's subjective intent, because that intent was irrelevant. Moreover, advertisements are not offers.

MCC-Marble Ceramic Center v. Ceramica Nuova d'Agostino (1998)

Facts: An agent for MCC-Marble signed a sale contract that incorporated by reference terms on the back of the contract document that were in a foreign language that the agent could not understand.

Issue: May written contract terms that the promisor cannot understand nevertheless be enforceable?

Rule: Yes. A sophisticated party dealing in a complex commercial transaction is bound by terms that he adopts, knowing that he cannot understand them.

Mesaros v. United States (1988)

Facts: The United States published an advertisement for the sale of Statute of Liberty commemorative coins. The advertisement stated that sales were subject to final approval of a government representative. Mesaros wanted to buy some of these coins and submitted his credit card number to do so, but the United States Mint rejected his credit card. Far more orders for the coins came in than the Mint could fill.

Issue: Is an advertisement for the sale of an item an offer to sell?

Rule: An advertisement generally merely invites or solicits offers and does not make an offer. Thus, Mesaros did not accept an offer to sell by the government when he submitted his credit card number. No contract was formed and therefore the government did not breach.

Houston Dairy, Inc. v. John Hancock Mutual Life Insurance Co. (1981)

Facts: John Hancock offered in writing to lend a sum of money at a stated interest rate to Houston Dairy. Houston Dairy had to sign and return its acceptance with a $16,000 deposit within seven days. It did so eleven days after the deadline. John Hancock cashed the deposit check. Houston Dairy found another lender whose interest rate was lower and demanded its deposit back from John Hancock, who refused.

Issue: Is a late acceptance sufficient to form a contract if the offeror does not object?

Rule: A late acceptance occurs after the offer has expired and therefore is a counteroffer that must itself be accepted by the original offeror. John Hancock's act of depositing the funds from the check did not clearly accept the counteroffer, and John Hancock did nothing else that clearly accepted it.

Seaview Ass'n of Fire Island, N.Y., Inc. v. Williams (1987)

Facts: Seaview was an unincorporated association of homeowners covering a certain geographic area. Seaview provided various services to all members who resided in that area, and simply owning a home within the area sufficed for membership in the private association of homeowners. Seaview charged all homeowners within the area an assessment to defer the cost of the services it provided. Williams bought several houses within the Seaview area, but denied he owed the assessment because he did not use the services and had not himself joined the association.

Issue: Is purchase of property within a geographic area served by an association of private homeowners enough to be bound to pay an assessment made by the association?

Rule: Buying property within an area served by a private association manifests assent to be bound contractually by the conditions of ownership of property in that area, including the payment of assessments by the association.

Empire Machinery Co. v. Litton Business Telephone Systems (1977)

Facts: Litton as seller gave a form sales agreement for the sale and installation of a telephone system to Empire. The form said that a contract would become effective between the parties when Litton's home office approved, accepted, and executed it. The home office did not sign the form, but Litton took steps to begin installation of the system, then after six months abandoned the project and returned Empire's deposit. Empire sued for breach.

Issue: May an offer that calls only for written acceptance be accepted through conduct?

Rule: Conduct by the offeree that manifests an intent to accept does accept the offer and form a contract, especially when the form on which the offer is made by the customer is supplied by the seller, who is the offeree.

Ionics, Inc. v. Elmwood Sensors, Inc. (1997)

Facts: Ionics bought thermostats from Elmwood to incorporate into water dispensers. Ionics used its purchase order for the transaction, which stated that the purchase order's terms governed the sale exclusively and which reserved all remedies available under state law. Elmwood used its acknowledgment form for the transaction, which stated that its terms governed the transaction exclusively and which contained a limitation of Elmwood's liability. Ionics alleged that the thermostats were faulty and caused fires, which caused losses to Ionics.

Issue: If buyer and seller use forms to document their sale that have terms that are in conflict, does the first form submitted control?

Rule: When terms in the forms used by contract parties conflict, neither party is deemed to accept the conflicting term of the other. The buyer's acceptance of the goods does not manifest acceptance of the seller's terms that conflict with the buyer's terms. UCC §2-207(1). The conflicting terms do not become part of the contract because each party has notified the other of the objection to the other's terms. UCC §2-207(2).

Therefore the contract is formed under the terms of the parties that agree. UCC §2-207(3).

A/S Apothekernes Laboratorium for Specialpraeparater v. I.M.C. Chemical Group, Inc. (1989)

Facts: The president of Apothekernes entered negotiations with the president of I.M.C. to acquire a division of I.M.C. They signed a letter of intent that was not a final contract but obliged each to seek the approval of his respective board of directors to the transaction. The I.M.C. board did not approve the transaction. Apothekernes sued.

Issue: Does a contract party have a duty to negotiate in good faith?

Rule: A letter of intent does not bind either party to the final contract but does bind the parties to negotiate in good faith, for example, not to demand concessions clearly inconsistent with the letter of intent. Here, I.M.C. did negotiate in good faith; the board was not obligated to approve the proposed transaction nor was the president of I.M.C. liable for failing to obtain the approval of the board of directors.

Chomicky v. Buttolph (1986)

Facts: Chomicky promised in writing to buy a tract of real estate from Buttolph, if government approval of a subdivision could be obtained. They agreed orally that if the government did not approve, then Buttolph would give Chomicky a right-of-way. Approval of the subdivision was denied and Buttolph refused to grant the right-of-way.

Issue: Must the modification of a contract to sell real estate be written?

Rule: Both the contract to sell real estate and modifications of that contract must be in writing to be enforced.

Sanchez v. Life Care Centers of America, Inc. (1993)

Facts: Life Care's Handbook of Employment Guidelines stated in a disclaimer that the handbook was not a contract. Sanchez, an employee, was terminated and brought a wrongful termination suit against Life Care.

Issue: May an employer rely on a provision of its employment handbook that disclaims any intent to create contractual obligations in the handbook?

Rule: An employer may not rely on an inconspicuous and ambiguous disclaimer to defeat a wrongful termination suit. Whether the handbook guidelines and procedures modified the state's presumption that all employment is at-will is a mixed question of law and fact to be tried by the judge.

Hoffman v. Horton (1972)

Facts: Hoffman bid at an auction of foreclosed property and the auctioneer signaled with his hands that Hoffman's bid had been accepted. But the auctioneer had missed a higher bid that had followed Hoffman's and so reopened the bidding. Hoffman eventually bought the property, but at a higher price.

Issue: May a bidder at an auction whose bid is accepted but who must pay more because the auctioneer reopens the bidding recover the difference between his final bid and the bid made before bidding was reopened?

Rule: When an auctioneer misses a bid just as another bid is being accepted, the auctioneer has discretion to reopen the bidding and unless such discretion is abused an auctioneer is not liable to a disappointed bidder.

State v. Malm (1956)

Facts: Plaintiff was assaulted and later read of a murder that occurred in a similar way. She gave a description of her assailant. Malm was apprehended as a result. After his arrest, the governor announced a reward for information leading to conviction of the murderer in the second case. Then Malm confessed, and Plaintiff sought to collect the reward.

Issue: May a person who provides the performance requested in a reward offer collect regardless of when the offer is made?

Rule: To be able to collect a reward the person who provides the performance must do so in response to the reward offer, which cannot occur if the reward offer is made after the person has performed.

Gem Broadcasting, Inc. v. Minker (2000)

Facts: Minker made a written offer to work as a consultant for Gem for $385 a day and in fact worked for 30 days. Gem did not accept Minker's offer.

Issue: May a party who proposes a written contract, which is not accepted, to work for so much per day recover based on a contract implied in fact?

Rule: A party who makes a written offer that the offeree does not accept but who works for the offeree in the way that the offer contemplated may allege a contract implied in fact and recover based on quantum meruit. To determine the offeror's compensation on that basis the proposed hourly rate is relevant.

Motel Services, Inc. v. Central Maine Power Co. (1976)

Facts: Motel Services contracted to build housing for a local Housing Authority. Motel Services changed the planned heating systems from oil to electricity based on the promise of a payment to owners of buildings who did so, and installed the electrical heating system while still the owner. Motel Services transferred title to the Housing Authority, and Central Maine Power sent the incentive payment to it and not to Motel Services. **Issue:** Does a power company that offers an incentive for using a certain kind of power system in a building propose a contract to be accepted by performance?

Rule: If an offer requests a performance and not a promise, the offer proposes a unilateral contract under which the acceptance is also the performance. The installation of the electrical heating system was complete while Motel Services was the owner, which entitled it to the incentive payment.

Cantu v. Central Education Agency (1994)

Facts: Cantu delivered her written resignation of employment by hand to her supervisor. The superintendent mailed a response, accepting her resignation. The next day, and before she received the superintendent's letter, Cantu delivered by hand a written retraction of her resignation.

Issue: Does delivering an offer by hand imply that the acceptance must also be delivered by hand?

Rule: For acceptance at a distance, acceptance occurs upon dispatch (the mailbox rule). Use of hand delivery does not by itself alter the rule. Without an express limitation of the means of acceptance to hand delivery, acceptance may occur by any medium reasonable under the circumstances.

Stepp v. Freeman (1997)

Facts: Stepp participated in a 20-member lottery pool with other employees for five years. Freeman managed the pool, reminding members to contribute to the purchase of tickets and bringing in a new member when one dropped out. Stepp and Freeman had a dispute unrelated to the pool. For the next drawing, Freeman didn't remind Stepp to contribute and he paid the price of the missing ticket himself. That pool won $8 million.

Issue: What are the elements of an implied-in-fact contract?

Rule: An implied-in-fact contract is proved by facts and circumstances, including consistent participation over five years and never failing to contribute his share of the ticket price.

Continental Laboratories v. Scott Paper Co. (1991)

Facts: Continental and Scott went through several drafts of a supply and distribution contract. Continental believed they had reached a binding agreement in a final telephone call, but Scott believed they would only be bound by a signed final document. Scott broke off negotiations.

Issue: Is a contract formed orally if one party believes that neither is bound until a written contract is signed by both?

Rule: Where one party does not intend to be bound until a final writing is signed, an oral agreement is not binding.

Marchionado v. Scheck (1967)

Facts: Scheck promised to keep his offer to sell real estate to a particular buyer open for six days and pay Marchionado a commission on the sale. Scheck revoked the offer on the sixth day. The offeree accepted later that day.

Issue: Is a promise to keep an offer open for a specific time enforceable?

Rule: A promise to keep an offer open for a specific time is enforceable as an option leading to a unilateral contract if the performance bargained for begins. Here, Marchionado is entitled to put on proof that he had begun performance so as to bind the offeror's promise to keep the offer open.

Loring v. City of Boston (1844)

Facts: Boston offered a reward for information leading to conviction of an arsonist. Several years later, after the arson outbreak in Boston had ended, Loring found the arsonist.

Issue: Is an offer of reward open indefinitely?

Rule: When an offer of reward is without time limit, a reasonable duration for the offer is implied.

Commerce & Industry Ins. Co. v. Bayer Corp. (2001)

Facts: Seller Bayer sold nylon tow to Buyer Malden Mills. Buyer's form contained an arbitration clause. Seller's form had no clause on dispute resolution but did impose its standard terms as a condition of contract. Fire destroyed Buyer's building; Buyer and its property insurer blamed Seller's nylon tow.

Issue: Is an arbitration clause in the buyer's form only enforceable if the seller's form conditions the contract on accepting its standard terms?

Rule: If the seller's invoice conditions the contract on agreement to its terms, the buyer's arbitration clause is not enforceable. The contract is formed by the parties' conduct under UCC §2-207(3). Terms common to the forms of buyer and seller are in the contract; terms not in both are not.

CyberCorp. v. Calldata Systems Development Inc. (1995)

Facts: Calldata had a contract to sell specially designed computer equipment to the federal government. Calldata submitted an offer to buy a part of it to Cyberchron, which Cyberchron did not accept, but Cyberchron began preparations to perform at the insistence of Calldata. Calldata later bought the same equipment elsewhere for less.

Issue: May a plaintiff who knows it does not have a contract bring an action based on promissory estoppel?

Rule: Where a promisor makes a clear, unambiguous promise, with foreseeable, reasonable reliance by the promisee who does so rely, and with injury in fact to the promisee, the promisee has an action against the promisor based in promissory estoppel for its expenditures made in reliance on the promise, especially where the injury to the promisee is unconscionable.

Armendariz v. Foundation Health Psychcare Services, Inc. (2000)

Facts: An employment contract contained an agreement to arbitrate all disputes arising out of termination. Employer told employee that her position was being eliminated and her employment terminated. Employee claimed sexual harassment.

Issue: Does lack of mutuality render an arbitration clause in an employment contract unenforceable?

Rule: So long as both employer and employee are bound to arbitrate any dispute, an arbitration clause in an employment contract does not lack mutuality, is not illusory, and is enforceable.

Simeone v. Simeone (1990)

Facts: Groom's attorney presented bride with prenuptial agreement not long before the wedding and bride signed. It limited her to a maximum of $25,000 upon divorce.

Issue: May a woman who signs a prenuptial agreement later claim she is not bound by it because it is substantively unfair to her?

Rule: A party who knowingly signs a contract without reading or fully understanding all its provisions is bound by them, even if they favor the other party. A prenuptial contract is treated like other contracts in this regard.

Slattery v. Wells Fargo Armored Service Corp. (1979)

Facts: After its agent was killed, Wells Fargo offered a reward for information leading to the killer's arrest and conviction. The government hired Slattery to do polygraph tests on other matters and he happened to question the killer, who confessed. Slattery sued Wells Fargo for the reward.

Issue: Is a person who provides the action requested in an offer of a reward entitled to collect it, if the person was contractually bound to provide the service?

Rule: One cannot collect a reward for actions one is already obligated by contract to perform, even to a third party. Performance of a pre-existing duty is not consideration sufficient to bind an offeror to a unilateral contract.

McMahon Food Corp. v. Burger Dairy Co. (1996)

Facts: McMahon bought dairy products from Burger Dairy that were delivered in plastic containers for which Burger charged a deposit that was credited to McMahon's account when they were returned. Burger believed that McMahon's account was in arrears but McMahon disputed that claim. McMahon had inconclusive discussions about the problem with Burger Dairy's general manager Bylsma. McMahon then represented to Burger Dairy's new general manager Carter that McMahon and Bylsma had settled the disputed debt. McMahon then submitted a check with a restrictive endorsement that purported to establish that McMahon's account was current and paid in full. Burger crossed out the restrictive endorsement and deposited the check.

Issue: Can a debtor who disputes the amount of his debt end the dispute by issuing a check to his creditor for payment in full?

Rule: In order to extinguish a debt through accord and satisfaction, a check with a restrictive endorsement must be issued in good faith. A debtor is not in good faith if it asserts that a debt has been settled when it in fact still remains in dispute.

Note: In addition to good faith by the debtor, accord and satisfaction requires that such a check clearly purport to discharge a debt and that the payee strike out the restrictive endorsement anyway knowing the purpose of the check.

In re the Marriage of Witten (2003)

Facts: Husband and Wife used in vitro fertilization that produced 17 frozen embryos, signing an "Embryo Storage Agreement." This agreement obligated the storage facility to keep the embryos until both Husband and Wife authorized release or destruction of the embryos; either Husband or Wife died; the storage fee was not paid; or ten years passed from the date of the agreement. The agreement did not mention whether Husband or Wife would control the embryos if they divorced.

Issue: Are contracts for the storage and release of frozen embryos enforceable as are other contracts?

Rule: The decision to bring a child into the world may be made in advance through embryo storage but a court will only enforce that decision if the intentions of both parents continue. Contracts to store and release frozen embryos may not be enforced if either parent no longer wants to proceed with the planned use of the embryos. Therefore, if one parent wishes to destroy the stored embryos but the other parent does not, then the embryos must remain in storage, at the expense of the parent who does not want them to be destroyed.

T. F. v. B. L. (2004)

Facts: A same-sex couple agreed that one would act as a parent and the other would conceive and bear a child through artificial insemination. After the pregnancy occurred, the couple split up. The child was born and the mother sought child support from the other member of the couple.

Issue: Can one make an enforceable promise to take on the responsibilities of a parent to the future child of another?

Rule: A promise to take on the responsibilities of a parent, including financial support, is not enforceable as a contract. The principle of freedom of choice permits the promisor to refuse to perform the promise.

Note: Courts are divided on whether such a promise to act as a parent is enforceable at all and if so on what basis. A separate opinion in this case suggested enforcing the promise of financial support based on estoppel through equity.

Polaroid Corp. v. Rollins Environmental Services (NJ), Inc. (1993)

Facts: Rollins contracted to dispose of Polaroid's chemical waste and agreed to indemnify Polaroid for any loss Polaroid suffered through acts of Rollins or its employees. Chemical waste under Rollins' control spilled, and Polaroid was fined. Polaroid sued Rollins based on the indemnity clause in their contract.

Issue: Does an offeree's promise to indemnify an offeror for losses have to be made as part of each acceptance of materials shipped by the offeror?

Rule: If an offeree accepts an offeror's performance without objecting to the offeror's essential terms, which the offeree is aware of, the offeree is presumed to accept those essential terms as part of the contract. It was unnecessary for Rollins to accept the indemnity clause in writing with each shipment, even if each shipment is viewed as a distinct contract.

Vogt v. Madden (1985)

Facts: Vogt sharecropped land owned by Madden on a year-by-year basis. Vogt wanted to renew the arrangement for the following year; the parties discussed it. Madden did not agree to continue the arrangement and leased the land to another, and insisted the parties had always had express, though oral, contracts in years past.

Issue: May silence on the part of the offeree indicate acceptance of an offer?

Rule: Silence of the offeree does not generally mean acceptance of the offer. Silence or inaction may indicate acceptance if the offeree accepts benefits from the offeror with the knowledge the offeror expected payment, if the offeror states that silence indicates acceptance, or if previous dealings of the parties make it reasonable for the offeree to notify the offeror that he rejects the offer.

Nursing Care Services, Inc. v. Dobos (1980)

Facts: Dobos's doctor ordered nursing care for her around the clock from Nursing Care Services while she was in the hospital and after she was released for about four weeks. Nursing Care Services presented Dobos with a bill for $3,732.90, which Dobos said she had never agreed to pay; she believed that Medicare would pay for it.

Issue: Does voluntary receipt of services that are not given gratuitously obligate the recipient to pay for them, even if the recipient has not promised or contracted to do so?

Rule: If services are given with an expectation of payment and the recipient of the services knowingly and voluntarily accepts them, the law implies a promise by the recipient to pay their reasonable value.

Academy Chicago Publishers v. Cheever (1991)

Facts: An author's widow contracted with Academy Chicago for the publication of an anthology of short stories by the author. Before the parties agreed on a final list of the stories to be included, the widow returned the advance paid by Academy Chicago and attempted to cancel the contract.

Issue: Where the parties intend to contract but fail to agree on essential terms, can the contract be enforced?

Rule: The parties must not only reach an agreement but also must make an agreement that is sufficiently definite so that a court can enforce it without supplying an essential term. In contract for the publication of an anthology of writings by an author, the works to be included is such an essential term, which the court cannot supply.

Teachers Insurance and Annuity Ass'n of America v. Tribune Co. (1987)

Facts: Tribune proposed borrowing money from TIAA as one part of a three-sided transaction. TIAA issued a commitment letter with a detailed term sheet describing the loan in some detail, after which items of less importance remained to be agreed upon. Despite TIAA's willingness to proceed, Tribune ceased negotiating with TIAA, and TIAA sued Tribune for breach.

Issue: Can a commitment letter be sufficiently definite in order to bind the parties contractually?

Rule: If the parties so intend, a commitment letter may bind them contractually, provided it covers all essential terms and leaves relatively minor issues to be resolved. Here, the parties agreed to the essential terms of the loan, leaving questions of documentation of the loan and other non-essential terms to be agreed upon.

Gardner Zemke Co. v. Dunham Bush, Inc. (1993)

Facts: The U.S. Department of Energy hired Gardner Zemke as its general contractor on a project. Gardner Zemke bought air conditioning equipment from Dunham Bush for that project. Gardner Zemke's order form stipulated a one-year manufacturer's warranty and certain specifications for the equipment. Dunham Bush's acknowledgment form disclaimed warranties and provided that the other party's silence should be deemed to be acquiescence to Dunham Bush's terms. When problems surfaced in some of the equipment after installation, Gardner Zemke notified Dunham Bush to make repairs under the warranty, and Dunham Bush refused, based on its disclaimer. The trial court held that Dunham Bush's acknowledgment form acted as a counteroffer that Gardner Zemke accepted by silence.

Issue: Where parties send writings to each other as part of the contract whose terms conflict, do the terms in the form that is sent last control?

Rule: If terms on the parties' forms conflict, each party is presumed to object the other's term and neither conflicting term becomes part of the contract. The contract binds the parties to the terms that they have negotiated and agreed to expressly, together with terms on their forms that do not conflict. Whether a party's acceptance is expressly conditioned on the other party's agreement to its own different or additional terms is a question of fact, on which the parties' conduct during the bargaining process and course of performance is relevant.

Note: See UCC §2-207.

Chateau des Charmes Wines Ltd. v. Sabaté USA Inc. (2003)

Facts: Chateau des Charmes, a Canadian business, had an oral contract to buy corks from Sabaté, an American business. Sabaté shipped the corks from France to Chateau des Charmes, and submitted invoices for the shipments with additional terms, including a clause selecting France as the forum for resolution of disputes. Chateau des Charmes sued Sabaté in California court, claiming the corks were defective.

Issue: Is a forum selection clause that the other party has not signed enforceable?

Rule: The oral contract of the parties was valid and enforceable, and it could be modified by another valid agreement. The proposal by Sabaté to modify the contract by including a forum selection clause was a material change to which the other party had to assent for a modification of the oral contract to occur. Including such a clause on invoices issued by the seller following shipment was insufficient to manifest assent by Chateau des Charmes to this change.

Note: The Convention on the International Sale of Goods applied in this case, which does not include consideration as an element of contract validity.

Izadi v. Machado (Gus) Ford, Inc. (1989)

Facts: A Ford dealer's newspaper advertisement made an offer in prominent text that very small print at the bottom severely qualified. Izadi tried to accept the offer without the qualifications, and the dealer refused, relying on the small print.

Issue: May an advertisement be treated as an offer to enter a contract?

Rule: If a reasonable person would read an advertisement as an offer, it may be accepted and form a contract even if the advertiser did not subjectively intend to make an offer.

Cook v. Coldwell Banker/Frank Laiben Realty Co. (1998)

Facts: Coldwell Banker offered its at-will employees a bonus based on commissions earned, which would be paid at the end of the year. Coldwell Banker announced in September that the year-end bonus would be paid the following March. Cook remained an employee until the end of the year, earning a bonus. She joined another firm in January. Coldwell Banker refused to pay her the bonus.

Issue: May the offeror of a bonus whose purpose is to retain employees revoke the offer if an employee quits?

Rule: The offeror of a bonus based on commissions earned may not revoke it once the bonus has been earned. An employee's continued employment binds the offeror not to revoke it while the employee is earning the right to a bonus.

Harlow & Jones, Inc. v. Advance Steel Co. (1976)

Facts: Buyer Advance agreed on the telephone with Broker VanAs to buy 1,000 tons of steel from Seller Harlow, with shipment in "Sept.-Oct. 1974." Seller and Buyer each confirmed the sale in writing but never acknowledged the other's form in writing. The parties did not set firm delivery dates. Buyer rejected a shipment in November as late. Seller resold it at a loss.

Issue: May a contract for the sale of goods be formed orally?

Rule: A contract for the sale of goods may be formed orally under the UCC and may be confirmed by the parties' conduct. The provisions of the forms the parties send after the contract is formed are memoranda that confirm the sale, and provisions in the forms that agree become part of the sale contract. Buyer may only reject a shipment for material delay, especially in an international sale.

Bretz v. Portland General Electric Co. (1999)

Facts: Bretz wrote a letter to Portland General offering to buy a Portland General Electric subsidiary; this letter laid out in detail how Portland could accept Bretz's offer. They exchanged a series of letters discussing the sale. Portland then wrote Bretz saying there were two more problems to resolve. Bretz answered with an amended offer that addressed those problems and captioned it "Acceptance of Offer." Portland denied that a contract had been formed and Bretz sued for breach.

Issue: May an exchange of letters that show agreement on the details of a proposed transaction be enforced as a contract?

Rule: For a party who denies that a contract was formed to be bound by a contract, that party's manifestations must reasonably be understood by the other party as assent to the contract. Here, Bretz could not reasonably have understood Portland's final letter to have manifested assent to the contract.

Note: The court affirmed a summary judgment for Portland General Electric.

Equitable Life Assurance Society of the U.S. v. First National Bank (1999)

Facts: Equitable Life as first mortgagee began foreclosure of its debtor's property, then transferred its interest to the second mortgagee, and instructed the sheriff to stop the public auction of the property. The sheriff continued the auction and sold the property.

Issue: May a mortgagee cancel a foreclosure sale after bidding starts but before a sale is complete to a buyer?

Rule: Yes. In an auction, the auctioneer is the seller's agent, and in a public auction the sheriff is the auctioneer, who must follow the seller's instructions.

A. Kemp Fisheries, Inc. v. Castle & Cookie, Inc. (1988)

Facts: Kemp negotiated the charter of a boat from Bumble Bee, believing that Bumble Bee had represented that the freezer system would meet Kemp's needs. The written contract from Bumble Bee did not say that, but Kemp signed it anyway.

Issue: If a promisee knowingly signs a contract that waives the promisor's liability, may the promisee submit extrinsic evidence that their contract did not waive that liability?

Rule: When a contract is reasonably susceptible to more than one meaning, extrinsic evidence is admissible to prove the meaning and the parol evidence rule does not bar such evidence. When the contract is clear and not ambiguous, extrinsic evidence is not admissible.

Ferguson v. Phoenix Assurance Co. of N.Y. (1962)

Facts: Phoenix Assurance insured Ferguson against burglary of his safe. The policy conditioned coverage on the presence of "visible marks" of forced entry on the outside of the safe. Ferguson's safe had an outside door, on which there were no visible marks, and an inside door, on which there were visible marks. Phoenix denied coverage.

Issue: May an insurance policy establish a rule of evidence tending to prevent fraudulent claims?

Rule: An insurance policy may establish rules of evidence necessary to prevent fraudulent claims, but such rules of evidence going beyond that purpose violate public policy. Here, Phoenix Assurance's rules acted to defeat a bona fide loss caused by burglary and went beyond what was necessary to defeat a fraudulent claim.

United States v. Winstar (1996)

Facts: The Federal Home Loan Bank Board induced solvent savings and loan associations to take over failed savings and loan associations, because this would reduce the financial liability of the Federal Savings and Loan Insurance Corporation. The Board in its agreements with such solvent associations granted them favorable regulatory treatment, including accounting rules. The agreements did not provide for what would happen if the regulations later changed for any reason. Winstar was such a solvent association that took over other associations, and it relied on the favorable accounting treatment the Board provided. Congress later wrote new legislation that eliminated the favorable accounting treatment.

Issue: May a party who contracts with the government urge that the government's unilateral change of the contract terms rendered performance impossible?

Rule: A claim of impossibility requires a party to show that an event occurred that was contrary to the basic assumptions underlying the agreement of the parties. A claim that a change in statute or regulations by the government is such an event must fail, as such changes are not only foreseeable but likely.

Johnson v. Utile (1970)

Facts: Johnson contracted to sell farm land to Utile with one working water well on it and with another well that Johnson would drill and test. The first well stopped working. Utile agreed to give up any claim to the first well in return for the equipment used to drill the second well and provided the second well met Utile's stated water requirements. The sale closed, Utile took possession, but the well never produced water at the rate needed and then went dry.

Issue: Must a party to a contract that is then followed by a compromise agreement upon breach of the compromise sue based only on the compromise?

Rule: A party to a contract that is followed by a compromise may elect to sue on the original contract or on the compromise. Here, the buyer brought a claim for the loss of the first well, which was a claim that the buyer had given up in the compromise agreement.

Directors Guild of America v. Harmony Pictures, Inc. (1998)

Facts: The Directors Guild and Harmony Pictures disputed the amount of Harmony's debt to the Guild. Harmony wrote a check to the Guild, with the words "full and final settlement" on the back. The Guild crossed out that restrictive endorsement and deposited the check.

Issue: If one party to a dispute writes a check with an endorsement that the check is full payment of its debt, may the other party cancel the endorsement and deposit the check?

Rule: No. Deposit of such a check accepts the accord and satisfaction offered by the debtor.

Adjustrite Systems, Inc. v. GAB Business Services, Inc. (1998)

Facts: Adjustrite was negotiating a sale of its assets to GAB. GAB submitted a two-page proposal for the purchase to Adjustrite. Adjustrite's right to use a certain database expired, which was an asset that GAB wanted to acquire. GAB withdrew from negotiations.

Issue: May a preliminary agreement be enforced as a contract?

Rule: The parties must intend to be bound by a preliminary agreement, and may be bound by it, provided that additional negotiations are on relatively unimportant points. Here, the parties did not yet intend to be bound by the preliminary agreement. It did not state that they were bound. Many terms had not been negotiated. Employment contracts that would go into effect after the transaction and that are customarily in writing had not been signed. Even though Adjustrite had performed in part, the preliminary agreement was not a binding contract.

St. Jude Medical, Inc. v. Medtronic, Inc. (1995)

Facts: St. Jude and Electromedics agreed to merge. St. Jude agreed to acquire Electromedics for $6.375 a share. Electromedics agreed to pay a termination fee if it breached. It did breach and merged with Medtronic instead for a higher price.

Issue: Must a termination fee meet the same test of validity as does a liquidated damages clause?

Rule: No. A termination fee must be reasonable in light of the size of the transaction. A $3 million termination is reasonable in a $90 million transaction.

CHAPTER 3

Consideration

Mnemonic for Requirements of a Contract:
  Mother Adores Cigars After Dinner

1.   Mutual Assent

2.   Consideration

3.   Absence of Defenses

I. ELEMENTS OF CONSIDERATION

Not every promise ought to be enforced. Some are not meant to be enforced legally, since they are merely social in nature, like a promise to meet someone for a date at a restaurant. Others occur in contexts where legal intervention doesn't ordinarily belong, for example, within the family.

Contract law uses the tool of *consideration* to draw a bright line between promises that are and promises that are not enforceable. Consideration is something given in exchange for something else. In a sale, the price is consideration for the thing sold, and vice versa. In a lease, the rent is consideration for the lessee's right to the premises. Thus, the essence of consideration is the notion of a bargain. Consideration can be thought of as two elements: *bargained-for exchange* and *legal detriment*. One party gets something; the other party gives something up. If a promise is made for no consideration, it might still be seriously intended, but without any consideration the law views it as gratuitous, as a promise of a gift that contract law does not enforce.

A. Bargained-for Exchange

A performance or return promise is bargained-for if it is sought by the promisor in exchange for his promise, *and* it is given by the promisee in exchange for that promise. (Rest. 2d §71(2).) The bargain requirement serves the purpose of distinguishing between enforceable promises and ordinary gifts.

1. Gifts

   A promise to make a gift is unenforceable, not only because it is not bargained-for but also because the offeree suffers no legal detriment. **Example:** A says to B, "I promise to buy you a new car." A is not legally bound to buy B a car because A's promise was not made as part of a bargain in exchange for some return benefit from B. There is no consideration for A's promise.

2. Bargain vs. Precondition

   Performance of a bargain benefits the promisor and therefore is valid consideration. Performance of a precondition does not benefit the promisor and is not consideration. **Example:** X promises his sister a place to raise her family if she comes to visit him. She incurs the expense of moving, but X changes his mind. X is not legally bound to keep his promise, because no consideration was given for it. The moving expenses were incurred as a precondition to fulfilling his request. X did not bargain that he would give his sister a place to stay **in exchange for** her incurring moving expenses.

3. Benefit

   a. The benefit a promisor receives as part of a bargain does not have to be economic in nature. **Example:** A promises B $100 if B does not smoke.

   b. But the benefit must be more than altruistic pleasure or love. **Example:** There is no consideration if A promises to pay B's debts as a gesture of gratitude for all the happiness B has given A. Moral obligation does not constitute legal consideration.

4. Sufficiency or Adequacy of Consideration

   In general, courts do not ask whether consideration is adequate, that is, whether the consideration given by the promisee is adequate when measured against the promise the promisee is trying to enforce. Instead, courts ask whether the consideration is legally sufficient, that is, whether the parties regarded the consideration as:

   a. Nominal Consideration

      Often an agreement between two parties will state something like "A promises B . . . in consideration of $1.00 paid to A." Although courts will not ordinarily examine the adequacy of consideration, courts will do so in cases involving purely token consideration, in order to thwart attempts to make gratuitous promises appear legally enforceable. Nominal or sham consideration is usually evidence that a gift is masquerading as a bargained-for exchange.

   b. Recited Consideration

      A majority of courts allow a promisor who is opposing enforcement of a contract to prove that the consideration recited in the agreement was not actually given. Nonpayment of recited consideration may be used as partial evidence that there was no bargained-for exchange.

   c. Past Consideration

As a general rule, past consideration is not consideration. Today's promise cannot be exchanged for some benefit that the promisor has already received. **Example:** A promises to pay B, A's employee, $100 a week "in consideration" of B's many years of hard work, or A promises to pay B $1 million after B has saved A's life. In both cases, A has received the benefit before he made the promise, and thus nothing was actually given in exchange for the promise. There are some exceptions to the general rule:

     i. Pre-existing Debt

A promise to repay a pre-existing debt that was excused because of a technical defense, such as the running of the statute of limitations, is enforceable without consideration. (Rest. 2d §§82, 83.)

     ii. New Promise for Benefits Received

A new promise to pay for benefits received will sometimes be enforceable without consideration on grounds of moral obligation to prevent injustice. (Rest. 2d §86.)

B. Legal Detriment

The second requirement for consideration is that it must constitute a **legal detriment** to the promisee. Legal detriment is liberally construed to mean either a promise to do anything that one is not legally obligated to do (e.g., cross the street) or to refrain from doing something that one has a right to do (e.g., stop smoking). There is no requirement that the promisee suffer any actual hardship. Likewise, the benefit that the promisor receives is not necessarily related to pleasure or advantage. All that is required is that the promisor does something he is not bound to do.

1. Minority View

Some courts broaden the test such that valid consideration exists if the promisor received a benefit, even if the promisee did not "suffer" a detriment.

2. Bilateral Contract

In a bilateral contract, the detriment is in the form of a return promise made by the promisee.

3. Unilateral Contract

In a unilateral contract, the detriment is in the form of an action or performance. No consideration exists prior to the taking of the action or the performance.

4. Pre-existing Duty Rule

Generally, there is no legal detriment if a party promises to do something that he is already obligated to do, or forbears from doing something that he is not legally entitled to do. (Rest. 2d §73.) **Example:** A promises not to use illegal drugs. Many courts dislike the pre-existing duty rule and have avoided its application in many ways. A promise to perform an act that one is already legally obligated to do may be consideration under certain circumstances.

Mnemonic: **DUCK PINS**

a. **D**ispute

If there is an honest dispute as to whether the promisor is already legally obligated to do the promised act, the promise or act may be consideration.

b. **U**nforeseen **C**ircumstances

Unforeseen circumstances make it "fair and equitable" to allow a promisor to modify an agreement without giving new consideration. (Rest. 2d §89.)

c. **K** Pre-existing Duty to a Third Party

The promise is made to a third party outside the contract. **Example:** A contracts with B to construct an elevator in the building that B is erecting for C. B quits the job, but A promises C that he will continue the job if C pays him. The promise is enforceable, even though A already had a legal obligation to build.

d. **N**ew or Different Consideration Promised

Even a slight change in the terms of a pre-existing duty will satisfy the requirement of consideration.

e. **S**ale of Goods

Under UCC §2-209, which applies only to the sale of goods, modifications of existing contracts can be made without new consideration.

5. Partial Payment as Satisfaction of a Debt

A promise to pay part of a debt, instead of the whole, is not consideration for a return promise by the creditor to relinquish the debt, because the debtor is obligated to pay anyway ("pre-existing duty"). This rule has been overruled by the UCC and by some jurisdictions. Also, courts will consider a promise of partial payment to be valid consideration if:

a. The payment terms are slightly changed.

b. The debtor refrains from declaring bankruptcy.

c. There is an honest dispute as to the debt.

d. A check marked "payment in full" is cashed.

       i. At common law, a creditor forfeited no rights to the rest of the debt still outstanding.

      ii. Under the UCC, the entire debt is discharged unless a creditor expressly reserves his rights by writing "with recourse," or something to that effect, on the check. (UCC §1-207.)

  6. Forbearance to Bring Suit

A promise not to sue, made in exchange for some return benefit, is valid consideration if either:

a. The claim was valid, or

b. The claim was not valid, and

       i. The parties reasonably believed the claim was valid (majority rule), or

      ii. The validity was uncertain or the promisor subjectively believed that it was valid (Rest. 2d §74.)

II. MUTUALITY

Mutuality requires that *each* party to a contract must provide consideration to the other in exchange for the other's promise.

A. Illusory Promises

An illusory promise is not sufficient consideration, because it only appears to bind the promisor when, in fact, it commits him to nothing at all. (Rest. 2d §77.) **Example:** A promises to be B's agent. B agrees, but reserves the right to terminate at any time. There is no mutuality, because A received no consideration for his promise.

B. Alternative Promises

A promise that allows the promisor to choose among several alternative performances will satisfy mutuality only if each alternative has valid consideration. (Rest. 2d §77.) **Example:** A promises to give B either $1,000 or his car in exchange for B's car. The promise is enforceable because both alternatives embody valid consideration.

C. Right to Withdraw from the Agreement

A promise that gives the promisor the right to terminate the agreement can still be valid consideration for a return promise if:

1. Termination is allowed after performance is rendered.

Example: A promises to be B's agent. B accepts (promises to hire A) but reserves the right to fire A upon 30 days' notice. B's promise is consideration for A's promise because the agency agreement must last at least 30 days before B can fire A.

2. Termination is dependent on ability to perform.

Example: A promises to sell his house to B. B promises to buy subject to his ability to obtain financing. B's promise satisfies mutuality because it is not dependent on his willingness to perform but rather on his ability.

3. Termination occurs with notice.

If the only limitation on termination is the requirement that notice be given, modern courts are likely to recognize such a promise as valid consideration. Some courts will even go so far as to imply a notice requirement, the idea being that if notice is required, performance must occur for the notice period, at least. **Example:** A promises to clean B's house in exchange for $100 a day, subject to A's right to terminate with seven days' notice. The promise is valid consideration because A must perform for at least seven days.

D. Voidable Promises

A promise that is voidable at a party's election (promises made by minors, incompetents, etc. are voidable if the promisor so chooses) is valid consideration and satisfies the requirement of mutuality. (Rest. 2d §78.)

E. Conditional Promises

A promise that makes performance of an act dependent on the occurrence of a future event is valid consideration if:

1. Condition Is Outside Promisor's Control

There is valid consideration, even if a promisor eventually does not have to perform, unless the promisor knows that the condition cannot occur. **Example:** A promises to pay B $100 for her baseball glove if it rains on Tuesday. This is valid consideration even if it does not rain on Tuesday.

2. Condition Is Partially Within Promisor's Control

A court will imply such a promise to mean that the promisor will use reasonable efforts to satisfy the condition. **Example:** B promises to sell his house to A if he can find a new house within a year. If A agrees, B's promise will be construed to mean that B will make best efforts to find a new home. Otherwise, B's promise is illusory.

F. Option Contracts

A promisee who receives an irrevocable offer (an option contract or a firm offer) is not always required to give consideration in exchange for that offer. (Rest. 2d §87; UCC §2-205.) Even in cases where consideration is recited, courts do not require that it be paid.

G. Requirements and Output Contracts

1. Traditional Rule for Requirements Contract

A promise to buy goods from a specific seller over a period of time was insufficient consideration for the return promise to supply those goods, if the quantity term was to be determined by what the buyer **required** over that period, and not a set amount. Mutuality was said to be absent because, although the seller had to provide the goods, the buyer did not have to buy if he didn't require or need them.

2. Modern/UCC Rule for Requirements Contracts

A promise to buy one's requirements is good consideration for the seller's promise to sell them. Mutuality of obligation is present. UCC §2-306 implies that the buyer has a good faith duty to:

a. Maintain reasonable requirement levels,

b. Buy exclusively from that seller, and

c. Not take advantage of the seller by increasing demand to benefit from fluctuating market prices.

3. Output Contract

Seller promises all of his output to one buyer. A mutuality problem exists because the seller never promised to have any output let alone a certain amount. Such contracts are now valid because UCC §2-306 implies that sellers have a good faith duty to maintain a certain level of output.

H. Unilateral Contract

Part performance of a unilateral contract is sufficient consideration to keep a promise open, even though the promisee is not obligated to complete performance. Once part performance is rendered, however, the promisor cannot withdraw his promise unless the promisee stops performing.

III. PROMISSORY ESTOPPEL

Promissory estoppel is an equitable doctrine that is used to avoid injustice by enforcing otherwise unenforceable promises. It "estops" the promisor from claiming that no consideration was given. (Rest. 2d §90.)

Promissory estoppel is based on equitable estoppel. Equitable estoppel keeps a party from making some claim. **Example:** Bank tells customer that a check the customer has deposited has cleared and the funds are available to use, but the check has not in fact cleared. The customer writes a check on the account, which bounces. Equitable estoppel prevents the bank from claiming that there were insufficient funds in the account, because the customer had relied reasonably on the bank's statement.

A. Requirements for Enforcement of a Promise with Estoppel

Mnemonic: **R**obin **H**ood **F**inds **D**anger **I**nviting

1. There was actual **R**eliance on the contract or promise

2. The reliance was **F**oreseeable to the breaching party

3. The reliance was clearly **D**etrimental and
4. Injustice can only be avoided by enforcement.
B. Examples of Promissory Estoppel
   1. Promise to Make Gift
      A promises to pay B, his son, $1,000 a week for life. B quits his job in reliance on the promise. A cannot revoke the offer if it would cause injustice, such as if B is unable to obtain new employment.
   2. Charitable Subscriptions
      Promises to make donations are enforceable absent consideration, even if there is no detrimental reliance.
   3. Bids by Subcontractors (Rest. 2d §87.)
      Subcontractor who submits a "sub-bid" to a general contractor for use in computing the general contract bid must give the contractor a reasonable amount of time to accept, even if no consideration is given to keep the offer (bid) open.

CASE CLIPS

Hamer v. Sidway (1891)

Facts: A young man's uncle promised to pay him $5,000 if he abstained from drinking, smoking, swearing and gambling until the age of 21. The uncle's executor refused to honor the promise, claiming that no consideration was given to the uncle in exchange for his promise.

Issue: Does voluntary forbearance of a legal right constitute consideration?

Rule: Forbearance of a right is a sufficient legal detriment to satisfy the requirement of consideration.

Fischer v. Union Trust Co. (1904)

Facts: A father deeded some property to his daughter and promised to pay the outstanding mortgages on it. The daughter jokingly gave her father $1 as consideration. At the father's death, the estate refused to continue the mortgage payments, claiming the promise was not binding for want of consideration.

Issue 1: Can a dollar that is transferred in jest to a promisor be consideration?

Rule 1: The passing of a dollar that is treated as a joke is not consideration.

Issue 2: Is a promisor's love and affection for his daughter and his desire to provide her with support consideration?

Rule 2: A promisor's love, affection and desire to provide support for his daughter is not sufficient consideration to render a promise enforceable.

Batsakis v. Demotsis (1949)

Facts: During World War II, Batsakis loaned Demotsis 500,000 Greek drachmas (worth about $25) to get back to America. Demotsis promised to pay Batsakis $2,000. Demotsis refused to repay the debt, claiming that inadequate consideration was given for her promise.

Issue: Is a contract void if the consideration furnished by one party is substantially disproportionate to that given by the other?

Rule: Inadequacy of consideration does not void a contract, as long as the consideration had some value. A party that receives the benefit it seeks will not be relieved from a bad bargain.

Duncan v. Black (1959)

Facts: Part of Black's contract to sell Duncan farm land included a clause specifying that Duncan was to receive a 65-acre cotton allotment.

Duncan was allotted a lesser area of cotton, and he threatened to sue. To settle the dispute, Black gave Duncan a $1,500 promissory note. Black stopped making payments when he discovered that under the existing cotton allotment quota, Duncan was not entitled to the amount of cotton for which he had contracted. Duncan sued to enforce the note.

Issue: May forbearance to bring a lawsuit constitute consideration for a promissory note?

Rule: Forbearance to assert an action is not sufficient consideration when the underlying claim is illegal and against public policy, such as a violation of the Agricultural Adjustment Act.

Martin v. Little, Brown and Co. (1981)

Facts: Martin offered proof to Little, Brown, a publisher, that a portion of one of its books had been plagiarized. When Little, Brown prosecuted the plagiarists, Martin sought one-third of the recovery amount. Although it had never promised Martin anything, Little, Brown gave him a $200 honorarium.

Issue: Absent any express promises, can a party recover for the value of services that were volunteered?

Rule: One who volunteers information or services is generally not entitled to restitution.

Mills v. Wyman (1825)

Facts: Mills provided board, nursing, and care to Wyman's 25-year-old son who became ill while traveling. After the services had been rendered, Wyman wrote to Mills, promising to pay for them. Wyman later refused to pay.

Issue: Is moral obligation sufficient consideration to support a promise?

Rule: Moral obligation is not sufficient consideration to enforce a promise to pay for services already rendered. Past consideration is no consideration.

Webb v. McGowin (1935)

Facts: Webb was crippled in the course of a heroic act to prevent harm to McGowin. Consequently, McGowin promised Webb $15 every two weeks for the rest of Webb's life. McGowin made payments until his death, whereupon his estate refused to honor the promise.

Issue: Is moral obligation sufficient consideration to enforce a promise?

Rule: Moral obligation is sufficient consideration to support a subsequent promise when the promisor received a material benefit.

Note: This is the minority rule; the majority view is that moral obligation is no consideration. (See *Mills v. Wyman.*)

Kirksey v. Kirksey (1845)

Facts: The defendant wrote to his sister-in-law, "If you will come down and see me, I will let you have a place to raise your family." Two years after her relocation, he changed his mind and made her leave. The plaintiff claims that the expenses she incurred in moving were valid consideration.
Issue: Is an act necessary to accept a promise simply a precondition to a gratuitous act or consideration given in exchange for the promise?
Rule: Acts that are required before fulfillment of a promise are preconditions to accepting the promise, not valid consideration.
Note: A famous example of this rule involved a man who told another, "If you go to the shop around the corner, you can buy a coat on my credit." The walk around the corner is a precondition to accepting the promise. It was not done "in exchange" for the coat.

Allegheny College v. Nat'l Chautauqua County Bank (1927)

Facts: Allegheny received a $5,000 pledge that was to become effective 30 days after the donor's death. It was agreed that the money would be used either as part of a general fund or to create a special fund named after the donor. The donor made a partial payment of $1,000 while she was still alive. Allegheny set the money aside until the rest of the pledge would be received. Before her death, the donor repudiated her pledge. Allegheny sued the donor's executor, National Chautaqua, to recover the rest of the pledge.
Issue: Does acceptance of part of a donation imply a promise to perform the donor's wishes, such promise being valid consideration to bind the promisor?
Rule: The acceptance of a charitable subscription is an implied promise by a college to comply with the wishes of the donor which, in turn, constitutes valid consideration to bind the donor.
Note: Consideration is not required to enforce a promise of a charitable contribution.

East Providence Credit Union v. Geremia (1968)

Facts: The Geremias secured a loan from East Providence by using their car as collateral. The loan agreement provided that if the Geremias' insurance lapsed, East Providence could make the payments and add the amount to the balance owed. On one occasion, the Geremias agreed to East Providence paying the premium, which it failed to do. The uninsured car was destroyed in an accident.
Issue: May the doctrine of estoppel be applied to promises to act in the future?

Rule: The doctrine of promissory estoppel, expressed in Restatement §90, provides that a promise to act in the future, that the promisor should reasonably expect to induce reliance, will be enforced, if the promise induced reliance, and injustice can only be avoided by enforcement of the promise.

Seavey v. Drake (1882)

Facts: Seavey, wishing to help his son, Drake, orally agreed to give him a strip of land. In return, Drake tore up a $200 debt his father owed him. Drake spent $3,000 to improve the land and paid all taxes on it. After Seavey's death, his executor sought to evict Drake, claiming no consideration was given for Seavey's promise because the oral agreement violated the Statute of Frauds.

Issue: Can an oral promise to convey land be enforced if the promisee has given the required performance?

Rule: A parol contract to convey land will be enforced in favor of the promisee if the failure or refusal to convey the land would operate as a fraud upon him. The bar of the Statute of Frauds is removed upon the grounds that it is a fraud for the promisor to insist upon the lack of a written document after he has allowed partial performance of the contract.

Stearns v. Emery-Waterhouse Co. (1991)

Facts: Defendant's president promised Stearns, 50 years old, employment to the age of 55 if he would quit his job of 27 years and start working for the defendant. Stearns was terminated before he reached the age of 55.

Issue: May an employee avoid the Statute of Frauds by claiming detrimental reliance on an oral contract that cannot be completed within one year?

Rule: Promissory estoppel may not be used to avoid the Statute of Frauds where there is an oral employment contract that requires longer than one year to complete, unless the employer engages in fraudulent conduct. In the absence of a written contract or proof of fraud, a multi-year employment contract is unenforceable.

Goodman v. Dicker (1948)

Facts: The defendant, a representative of a franchisor, encouraged the plaintiff to apply for a franchise and incorrectly told him that it would be granted. Relying on the defendant's assurance, the plaintiff invested money in setting up a store.

Issue: Can a party be compensated for expenses that were incurred because of reasonable reliance on the words or actions of another party?

Rule: A party that incurs expenses as a result of reasonably foreseeable reliance on the statements of another party can recover the value of those expenses under the theory of promissory estoppel, even in the absence of an actual contract between the parties. However, the plaintiff can only recover for expenses made in reliance, not for the value of lost profits.

Obering v. Swain-Roach Lumber Co. (1927)

Facts: Both Obering and Swain-Roach were interested in purchasing the same parcel of land for different purposes. They agreed that if Swain-Roach succeeded in buying the land, it would sell it immediately to Obering, with some rights reserved. Obering refused to honor the agreement after Swain-Roach purchased the land and tendered it to him. Obering claimed that the condition precedent, Swain-Roach obtaining the land, made their contract too indefinite to be valid.

Issue: Is a contract that cannot become effective without the occurrence of a condition precedent too indefinite to be enforceable?

Rule: A contract that cannot become effective absent a condition precedent does not fail because of indefiniteness.

Wood v. Lucy, Lady Duff-Gordon (1917)

Facts: Lady Duff-Gordon, a famous designer, agreed with Wood that he would have exclusive agency to place her endorsements on clothing designs, to place her designs on sale and to license others to market them. In exchange, Wood promised to keep the books and to split the profits evenly with Duff-Gordon. Duff-Gordon breached by endorsing designs herself and keeping the profits. In defense, she claimed that Wood's promise was illusory, as she had granted him exclusive agency, but he was not obligated to find designs or to sell her labels.

Issue: Is a contract void for lack of mutuality because one party did not promise to use reasonable efforts to perform his duties?

Rule: A promise to use reasonable efforts can be implied from a contract and, therefore, a contract does not fail for lack of mutuality because it does not contain explicit clauses requiring good faith efforts (UCC §2-306(2)).

Feld v. Henry S. Levy & Sons, Inc. (1975)

Facts: The defendant agreed to sell to the plaintiff the entire output of bread crumbs at its factory for one year. Each party had the right to cancel upon six months' notice. The defendant stopped production because his obsolete equipment was uneconomical, and offered to resume production at a higher price.

Issue: Must a seller who signs an output contract continue to produce goods for the term of the contract?

Rule: A party to an output contract is obligated to act in good faith and may cease production as long as it is acting in good faith. Whether a party acted in good faith is a jury question.

Note: The case was remanded for further proceedings.

Sheets v. Teddy's Frosted Foods, Inc. (1980)

Facts: Sheets claimed he was wrongfully discharged in retaliation for his efforts to ensure that Teddy's products would comply with statutory health requirements.

Issue: Does an employer have a complete and unlimited right to terminate the services of an at-will employee?

Rule: An employer can terminate an at-will employee without showing just cause, unless the employee can show that the termination was against public policy.

Schwartzreich v. Bauman-Basch, Inc. (1921)

Facts: Bauman-Basch hired Schwartzreich for one year at $90 a week. Before beginning the work, Schwartzreich was offered $115 a week by another employer. Bauman-Basch offered to raise Schwartzreich's weekly salary to $100, which he accepted. Another contract was made reflecting the new salary provision, and the old one was simultaneously torn up. Bauman-Basch fired Schwartzreich before the year passed, claiming the second contract was unenforceable for lack of consideration.

Issue: Is a new contract that replaces a prior contract with terms that are similar, but more favorable to one party, enforceable?

Rule: Any change from an existing contract must have new consideration to support it. Where an existing contract is terminated by mutual consent, and a new one is executed in its place, the mutual promises of the parties constitute consideration.

Great Northern Ry. v. Witham (1873)

Facts: Great Northern entered into a one-year contract to buy "any quantity that they may need" of train fenders from Witham. Witham later refused to perform, claiming the contract was invalid for lack of mutuality (i.e., Great Northern was not obligated to buy any set amount and could, if it wished, buy nothing, whereas Witham had to sell if Great Northern asked).

Issue: Does a requirements contract fail for lack of consideration if a party was not obligated to place an order?

Rule: Placing an order is sufficient consideration to bind a party to a requirements contract.

Eastern Airlines v. Gulf Oil Corp. (1975)

Facts: Gulf contracted to fulfill Eastern's jet fuel requirements on a long-term basis. The parties agreed that price would be determined by an index of posted fuel prices. In 1974, when oil prices skyrocketed as a result of an OPEC embargo of foreign fuel sources, posted prices were kept below the market level by government regulation. Gulf refused to perform, claiming lack of mutuality because Eastern was not obligated to buy a set amount.

Issue: Are requirements contracts void for lack of mutuality?

Rule: Requirements contracts, entered into in good faith, are not void for lack of mutuality. According to UCC §2-306, such contracts are valid so long as the requirements are not varied in bad faith or grossly disproportionate to a reasonably foreseeable figure.

Sylvan Crest Sand & Gravel Co. v. United States (1945)

Facts: Sylvan was awarded a contract to supply traprock for an airport. The contract specified that the United States could cancel at any time. Other provisions, including penalties for refusal or failure to perform, clearly indicated that the parties supposed they were entering an enforceable contract. The United States later refused to take custody of a delivery of rock, claiming its reservation of an unrestricted power of termination made the contract wholly illusory and nonbinding.

Issue: Is a contract that allows cancellation at any time void for lack of consideration?

Rule: A contract provision allowing cancellation at any time is to be interpreted as an implied promise to either perform according to the contract or to give notice of cancellation within a reasonable time. The alternative of giving notice, while not usually difficult, is sufficient consideration to support a contract.

Roberts-Horsfield v. Gedicks (1922)

Facts: Horsfield's aunt, Gedicks, gave Horsfield land and helped her to build a house on it. Horsfield occupied the house and made improvements. After Gedicks died, her husband's second wife tried to evict Horsfield.

Issue: Is an oral gift of realty enforceable if the donee occupied the realty and paid for improvements?

Rule: A parol gift of land is invalid, but when the gift is accompanied by possession, and the donee has been induced by the promise of the gift to make valuable improvements of a permanent nature, the gift will be enforced on equitable principles.

Devecmon v. Shaw (1888)

Facts: While working for his uncle, Devecmon took a trip unrelated to business to Europe at his uncle's request after his uncle promised that he would be reimbursed. The uncle's estate refused to pay.
Issue: Is a party bound by a promise from which no direct benefit was received?
Rule: A gratuitous promise that induces the promisee to incur an expenditure in reasonable reliance on the promise is enforceable even if no benefit is received by the promisor.

Ricketts v. Scothorn (1898)

Facts: Ricketts signed a note promising his granddaughter $2,000 on demand so that she would not have to work. She quit her job in reliance on the promise. The administrator of Ricketts' estate refused to honor the note after Ricketts' death, claiming that no consideration was given for his promise.
Issue: When will a gratuitous promise bind a promisor?
Rule: The doctrine of equitable estoppel provides that a right may accrue to a promisee if the promisee changed her position in accordance with the real or apparent intention of the promisor.

De Cicco v. Schweizer (1917)

Facts: Schweizer promised his daughter's fiancé $2,500 per year if they married. Schweizer paid the annuity for ten years after the marriage before stopping. When the husband sued, Schweizer claimed the promise was unenforceable for lack of consideration.
Issue: Is a promise made by a third party to encourage two parties to marry enforceable?
Rule: A promisee who forbears from the right to modify or withdraw from an agreement has incurred legal detriment.

Gillingham v. Brown (1901)

Facts: The defendant gave the plaintiff a promissory note, which he never paid, and the statute of limitations expired. The defendant later gave the plaintiff part of the money and promised to pay the rest in installments, which he did not do. The jury found that the defendant had to pay all of the outstanding debt. The defendant claimed he only had to abide by the terms of his new promise and pay for those installments that were actually overdue.

Issue: Is a party who promises to pay a debt that is unenforceable due to a legal technicality required to abide by the conditions of the old debt?

Rule: A new promise to pay an old debt will be enforceable only according to the terms of the new promise.

Lampleigh v. Brathwait (1615)

Facts: After he was convicted on murder charges, Brathwait asked Lampleigh to try to obtain a pardon from the King. Brathwait made no reference to payment. Lampleigh expended great effort on behalf of Brathwait, but was unsuccessful. After Lampleigh's efforts, Brathwait promised to reimburse him, then later changed his mind.

Issue: Is a promise to pay for services voluntarily performed in the past enforceable?

Rule: A promise to pay for services voluntarily performed in the past will usually fail for lack of consideration unless such services were performed pursuant to the request of the promisor.

Haigh v. Brooks (1840)

Facts: Brooks gave Haigh and another a promissory note for £10,000 owed to them by a third party. Neither party realized that the note was void because it lacked a proper seal. Brooks promised Haigh £10,000 for the return of the note but refused payment when he found out the document was worthless, claiming that he received no consideration for his promise.

Issue: Is an agreement void for lack of consideration if the "value" given by one party turns out to be worthless in fact?

Rule: Consideration exists when a party is induced to part with something he might have kept, even if the parties later discover that the "value" of the inducement was not as expected.

United States v. Bethlehem Steel Corp. (1942)

Facts: Bethlehem was able to negotiate extremely favorable contract terms to build ships for the United States because it owned the only plant with the necessary facilities to fulfill its needs, and because an overall shipping shortage existed due to World War I. The United States sued in equity for an accounting and for a refund of amounts paid in excess of just and reasonable compensation. Bethlehem sued for breach of contract.

Issue: Is a contract enforceable if it allows one of the parties to realize excessive profits?

Rule: Without a showing of fraud or duress, a contract is valid even if one of the parties enjoys excessive profits to the detriment of the other.
Dissent: Taking advantage of desperate circumstances constitutes duress, which leads to unconscionable contract terms. (UCC §2-302.)

Thomas v. Thomas (Eng. 1842)

Facts: Husband promised his wife that upon his death she could choose either payment of £100 from his personal estate or the use of their residence unless she remarried. He died. She chose the house. His executor alleged that the husband's promise lacked consideration.
Issue: Is there consideration for a husband's promise to convey a residence to his wife upon his death?
Rule: The motive of one who promises to transfer real estate is not sufficient consideration for the promise.
Note: The widow could continue to live in the house because the promise of the executor to permit her to do so in return for £1 per year was held sufficient consideration.

Krell v. Codman (1891)

Facts: A deceased signed a covenant under seal to bind her estate to make cash distributions after her death to certain parties, including the plaintiff. The defendant refused to honor the covenant, claiming no consideration was given.
Issue: Is a covenant to pay money after one's death valid?
Rule: A covenant for the payment of money after one's death will be valid, even if the requirements of a will are not met, if the covenant was written and signed.

Goulet v. Goulet (1963)

Facts: The plaintiff executed a covenant under seal that she would not sue her husband for injuries sustained in a car accident. The plaintiff was given $1 as consideration. She later decided to bring suit.
Issue: Must consideration be given when a contract is executed under seal?
Rule: Neither the absence nor the failure of consideration will overcome the binding legal effect of a seal.

Aller v. Aller (1878)

Facts: The defendant executed a promissory note to his daughters under seal. He did not receive consideration.

Issue: Is a note executed under seal enforceable, despite the absence of consideration?

Rule: A note executed under seal is enforceable regardless of whether consideration was exchanged.

Schnell v. Nell (1861)

Facts: Nell was granted $200 in a will made by Schnell's wife. The will was invalid, but Schnell promised to make the payment in exchange for one cent consideration. Schnell revoked his promise.

Issue: May one cent be acceptable consideration?

Rule: Plainly nominal consideration is not effective.

Cochran v. Taylor (1937)

Facts: The defendant gave an option for the purchase of land for $1 consideration. The option was executed under seal.

Issue: Must consideration be more than nominal if an option is given under seal?

Rule: An option executed under seal is enforceable, regardless of whether actual or nominal consideration is given.

Pillans & Rose v. Van Mierop & Hopkins (1765)

Facts: Pillans & Rose extended credit to a third party in reliance on Van Mierop & Hopkins' written promise to guarantee the debt. The latter was given no consideration for its promise. Both parties were financial institutions.

Issue: Is a written contract between merchants valid without the exchange of consideration?

Rule: A commercial contract between merchants does not fail because consideration was not given (UCC §2-209).

Dougherty v. Salt (1919)

Facts: The plaintiff received a promissory note from his aunt for $3,000. The note was on a printed form that contained the words "for value received." No consideration was in fact given.

Issue: Is the printed clause "value received" sufficient evidence of consideration to render a note enforceable?

Rule: An inference of consideration that is drawn from the form of a note can be overcome by other evidence suggesting that no consideration was in fact given.

Hancock Bank & Trust Co. v. Shell Oil Co. (1974)

Facts: Shell had a lease that included a clause providing that "Shell may terminate this lease at any time by giving lessor at least ninety days notice." Hancock tried to invalidate the lease on grounds of lack of mutuality.
Issue: Will a lease be void due to a lack of mutuality when one party has the option of canceling upon providing 90 days' notice?
Rule: When a contract is supported by some consideration, the contract will not be voided because of a bad or uneven bargain.

Newman & Snell's State Bank v. Hunter (1928)

Facts: Hunter's husband owed money to Newman & Snell's, and at his death, his insolvent estate could not repay his debts. Hunter made an agreement to repay her husband's debt to Newman & Snell's, in exchange for the bank surrendering her husband's promissory note and interest due.
Issue: Does a spouse's promise to pay the debts of a deceased, insolvent spouse fail for lack of consideration?
Rule: A spouse's promise to pay the debts of her insolvent, deceased spouse will not be enforced if she did not receive consideration for her promise. The submission of a worthless debt does not constitute consideration.

Springstead v. Nees (1908)

Facts: Springstead, Nees and others were siblings. Their father died intestate (without a will) leaving behind two parcels of real estate. One was held in trust exclusively for Nees and another defendant. The other was to be divided equally among all the parties. In reaction to Springstead and others' disapproval, Nees and another defendant promised to give their share of the common property to Springstead and the others if the plaintiffs would not bother them about their inheritance (to which they had no right). The defendants later changed their mind.
Issue: Does forbearance from asserting an invalid claim constitute consideration?
Rule: Forbearance of a claim does not constitute consideration if the party forbearing the claim was aware that the claim was unfounded.

Miller v. Miller (1887)

Facts: A husband and wife contracted to "refrain from scolding, fault-finding and anger." The wife agreed to "keep her home and family" in return for the husband's promise to support the family and provide his wife with $200 per year for her "individual use." The wife sued because her husband spent money on other women and did not meet the terms of their financial agreement.

Issue: Is a marriage contract invalid because it is without consideration and against public policy?

Rule: Although a marriage contract does not fail for lack of consideration, it will fail because public policy prohibits a judicial inquiry into matters between husband and wife.

Scott v. Moragues Lumber Co. (1918)

Facts: Scott agreed to charter a vessel to Moragues on the condition that Scott was able to buy it. Scott purchased the vessel, but rented it to a third party. Scott claimed its agreement with Moragues was void for lack of mutuality because it was not obligated to buy the vessel, but Moragues was obligated to rent it if it was available.

Issue: Is a contract void for lack of mutuality of consideration when it is conditioned upon an event whose occurrence is at the will of one of the parties?

Rule: A contract that is conditioned upon the occurrence of an event, which is at the will of a party to the contract, is not void for lack of consideration. Once the condition is met, an obligation to fulfill the contract exists.

Wickham & Burton Coal Co. v. Farmers' Lumber Co. (1920)

Facts: Wickham & Burton agreed to supply Farmer's with the coal it "would want to purchase." Wickham & Burton later renounced the contract, claiming lack of mutuality of obligation. Farmer's counterclaimed for damages.

Issue: Does a contract lack mutuality of obligation if it allows one party to choose the quantity it will purchase?

Rule: A requirements contract is void for want of mutuality if the quantity to be delivered is conditioned entirely on the will, wish or want of the buyer and not dependent on the buyer's needs.

Grouse v. Group Health Plan, Inc. (1981)

Facts: Grouse resigned from his job because he received an employment offer from Group Health. The offer was later revoked.

Issue: Are damages resulting from revocation of an at-will employment offer recoverable?

Rule: Under the doctrine of promissory estoppel, a promise that the promisor should reasonably expect to induce action or forbearance on the part of the promisee, and that does induce such action, is binding if nonenforcement would result in injustice.

Lingenfelder v. Wainwright Brewery Co. (1891)

Facts: Wainwright hired an architect to build its new brewery. The architect walked off the job after Wainwright awarded a different job to his competitor. Pressed for time, Wainwright promised to pay him extra compensation if he resumed work. Wainwright reneged on this promise, claiming it received no consideration for its promise.

Issue: Does the resumption of work one was contractually obligated to perform constitute sufficient consideration for a promise that induced the return to work?

Rule: A new contract that was signed to prevent one party from breaching an earlier agreement will fail for lack of consideration.

Note: This is the "pre-existing duty" rule.

Foakes v. Beer (1884)

Facts: Beer agreed to forgive all the interest on Foakes' debt if he paid a quarter of the principal at once and the rest in installments. After Foakes completed the installments Beer sued for the interest.

Issue: Will an agreement to forgo the interest due on a loan in exchange for payment of the principal fail for lack of consideration?

Rule: A creditor's agreement to forgo interest on a debt in exchange for repayment of principal fails for lack of consideration because the debtor only agreed to do that which he was already obligated to perform (pre-existing duty rule).

Angel v. Murray (1974)

Facts: After he signed a five-year garbage collection contract, Maher requested an increase in pay because a construction boom substantially increased the number of homes from which he had to collect garbage. The city council agreed to pay Maher more. Several years later, Angel and other taxpayers brought suit claiming that no consideration was given for the promise to pay more.

Issue: Can a contract be modified because of unanticipated difficulties?

Rule: If a party to a contract encounters unanticipated difficulties, and the other party, not influenced by coercion or duress, voluntarily agrees to pay additional compensation for work already required to be performed under the contract, the contract will be enforced despite the pre-existing duty rule.

Central London Property Trust Ltd. v. High Trees House Ltd. (1946)

Facts: High Trees leased premises from Central London at a rate of £2,500 a year. During World War II, Central London agreed to halve the rent because of the poor economic situation. After the war, it sought to restore the rent and to recover the discount it gave High Trees.

Issue: Can an agreement to lower the rent of a written lease be enforced if the lessee relies on the modification?

Rule: A promise to accept a smaller sum in discharge of a larger sum is binding if the promisee relied on the promise despite failure of consideration.

Roth Steel Prod. v. Sharon Steel Corp. (1983)

Facts: Sharon threatened to breach its contract to supply steel if Roth did not agree to price increases. Although Sharon's motive was rising costs, it did not offer this explanation until the case came to trial.

Issue: Is an attempted contract modification to compensate for rising costs ineffective if the party did not act in good faith?

Rule: Contract modification must be obtained in good faith, by conduct that is both consistent with "reasonable commercial standards of fair dealing in the trade" and "honesty in fact," to be enforceable. (UCC §2-103(1)(b).)

Clark v. West (1908)

Facts: West Publishing promised to pay Clark $6 per page for an acceptable manuscript if he did not drink and $2 per page if he did. West discovered that Clark was drinking alcohol during the term of the contract but told him not to worry. After the book was finished West offered to pay only $2 per page. Clark claimed that the alcohol provision was a condition to the contract, which was expressly waived by West. West claimed abstinence was consideration for the contract.

Issue: May a condition to a contract be waived?

Rule: A condition to a contract can be expressly waived. Merely accepting a party's performance does not constitute waiver, but if an express waiver is made, it is valid.

Wisconsin Knife Works v. National Metal Crafters (1986)

Facts: Wisconsin's purchase order included a provision that stated that the contract could not be modified without its written assent. National missed the delivery deadlines, but Wisconsin accepted the late shipments and issued a new set of orders (later rescinded). Wisconsin later terminated the contract after National missed more of the original deadlines. National claimed Wisconsin "waived" the written modification requirement by acceptance of late shipments. In consequence, National continued to produce the goods.

Issue: Absent a writing, when does a contract modification "operate as a waiver" (UCC §2-209(4)) so as to be effective despite a clause that forbids modification other than in writing?

Rule: Absent a writing, an attempted modification of a contract that contains a clause forbidding modifications other than in writing is effective as a waiver only when it is reasonably relied upon.

Langer v. Superior Steel Corp. (1932)

Facts: Upon his retirement Langer was promised a pension "as long as [he] preserve[d] his present attitude of loyalty to the company and its officers and [was] not employed in any competitive occupation." Pension payments were discontinued after four years. Superior claimed that its promise was unenforceable due to lack of consideration.

Issue: Can forbearance of a right constitute consideration?

Rule: Forbearance of a right, such as the right to be employed by a former employer's competitor, is a detriment of a definite and substantial character and is valid consideration.

Bogigian v. Bogigian (1990)

Facts: When David and Hazel Bogigian dissolved their marriage, Hazel received a judgment on the family home of $10,300, to be paid when David sold the real estate. David sold the home, but because he had no equity in the property, he gave Hazel a paltry $5, and Hazel released her judgment. Hazel brought suit the following year to reinstate the judgment, claiming that her release was not supported by consideration because she did not understand what she was doing.

Issue: Can parties give or receive valid consideration if they are not aware that they are doing so?

Rule: Because consideration must actually be bargained for, a benefit received or a detriment suffered cannot be consideration unless the parties agree that the benefit or detriment is consideration.

Jones v. Star Credit Corp. (1969)

Facts: Jones and other welfare recipients were to pay over $1,400 (including tax, finance charges, and insurance) for a freezer that ordinarily retailed for less than $300. UCC §2-302 provided that a court may refuse to enforce a contract or excise an objectionable clause if it finds that the contract or clause was unconscionable at the time it was made.

Issue: Can a contract be void for unconscionability because the price term is excessive?

Rule: A court may refuse to enforce an excessive price term on the grounds of unconscionability.

In Re Greene (1930)

Facts: Greene, a married man, signed an agreement to pay his mistress $1,000 monthly plus insurance and rent upon the termination of their relationship. Consideration of $1 was recited in the agreement.

Issue: Does nominal consideration suffice to bind a promise?

Rule: Token consideration will not suffice to make an agreement binding. The past "illicit intercourse" of the parties is not consideration either.

Fiege v. Boehm (1956)

Facts: Fiege agreed to pay medical and other expenses of Boehm provided that Boehm would not institute a paternity suit. After Boehm gave birth, Fiege used blood tests to prove he was not the father. He then refused to honor his promise, claiming absence of valid consideration.

Issue: Does forbearance to bring suit qualify as consideration if the suit would not have been successful?

Rule: Forbearance to assert an invalid claim is sufficient consideration if the forbearing party had an honest intention to prosecute the litigation and reasonably believed it was valid.

Levine v. Blumenthal (1936)

Facts: The defendant contracted to lease a store for two years at a rate of $175 per month in the first year and $200 per month in the second. At the end of the first year, the defendant claimed that due to financial difficulties, he would have to go out of business if his rent was increased. The plaintiff accepted $175 per month, then sued for the balance.

Issue: Is an agreement to accept payments below the agreed upon amount binding when a party is in financial difficulties?

Rule: Partial payment of a larger debt is not consideration for an agreement to excuse the full debt, because the debtor is obligated to repay his debt anyway (pre-existing duty). The fact that a financially weak debtor agreed not to breach is not adequate consideration.

Alaska Packer's Assoc. v. Domenico (1902)

Facts: Sailors contracted to work for Alaska Packer's as fishermen in Alaska at a rate of $50 for the season, plus two cents for each fish caught. Upon arrival in Alaska, they refused to work unless they received higher wages. Alaska Packer's agreed because of the unavailability of alternative fishermen, and subsequently refused to pay the higher wages.

Issue: Is an agreement to increase compensation for services that the promisee is already contractually obligated to perform enforceable?

Rule: A new promise to increase the compensation of one already contractually obligated to perform is invalid if new consideration is not given (pre-existing duty rule).

Rehm-Zeiher Co. v. F.G. Walker Co. (1913)

Facts: Rehm-Zeiher, a seller of whiskey, entered into a four-year contract to purchase whiskey from F.G. Walker, a distiller. A clause in the contract provided that if Rehm-Zeiher "finds they cannot use the full amount of the above-named goods," they would only be required to buy what they wanted. Walker broke the agreement, claiming lack of mutuality of consideration made it void.

Issue: Is a contract that allows one party to refuse to purchase void for lack of mutuality?

Rule: A contract that allows one party to perform at its own discretion fails for lack of mutuality.

McMichael v. Price (1936)

Facts: Price, an experienced sand salesman, formed a new company and contracted to buy all the sand his company would be able to resell from McMichael for 60 percent of the market price. Although Price's company was not established, McMichael was aware of Price's experience.

Issue: Is an agreement to purchase all of one's requirements void for lack of mutuality?

Rule: A contract to buy all of one's "requirements" will not be void for lack of mutuality when both parties assume that a purchase would be made.

Note: In light of Price's experience and likely connections, it is sufficiently probable that his business would have requirements.

Omni Group, Inc. v. Seattle-First Nat'l Bank (1982)

Facts: Omni contracted to buy land from the Clarks subject to the requirement that Omni would be satisfied with a feasibility report made by its engineers and architects. The Clarks refused to sell, claiming lack of consideration because Omni's promise was illusory.

Issue: Does a condition precedent involving the satisfaction of a party render the said party's promise to perform illusory?

Rule: A condition precedent that requires a party's subjective satisfaction does not render a contract unenforceable, because it imposes a duty of good faith upon the said party in exercising good judgment.

Bailey v. West (1969)

Facts: The defendant bought a lame horse, which he tried to return to the seller. During several months of arguments between the defendant and the seller, the plaintiff, aware of the dispute, voluntarily cared for the horse and sent bills to both. The plaintiff sued the defendant for the value of the services rendered.

Issue: Is a person who voluntarily renders a service entitled to recovery in quasi-contract?

Rule: A person who voluntarily renders a service is usually not entitled to restitution.

Manwill v. Oyler (1961)

Facts: Defendant orally agreed to pay a debt that had been barred by the statute of limitations. The defendant later claimed that his promise was unenforceable due to lack of consideration.

Issue: Is a promise to repay a debt that is legally unenforceable due to a technicality void for lack of consideration?

Rule: Moral obligation does not suffice as consideration.

Note: Courts are split on this issue.

Harrington v. Taylor (1945)

Facts: The defendant's wife took refuge in the plaintiff's home after the defendant assaulted her. The defendant entered the plaintiff's house. His wife succeeded in knocking him down and was about to hit him with an axe when the plaintiff deflected the blow, mutilating her hand as a result. The defendant promised to pay for the plaintiff's damages but reneged after making a few payments, claiming that no consideration was given for his promise.

Issue: Is a promise to pay for damages made subsequent to an accident unenforceable for lack of consideration?

Rule: A voluntary humanitarian act is not consideration for a promise made at a later date. Past consideration is no consideration.

Kibler v. Frank L. Garrett & Sons, Inc. (1968)

Facts: In response to a dispute over how much money he owed the plaintiff for harvesting wheat, the defendant sent a check for what he felt he owed. A clause, written in fine print, stated that cashing the check would constitute full satisfaction of the debt. The plaintiff accepted the check without noticing the fine print and sued for the rest of the debt.

Issue: If there is a disputed claim, is it necessary to show that the defendant actually manifested his intention not to pay more than he remitted?

Rule: When partial payment of a debated debt is intended to be full satisfaction, it must be clearly brought to the attention of the payee.

Austin Instrument, Inc. v. Loral Corp. (1971)

Facts: Loral had a contract to produce radar sets for the Navy. The sets had 40 parts of which Austin, a subcontractor, produced 23. When Loral received a second contract from the Navy, Austin bid on all 40 parts, threatening to stop delivery of all parts on the first contract if it did not receive a price increase and the subcontract for all 40 parts of the second contract. After unsuccessfully checking with all the other subcontractors on its approved list, Loral acceded to Austin's demands so as to avoid breaching its contract with the Navy.

Issue: Is a contract modification enforceable if it was agreed to by a party who was deprived of free will under circumstances amounting to economic duress?

Rule: A contract is voidable if the party claiming duress was forced to agree by means of a wrongful threat precluding the exercise of its free will. The existence of economic duress is demonstrated by proof that immediate possession of needed goods is threatened and that the goods could not be obtained from another source.

Texas Gas Utilities Co. v. S.A. Barrett (1970)

Facts: Texas Gas was assigned a contract to supply natural gas to Barrett and others. The lower court held that the contract was unenforceable for lack of mutuality of obligation because an article of the contract relieved Texas Gas of its obligation to furnish gas in specific situations.

Issue: Does an exculpatory clause that excuses a party from performance of the contract automatically violate the requirement of mutuality of obligation between the parties?

Rule: The requirement that a contract be mutually binding is not violated by an exculpatory clause that provides specific circumstances in which a party is not bound to perform.

Mezzanotte v. Freeland (1973)

Facts: Mezzanotte contracted to purchase a tract of land together with improvements and facilities. The contract was contingent on Mezzanotte securing a second mortgage under conditions that would enable it to satisfactorily complete the contract. Freeland contended that the promise to buy was "illusory" since it depended on Mezzanotte's efforts to obtain financing.
Issue: Can there be valid consideration in a contract that is contingent on a conditional promise of one of the parties?
Rule: A conditional promise accompanied by an implied promise of good faith and reasonable effort constitutes valid consideration.

Miami Coca Cola Bottling v. Orange Crush Co. (1924)

Facts: Under a licensing agreement, Miami Coca Cola had the exclusive right to manufacture and distribute Orange Crush soda. In return, it was required to purchase a specified quantity of concentrate and promote and sell the soda. The license was perpetual but contained a provision allowing Orange Crush to cancel at any time. A year later, Orange Crush canceled the agreement.
Issue: Is a contract void for lack of mutuality when one party is given an option to terminate without providing any consideration to the other party for this term?
Rule: For an unlimited cancellation provision to be valid it must be supported by consideration.

Central Adjustment Bureau, Inc. v. Ingram (1984)

Facts: After being hired at CAB, a collection agency, Ingram and two colleagues were made to sign noncompetition agreements if they wished to continue working there. Several years later, they resigned and formed a competing collection agency with CAB's client lists, claiming that the noncompetition agreement was void for lack of consideration.
Issue: Is a noncompetition agreement invalid for failure of consideration if it was signed after at-will employment had begun?
Rule: Continued employment constitutes valid consideration for a noncompetition agreement signed after at-will employment has begun.
Note: Despite this rule, courts are generally hostile to noncompetition agreements that are not sufficiently limited in scope of location and time.

Sheldon v. Blackman (1925)

Facts: The deceased, Wilkinson, left a written promise to pay Sheldon a large sum of money in compensation for services rendered. Sheldon had cared for the elderly Wilkinson and his wife for many years.

Issue: When the value of a deliberately made agreement is indefinite or indeterminate, should the court substitute its own judgment for what constitutes valid consideration?

Rule: When the value of services is largely a matter of opinion, the court will not substitute its own judgment for that of the contracting parties because it would be a denial of the right of parties to make their own contract.

Feinberg v. Pfeiffer Co. (1959)

Facts: Pfeiffer agreed to pay Feinberg $200 per month for life when she retired. Feinberg worked for a few more years and retired. Her pension was terminated after several years when she refused to have it reduced to $100 per month.

Issue: Can a promisor withdraw a promise that was given without consideration?

Rule: Past employment is considered past and invalid consideration. However, if one acts to her detriment (quitting work) in justifiable reliance on a promise, the promise will be enforced if an injustice would otherwise result.

Salsbury v. Northwestern Bell Telephone Co. (1974)

Facts: Northwestern pledged a sum of money to support the establishment of a new city college. Salsbury, chairman of the college's board of trustees, sued to enforce the pledge.

Issue: Can a charitable subscription be enforced?

Rule: As a matter of public policy, charitable subscriptions are enforceable even without a showing of consideration or detrimental reliance.

Note: The court takes a modern approach to charitable subscriptions by applying the tentative draft of the Restatement (Second) of Contract §90(2).

Drennan v. Star Paving Co. (1958)

Facts: Drennan, a contractor, used a bid from Star Paving, a subcontractor, to calculate the costs of a larger bid it submitted to a third party. After Drennan was awarded the job, Star informed it that its "sub-bid" was erroneously low and refused to work at that price. Although Drennan had not formally accepted the offer, it had relied on the price, as is customary in the construction industry. Drennan sued to recover the difference between Star's original price and the amount paid to another subcontractor to do the work.

Issue: May a party be required to perform by the terms of an offer that was never actually accepted?

Rule: If an offeror should reasonably expect that his offer will induce reliance by the offeree to take an action or forbearance of a substantial and definite character (such as basing a contract price on subcontractor bids), the offer is enforceable even if the reliance occurs prior to a formal acceptance of the offer.

Werner v. Xerox Corp. (1984)

Facts: A district court held that Werner had reasonably relied upon the representation of a Xerox agent that Werner would become a parts manufacturer for Xerox. Having received parts-producing machines from Werner, Xerox terminated their relationship and prepared to make the parts in its own factory. The court awarded reliance damages having found that the reliance was foreseeable to Xerox, that Werner actually relied and that nonenforcement of the promise would be unjust.

Issue: What standard will a court apply in reviewing the three elements of promissory estoppel?

Rule: Foreseeability of reliance and actual reliance are matters of fact that will not be reversed unless clearly erroneous; whether injustice will result from nonenforcement is a matter of law to be reversed only in a case of abuse of discretion.

Greiner v. Greiner (1930)

Facts: Mrs. Greiner promised to give her son some land if he and his family would move from one county to another and live in a house that she owned. Frank and his family moved. His mother then told him that if he would move the house to another 80-acre tract that she owned, she would give him both the house and the tract. Frank moved the house and spent money on improvements. Mrs. Greiner then promised to leave the land to Frank in her will, but later agreed to give him the deed outright. A family squabble occurred and the deed was never given to Frank. Instead, Frank's mother tried to evict Frank and his family from the land. Frank counterclaimed for the deed.

Issue: If a promisee acts in reasonable reliance on a promise, is the promisor obligated to perform?

Rule: A promise binds the promisor if the promisee acts in reasonable reliance on the promise and injustice can only be avoided by enforcement of the promise.

Katz v. Danny Dare, Inc. (1980)

Facts: Katz worked for Dare. Katz was injured attempting to foil a robbery attempt at one of Dare's stores, and Dare tried to convince Katz to retire. After negotiating for over a year, Katz agreed to retire upon Dare's promise of a lifetime pension. Dare would have fired Katz had he not agreed to retire. Dare paid Katz the pension for three years and then stopped.

Issue: Does the doctrine of promissory estoppel require a promisee to give up something to which the promisee is legally entitled before a promise can be enforced?

Rule: Promissory estoppel does not require a promisee to give up something to which the promisee is legally entitled before a promise can be enforced. If a promisee reasonably relies on a promise to the promisee's detriment and injustice can only be avoided by enforcement of the promise, the promise is enforceable.

Universal Computer Systems, Inc. v. Medical Services Ass'n (1980)

Facts: Medical Services solicited bids for the lease of a computer and specified a deadline for receipt of all proposals. To meet the deadline, Universal arranged to send the bid by airplane and asked Gebert, Medical Service's agent, if he could arrange to have the bid picked up at the airport. While the bid was in flight, Gebert told Universal he had changed his mind and could not pick up the bid. Universal attempted to find an alternate courier, but was unable to meet Medical Services' deadline. Medical Services returned Universal's bid unopened.

Issue: If a company's agent makes a promise and the promisee detrimentally relies on that promise, is the company bound by the agent's promise?

Rule: If a promisee reasonably believes that a company's agent has the authority to make a promise and detrimentally relies on that promise, the company is bound by the agent's promise.

Ray v. William G. Eurice & Bros., Inc. (1952)

Facts: Eurice submitted a three-page proposed contract to build Ray's house. Ray did not approve of Eurice's proposal, so he had his own lawyer draft a contract, consisting of five pages of specifications that differed from Eurice's proposal. Both Ray and Eurice signed this contract. Subsequently, Eurice refused to perform, arguing that when John Eurice signed the contract, he thought it was identical to the three-page proposal that Eurice had submitted and did not contain any new specifications.

Issue: Does a unilateral mistake as to the contents of a contract discharge the party from his contractual obligations?

Rule: A unilateral mistake as to the contents of a contract does not discharge the party from his contractual obligations. Absent fraud, duress or mutual mistake, a party who has the capacity to understand a written document is bound by his signature.

Plowman v. Indian Refining Co. (1937)

Facts: Indian promised to pay retirement benefits to Plaintiffs, and stopped paying after one year. Plaintiffs claimed that Indian promised that the payments would continue for life, and that their past performance and their promise to pick up the checks themselves constituted consideration.
Issue 1: Can consideration be based on past performance?
Rule 1: Past performance cannot be consideration for a promise, because consideration is something given in exchange for a promise or in reliance on a promise.
Issue 2: Can consideration be based on moral obligations?
Rule 2: Moral consideration cannot be used to enforce a promise.
Issue 3: Can consideration be based on an act imposed on the promisee as a condition for the promise?
Rule 3: Acts imposed on the promisee, which are merely necessary conditions for obtaining the gratuitous promise, are not consideration. These conditions are benefits to the promisees, not detriments.

Berryman v. Kmoch (1977)

Facts: Berryman and Kmoch signed an option contract that stated that Berryman, for $10 and "other valuable consideration," would grant Kmoch a 120-day option to purchase real estate. However, the $10 was never paid. Kmoch attempted to exercise his option after he learned that Berryman sold the land to someone else.
Issue: When is an option contract valid?
Rule: An option contract is valid only when there is sufficient consideration, or when promissory estoppel can be invoked as a substitute for consideration. If the option contract is void, then there is merely an offer to sell, revokable anytime before the offeree accepts.

De Los Santos v. Great Western Sugar Co. (1984)

Facts: De Los Santos agreed to transport all the beets loaded into its trucks by Great Western to designated factories. Before all the beets had been transported, Great Western terminated its contract with De Los Santos.
Issue: Can a promisor be held liable for terminating a contract that does not specify a quantity of goods?

Rule: Where a promisor agrees to purchase services from a promisee on a per unit basis, but the agreement does not specify a quantity or an intent to have the promisee perform all of the promisor's needs, the promisor may terminate the agreement at any time.

Mattei v. Hopper (1958)

Facts: Mattei agreed to buy Hopper's shopping center. The agreement called for a $1,000 down payment and the balance to be paid within 120 days subject to Mattei obtaining satisfactory leases. Hopper refused to complete the sale, claiming Mattei's promise was illusory because he was not actually bound: Hopper was obligated to sell, but Mattei only had to buy if he was satisfied with the leases.

Issue: Does a contract lack consideration if the assent of one party to the agreement is conditioned by a satisfaction clause?

Rule: An agreement that contains a satisfaction clause is not illusory (lacking consideration or mutuality of obligation) if performance of the condition can be judged by a reasonable person standard or if the party subject to the satisfaction clause acts in good faith.

Charter Township of Ypsilanti v. General Motors Corp. (1993)

Facts: Ypsilanti granted numerous tax abatements to General Motors, based on promises by General Motors that its production line would remain in the area. When General Motors announced that it was going to move its production line elsewhere, Ypsilanti alleged that the company breached a contract created by the tax abatement statute.

Issue: Do promises made in an effort to solicit tax abatements constitute an enforceable contract?

Rule: The fact that a corporation solicits a tax abatement and persuades a municipality to grant them with assurances of jobs cannot be evidence of a promise, and thus may not be used to estop action by the beneficiary of the tax abatement.

Keller v. Holderman (1863)

Facts: Keller gave Holderman a $300 check for a watch owned by Holderman. The watch had an actual value of $15, and Keller had never expected to actually be held to the deal, as evidenced by the lack of funds in his account. The check was not honored, and Holderman sued.

Issue: Is a contract enforceable when the parties contracted in jest?

Rule: When a trial court finds that a transaction is a "frolic and a banter," such that the plaintiff does not expect to sell a good, and the defendant does not intend to buy it, no contract has been made.

Brown v. Finney (1866)

Facts: The parties met at a restaurant, and their conversation turned to coal prices. Although there was no mutual intent to contract, the plaintiff made a "bantering proposition" to the defendant that was orally accepted. Plaintiff brought action for breach of the contract.

Issue: Is a contract formed when two parties meet, and an agreement is proposed in the absence of the intent to create a binding contract?

Rule: If a proposition is made and accepted, and no expectation to create a binding contract exists, a court must look at the specific circumstances of the case to decide if there was mutual assent to the agreement.

Clark v. Elza (1979)

Facts: Plaintiffs brought suit against defendants for injuries sustained in a car accident. The parties verbally agreed upon a settlement figure, which was later rescinded by the plaintiffs. Defendants filed a motion to enforce the settlement.

Issue: When does a settlement agreement become binding on the parties?

Rule: In order to enforce a settlement agreement, a court must decide whether it constituted an agreement for the future discharge of an existing claim (an executory accord), or one that immediately discharged the original claim (a substitute contract). Unless there is clear evidence to the contrary, an agreement to discharge a pre-existing claim is regarded as an executory accord, and thus will not discharge the underlying claim until it is performed.

Mazer v. Jackson Insurance Agency (1976)

Facts: Homeowners, represented by Mazer, sued for an injunction against developers of an office park. The homeowners claimed that the action proposed by the developers to clear-cut woodlands constituted a breach of a promise to maintain the area as a 100-foot buffer zone between the office park and their property, and contended that the developer was estopped from developing in a manner inconsistent with its previous assurances.

Issue: May a party claim estoppel due to detrimental reliance on another's actions?

Rule: A party is estopped from denying the validity of a promise when the promise is reasonably expected to induce action or forbearance on the part of the promisee and does induce such action or forbearance, if injustice can be avoided only by enforcement of the promise. (Rest. 2d §90.)

D & G Stout, Inc. v. Bacardi Imports, Inc. (1991)

Facts: Plaintiff, General, had an at-will agreement with Bacardi to distribute Bacardi liquor in Northern Indiana. Because Bacardi promised to faithfully continue to supply General with liquor, General rejected a pending deal to sell its assets. However, Bacardi reneged on its promise and General was forced to sell its assets at a much lower price than it was first offered.
Issue: Can promissory estoppel be used to enforce a promise made between two parties already in an at-will relationship?
Rule: If a promise can reasonably induce reliance, then the promise can be enforced by promissory estoppel despite an existing at-will relationship. Plaintiffs can recover for reliance damages, not expectation damages.

Hayes v. Plantation Steel (1982)

Facts: After employee Hayes announced he would retire, but before he in fact retired, his employer promised him a pension without specifying an amount. After the retirement, the employer paid Hayes $5,000 for three years but made no more payments thereafter. Hayes sued for breach.
Issue: Assuming that the employer promised the employee a definite pension, is the promise enforceable if the employee did not rely upon it in deciding to retire?
Rule: A promise of a pension is not an enforceable contract if the employee provides no consideration for it. There would be consideration for the promise if the employer made the promise to motivate the employee to retire, for example, or to continue working when he otherwise could retire. A promise of a pension may not be enforced under promissory estoppel if the employee does not rely on the promise at all in leaving his job.

Dyer v. National By-Products (1986)

Facts: Employee Dyer lost a foot in a workplace accident. Dyer claimed that he agreed to give up his claim in tort against his employer for his employer's promise to employ him for life. The employer eventually laid him off and Dyer sued for breach of the promise of employment. The employer in defense urged because Dyer's only legal remedy was in workers' compensation a promise not to sue in tort, which Dyer could not do, was not consideration that could make the employer's promise of lifetime work enforceable. The employer obtained a summary judgment on that basis and Dyer appealed.

Issue: Is a good faith promise to forbear bringing a suit that one cannot legally make nevertheless consideration for a promise made in return?

Rule: Forbearance to bring a suit that the claimant in good faith does not know is invalid may be consideration for a promise. Reversed and remanded for evidence on Dyer's good faith. (Rest. 2d §74.)

Apfel v. Prudential Bache (1993)

Facts: Apfel sold Prudential Bache a system for selling municipal bonds by using computers. Prudential Bache later denied it was obligated to pay for the system as promised, because Apfel had no property interest in the idea and therefore could not sell it.

Issue: Is a promise to pay for a system not supported by consideration if the seller has no property interest in it?

Rule: The investment bank's contract to purchase an idea for issuing and selling municipal bonds through computerized entries was supported by consideration, and an idea does not have to be novel for the promise to buy it to be supported by consideration.

Gottlieb v. Tropicana Hotel and Casino (2000)

Facts: Gottlieb was a member of Tropicana's Diamond Club, a free club she joined simply by submitting her name, address, phone number, and email address, in return for which the Tropicana gave her a card that would identify her when she gambled at certain games. She played a $1 million game that was part of an advertising promotion of the Tropicana. She claimed to have won the game and sued the Tropicana in contract for breach of its duty to pay as promised in the promotional advertising.

Issue: Is the promise made by a casino in connection with a particular game enforceable?

Rule: When a casino makes a promise in connection with a promotional game, that promise is supported by sufficient consideration in the form of the detriment of the promisee in traveling to the casino location, waiting to play the game, and permitting the casino to use her card to track her gambling preferences, even though such detriment is minimal.

Ridge Runner Forestry v. Ann M. Veneman, Secretary of Agriculture (2002)

Facts: Ridge Runner contracted with the Department of Agriculture to provide equipment during emergencies "to the extent" that Ridge Runner "is willing and able" to do so. The Department of Agriculture never made a request and Ridge Runner sued for breach.

Issue: Is a promise to provide equipment if "willing and able" enforceable as a contract?

Rule: A promise that depends upon the will of the promisor is illusory because it does not bind the promisor and is therefore unenforceable.

Canusa Corp. v. A & R Lobosco, Inc. (1997)

Facts: Lobosco agreed to sell old newspaper to Canusa. The parties put their agreement in the form of an output contract. Canusa agreed to accept all of Lobosco's newspaper output; Lobosco promised a minimum monthly tonnage, which it never met. Canusa sued for breach.

Issue: Is a seller under an output contract who never meets the minimum quantity promised in breach of contract?

Rule: A seller who agrees to sell all its output and to sell a stated minimum is bound to measure its output in good faith. The amount delivered cannot be unreasonably disproportionate to the stated minimum, which is treated as an estimate for deciding whether there is a breach. Seller here attempted to explain the shortage by the additional expense it would have incurred to meet the monthly minimum, which does not satisfy good faith.

Estate of Lovenkamp (2001)

Facts: Louise Serrato and Donald Lovenkamp divorced; all real estate they had owned went to him. Soon, they began to live together as before. Donald wrote her a check for $60,000 "in case something happened." When he died several years later, the check was stale. She tried to enforce the decedent's promise to pay $60,000 against his estate.

Issue: Is a man's promise to pay money to a woman in recognition of her having lived with him supported by consideration?

Rule: A man's promise to a woman made in recognition of her having cohabited with him is a promise made for past consideration and is therefore unenforceable. It is a promise based on the motive of the promisor only.

Deli v. University of Minnesota (1998)

Facts: An athletic team coach videotaped herself and her husband having sex on the same tape that they used to videotape a team competition. She alleged a promise by the athletic director not to look at the tape, which she alleged was breached, causing her emotional distress.

Issue: Can a claim of promissory estoppel support an award of damages for emotional distress?

Rule: Because promissory estoppel is a contractual claim, it cannot support an award of damages for emotional distress. The promisee must plead and prove an independent tort to support such damages.

Harris v. Watson (1791)

Facts: A seaman, Harris, demanded extra compensation from the ship commander, Watson, to guide the vessel out of danger during a storm, which Watson promised to pay.

Issue: Is a promise of additional consideration enforceable?

Rule: There was no consideration for the promise of additional pay, because the seaman was already obligated to do the work he did.

Pennsy Supply, Inc. v. American Ash Recycling Corp. of Pa. (2006)

Facts: American Ash gave a product called AggRite to Pennsy, a paving contractor. AggRite is classified as hazardous waste. Pennsy did not pay for it but agreed to dispose of it by using it as a paving material, but it did not work for this purpose and it had to be removed from roads and disposed of as hazardous waste. Pennsy sued American Ash for costs of disposal based on breach of contract and of warranty.

Issue: Is there consideration for a warranty by a transferor of waste where the transferor is not given anything of direct value either for waste itself or for a warranty?

Rule: The promise to dispose of waste, thus saving the manufacturer the cost of disposal, is consideration for the transferor's contract and warranty obligations.

Pop's Cones, Inc. v. Resorts International Hotel, Inc. (1998)

Facts: Hotel promised space to frozen yogurt seller and withdrew the promise.

Issue: May a promisee assert a claim for reliance damages based on promissory estoppel when it knows it does not have a contract?

Rule: A claim under promissory estoppel exists when defendant makes a promise that promisor should reasonably expect to induce action or forbearance by promisee, which does induce action or forbearance, if enforcement of the promise is necessary to avoid injustice. Here, the promise of a space to lease in the hotel induced the promisee to terminate an existing lease and to put equipment in storage.

Wright v. Newman (1996)

Facts: Wright promised to support Newman's son. Wright and Newman were unmarried, and Wright believed that he was the natural father. He later learned he was not the natural father.
Issue: May a promise to support a child create a claim under promissory estoppel?
Rule: A claim under promissory estoppel exists when defendant makes a promise that promisor should reasonably expect to induce action or forbearance by promisee, which does induce action or forbearance, if enforcement of the promise is necessary to avoid injustice. Here, Newman relied on Wright's promise and his conduct in continuing support for the child.
Note: The dissent reasoned that Newman had not proved detriment because she had not shown that the true father was unavailable or unable to support the child.

King v. Trustees of Boston Univ. (1995)

Facts: Martin Luther King, Jr., gave possession of his papers to Boston University and wrote a letter concerning eventual transfer of title to the papers to Boston University at his death.
Issue: May a promisee reasonably rely on a donor's promise to transfer title in the future, given the donor's retention of title in fact?
Rule: A jury may reasonably conclude that a letter concerning an eventual transfer of title to goods is a promise of a gift enforceable as a charitable pledge supported by consideration or reliance, even if the jury finds that the letter is not a contract.

Best Construction Co. v. Southland Construction Co. (1977)

Facts: Southland promised to lend plywood to Best "as a favor." Before delivering any plywood to Best, Southland sold all its plywood to a third party. Best sued Southland for breach of contract.
Issue: Is a business's gratuitous promise to lend goods to another business enforceable?
Rule: No. A gratuitous promise even in a business context that is without consideration is not enforceable.

Technical Assistance Int'l, Inc. v. United States (1998)

Facts: The General Services Administration (GSA) of the federal government contracted to hire Technical Assistance to maintain and repair certain vehicles owned by the GSA according to the GSA's requirements.

The GSA had overestimated the amount of its requirements for this contract and Technical Assistance sought to modify the contract because of the GSA's mistake. Technical Assistance obtained summary judgment against the GSA for breach of contract.

Issue: Does a buyer who binds itself to purchase its requirements breach if the buyer has overestimated its requirements to the detriment of the seller?

Rule: A requirements buyer is bound to measure its requirements in good faith, and falling short of an estimate does not prove bad faith. To remain in good faith, the buyer must have a good business reason for determining its requirements and cannot reduce its requirements solely to avoid its contractual duties.

Passant v. McWilliam (1997)

Facts: Attorney (Passante) for a corporation and some directors secured a needed loan for the corporation when McWilliam, a shareholder and director, failed to do so. The board of directors then approved giving 3 percent of the corporate stock to Passante for getting the loan, but did not follow through and later fired Passante.

Issue: Is a corporation's promise to transfer shares for services to the corporation that have already been performed enforceable?

Rule: No. Services already performed are not consideration for a later promise.

Autorol v. Continental Water Systems Corp. (1990)

Facts: Plaintiff and Defendant contracted to produce and sell a water purification system. The contract provided that Plaintiff and Defendant would agree by a date certain on specifications of the system, and it provided that if they could not in good faith agree, either Plaintiff or Defendant could terminate the contract. The date passed without an agreement and without termination. The contract provided that any modification must be in writing. Plaintiff sued for breach.

Issue: If a written contract provides that any modification of the contract must also be written, is an oral modification enforceable?

Rule: A written contract with a no-oral-modification clause may be modified without a writing if the modification is supported by consideration and the other party relies on the modification. Here, there was both consideration and reliance on the oral modification that extended the deadline.

CHAPTER 4

Remedies

INTRODUCTION

If a promisor breaches his contract, the law provides the promisee with several possible remedies. First, the court may enter an order compelling the promisor to perform the promise, that is, to do exactly what he promised to do. This remedy is known as specific performance. Second, the law may grant the promisee an award of money, known as damages, whose amount is set so as to compensate the promisee for the loss of the performance that had been promised. Damages are therefore a remedy that substitutes for the performance itself. Damages for contract breach may be measured according to the value of the expectation the promisee had in the promise or according to costs the promisee paid out in reliance upon the promise. Specific performance and damages are the two main types of remedy in contract. Third, a court may order a remedy for the promisee in restitution. A remedy of restitution often requires the promisor to return any benefit the promisor received from the promisee, but restitution may also require the promisor to return any profits he earned by use of the promisee's property. Those are the main categories of remedy in contract.

In addition, contracts courses also deal with a few other topics connected with remedies. First, they deal with remedies for breach that the parties agree on in the contract, known as liquidated damages, because dollar amounts are named or "liquidated." Second, they deal with remedies in so-called quasi-contract, which are not truly contracts at all, but situations in which courts supply a remedy similar to a contract remedy. Finally, courses sometimes deal with situations in which courts deny a contract remedy where one is legally possible, so-called non-recoverable damages.

I. EQUITABLE REMEDIES

Although the standard relief for breach of contract is monetary damages, they may be inappropriate in certain situations, such as where the amount of damages is too speculative, or the contract was for unique goods. In such cases, courts will grant primarily two forms of equitable relief: injunctions and specific performance. Originally, there were two court systems, law and equity. Today, the distinction has been abolished and all courts can grant either form of remedy. A primary consideration in granting equitable relief is the issue of justice and fairness.

A. Specific Performance (Rest. 2d §359; UCC §2-716)

Instead of giving monetary damages, a court can force the breaching party to perform as promised in the contract. Specific performance is usually granted where a contract involves a unique good, such as land. Before granting this remedy a court will consider several issues:

1. Indefiniteness (Rest. 2d §362)

The agreement between the parties must be sufficiently definite and certain to be specifically performed, all material terms included.

2. Extensive Supervision (Rest. 2d §366)

If specific performance of the agreement requires extensive supervision by the court to ensure that each party is fulfilling its duties properly, the court will avoid awarding this measure of damages. Judicial time is scarce enough without such additional burdens. Building contracts generally involve much supervision.

3. Adequacy of Alternative Remedies (Rest. 2d §360)

Specific performance is an attractive remedy if other remedies do not appear adequate. Relevant considerations include:

a. The difficulty of proving monetary damages,

b. The availability of satisfactory substitute goods, and

c. The likelihood the plaintiff will be able to collect a monetary judgment from the defendant.

4. "Do Equity to Get Equity" (Rest. 2d §364)

A court may refuse to grant equitable relief if the party requesting such relief did not act fairly in forming the contract or if denial of equitable relief would cause great hardship to the breaching party.

5. Land

Traditionally, courts have had a strong preference for requiring specific performance in land contracts because each parcel of land is unique.

6. Personal Service Contract (Rest. 2d §367)

Contracts made for the personal services of a party are rarely specifically enforced because courts dislike the idea of forcing people to work in places not of their choosing. However, injunctions are used to prohibit the breaching employee from working for his employer's competitors for the duration of the contract.

B. Injunctions (Rest. 2d §361)

As another alternative to monetary damages (and to specific performance), a court may prohibit the breaching party from rendering the contracted-for performance to anyone but the non-breaching party. Courts will grant an injunction if:

1. A noncompetition clause is in the contract.
2. The contract is for unique services.

   The employer must prove that the employee's services or abilities are special or unique. This relates to the issue of availability of alternate remedies.
3. The employee's livelihood is not threatened.

   A court will not grant an injunction if doing so would leave the employee with no other reasonable means of making a living.

II. REMEDIES AT LAW

At law, the nonbreaching party is awarded monetary damages to compensate for the loss incurred. Courts seek to protect three interests when awarding monetary damages:

1. Expectation

2. Reliance

3. Restitution

III. EXPECTATION

Courts have a strong preference for awarding damages measured by the expected value of the promise/contract. The object is to put the party in the same position he would be in if the contract were performed as expected. This includes both the value of expenses incurred and expected profits.

A. Computing the Value of Expectations (Rest. 2d §347)

Professor Farnsworth's formula for calculating expectation damages is:

$$\text{General Damages} = \text{Loss in Value} + \text{Other Loss} - \text{Cost Avoided} - \text{Loss Avoided}$$

1. Loss in Value
   a. The difference between the *value to the injured party* of the performance he should have received and that of any performance he did receive. **Example:** If the defendant paid the plaintiff $100 of a $1,000 debt, the loss in value is $900.

b. If defective service was rendered, then loss in value is value of flawless service less value of the defective service. This is a subjective standard (the value is the value to the plaintiff).

2. Other Loss

Other loss involves two types of damages, incidental and consequential.

   a. Incidental

   Costs incurred in a reasonable attempt to avoid loss, even if unsuccessful.

   b. Consequential

   Costs or injury to persons or property resulting from breach.

3. Cost Avoided

Savings to the plaintiff from not having to perform further.

4. Loss Avoided

Any loss avoided by the salvaging or reallocation of resources that would have been devoted to performance.

5. Example

A contracts to build B a residential house for $100,000, payable as work progresses. A's expenses for labor and materials would be $60,000 if he completed construction. A does half the work ($50,000 due) incurring $35,000 in expenses. B refuses to pay. A uses the unused lumber and other materials, worth $10,000, on another job.

A's loss in value is $100,000 (what B promised him overall). He has incurred no other loss. By stopping work midway, A avoids spending an additional $25,000 of his expenses. Therefore, A's expectation damages are $100,000 − 25,000 − 10,000 = $65,000.

B. Promised Performance (Nonmonetary) (Rest. 2d §348)

There is difficulty in measuring loss in value when the performance not rendered involves services, e.g., builder refuses to complete work, seller does not deliver goods, etc. In such cases, courts utilize one of two measures of damages:

1. Cost of Completing Performance

Damages are awarded in the amount it would cost plaintiff to properly complete the work that the breaching party began.

2. Diminution in Value/"Benefit of the Bargain"

Damages are calculated as the difference between the value of a complete performance and the value of defendant's defective performance.

   a. This measure in damages is favored when the cost of completing performance is clearly disproportionate to the probable loss in value resulting from the incomplete or defective work.

Example: A builds a pool but erroneously uses blue tile instead of green tile. The diminution in the pool's market value is $1, but the cost of properly completing the work is $1,000. It would be economically wasteful to force A to expend $1,000.

    b. However, willful breach or public policy may induce a court to award cost of completion damages; such considerations may override economic waste.

Example: A knows the pool was supposed to have green tile, but he installs blue tile anyhow because he has too much of it lying around. A may be required to remedy the defective performance or pay for someone else to do it.

C. Examples of Expectation Damages
    1. Sale of Goods Contracts
        a. Breach by Buyer (remedies of seller) (UCC §2-703)
        Mnemonic: **ROW SCRAP**
          i. **R**ecover **O**rdinary contract damages, i.e., contract price less market price plus incidental damages (without reselling the goods).
          ii. **W**ithhold delivery of goods.
          iii. **S**top delivery by bailee or carrier.
          iv. **C**ancel entire contract.
          v. **R**esell **A**ll goods and recover any loss from the contract price.
          vi. Recover **P**rice of goods that were actually accepted by the buyer.
        b. Breach by Seller (remedies of buyer) (UCC §2-711)
        Mnemonic: **MSG** Causes Cancer
          i. Recover **M**onetary damages (market price at breach less contract price plus incidental and consequential damages).
          ii. Obtain **S**pecific performance.
          iii. Recover contracted for **G**oods (if total or partial payment was made).
          iv. **C**ancel the contract.
          v. **C**over — buy substitute goods and recover the difference between the contract price and market price.
    2. Sale of Land Contracts
    Damages are awarded based on the difference between the contract price and the fair market value of the real property at the time of breach.
    3. Employment Contracts
    In equity, an injunction may be granted. At law:

       a. Employer Breaches

       Employee recovers full contract price for the remainder of the employment term.

       b. Employee Breaches

       Employer recovers cost of obtaining a substitute if it is above the contract price. There are two types of breaches by employee:

         i. Intentional

         Employee is barred from recovering expectation damages but may recover restitution in quantum meruit for substantial performance.

         ii. Unintentional

         Employee is allowed to recover in quasi-contract the value of work done prior to unintentional breach.

    4. Construction Contracts

       a. Breach by Builder

         i. Before Construction Commenced

         Owner of the premises can recover excess cost of building above the contract price and the reasonable cost of delays.

         ii. During Construction

         Cost of completion and reasonable damages for delay.

         iii. Late Performance

         Subjects builder to liability for damages caused by delay.

         iv. A builder can recover in quasi-contract for the value of work done if the breach was unintentional.

       b. Breach by Property Owner

         i. Before Construction Began

         Builder recovers lost profits.

         ii. During Construction

         Builder recovers lost profits and expenses incurred.

         iii. After Construction Is Completed

         Builder recovers contract price plus interest.

D. Limitations on Recovery of Expectation Damages

  1. Foreseeability (Rest. 2d §351; UCC §2-715)

  Generally applies to consequential and incidental losses. The damages must be foreseeable to the breaching party at the time the contract was made, not at the time of breach. A loss is foreseeable if it naturally follows from the breach or if the breaching party had actual notice that such a loss would result from a breach. (See *Hadley v. Baxendale*.)

  2. Certainty (Rest. 2d §352)

  A party must establish with reasonable certainty the amount of its loss and the fact that it would have avoided the loss but for the breach. Some types of damages are generally considered to be uncertain, such as lost profits or lost publicity.

3. New-Business Rule

Courts are not very receptive to claims for lost profits made by new businesses that have no prior history of profitability, but a court will consider such claims in light of the plaintiff's experience in the industry and the diligence of his efforts in running the business.

4. Mitigation (Rest. 2d §350)

The injured party is not compensated for damages resulting from a breach that the nonbreaching party could have reasonably avoided. Compensation will be granted if an unsuccessful, but reasonable, effort to avoid the loss was made.

a. Comparable Alternatives

If a comparable opportunity exists, the plaintiff must accept it and use it to mitigate damages caused by the defendant's breach. If the plaintiff fails to accept a comparable alternative, the court will not award him the damages that could have been avoided. Criteria for comparability include location, type of services, hours of work, status, etc.

b. Incomparable Alternatives

The existence of incomparable alternatives will not reduce damages unless they are actually accepted by the plaintiff. Money earned at a new opportunity will be used to mitigate the damage award if the party in breach proves that the plaintiff would not have accepted this opportunity but for the breach. (This is more likely to occur if the contract was for the personal services of the plaintiff.) However, if the plaintiff shows that he could have accepted both opportunities, there will be no reduction of damages.

c. The breaching party has the burden of proving that the plaintiff failed to mitigate and that a comparable opportunity existed.

d. UCC: If a seller breaches a sales contract, the buyer must try to "cover" by buying substitute goods. If the buyer breaches, the seller does not have a duty to mitigate. He may choose from a number of remedies.

IV. RELIANCE

There are two types of reliance damages that a party can incur. The first type involves actions done in reliance upon a valid and binding contract that is subsequently breached. In either case, the goal of the court is to put the nonbreaching party in as favorable a position as he enjoyed prior to the contract. Reliance damages are usually awarded if expectation damages are too uncertain. The second type involves the doctrine of promissory estoppel and results when there is no valid contract, but a party detrimentally relied on another's promise, and it is unfair not to enforce the promise. (Rest. 2d §90.)

A. Requirements

Mnemonic: **R**obin **H**ood **F**inds **D**anger **I**nviting

To recover damages based on reliance a party must show:

1. There was actual **R**eliance on the contractual promise
2. The reliance was **F**oreseeable to the breaching party
3. The reliance was clearly **D**etrimental to the promisee and
4. **I**njustice can only be avoided by enforcement of the contract.

B. Reliance upon a Contract (Rest. 2d §349)

1. Types of Reliance Damages

   a. **Expenses** Incurred in Preparation of Performance

   These are not part of the contract but are necessary to perform it.

   b. **Expenditures** Made in Performance Prior to Breach

   c. Forgone Opportunities (Opportunity Costs)

   Example: The value of wages a party would have received had he remained at a prior job and not entered into the contract.

2. Limitations on Reliance Damages

   a. Net Loss

   If full performance by the breaching party would have resulted in a net loss to the nonbreaching party, the amount of the loss is deducted from the reliance damages award.

   b. Foreseeability and Certainty

   Reliance damages must be foreseeable to the breaching party and must be proved with certainty.

   c. Mitigation

   The nonbreaching party has an obligation to mitigate his damages if possible.

   d. Cost to Plaintiff

   The amount of reliance damages is determined by the costs incurred, regardless of the value of the benefit the breaching party received.

   e. Essential vs. Incidental Reliance Damages

   Under the classical view, reliance damages were limited to a maximum of the full contract price. In such cases, a party could recover only essential reliance damages, i.e., expenses made in preparation for or in actual performance of the contract. The modern view allows recovery beyond the contract price in cases where incidental reliance naturally and foreseeably follows from the contract. Incidental expenses are those made in reliance upon having a contract, although they are not actually incurred in preparation or performance of the contract. **Example:** A rents a store from B for $100 and buys inventory worth $500. B breaks the lease before A takes possession. A can recover (1) rent paid to date ($100) in performance of the contract and (2) unsold inventory purchased in reliance on the lease (incidental).

V. RESTITUTION

A court may require the breaching party to disgorge the value of any benefits received from the nonbreaching party. Unlike reliance damages, restitution is based upon the value of the benefit to the defendant rather than the cost to plaintiff. Restitution is granted when expectation damages are uncertain and reliance damages do not properly reflect the value defendant has received. The main goal of such damages is to avoid unjust enrichment. (Rest. 2d §370.)

A. Value of Benefit to Defendant (Rest. 2d §371)

The value of the benefit a party has received is measured in one of two ways:

1. The reasonable value of such a "benefit" as measured by the market value of obtaining it from another source (not the subjective value to the defendant).

2. The extent to which the party's property has increased in value or other interests have been advanced where the benefit is not readily obtainable from another source.

B. Limits on Restitution

1. Restitution can exceed the contract price if defendant was actually "enriched" beyond that amount.

2. If plaintiff has completed performance, then expectation damages are given, and restitution is not available.

VI. QUASI-CONTRACTS, AGREED REMEDIES AND NON-RECOVERABLE DAMAGES

A. Recovery in Quasi-Contract

Recovery in quasi-contract occurs in any one of three general situations: (1) if a contract never existed but justice requires that the plaintiff be compensated; (2) if there was an unenforceable contract (due to the Statute of Frauds, illegality, etc.); and (3) if the plaintiff has materially breached an existing, valid contract and has conferred a benefit on the other party. Courts generally award either restitution or reliance damages, depending on fairness and equity.

1. Requirements of Quasi-Contract:

a. One party provided a benefit to another.

      b. The benefit was provided with the "reasonable expectation" of compensation.

      c. There was an express or implied request for the benefit.

      d. The party receiving the benefit would be unjustly enriched if he was not forced to compensate the party providing the benefits.

  2. The size of recovery in quasi-contract (also called quantum meruit) is determined by the degree of the plaintiff's detriment.

  3. If a party willfully breaches a contract, it is less likely that a court will grant quasi-contractual recovery, although this restriction is somewhat eased in cases of employment contracts in which an employee intentionally breaches.

  4. UCC §2-718

    A breaching buyer may recover the value of payments made to the seller before the breach that exceed any liquidated damages clause or, if there is no such clause, the value of such payments in excess of 20 percent of the contract price or $500, whichever is less. The seller can offset such recovery by any damages suffered.

B. Agreed Remedies/Liquidated Damages

In some cases, the parties have included a liquidated damages clause in their contract. Such a clause provides a remedy, should either party breach the contract. Such agreements take the place of expectation, reliance, restitution, and quasi-contractual remedies.

  1. Enforceable if:

      a. Actual damages caused by the breach were difficult to ascertain at the time the contract was executed, and the remedy clause represents a good faith attempt by the parties to provide for the case of breach.

      b. The amount of stipulated or liquidated damages is reasonable as judged either at the time the contract was made or in light of the actual damages incurred (Rest. 2d §356; UCC §2-718.) A reasonable clause at the time of contracting is valid even if actual damages turn out to be lower than expected. Some courts will enforce a reasonable clause even if no actual damages occur. Other courts and the Restatement take the opposite view.

  2. Unenforceable

    a. Penalties

      Courts oppose any liquidated damages clauses that penalize a party for not performing. Such clauses typically compensate the nonbreaching party far in excess of any actual damages suffered. However, if a liquidated remedy clause is reasonable, courts will generally not examine the intent of the parties.

    b. Disclaimers
       Clauses limiting a party's liability will not be enforced if the amount of liability allowed is unreasonably small given the foreseeable consequences of a breach.
C. Nonrecoverable Damages
  Certain types of damages are generally nonrecoverable. Mnemonic: **APE**
  1. **Attorneys' Fees**
    Under the American rule, the value of attorneys' fees expended as a result of the breach is generally not recoverable. There are a few exceptions:
    a. In certain situations involving class actions
    b. "Private Attorney General Theory"
       Litigation that involves important public policies.
    c. Abusive Litigation Practices
       If either party maintained an "unfounded claim or defense in bad faith, or for oppressive reasons."
    d. Statutory Exception
  2. **Punitive Damages (Rest. 2d §355)**
    Generally, damages serve a compensatory purpose only. Punitive damages are awarded only in certain situations:
    a. The breaching party acted in a way that is a tort (i.e., gross negligence) for which punitive damages are available.
    b. An insurance company refuses to give any reason for not honoring an insurance claim (bad faith breach).
    c. Breach of fiduciary duty.
    d. Fraudulent conduct.
  3. **Emotional Distress (Rest. 2d §353)**
    Recovery for emotional distress is denied unless the breach causes serious bodily harm or if serious emotional disturbance is a particularly likely result of breaching such a contract. Contracts where emotional distress will be compensated in case of breach include:
    a. Breach of contract to marry.
    b. Loss of cherished object. **Example:** A film developer loses the plaintiff's film, which covered his life over many years.
    c. Failure to properly transmit a message concerned with death or illness.
  4. **Nominal Damages (Rest. 2d §346)**
    When a contract is breached, but the plaintiff has not suffered actual damages, a court may grant nominal damages.

CASE CLIPS

Hawkins v. McGee (1929)

Facts: The palm of plaintiff's hand had been badly scarred in an accident, limiting the hand's use substantially. A surgeon promised that an operation would restore the hand completely. The surgeon performed a skin graft, which was unsuccessful: the palm was worse than before the operation, and even began to grow hair. The plaintiff sued for breach of the express warranty.

Issue: How are damages calculated in a case of breach of contract?

Rule: The measure of damages in a breach of contract case is the **difference** between the plaintiff's actual position after breach and the position he would have been in if the promisor had performed the contract without any breach.

Peevyhouse v. Garland Coal & Mining Co. (1962)

Facts: Garland leased the Peevyhouse's farm for strip-mining operations and promised to restore the land to its previous condition. After mining it, Garland refused to restore the land. Although restoration would cost $29,000, the actual value of the land would only rise by $300 after such work.

Issue: Is "cost of completion" or "diminution in value" used to measure damages for breach of a promise to restore land to its prior state?

Rule: Diminution in value. The usual measure of damages for breach of a construction obligation is the reasonable cost to complete the work properly, unless the obligation is only incidental to the main purpose of the contract, and the cost of performing is grossly disproportionate to any economic benefit it will yield. In that case, damages are limited to the diminution in value of the property as a result of the breach in order to avoid "unreasonable economic waste."

Note: *Groves v. John Wunder Co.* reaches the opposite result.

Groves v. John Wunder Co. (1939)

Facts: John Wunder leased land from Groves to remove sand and gravel, and Wunder promised to restore the property to a level grade afterwards. Wunder deliberately did not restore the land's grade.

Issue: How are damages assessed when a party's intentional breach of contract damaged another's land, but the cost of completion is greater than the value of the land?

Rule: One who wrongfully and willfully breaches a construction contract is liable for the reasonable cost of completing the required work, rather than the value that completion would add to the land (as held in the lower court).

Acme Mills & Elevator Co. v. Johnson (1911)

Facts: Johnson breached a contract by failing to deliver wheat to Acme Mills. Market prices for wheat were lower than the contract price at the time of the breach.
Issue: What is the measure of damages to the buyer from a breach of a sales contract?
Rule: A buyer can recover the difference between the contract and market prices at the time the breach occurs.
Note: In this case, no damages were actually suffered, as the market price was lower than the contract price.

Louise Caroline Nursing Home, Inc. v. Dix Constr. Co. (1972)

Facts: Dix contracted to build a nursing home for Louise Caroline but ceased work before the building was complete. Louise Caroline hired another contractor to finish the work. The total paid to Dix and the second contractor was less than the contract price on Dix's contract. Louise Caroline claimed it was entitled to damages against Dix of the difference between the value of the building Dix had promised to build and the value of the incomplete building when Dix ceased work.
Issue: When a builder ceases work on a construction project, may the job owner recover as damages only the costs to complete if they exceed the contract price?
Rule: Damages awarded for failure to complete a construction contract are based on the reasonable cost to complete the contract and repair any defective performance less the unpaid part of the contract price.

Rockingham County v. Luten Bridge Co. (1929)

Facts: Rockingham County contracted with Luten to construct a bridge. After Luten began the work, Rockingham County gave Luten notice of cancellation of the contract. (The membership on the county board had changed.) Luten nevertheless continued the work, completed the bridge, and sued for the entire contract price.
Issue: Despite notice of repudiation, may the nonbreaching party complete performance and sue for the contract price?
Rule: Once a party is notified of repudiation of or refusal to perform a contract, that party may not continue to perform and recover damages based on full performance. Damages are computed as of the time of

repudiation, and include in principle compensation for the profit the nonbreaching party would have earned on the contract.

Parker v. Twentieth Century-Fox Film Corp. (1970)

Facts: Shirley MacLaine contracted to star in a musical for Twentieth Century-Fox to be filmed in California. Twentieth Century-Fox later canceled the movie and offered MacLaine a starring part in a Western to be filmed in Australia for the same amount of money, which she refused. She sued for breach. The defendant claimed she had failed to mitigate her damages.

Issue: Must a party mitigate damages by accepting alternate employment?

Rule: A wrongfully discharged employee is entitled to recover the agreed upon compensation less any amount the employer proves the employee has earned or with reasonable effort might have earned from other employment. The employer must show that the other employment was comparable, or substantially similar, to that of which the employee has been deprived. Here, the proposed substitute employment was different from and inferior to the contracted employment, and the actress's damages were not reduced for failure to mitigate.

Missouri Furnace Co. v. Cochran (1881)

Facts: Missouri Furnace contracted to buy coke (coal) from Cochran at $1.20 per ton. After delivering about one-tenth of the agreed upon quantity, Cochran breached the contract. Missouri was forced to "cover" by buying coke elsewhere for $4.00 per ton, which was higher than the market price.

Issue: What is the measure of the buyer's damages when the seller breaches a sales contract?

Rule: When a contract for the sale of chattels is breached by a vendor who fails to deliver, the measure of damages is the difference between the contract price and the market value of the article at the time it should have been delivered, regardless of the actual costs to "cover."

Note: This case was decided prior to and differs from UCC §2-712, which permits the buyer on a seller's breach either to cover reasonably or to seek damages based on the market price at the place of tender.

Neri v. Retail Marine Corp. (1972)

Facts: Neri wrongfully repudiated a contract to buy a boat. Retail Marine sold the boat to a third party at the same price, but refused to return Neri's deposit. Retail Marine claimed damages for the lost profits.

Issue: Can a seller recover lost profits from a breaching buyer if he later sells the item at the same price?

Rule: A seller can recover lost profits from a breaching buyer even though the item was later sold at the same price because the seller could have sold two of the items but for the breach. See UCC §2-708(2) and comment 5 to revised model version on the lost volume seller.

Hadley v. Baxendale (1854)

Facts: A mill shaft broke, shutting down the mill, and the mill operator shipped the broken shaft on a common carrier to an engineer as a model for a replacement shaft. The carrier negligently delayed delivering the shaft, forcing the mill to remain shut down longer, causing the mill operator additional lost profits as a consequence of the carrier's error. The jury gave a verdict against the carrier that included lost profits.

Issue: May a jury award damages that include lost profits against a carrier who breaches a shipping contract by unnecessary delay?

Rule: No. First, damages are those that arise naturally or usually from breach of a contract of that kind (damages the parties are deemed to contemplate, that are foreseeable, general damages). Second, damages are also those that may be supposed to have been in the contemplation of both parties because of particular circumstances communicated to the defendant (special or consequential damages). Here, lost profits do not naturally or usually flow from a delay in delivery of a mill shaft (the miller might have had another shaft to use, so far as the carrier knew). Nor had the miller told the carrier that mill could not operate until another shaft arrived.

Note: This landmark case is widely accepted. The reporter might have been mistaken in stating that the miller had not communicated the special circumstances to the carrier. Or if the special circumstances were communicated to the carrier's clerk, under the law of agency at the time the clerk's mere knowledge might not have been imputed to his principal, the carrier firm.

Valentine v. Gen. American Credit, Inc. (1984)

Facts: Valentine sued to recover for the mental distress she suffered as a result of being wrongfully fired by the defendant.

Issue: Is a wrongfully discharged employee entitled to damages for mental distress?

Rule: No. Mental distress damages are not recoverable for breach of an employment contract even if the distress was foreseeable.

Freund v. Washington Square Press (1974)

Facts: Washington Square Press breached its contract to publish Freund's book manuscript. Freund sued for damages claiming lost royalties, a delay in his academic promotion.

Issue: When a publisher breaches a contract to publish a book, may the author recover as damages for the royalties he would have earned on sales of the book, for the delay in promotion?

Rule: No. Damages must relate to injuries that were the foreseeable consequences of a breach and that can be measured with a reasonable degree of certainty. Lost royalties and delay in promotion were not sufficiently certain.

Note: Only nominal damages were awarded because Freund failed to prove his damages with reasonable certainty, i.e., the amount of lost royalties.

Chicago Coliseum Club v. Dempsey (1932)

Facts: Dempsey, a world champion boxer, contracted to fight in Chicago Coliseum. As part of the contract, the Coliseum was obligated to spend a lot of money to promote the fight. Dempsey repudiated the contract a month before the fight.

Issue: How are damages calculated for the breach of a performance contract?

Rule: When a performance contract is breached, lost anticipated profits are only recoverable if they can be proved with certainty, which is not the case where profits would be affected by multiple factors (i.e., weather, reputation of fighters, promotion, etc.). Attorneys' fees and other costs incurred in negotiating and preparing the contract are also not recoverable. However, expenses made in preparation for performance are recoverable.

Boone v. Coe (1913)

Facts: Coe agreed to provide a dwelling for the plaintiffs on the condition that the plaintiffs would move from Kentucky to Texas and cultivate his farm for one year, but Coe did not honor his promise. The Statute of Frauds made his promise unenforceable unless written because it could not be performed within one year from the date of its inception. The plaintiffs sued to recover their traveling expenses.

Issue: Can a party recover the value of expenses incurred in reliance on a contract that is unenforceable under the Statute of Frauds?

Rule: Damages may not be awarded for breach of a contract that is unenforceable under the Statute of Frauds.

Note: Today such reliance damages would probably be awarded to avoid injustice.

United States ex rel. Coastal Steel Erectors v. Algernon Blair, Inc. (1973)

Facts: After Blair breached by its failure to pay for part of Coastal Steel's (suing under the name of the United States) operating costs, Coastal ceased work and sought restitution for the work performed. Coastal would have lost money if the contract was fully performed.

Issue: Is a party who justifiably stops work under a contract entitled to restitution for work done, if it would have lost money had the contract not been breached?

Rule: A party can recover in quantum meruit (what is deserved) for the value of labor and equipment furnished pursuant to a contract that it justifiably breached, irrespective of whether it would have lost money.

Note: A party suffering a loss under a contract will not recover damages in a suit on the contract, but may always forgo a suit on the contract and claim only the reasonable value of the performance rendered.

Britton v. Turner (1834)

Facts: The plaintiff contracted to work for the defendant for one year, with payment to occur at the end of the year. Plaintiff quit during the tenth month, and the defendant refused to pay him at all.

Issue: Can an employee who breaches an employment contract by quitting before its term is over recover for the value of work actually done?

Rule: Yes. An employee who fails to work to the end of his contract term may recover a pro rata share of his compensation under the theory of quantum meruit.

Pinches v. Swedish Evangelical Lutheran Church (1987)

Facts: Pinches inadvertently deviated from the plans for the defendant's church by building the ceiling two feet lower and the windows shorter and narrower and by making other omissions. Even though the defendant objected to the defects, the church was reasonably adapted to the defendant's needs, and the cost of correcting the problems was prohibitively high. The defendant withheld payment.

Issue: If a builder breaches a construction contract by delivering a building that is usable but not in conformity with the contract, is the building owner freed from his promise to pay for it?

Rule: A party must pay the contract price less an amount for the diminution in value of the building if the builder inadvertently deviates from plans, and the structure is still reasonably fit for its intended purpose.

Note: The church accepted the building and was using it, despite the nonconformities.

Vines v. Orchard Hills, Inc. (1980)

Facts: Vines contracted to buy a condominium from Orchard Hills and made a down payment. Vines later repudiated the contract and Orchard

Hills kept the down payment as liquidated damages, as the contract provided. The value of the property later appreciated to the benefit of Orchard Hills.

Issue: If the seller under a contract to sell real estate is made better off by the buyer's breach because the value of the property appreciates, may the seller retain liquidated damages under the contract?

Rule: Yes. A breaching buyer in a land-sale contract may recover his down payment on a theory of unjust enrichment, if he can prove that the seller was not financially damaged by the breach.

City of Rye v. Public Service Mutual Ins. Co. (1974)

Facts: Developers contracted with the City of Rye to build 12 apartment buildings. After six of the buildings were completed, developers provided a surety bond with the City in the amount of $100,000 for timely completion of the project. Defendant provided the bond. The developers also agreed to liquidated damages for delay of $200 for each day the buildings remained incomplete beyond the contract date, up to the amount of the bond. The buildings were not complete more than 500 days after the contract date. The City sued the defendant surety on the bond for the entire amount based on the liquidated damages clause the developers agreed to.

Issue: May a court refuse to enforce a liquidated damages clause against a surety who guaranteed performance of the underlying contract?

Rule: Yes. A provision fixing damages in advance will not be enforced if the amount fixed is grossly disproportionate to the anticipated probable harm. This type of clause will be considered a penalty or forfeiture, and is unenforceable without statutory authority. Here, the City provided no evidence of any harm due to delay on completion of the remaining buildings.

Wilt v. Waterfield (1954)

Facts: The defendant contracted to sell his farm to the plaintiff but breached the contract by selling the farm to a third party. A liquidated damages clause provided that 10 percent of the purchase price ($1,900) would be paid in case of breach. The plaintiff proved damages of $7,000.

Issue: Is a liquidated damages clause invalid if it was arbitrary?

Rule: A liquidated damages clause is unenforceable as a penalty if it is arbitrarily made. The reasoning behind this rule is that a liquidated damages clause must be a reasonable forecast of likely damages.

Fretwell v. Protection Alarm Co. (1988)

Facts: Defendant installed a burglar alarm system in the plaintiff's residence. The residence was burglarized of property totaling $91,379.93. The contract between the parties limited the liability of the defendant to $50, and indemnified the defendant from any claims arising against it by third parties.

Issue 1: May a court enforce a contractual clause that sets forth a limitation on liability for damages?

Rule 1: An agreement limiting the amount of damages recoverable for breach is not an agreement to pay either liquidated damages or a penalty, as long as it does not purport to make an estimate of possible harms caused by breach, or operate to induce performance through fear. Accordingly, a damage limitation clause is enforceable in a majority of jurisdictions.

Issue 2: May a court enforce a contractual clause that serves to indemnify one party against all future claims, and relieve it from liability for future acts?

Rule 2: A promise of indemnity for the performance of an act is valid, as long as the act is not illegal, immoral, or against public policy, and the intention to indemnify is clearly provided for in the contract.

Van Wagner Advertising Corp. v. S & M Enterprises (1986)

Facts: Plaintiff rented space on a wall of a building in Manhattan from Michaels for the purpose of erecting a billboard. Plaintiff erected a billboard and subleased it to a third party. Michaels later sold the building to the defendant, S & M. Defendant breached the contract by canceling the lease.

Issue: Should a court award specific performance for breach of a real property lease, when the property is considered unique?

Rule: No. A tenant may not specifically enforce a lease of real property if damages are an adequate remedy to compensate the tenant. Here, there was a strong market in such billboard space and damages could be calculated. And equitable relief would impose a disproportionate burden on the landlord. Merely because a given property is unique does not entitle the tenant to specific performance, unless the value of the property cannot be calculated with reasonable certainty.

Fitzpatrick v. Michael (1939)

Facts: Michael promised to give Fitzpatrick, a nurse, a salary, room, board and a significant part of his estate if she cared for him until his death. Michael fired Fitzpatrick without cause after she worked for a year.

Issue: Is specific performance of an employment contract allowed?

Rule: No. Specific performance of a personal services contract is generally denied, because it would require excessive and burdensome supervision by the court.

American Broadcasting Co., Inc. v. Wolf (1981)

Facts: Warner Wolf, a sportscaster, breached his contract with ABC by negotiating with another network (CBS) during the 90-day period of contract negotiations and did not honor the right of first refusal clause in the existing contract. ABC sought an injunction forbidding Wolf to work for CBS and specific enforcement of ABC's right of first refusal as to any offer Wolf received.

Issue: What form of equitable relief is available for the breach of an employment contract, if specific performance is denied?

Rule: An injunction prohibiting the employee from working for his employer's competitor may be granted against a breaching employee during the original contract term. After that term ends, such an injunction will only be granted if there is an express agreement not to compete or if necessary to avoid unfair competition, e.g., if employee threatens to reveal trade secrets, neither of which is the case here.

Northern Delaware Indus. Dev. Co. v. E.W. Bliss Co. (1986)

Facts: Bliss contracted to refurbish Northern Delaware's steel mill. The contract obligated Bliss to hire additional workers on the night shift during certain parts of the work. Northern Delaware sought specific enforcement of that clause when Bliss fell behind schedule.

Issue: Will equity specifically enforce a single provision of a complex construction contract?

Rule: Specific enforcement of a complex construction contract is generally denied because it would require impracticable supervision of the contract by the court. This is true even for enforcement of part of the contract.

Congregation Kadimah Toras-Moshe v. DeLeo (1989)

Facts: DeLeo, on several occasions, orally promised to give the Congregation a $25,000 gift. The Congregation unilaterally made plans to use the money for a library named after DeLeo, and included the money in its budget. The oral promise was never reduced to writing, and DeLeo died intestate. DeLeo's estate refused to honor the promise.

Issue: May an oral promise of a gift be enforced against the estate of the promisor?

Rule: An oral pledge of a gift is unenforceable as a contract because it lacks consideration; there is neither benefit to the promisor nor detriment to the promisee. Reliance on the promise by the promisee may make the promise enforceable through promissory estoppel, but putting the amount of the gift into the budget is not sufficient reliance.

Note: A majority of states have enacted statutes that enforce written gratuitous promises (charitable subscriptions) without consideration.

Lumley v. Wagner (1852)

Facts: Wagner, an opera singer, breached an exclusive employment contract with Lumley and performed at a competing theater. Lumley sought equitable relief, including an injunction forbidding her to sing for the competitor.

Issue: May a court order specific performance of an agreement not to sing for another employer?

Rule: Yes. Courts rarely order specific performance of a personal services contract but may issue an injunction preventing the breaching employee from performing for a competitor, even if this indirectly forces employee to provide the services as promised to the plaintiff.

Stokes v. Moore (1955)

Facts: Stokes contracted to manage Moore's loan company. The contract provided that Stokes would owe liquidated damages for any breach and would not compete with Moore in the same city for one year if he quit. Stokes quit and opened a rival company within the year. Moore sued for an injunction.

Issue: Will an injunction be granted to enforce a covenant not to compete, despite the presence of a liquidated damages clause?

Rule: A covenant not to compete, sustained by adequate consideration, is valid if it is reasonably limited in time and geography. Such a covenant will be enforced by an injunction if legal remedies are inadequate because of uncertainty as to the extent of monetary damages caused by the breach. A liquidated damages clause will not prevent the granting of an injunction against a solvent party if it is clear that liquidated damages were not intended to be the exclusive remedy for breach.

Jacob & Youngs v. Kent (1921)

Facts: Kent hired Jacob & Youngs to build a home. The contract specified a brand of pipe to install, but the contractor inadvertently used a different brand, though of comparable price and quality to the specified brand. Kent refused to make the final payment to Jacob & Youngs unless the pipes were replaced with brand in the contract.

Issue: What is the measure of damages against a party who inadvertently breaches a contract in a nonmaterial manner?

Rule: When a party inadvertently breaches a contract in a nonmaterial manner, the measure of damages will be the difference in value between the specified and the actual performances, rather than the cost to correct. Since Kent proved no difference in value between the kinds, he owed the final payment.

Note: Judge Cardozo applies the doctrine of substantial performance.

Gainsford v. Carroll (King's Bench 1828)

Facts: Seller breached three contracts for the sale of bacon by failing to deliver. The trial court fixed damages as of the date of judgment.

Issue: In calculating damages for a breach by a seller should the court use the market price on the day delivery was to be made or the day judgment was entered against the seller?

Rule: When a seller breaches, damages should be calculated based on the difference between the contract price and the market price on the agreed delivery date when breach occurred.

Note: Presumably, the seller breached because the market price of bacon had increased above the contract price, and the price kept rising until the date of judgment. But the effect of the rule in this classic case is to encourage the buyer to cover as of the date of breach, and to mitigate his damages. If the buyer could choose the date of breach or the date of judgment to set damages, that would permit him to speculate at the expense of the seller.

Tongish v. Thomas (1992)

Facts: Tongish contracted to supply sunflower seeds to Coop, at a set price per hundredweight. The market price of the seeds doubled, and Tongish sold his crop to Thomas for a price reflecting the change. Coop had previously entered into a resale agreement with a third party from which he was to receive a set 55 cent profit per hundredweight, regardless of price. Coop sued for the damages resulting from Tongish's breach.

Issue: What measure of damages should be used in the case of a seller breach?

Rule: In the case of a seller breach, a buyer should be awarded damages in the amount of the difference between the market price and the contract price at the contracted time of performance. This method encourages the honoring of contracts and market stability.

Note: The minority rule would only award lost profits, as this method more accurately reflects actual loss.

Globe Ref. Co. v. Landa Cotton Oil Co. (1903)

Facts: Landa breached a contract to sell and deliver crude oil to Globe. Globe sued to recover the difference between the contract and market prices at the time of breach, the cost of sending tankers to pick up the oil, and damages for failure to supply its customers with oil. The contract stated that Globe's tankers would go to Landa's mill.

Issue: Is a party liable for all consequences of a breach of which it has knowledge?

Rule: Mere knowledge by the seller of the buyer's possible special damages is not enough to make the seller liable for them. The seller must take the contract understanding that the buyer reasonably believed the seller's responsibility for those special damages was part of the contract.

Note: This opinion by Justice Holmes represents the "tacit agreement" view of consequential damages, which did not attract followers and was not adopted in the Restatement.

Kerr S.S. Co., Inc. v. Radio Corp. of America (1927)

Facts: Kerr gave Radio Corp. a coded telegram to transmit to the Philippines ordering that a vessel be loaded on which Kerr would earn freight charges. Defendant failed to send the cable, and Kerr alleged a loss of about $7,000; the telegram cost about $27.

Issue: Is one liable for damages beyond the price of providing the service, if its negligent performance of the service leads to unforeseeable losses?

Rule: A party is not liable for damages caused by its negligence if it had no reason to know the extent of the harm that would result.

Note: This opinion by Cardozo applies *Hadley v. Baxendale*: because the message was coded, Radio Corp. had no idea of the particular nature of the message, merely that it related to business in some way.

Security Stove & Mfg. Co. v. American Rys. Express Co. (1932)

Facts: Security, a furnace manufacturer, contracted to have American ship its furnace to an exhibition, for promotional purposes. Security rented a booth, sent its president, and incurred other expenses in preparation for the exhibition. American, fully aware of Security's plans, had assured it that it could make delivery within four days. American failed to deliver a key part of the stove on time.

Issue: What is the measure of damages against a carrier who fails to deliver on time?

Rule: Ordinarily a carrier who fails to deliver within a reasonable time is liable for any drop in the market value of the goods between the time set for delivery and the actual time of delivery. When lost profits are too speculative, however, and a carrier has notice of a shipper's special needs, the carrier must pay for the actual expenses incurred in reliance upon timely delivery.

L. Albert & Son v. Armstrong Rubber Co. (1949)

Facts: Albert breached its contract by delaying shipment of two out of four machines. Armstrong rejected all four and sued for reliance costs incurred in building foundations for the machines. If Armstrong had used the machines to recondition old rubber, as planned, it would have lost money on the venture.

Issue: Is a buyer entitled to full compensation for expenses made in reliance upon the receipt of goods if it would have lost money had the contract been fully performed?

Rule: Normally, a promisee is entitled to the value of the promised performance less any outlays avoided because of breach. But if full performance would not cover the promisee's outlays, the promisor may reduce recovery for the outlays by as much as he can prove the promisee would have lost if the contract were performed.

Kemble v. Farren (1829)

Facts: The defendant's contract to perform in the plaintiff's theater provided £1,000 in damages in case of any breach. The defendant breached, causing actual damages of £750.

Issue: Is a liquidated damages clause enforceable if it is broadly worded to apply to all breaches?

Rule: A liquidated damages clause that applies to all breaches, no matter how minor, is unenforceable, and actual damages will be awarded.

Klar v. H. & M. Parcel Room, Inc. (1947)

Facts: Klar paid ten cents to check furs and received a ticket that had a liability limiting clause ($25) printed in fine print on the back. The furs were lost.

Issue: Can a bailee limit liability by use of an inconspicuous clause printed on its tickets?

Rule: To limit its liability, a bailee must establish a special contract of which the bailor received reasonable notice and to which he assented.

Daniels v. Newton (1874)

Facts: The defendants breached an agreement to purchase land before the end of the 60 days allowed for performance.

Issue: Can suit be brought against a party who renounced a contract before the time for performance has arrived?

Rule: One can only recover for actual injuries. Therefore, a party cannot recover for anticipated injuries when the other party announces his intention not to render a future performance. Suit can only be brought after the time for performance has passed.

Phelps v. Herro (1957)

Facts: Herro contracted to transfer interests in real estate and stocks to Phelps in 1955 in exchange for Phelps' promissory note that would be due in 1961. After Herro conveyed his interests, Phelps refused to issue the note and claimed he could not be sued for breach before 1961.

Issue: Does the doctrine of anticipatory repudiation apply to situations where the payment of money is the only obligation still due?

Rule: The doctrine of anticipatory repudiation has no application to simple unilateral contracts (or bilateral contracts that have become unilateral by full performance on one side) for the payment of money in the future, without surety or other conditions involved. Suit can only be brought at the time set for performance.

Oloffson v. Coomer (1973)

Facts: Oloffson contracted to buy corn from Coomer, a farmer, to be delivered in October and December at approximately $1.12 per bushel. In June, Coomer notified Oloffson that he would not be planting any corn that year. The market price of corn was $1.16 per bushel. The plaintiff waited until the dates on which delivery was due before buying corn elsewhere at prices of $1.35 and $1.49 a bushel.

Issue: Can a buyer recover the value of additional damages that accrued between the times of the anticipatory and actual breaches?

Rule: Under UCC §2-610, a buyer is allowed to await a "commercially reasonable time" before taking action in response to an anticipatory breach. Where a repudiation is unequivocal and "cover" is easily and immediately available, however, no waiting period is reasonable.

Clark v. Marsiglia (1845)

Facts: Marsiglia continued to clean and repair Clark's paintings after Clark had repudiated their agreement.

Issue: Can a party recover for services rendered after a contract has been repudiated?

Rule: One who repudiates a contract must only compensate the other party for the performance rendered prior to repudiation and anticipated loss in regard to the unexecuted portion (i.e., lost profits minus cost avoided) and not for actions that only served to increase the amount of damages.

Mount Pleasant Stable Co. v. Steinberg (1921)

Facts: Mount Pleasant agreed to supply Steinberg with horses for trucking goods. Steinberg breached and claimed in response to Mount

Pleasant's suit for lost profits that Mount Pleasant had a duty to mitigate its damages by securing another contract.

Issue: Is the nonbreaching party required to mitigate its damages?

Rule: The rule that one must use reasonable effort to obtain other employment and thereby mitigate damages has no application to a situation where a plaintiff could simultaneously perform as many contracts as it could sign.

Aiello Constr., Inc. v. Nationwide Tractor Trailer Training & Placement Corp. (1980)

Facts: Nationwide was to pay Aiello in installment payments for construction work. When Nationwide stopped making full payments, much of the work was already completed, and Aiello won a judgment for breach of contract.

Issue: How are damages assessed for breach of a construction contract by the property owner after a portion of the contract has been performed by the builder?

Rule: Damages for a job partially completed where the contracting party has breached are set at the cost to the promisee for the work done, plus the profit to be gained, minus the amount already paid in installments by the promisor.

Sullivan v. O'Connor (1973)

Facts: Sullivan sued her surgeon for breach of contract after the plastic surgery performed on her nose failed to "enhance her beauty and improve her appearance" as expressly promised.

Issue: Does a doctor breach a contract if a medical procedure does not produce the desired results?

Rule: If a doctor expressly promises that a procedure will produce certain results, a patient may recover damages if that promise is not fulfilled. Restitution (e.g., doctor's fees) and reliance (loss of the value of the organ operated upon) will be given, but not expectation (increased value had the operation been successful).

Note: Because of the fear that patients will elevate a doctor's opinion to a promise, some courts require written proof of the promise. Other courts completely deny recovery in such cases.

Truck Rent-a-Center, Inc. v. Puritan Farms, Inc. (1977)

Facts: Puritan leased a fleet of trucks from the plaintiff. Puritan agreed that if it were to terminate the lease early, it would pay the plaintiff 50 percent of the rental price for the rest of the term. The agreement cited that the parties had considered the lessor's substantial initial investment in the trucks and their need for reconditioning prior to subsequent leasing.

Issue: Is a provision in a lease agreement that requires the payment of a specified amount of money to the lessor in the event of the lessee's breach an enforceable liquidated damages clause or an unenforceable penalty?

Rule: If the amount stipulated by the parties bears a reasonable relation to the amount of probable actual harm, it is not a penalty and is enforceable as a liquidated damages provision.

Lake River Corp. v. Carborundum Co. (1985)

Facts: Lake River contracted to bag and ship "Ferro Carbo" for Carborundum. Because it had to invest in new machinery, Lake River required Carborundum to supply it with at least 22,500 tons of Ferro Carbo or pay prevailing rates for the difference between the quantity bagged and the quantity guaranteed. Carborundum failed to ship Lake River the minimum because of falling demand for its product. Lake River sued for the sum promised.

Issue: Is a clause requiring payment for a minimum guaranteed quantity a penalty and therefore unenforceable?

Rule: A liquidated damages provision is a penalty and unenforceable unless it reflects an estimate of the actual damages incurred. A minimum guarantee clause penalizes the breaching party based on when the breach occurs rather than on the gravity of the breach. It reflects neither the operating costs saved nor the actual profit forgone by the nonbreaching party, but simply rewards the nonbreaching party with a windfall.

Note: The court held that Lake River was entitled to the money due on the contract if it had been completed, less operating costs saved.

London Bucket Co. v. Stewart (1951)

Facts: Stewart sought specific performance of a contract to install a heating system in his motel.

Issue: Is specific performance granted if it would require extensive judicial supervision?

Rule: Contracts for building construction are generally not specifically enforced, because ordinary damages are an adequate remedy and because courts are reluctant to expend resources on the extensive supervision of performance that is necessary.

Laclede Gas Co. v. Amoco Oil Co. (1975)

Facts: Amoco breached a long-term contract to supply Laclede with propane. Although other propane suppliers were readily available, none was willing to enter into a long-term contract because of uncertainty as to future energy supplies and prices.

Issue: Can a sales contract be specifically enforced if there is no adequate alternative remedy at law?

Rule: Specific performance is granted if a remedy at law is inadequate because such remedy is not as certain, prompt, complete and efficient to attain the ends of justice as specific performance.

Osteen v. Johnson (1970)

Facts: Johnson contracted to promote Osteen, a country singer, in exchange for $2,500. Johnson failed to press and distribute the singer's second record after her first was a success. Osteen sued for breach, but was unable to prove damages and recovered only nominal damages of $1 in the trial court.

Issue: May a plaintiff able to prove breach but unable to prove damages recover based on restitution?

Rule: Yes. If the breach is substantial, going to the essence of the contract, the court may grant restitution. Johnson did not perform as promised, and the court ordered him to return the $2,500, less the value of the services he did render, to be determined on remand.

Hochster v. De La Tour (1853)

Facts: De La Tour contracted with Hochster for services that Hochster was to begin providing on June 1. On May 11 De La Tour told Hochster he would not be hired on June 1. Hochster sued for breach on May 22.

Issue: Can a party sue for breach of contract before the date of performance (i.e., June 1) arrives?

Rule: A renunciation of a contract by one party may be treated as a breach of contract by the other party who is immediately relieved of his duty to perform and need not wait before filing suit.

Note: Currently one may suspend performance upon the other party's repudiation but may not bring suit until actual breach has occurred.

Taylor v. Johnston (1975)

Facts: Johnston contracted to provide his stallion to breed with Taylor's two mares. The contract provided that if the encounter was unsuccessful, Taylor would be entitled to another chance the following year. Before it was time to breed, Johnston sold his stallion and told Taylor the contract was canceled. Under threat of suit, Johnston agreed to let Taylor's mares breed, but the stallion was constantly "booked" by its new owners and thus unavailable for Taylor's mares. Taylor bred his mares with another stud before the year was up, but had to abort the foals.

Issue: What are the remedies available to a promisee who disregards a repudiation that is later retracted prior to the time of performance?

Rule: If a promisee disregards an anticipatory repudiation that the promisor then retracts before the time of performance, the repudiation is nullified, and the injured party is left with his remedies, if any, that he could invoke at the time of performance.

AMF, Inc. v. McDonald's Corp. (1976)

Facts: AMF agreed to sell 22 computerized cash registers to McDonald's. McDonald's canceled the contract after AMF's prototype performed unsatisfactorily, projected delivery of the units was extended, AMF's plant was incapable of assembling the units, and it failed to provide adequate performance standards.

Issue: Can a party repudiate a contract if it has "reasonable grounds for insecurity"?

Rule: A contract can be repudiated if a party has reasonable grounds to believe the other party will not perform, and adequate assurances of performance are not given. (UCC §§2-609 & 2-610.)

Plotnick v. Pennsylvania Smelting & Refining Co. (1952)

Facts: Plotnick sold battery lead to Pennsylvania Smelting in several installment contracts. Seller sometimes was late in shipping and Buyer sometimes late in paying, but both eventually performed the contracts in full. In the final contract, however, Seller refused to complete the shipments until the Buyer paid in full for a prior shipment; Buyer requested full delivery before it would make the final payment. Seller canceled the contract and sued the Buyer for breach.

Issue: Is a delay in payment a sufficient breach to constitute a repudiation justifying rescission by the other party?

Rule: Failure to make installment payments may constitute a constructive breach of contract only if the buyer's delay makes the contract unreasonably financially burdensome or risky for the seller to perform because of fear of future default. Whether an unreasonable risk of default exists partly depends on the prior behavior of the parties, and there was no such risk given Pennsylvania Smelting's behavior. Thus, the Seller Plotnick committed a material breach.

F.D. Borkholder Co., Inc. v. Sandock (1980)

Facts: Borkholder was hired to build an addition to Sandock's building, which was to be used as a retail carpet showroom and warehouse. Borkholder intentionally deviated from the contract plans, creating a recurring moisture problem. Borkholder promised that it would remedy the situation, but never did so. Sandock won a judgment for compensatory and punitive damages.

Issue: Will punitive damages be awarded for breach of contract?

Rule: Punitive damages may be awarded for breach of contract if separate torts accompany the breach and the public interest is served by imposing punitive damages.

Note: In the instant case, the award of punitive damages was upheld because the plaintiff engaged in wrongful acts constituting fraud, misrepresentation, deceit, and gross negligence, and because people generally lack knowledge of the construction industry and must be able to rely on the expertise and trustworthiness of builders.

Boise Dodge, Inc. v. Clark (1969)

Facts: Boise Dodge, a car salesman, reset a car's odometer and sold it to Clark as "new." Boise Dodge sued after Clark stopped payments, but was forced to pay $350 in actual damages and $12,500 in punitive damages.

Issue: Are punitive damages awarded in a contract action?

Rule: Punitive damages are awarded for breach of contract if the defendant has committed fraud, and the punitive damages bear a "reasonable relation" to the amount of actual damages. In addition to the actual loss, a jury can consider the need for deterrence, the defendant's motives, degree of disregard of the rights of others, and the sophistication of the scheme.

John Hancock Mutual Life Ins. Co. v. Cohen (1958)

Facts: After making monthly payments for 15 years on a life insurance policy issued to Cohen's deceased, John Hancock claimed the policy was expired and that its 20-year duration was in error. The lower court ruled that John Hancock had anticipatorily breached the contract and that Cohen was immediately entitled to all future payments.

Issue: Is an attempted refusal to make future payments an anticipatory repudiation of a contract?

Rule: The doctrine of anticipatory breach is not applicable when the only remaining obligation is the payment of money. Future installments have to be paid when they fall due.

American Mechanical Corp. v. Union Machine Co. (1985)

Facts: American Mechanical was having trouble meeting its mortgage payments and contracted to sell property and equipment to Union for $135,000. Union repudiated the contract and forfeited a $5,000 down payment. American Mechanical's bank foreclosed and the property was sold for $90,000. American Mechanical alleged that it lost the $45,000 difference between Union's price and the foreclosure price due to Union's breach.

Issue: What is the measure of damages for breach of an agreement to purchase real estate?

Rule: The generally applicable rule for measuring damages for breach of an agreement to purchase real estate is the difference between the contract price and the fair market value of the property on the date of the breach. However, if the party suing for breach has sustained a reasonably foreseeable loss that exceeds the difference between the contract price and the market value, then the actual loss may be recovered.

Lowy v. United Pacific Ins. Co. (1967)

Facts: The defendant was hired to excavate, grade and improve a street. Payment for each type of work was listed separately, and the defendant gave a different surety bond for each phase of the work. The defendant performed 98 percent of the grading work before a dispute arose, and he stopped performance. The plaintiff hired another contractor to do the paving work. The plaintiff claimed the defendant should not be paid because performance of both phases was a condition to payment.

Issue: Can a contractor recover for work it has completed if it has substantially performed one phase of a severable contract and was prevented from completing the other phase by the other party?

Rule: A contractor may recover on a contract for work it has completed if it has substantially performed one phase of a severable contract and was prevented from completing the other phase by the other party. (Rest. 2d §240.)

New Era Homes Corp. v. Forster (1949)

Facts: New Era's contract to remodel Forster's home required Forster to pay in four installments unrelated to the amount of work completed at each stage. Forster did not make the third payment, and New Era sued for its value.

Issue: Does an agreement to pay the contract price in several installments at the completion of distinct stages make the contract divisible?

Rule: A contract is not divisible if its language suggests that it is one entire contract, with one consideration for doing the whole work, to be paid in several stages mutually convenient to both parties. Thus, New Era cannot enforce a single payment. It may sue based on quantum meruit for the value of the work done. Or it may sue on the contract for the contract price, minus the payments received and minus the cost of completion.

Bernstein v. Nemeyer (1990)

Facts: Plaintiffs were limited partners in a real estate venture from which they sought capital appreciation and tax benefits on an investment of $1,050,000. The defendants, who organized and controlled the venture, promised Plaintiffs a negative cash flow for a certain time, and Defendants promised to lend the partnership the excess of expenses over cash receipts. Those loans reached $3 million but losses became so great the mortgagee foreclosed upon, wiping out all investments by Plaintiffs and Defendants. Plaintiffs sued for rescission of the contract and restitution of their investment.

Issue: Should rescission of the contract and restitution be granted where the breaching party has not been enriched?

Rule: Rescission may be granted when there is a material breach, and Defendants materially breached the contract's negative cash flow guaranty. Because the object of restitution is to put the party in breach back in the position he would have been in if the contract had not been made, rather than to restore the injured party's position, restitution should not be granted where the breaching party has realized no benefit. And here, the defendants got no benefit and restitution was denied.

Locks v. Wade (1955)

Facts: After the defendant lessee breached a two-year lease of a jukebox, the plaintiff lessor recovered damages for lost rent less costs avoided. The lessor then rented the jukebox to a third party. Although jukeboxes were easily available at the time, prospective renters were scarce.

Issue: Are damages for breach of a lease reduced by the amount the lessor could realize from reletting the article?

Rule: When a lessee breaches the lease of a thing whose supply is not limited, the lessor's damages are not reduced by the amount he did or could earn by reletting the thing, because he could make a second lease, irrespective of the breach.

R.E. Davis Chem. Corp. v. Diasonics, Inc. (1987)

Facts: Davis breached a contract to buy medical equipment from Diasonics. Diasonics eventually sold the equipment to a third party at the price Davis had agreed to pay. Diasonics claimed it was entitled to offset its lost profits against Davis's deposit before returning the balance.

Issue: Are damages for lost profits awarded to a seller who later resells the goods to a third party?

Rule: A seller can recover lost profits against a breaching buyer even if the goods were resold at the same price if the seller can prove that, but for the breach, he would have made two profitable sales.

Reliance Cooperage Corp. v. Treat (1952)

Facts: Treat agreed to sell and deliver barrel staves to Reliance by December 31. In August, Treat notified Reliance that it would not make the sale because the market price had risen. Treat waited until December 31, when the price rose even more, and sued for breach.

Issue: Is the measure of damages for breach of a sales contract affected by the fact that the seller gave the buyer notice of its intent to repudiate prior to the date set for performance?

Rule: A breaching seller is liable for the difference between market price and contract price on the date delivery was due; damages are not affected by a seller's anticipatory repudiation.

Note: UCC §2-713 gives a different rule. It measures damages by the difference between contract price and market price when the buyer learns the seller has breached or repudiated.

American Standard, Inc. v. Schectman (1981)

Facts: American Standard owned an industrial plant and land. It sold the plant and equipment to Schectman for $275,000, and on condition that Schectman would remove all structures and grade the property one foot below grade. Schectman did some of the work but refused to complete performance. American Standard sold the property for $183,000, $3,000 less than its fair market value, and sued Schectman for the cost of completion ($90,000). Schectman claimed that damages should be measured by the drop in the property's value ($3,000).

Issue: Is diminution in value used to measure damages for breach of a construction contract if the cost of completion is disproportionately high?

Rule: The general rule of damages for defective performance of construction contracts, "cost of completion," is replaced by the "diminution in value" rule to avoid causing "economic waste" where the cost of completion is disproportionately higher than the benefit that would be derived. This rule is not applicable when the promisor intentionally breaches, as did Schectman.

Chatlos Sys. Inc. v. National Cash Register Corp. (1982)

Facts: NCR sold Chatlos a defective computerized payroll system. Chatlos claimed its damages should be measured by the difference between the contract price and the actual fair market value of the computer.

Issue: Will contractual price solely ever be used to determine damages without reference to market price?

Rule: The measure of damages in case of breach of warranty is the difference between the fair market value of the goods accepted and their value had they been as warranted. Evidence of the contract price may be relevant to the fair market value, but it is not controlling.

Spang Indus., Inc. v. Aetna Cas. & Surety Co. (1975)

Facts: Spang delayed delivery of steel to Torrington for the building of a bridge, which forced Torrington to incur additional expenses, because the concrete had to be poured in one day to avoid oncoming freezing temperatures. Spang sued Torrington's surety when Torrington withheld Spang's payment as damages. It is common knowledge that construction has to be delayed once the temperature drops significantly.

Issue: Can knowledge of the consequences of a delay in performance be imputed to a breaching party if the consequences were not expressly communicated?

Rule: A party is liable for all direct damages that both parties to the contract, had they been fully informed and given the issue proper attention, would have anticipated as flowing from a breach at the time they made the contract.

Note: The court recognized Torrington's right to recover the additional expenses Spang caused it to incur.

Patterson v. Meyerhofer (1912)

Facts: Plaintiff agreed to sell four houses to Defendant. Both knew that Plaintiff did not own the houses but intended to buy them at a foreclosure sale. Before the foreclosure occurred, Defendant repudiated the contract and outbid Plaintiff for each house during the sale. Defendant also bought a fifth house, which they had orally agreed Plaintiff would keep. Plaintiff sued for damages. Defendant claimed Plaintiff breached the contract because he never conveyed the properties to her.

Issue: Can a party who causes the other party not to perform raise that nonperformance as a defense to a suit for damages?

Rule: Every contract contains an implied promise by each party not to intentionally and purposely prevent the other party from performing the contract. One who causes the breach of an agreement is precluded from recovering damages for nonperformance or from interposing it as a defense to an action on the contract.

Iron Trade Products Co. v. Wilkoff Co. (1922)

Facts: Plaintiff contracted to buy rails from Defendant. Supply of the rails was limited to two sources, and Plaintiff's subsequent purchase of part of its needs from one of them drove market supply down and prices up. As a result, Defendant was unable to acquire rails for Plaintiff as promised.

Issue: Is a party to a contract excused from performance because the other party made its obligation more difficult?

Rule: Conduct by one party to a contract that makes performance by the other more difficult, but not impossible, will not excuse performance.

Billman v. Hensel (1979)

Facts: The Billmans made a deposit on the Hensels' home and agreed to buy it provided they succeeded in getting a mortgage. The Billmans could not get a mortgage for the full amount, and refused the Hensels' offer to lower the price so that the mortgage would suffice. The Billmans sued for the deposit, which was treated as liquidated damages.

Issue: If a contract is subject to a condition, must a party make a good faith effort to meet the condition?

Rule: When a contract is subject to a condition, a party has an implied obligation to make a reasonable and good faith effort to satisfy the condition.

Vanadium Corp. of America v. Fidelity & Deposit Co. of Maryland (1947)

Facts: Vanadium agreed to buy a mining lease from Redington, which would require approval by the Secretary of the Interior. If the Secretary denied approval, then Redington had to return the price to Vanadium, and Fidelity was surety for that obligation to return the price. The Secretary did not initially approve the sale, Vanadium abandoned efforts to obtain the approval, and it sued Fidelity for the return of the price.

Issue: When the cooperation of one of the parties is necessary to obtain approval of the transaction, is there an implied condition of cooperation?

Rule: Whenever the cooperation of a promisee is necessary to performance of the contract, there is a condition implied in fact that the cooperation will be given. Here, Vanadium was not entitled to return of the price; only Vanadium could apply for approval, and it unilaterally decided to abandon the effort.

Curtice Bros. Co. v. Catts (1907)

Facts: A cannery contracted to buy Catts' tomato crop. When Catts repudiated the contract, the cannery was unable to find a substitute source of tomatoes and sued for specific performance of Catts' contract.

Issue: Is specific performance of a contract to sell personal property granted when monetary damages are inadequate, and substitute goods are unavailable?

Rule: Specific performance is granted for breach of a sale of goods if the facts surrounding the breach indicate that an award of monetary damages would not do justice to the nonbreaching party, and substitute goods are unavailable.

Northern Indiana Pub. Serv. Co. v. Carbon County Coal Co. (1986)

Facts: NIPSCO, a public utility selling electricity to consumers, entered into a long-term fixed-price contract to buy low-sulfur coal from Carbon County for use in generating electricity. New state government regulations required that if NIPSCO could acquire electric power from other suppliers cheaper than it could generate electricity using coal it bought, it must charge its consumers a lower price, even if it in fact paid more for Carbon County coal. The contract contained a clause that provided that NIPSCO could stop taking delivery of coal for any cause beyond its control, including acts of civil authority, which wholly or partly prevented utilizing the coal. NIPSCO sought a declaratory judgment that the contract was commercially impracticable to perform; the demand was rejected. Carbon County counterclaimed for specific performance of the contract and damages. Specific performance was denied; damages of $181 million were granted.

Issue: Are damages an adequate remedy for a seller under a long-term contract for sale of a basic commodity?

Rule: Damages are adequate when the award was a reasonable estimate of the loss suffered. Specific performance is also not called for when the buyer's breach was efficient (its energy generation plan had become inefficient). The buyer was not excused from performance on the grounds of impracticability because it accepted the risk of a fixed price over a long term in order to be assured of a supply.

City Stores Co. v. Ammerman (1967)

Facts: Ammerman promised to grant City Stores a lease on equal terms to those of other tenants in its proposed shopping mall in exchange for City's letter of commitment to open a store in Ammerman's mall. Ammerman used City's letter, among others, to secure approval of the project from the county council, but later refused to give City a lease. City sued for specific performance.

Issue: May an option to lease a store be specifically enforced?

Rule: Where monetary damages are inadequate to compensate a party's loss, and the terms of a contract can be verified or reasonably implied, a court will enforce despite supervisory problems, because leases, like land, are unique.

Karpinski v. Ingrasci (1971)

Facts: An oral surgeon hired another oral surgeon and made him agree not to practice dentistry or oral surgery in five counties if he quit the plaintiff's employ. The defendant quit and opened his own business.
Issue: Does a covenant not to compete bind a professional?
Rule: An agreement of a professional not to compete with his employer is enforceable even if it is for an unlimited period of time if the geographical area is limited and reasonable. However, a prohibition of a type of work that is not in competition can be struck from the covenant.

Southwest Engineering Co. v. United States (1965)

Facts: Pursuant to the terms of a contract, the United States deducted "late charges" from payments for construction work by Southwest that was partially delayed. No actual harm was suffered because of the delay.
Issue: Is a liquidated damages clause enforceable if actual damages were not incurred?
Rule: A liquidated damages clause will be enforced even though actual damages were not incurred if the clause was a reasonable forecast at the time of contracting and the harm is of a type that is impossible or difficult to estimate.

United Airlines, Inc. v. Austin Travel Corp. (1989)

Facts: United brought suit to recover accrued rents receivable and damages for breach of leases entered into for a computerized reservation and accounting system. Austin counterclaimed, asserting that United violated federal antitrust laws and that liquidated damages are unenforceable penalties.
Issue: What factors will a court consider to determine whether a liquidated damages clause is enforceable?
Rule: A liquidated damages clause generally will be upheld unless the liquidated amount is considered to be a penalty because it is grossly disproportionate to the probable loss anticipated when the contract was executed. A court will often uphold liquidated damages if it is difficult or impossible to accurately estimate the amount of actual loss.

Leeber v. Deltona Corp. (1988)

Facts: Leeber invested in a condominium unit being constructed by Deltona. He put down $22,530 (15 percent) against the $150,200 purchase price, with the balance due at closing. After Deltona gave Leeber several extensions, he failed to close. Deltona canceled the agreement, retained the down payment and sold the property to another party for $167,000. Leeber sued to recover his deposit. The lower court awarded Leeber $15,000, which was the amount of the deposit reduced by expenses incurred by Deltona in connection with the transaction.

Issue: Are liquidated damages unenforceable if they are far in excess of the nondefaulting party's actual damages, and the nondefaulting party actually profits from the breach?

Rule: A seller may retain liquidated damages if the amount is reasonable, because liquidated damages are preferred to litigation as a mechanism for resolving conflicts. Reasonableness is determined at the time of the breach. The fact that a seller subsequently resells property for a greater amount does not convert otherwise reasonable damages to unreasonable damages. Damage sums in the range of 15 percent of the contract price are reasonable.

Lewis Refrigeration Co. v. Sawyer Fruit, Vegetable and Cold Storage Co. (1983)

Facts: Sawyer was awarded lost profits and excess costs caused by a defective freezer bought from Lewis. The contract provided that Lewis was only obligated to repair or replace a defective product. Rescission was also available.

Issue: Can consequential damages be limited by express agreement in a contract?

Rule: Consequential damages may be limited by contract as long as the limitation is not unconscionable.

Mader v. Stephenson (1976)

Facts: Mader won a judgment on a contract action against Stephenson, but he also sought damages for various expenses pertaining to the lawsuit.

Issue: May a party recover for attorneys' fees and other expenses in connection with a lawsuit?

Rule: Absent statutory authority or contractual agreement, neither attorneys' fees nor litigation expenses are recoverable.

Guard v. P & R Enterprises, Inc. (1981)

Facts: Guard contracted to sell the Edgewater lounge, restaurant and motel to P & R but was unable to acquire title to the property. Another party acquired title, and P & R sued Guard for damages.

Issue: When may lost profits be awarded as consequential damages?
Rule: Reasonably certain lost profits, which can be established by the profit history of the party's similar business at a different location or the business in question if it was successfully run by someone else, may be awarded as consequential damages.
Note: Lost profits were denied to P & R.

Gruber v. S-M News Co. (1954)

Facts: Gruber contracted to distribute 90,000 sets of Christmas cards through S-M News. S-M News was bound to exercise reasonable diligence to promote and sell the cards. Gruber claimed S-M News breached, but S-M News claimed Gruber would have lost money on the venture if S-M had performed fully. Gruber sought recovery of his out-of-pocket expenditures.
Issue: Under "essential reliance," may a party recover out-of-pocket expenses even if the party would have suffered a loss had the defendant fully performed on its promise?
Rule: A party's recovery for out-of-pocket expenses must be diminished by any loss that would have resulted from the defendant's full performance.
Note: The burden of proving this loss in event of performance rests on the defendant, which S-M News did not meet here.

Ballard v. El Dorado Tire Co. (1975)

Facts: Ballard had a five-year employment contract with El Dorado to serve as Executive Vice President and General Manager of its Florida subsidiary. El Dorado breached by selling all of its stock in the subsidiary.
Issue: Must an employee's damages from an employer's breach be mitigated by the amount he might have earned in other similar employment?
Rule: The employee's damages will be reduced for failure to mitigate only if the employer proves a similar employment opportunity was available.

Laredo Hides Co. v. H & H Meat Products Co. (1974)

Facts: H & H breached a contract to sell cattle hides to Laredo. Laredo purchased hides on the open market and sued for the difference in prices.
Issue: If the seller breaches, is a buyer entitled to recover the difference between the cost of "cover" and the contract price?
Rule: When a seller wrongfully breaches a contract, the buyer can "cover" by purchasing the goods elsewhere in good faith and recover the difference between the price of the substituted goods and the contract price. (UCC §2-712.)
Note: The buyer is also entitled to incidental and consequential damages.

Emery v. Caledonia Sand and Gravel Co., Inc. (1977)

Facts: The Emerys, husband and wife farmers, sold Caledonia the right to remove earth from their land provided that Caledonia restored the land to its productive capacity at the completion of operations.

Issue: How are damages for breach of contract different from tort damages that simply try to undo the wrong committed?

Rule: In the case of breach of contract, the goal of compensation is to place the plaintiff in the position he would have been in if the contract had been performed; in tort it is to return the plaintiff to the position he was in before the plaintiff encountered the defendant. Here, that meant granting the Emerys the cost of completion.

Note: The court held the injury to the Emerys was foreseeable and not disproportionate to the compensation damages awarded.

Patton v. Mid-Continent Systems, Inc. (1988)

Facts: Patton agreed to accept Mid-Continent's credit cards at Patton's truck stops if Mid-Continent promised to make the same arrangement with Patton's competitors in a given territory. Mid-Continent made that promise of exclusivity but breached it. Patton sought punitive damages based on Mid-Continent's intentional breach.

Issue: When may punitive damages be awarded in a contract action?

Rule: Punitive damages may be awarded in suits when the breach is malicious, fraudulent, oppressive, grossly negligent or otherwise blame-worthy. The breach is blameworthy if it was opportunistic, voluntary and inefficient in the sense that the loss suffered by the plaintiff was greater than the profits gained by the breaching party, which was not the case here.

Hibschman Pontiac, Inc. v. Batchelor (1977)

Facts: Batchelor bought a Pontiac GTO from the Hibschman dealership. The car was under warranty and Batchelor relied on assurances from three Hibschman employees regarding the high dependability of the service department. He had constant problems with his car, which Hibschman's service department repeatedly failed to fix. Eventually, the warranty expired and Batchelor had many of the defects corrected at another garage.

Issue: When is an award of punitive damages proper?

Rule: A jury may award punitive damages if in addition to breach of warranty the jury finds evidence of fraud, malice, gross negligence or oppression. The amount of punitive damages may not be so high that at first blush it appears outrageous, excessive or improper.

Wedner v. Fidelity Security Systems, Inc. (1973)

Facts: Wedner suffered a loss of over $46,000 due to Fidelity's wrongful failure to perform under a burglary service contract. The contract contained a provision allowing recovery only up to a sum equal to the yearly service charge, which was $312.

Issue: Is a contract provision valid when it exculpates or limits a party from liability for its own acts of negligence?

Rule: Consequential damages may be limited or excluded by contract except when the limitation or exclusion is unconscionable, which was not the case here as the parties had equal bargaining power.

Note: Such provisions are prima facie unconscionable when they concern consumer goods.

Centex Homes Corp. v. Boag (1974)

Facts: Centex sold a condominium to Boag, who paid a $525 deposit and wrote a check for the balance of $6,870. When Boag's employer transferred him out of state, he canceled payment on the check and notified Centex "he would be unable to complete the purchase agreement." Centex sought specific performance.

Issue: When is specific performance an available remedy?

Rule: Specific performance is confined to those special instances where a vendor will otherwise suffer an economic injury for which his damage remedy at law will not be adequate, or where other equitable considerations require that the relief be granted. While a buyer of real estate is always entitled to specific performance, the vendor of real estate is not.

Note: The court rejected the contention that mutuality of remedy is an appropriate basis for granting specific performance.

American Brands, Inc. v. Playgirl, Inc. (1974)

Facts: American, a tobacco manufacturer and distributor, had a contract with Playgirl to advertise its products on the back cover of each issue. A provision provided that American could buy the back cover space for as long as Playgirl would be published. After a year, Playgirl informed American that it planned to diversify the advertisers on its back cover. American sought an injunction claiming that Playgirl appealed to a unique market and that an injunction prohibiting Playgirl from denying American the back cover was necessary to avoid irreparable harm for which monetary damages would not be compensable.

Issue: When may a preliminary injunction be granted in a contract dispute?

Rule: Before a preliminary injunction may be granted, the moving party has the burden of demonstrating that its damages cannot be calculated and that consequently it cannot be made whole by monetary relief. The burden was not met here.

Schlegel v. Moorhead (1976)

Facts: Moorhead owned the oil and gas lease to 120 acres in Montana where he maintained one oil well. The well did not produce much revenue, so he had previously attempted to sell the lease. Schlegel determined that Union Oil had been very active in the area and that the property could be very valuable. Schlegel sought to buy the lease. Moorhead asked him why he was interested, and Schlegel told him he had a general interest in the area. Schlegel signed an option to purchase the lease but Moorhead breached.

Issue 1: Absent a finding of fraud, must a court grant specific performance where the party seeking the remedy has concealed information or circumvented questions?

Rule 1: A court may refuse to grant specific performance if it would be unjust and unreasonable.

Issue 2: When should a lower court's refusal to grant specific performance be overruled?

Rule 2: The application of specific performance is left to the sound legal discretion of the court and should be overruled only in the case of an abuse of discretion.

Note: The court did not award Schlegel specific performance. The court denied Schlegel's later suit for damages, ruling that consideration was inadequate and that Moorehead's consent had been obtained through concealment.

Meyer v. Benko (1976)

Facts: Benko wanted to sell his residence quickly and agreed to sell it to Meyer for $23,500, which was below the market value. Benko breached.

Issue: Should specific performance be denied because of inadequate consideration?

Rule: Adequacy of consideration should be examined when deciding whether a contract was formed rather than when deciding what remedy is appropriate for breach. Here it was not inadequate.

Duane Sales, Inc. v. Carmel (1977)

Facts: A court granted specific performance of an option agreement for the purchase and sale of real property.

Issue: In awarding specific performance, should a court take into account the respective losses and gains during the period of litigation?

Rule: Equity requires both that the contract provisions be enforced and that the consequences of specific performance be just and equitable. Thus, the court may consider the parties' losses and gains during the litigation.

Howard Schultz & Associates v. Broniec (1977)

Facts: Howard Schultz & Associates sought an injunction against Broniec to enforce a covenant not to compete contained in his employment agreement. The plaintiff also sought to restrain him from divulging confidential and privileged information received during employment.

Issue: When is a covenant not to compete contained in an employment contract enforceable?

Rule: A covenant not to compete is enforceable only where it is strictly limited in time and territorial effect and is otherwise reasonable considering the business interest of the employer and the effect on the employee. The territorial restriction generally may include only the area where the employee was employed. The activities prohibited must also be specified. Nor will the court rewrite an overbroad covenant not to compete.

Handicapped Children's Education Board v. Lukaszewski (1983)

Facts: Lukaszewski had a one-year teaching contract with the Board. Lukaszewski quit her job mid-year, and the Board had to hire a replacement at a higher salary.

Issue: What is the proper measure of damages for breach of an employment contract by an employee?

Rule: Expectation damages should be awarded to put the employer in the same position he would have been in had the contract been performed. Expectation damages include the cost of obtaining other services equivalent to those promised but not performed, plus any foreseeable consequential damages. The employer can still recover the extra cost of a replacement even if the replacement gives the employer added benefits.

Native Alaskan Reclamation & Pest Control, Inc. v. United Bank Alaska (1984)

Facts: Defendant breached a loan agreement to help finance plaintiff's purchase of military aircraft. Plaintiff could not find replacement financing and his attempts to purchase the aircraft failed. Plaintiff argued that it should recover the money it would have earned had the defendant performed.

Issue: What limits should be placed on expectation damages?

Rule: Damages must be foreseeable, proven with reasonable certainty, and be caused by the breach. Restatement (Second) §352 defines foreseeability as being foreseeable as a probable result of the breach when the contract was made. This occurs if the loss follows from the breach in the ordinary course of events, or is a result of special circumstances beyond the ordinary course of events that the party in breach had reason to know.

Stewart v. Board of Educ. of Ritenour Consol. School Dist. (1982)

Facts: Stewart, a tenured teacher, was wrongfully discharged for excessive absence. Five years later, pursuant to a court order, she was reinstated and awarded money damages in the form of back pay plus interest. During the time she was unemployed, Stewart made no effort to attain a comparable teaching position, although there were some teaching positions available. The school board appealed the damage award, claiming that Stewart had made no effort to mitigate damages, and was thus not entitled to the full amount of the award.

Issue 1: Which party bears the burden of proof as to failure to mitigate damages?

Rule 1: The breaching party bears the burden of proving that the opportunity to mitigate existed, as well as the amount of damages that could have been avoided.

Issue 2: How should a court determine the feasibility of mitigation?

Rule 2: Feasibility of mitigation is proven when the breaching party can show that feasible alternatives (e.g., employment openings) were available and that the nonbreaching party could have obtained one of those alternatives using reasonable effort.

Bunnett v. Smallwood (1990)

Facts: Smallwood wished to sever his ties to a company he owned with Bunnett. Smallwood gave his share of the company's stock to Bunnett in exchange for a release from all future claims. Nevertheless, Bunnett sued Smallwood.

Issue: Can the prevailing party in a lawsuit recover attorneys' fees and costs for breach of an agreement not to sue?

Rule: Violation of an agreement not to sue does not entitle the non-breaching party to attorneys' fees and costs. This would violate the American rule requiring each party to pay its own legal expenses. Attorneys' fees can only be imposed by contractual agreement, statute, or court rule.

Gaglidari v. Denny's Restaurants, Inc. (1991)

Facts: Gaglidari was a bartender at defendant's restaurant and was fired when she fought with a patron. Gaglidari claimed that Denny's breached her employment contract and caused her emotional distress.

Issue: Are emotional distress damages recoverable for breach of an employment contract?

Rule: Tort damages for emotional distress caused by breach of an employment contract are not recoverable because the primary purpose of employment contracts is economic, and adequate pecuniary compensation is available.

Dissent: Damages for emotional distress caused by breach of an employment contract should be recoverable if the employer's conduct is wanton or reckless.

Roth v. Speck (1956)

Facts: Roth, the owner of a beauty salon, hired Speck as a hairdresser. The contract was for one year and Speck's salary was the greater of $75 per week or 50 percent of the gross receipts from his work. Although Speck proved to be an exceptional hairdresser, he quit after six and one-half months and was hired by another salon for $100 per week. Roth, in an attempt to mitigate damages, hired two replacements, both of whom lost money for Ross due to their lesser skills. Roth sued for damages stemming from breach of the employment contract.

Issue: What is the proper measure of damages for breach of an employment contract by an employee?

Rule: Damages for breach of an employment contract by an employee are measured by the cost to the employer of obtaining services comparable to the ones that were unperformed due to the breach. The fair value of the employee's services may be deduced from, among other things, the salary received in a similar position elsewhere.

Wartzman v. Hightower Productions, Ltd. (1983)

Facts: Plaintiffs concocted a promotional venture whereby an entertainer, "Woody Hightower," would set a Guinness World Record for the longest time spent on top of a flagpole. Woody was to live in a specially constructed mobile flagpole perch for nine months, have his own theme song, and be displayed throughout the country at state fairs and shopping centers. He was to descend the flagpole on New Year's Eve in New York's Times Square. Plaintiffs hired the defendant law firm to incorporate their flagpole venture. Defendants structured the corporation improperly and plaintiffs' investments were lost.

Issue: What are the damages when breach of contract prevents a highly speculative venture from being performed?

Rule: When expectation interests are not provable or cannot be ascertained because of the speculative nature of a venture, reliance damages should be awarded. Reliance damages may include expenditures made in preparation for performance, less any loss that the breaching party can prove with reasonable certainty the injured party would have suffered had the contract been performed.

Colonial at Lynnfield, Inc. v. Sloan (1989)

Facts: Defendant contracted to buy an interest in plaintiff's hotel. Defendant breached the contract and plaintiff sued to recover $200,000 in liquidated damages.

Issue: Are liquidated damages provisions enforceable?

Rule: Liquidated damages provisions are enforceable if the amount is a reasonable estimate of difficult-to-ascertain damages at the time of the agreement. If the actual damages turn out to be easily ascertainable, a court must consider whether the stipulated sum is unreasonably disproportionate to the real damages from the breach. If the liquidated damages are unreasonable based on the actual damages, the liquidated damages clause is unenforceable because it constitutes a penalty.

Woods v. Fifth-Third Union Trust Co. (1936)

Facts: Wood sued the executor of his mother's will to collect for personal services Wood had rendered to his mother prior to her death.

Issue: Is a child entitled to compensation for rendering services to a parent?

Rule: No contract arises from the performance of personal services by a child for the benefit of a parent. Because the relationship between a parent and child is close, any service is presumed to be rendered without the expectation of compensation. An individual may obtain payment only by showing clear and convincing evidence that there was an express promise under circumstances that manifest an intention to contract.

Clausen & Sons, Inc. v. Theo Hamm Brewing Co. (1968)

Facts: Clausen & Sons alleged that it orally contracted to become Hamm's exclusive beer distributor in a certain area. Clausen discontinued all competitor's products and made further expenditures in reliance on the contract. When Hamm terminated the agreement, Clausen brought this suit for breach of contract based on reliance. Hamm asserted that the contract was unenforceable due to a lack of mutuality of obligation.

Issue: Does an exclusive franchise dealer have a claim for breach of contract for an unreasonable termination of the contract?

Rule: Where an exclusive franchise dealer is under a contract that is terminable at will, and has at the manufacturer's or supplier's insistence invested substantial resources, the supplier may not unreasonably terminate the contract without giving the dealer the opportunity to recoup his investment. Termination without notice gives rise to an action in breach, based on reliance.

White v. Benkowski (1967)

Facts: The Whites contracted to buy water from their next-door neighbors, the Benkowskis, that would be piped from their well to the White's house. The Benkowskis maliciously shut off the water supply for short periods of time after the initially friendly relationship of the parties deteriorated. The Whites sought compensatory and punitive damages.

Issue 1: May a court reduce a jury award for compensatory damages in the belief that such damages were not adequately proven?

Rule 1: Compensatory damages need not be proven with precision; evidence of damages shall be reviewed in the light most favorable to the plaintiff.

Issue 2: Are punitive damages awarded for a breach of contract?

Rule 2: Punitive damages are not available in breach of contract actions.

Thorne v. White (1954)

Facts: Thorne contracted to install a new roof on White's house. Thorne began the work, but stopped because of inclement weather and never returned. White hired a new roofer, who did more work than was to be done under Thorne's contract, and for a higher cost. White sued Thorne for the difference in cost under the two contracts.

Issue: What is the proper measure of damages for a breach of contract, when substitute performance is obtained that calls for performance above and beyond the original contract?

Rule: A party damaged by a breach may recover for losses that are the natural consequence and proximate result of that breach. The nonbreaching party in a contract should only get damages up to the difference in the cost of obtaining identical substitute performance.

Anglia Television Ltd. v. Reed (1971)

Facts: Anglia hired Robert Reed to star in a television film after it had incurred numerous other production expenses. Reed later repudiated the contract. Anglia, unable to find a substitute, was forced to abandon production. Anglia then sued Reed for damages, including expenditures made before Reed signed his contract.

Issue: May a nonbreaching party obtain damages for expenses incurred before a contract with the breaching party was formed?

Rule: Reliance damages are awarded for expenditures incurred after a contract is made, but may also be awarded for costs incurred before the contract, if it was within the reasonable contemplation of the parties at the time of the contract that such prior expenditures would be wasted if the defendant breached.

Sutherland v. Wyer (1877)

Facts: Wyer hired Sutherland as a theatrical actor for 36 weeks at $35 per week. Halfway through the term, Sutherland refused to accept the one-third pay cut Wyer demanded of all the actors and Wyer fired Sutherland. Sutherland found another acting job for less money, which he left in order to attend this breach of contract trial in April. (The court noted that the trial could just as easily have been held in May, after the end of Sutherland's new job.)

Issue: What remedies are available to an employee who has been wrongfully terminated?

Rule: When an employee has been wrongfully discharged, he is entitled to the salary that he would have earned during the remainder of his contract, reduced by the income that he has earned or could have earned through reasonable diligence during that period of time. Thus, damages here are reduced by what the employee here did earn and could have earned in mitigation.

R.B. Matthews, Inc. v. Transamerica Transportation Services, Inc. (1991)

Facts: Matthews agreed to purchase 300 used trailers from Transamerica, which was supposed to use its "best efforts" to make the trailers available for each of two years. By the end of the second year, Transamerica had only delivered a portion of the required trailers, and although it continued to express its intention to comply, it failed to deliver the remaining goods. Matthews brought suit, alleging breach of contract, fraud, misrepresentation, and bad faith.

Issue: What remedies are available to a buyer if a seller breaches?

Rule: When a seller breaches, the buyer may either (a) attempt to "cover" and obtain substitute goods, after which time he may recover the difference between the cost of cover and the contract price, plus any incidental or consequential damages, or (b) recover the difference between the market price and the contract price. If a buyer chooses the second remedy but could have covered, he cannot receive consequential damages.

Center Chemical Co. v. Avril, Inc. (1965)

Facts: Avril contracted to sell cleaning products to Center and granted Center exclusive rights to sell the products in Florida for 20 years. Center was to buy only from Avril. Avril could terminate the contract if Center's sales fell below exact monthly minimums. Center breached the contract in the fourth year. Avril sued for damages based on lost profits for the remaining years of its contract.

Issue: May seller recover lost profits as damages upon breach by a buyer under an exclusive requirements contract for its remaining term?

Rule: No. Lost profits must be proved with reasonable certainty. Here, the projected profits over 16 years were not certain because the price was not certain, the duration was not certain because of the right of termination, and buyer's future requirements were not certain.

Mooney v. York Iron Co. (1890)

Facts: Mooney contracted to sink a mineshaft for York, but York terminated Mooney just before the job was complete. Mooney sued in quantum meruit for the cost of the work to him.

Issue: Can a party without fault recover in quantum meruit if he is prevented from completing performance?

Rule: A party without fault who is prevented from performing a contract by the other's breach is entitled to recover the value of his work and the cost of his materials. A party who terminates his own performance may only recover the value to the other party of the work completed.

United States for the Use of Palmer Construction v. California State Electric, Inc. (1991)

Facts: Cal State contracted with the U.S. Army Corp of Engineers to construct a power plant and hired a subcontractor, Palmer, who breached its contract. Cal State had to spend $6,000 more than the price of the Palmer contract to obtain substitute performance.

Issue: What is the measure of damages when a breach causes the non-breaching party to incur extra costs for substitute performance?

Rule: The nonbreaching party may recover the extra costs incurred to obtain substitute performance. Recovery by the breaching party in quasi-contract is precluded where it would cause the nonbreaching party to pay more than the actual contract price.

Petropoulos v. Lubienski (1959)

Facts: Owner hired Builder to build a house for a set price. Builder asked to be paid for extra work, Owner refused, and the issue was submitted to arbitration, which resulted in an award favorable to Builder. Owner still refused to pay and hired another contractor.

Issue: What amount of damages is available to a contractor when there is a breach of contract by the other party?

Rule: There are three measures of damages for breach of building contracts. First, award the contractor the total price of the contract, less the amount saved by the breach. Second, award the contractor the actual expenditure to the date of breach, less the value of materials that can be reused, plus the profit he can prove with reasonable certainty would have been realized given full performance. Third, award quantum meruit for the reasonable value of work, labor, and materials used in performance of the contract before breach. The court applied the third measure. The court below erroneously included lost profits on a quantum meruit claim.

Watson v. Wood Dimension, Inc. (1989)

Facts: WDI lost its main customer. Fisher, and hired Watson to help reacquire Fisher's business. WDI orally promised Watson a commission on all of Fisher's orders if Watson succeeded. Fisher resumed ordering from WDI, and Watson continued to wine and dine Fisher management. Watson received his commission until he was fired.

Issue: When an employee procures an ongoing business relationship for his employer, for how long is the employer obligated to compensate his employee after termination?

Rule: Based on quantum meruit, an employee must be compensated for a reasonable period of time beyond his termination or alliance with the employer. The court determines a cutoff point for compensation based on what is reasonable under the circumstances.

Hargrave v. Oki Nursery, Inc. (1980)

Facts: Hargrave, president of Long Island Vineyards, sued Oki, alleging that Oki had fraudulently represented the quality of vines that Long Island Vineyards had purchased as healthy when they were diseased.

Issue: Can a plaintiff convert a breach of contract into a claim for tortious liability?

Rule: Where a legal duty exists independent of a contractual obligation, a plaintiff may recover in tort. The court ruled that Hargrave could maintain a tort fraud action.

J'Aire Corp. v. Gregory (1979)

Facts: The County of Sonoma hired Gregory, a general contractor, to work on property the County had leased to J'Aire. J'Aire sued Gregory in tort because Gregory failed to complete the work in a reasonable time, causing J'Aire economic loss.

Issue: Does a contractor owe a duty of care to a tenant of a building undergoing construction work, when the contract is with the landlord, not the tenant?

Rule: A contractor owes a duty of care to the tenant of a building undergoing construction work. The contractor must act in a reasonable and timely fashion so as not to cause reasonably foreseeable losses to business and profits, which would occur if the project is not undertaken with due diligence.

Foley v. Interactive Data Corp. (1988)

Facts: Foley was fired from Interactive. Foley alleged that he was wrongfully discharged because Interactive's "Termination Guidelines" stated that employees would only be discharged for good cause. Foley claimed tort damages because he refrained from pursuing other possible job opportunities in reliance on Interactive's "Termination Guidelines."

Issue 1: May an at-will employment agreement be modified by evidence of implied terms?

Rule 1: The presumption of at-will employment may be modified by express or implied terms in an employment agreement.

Issue 2: Can a party recover tort damages for breach of an implied covenant in an employment contract?

Rule 2: Since the nature of an employment contract is fundamentally contractual, relief for the breach of an implied covenant of good faith and fair dealing should be limited to contract remedies.

Jarvis v. Swans Tours Ltd. (1973)

Facts: Jarvis booked a holiday based on representations in Swans' brochure. However, the contents of the brochure were false, and Jarvis was disappointed by his trip.

Issue: What is the proper measure of damages when a party suffers disappointment, frustration, or distress because the other party breached a contract to provide entertainment and enjoyment?

Rule: Where a party breaches a contract for entertainment or enjoyment, damages should compensate the plaintiff for the disappointment suffered and the loss of entertainment that should have been received. The court should take into account the mental distress suffered by the plaintiff.

California and Hawaiian Sugar Co. v. Sun Ship, Inc. (1986)

Facts: California hired Sun Ship to build a barge. A liquidated damages clause was included in the contract, requiring payment if the barge was not completed by a specified date. Sun missed the deadline and began to pay the daily liquidated damages charges, but ultimately denied liability for any damages.

Issue: When will a court uphold a liquidated damages clause?

Rule: Liquidated damages are permitted when informed parties with equal bargaining power have agreed to pay a reasonable measure of damages, and the actual injury is difficult to ascertain at the time the contract was formed.

Oliver v. Campbell (1955)

Facts: Oliver agreed to represent Campbell in his divorce for $750, payable after trial. The trial took 29 days. Before a final judgment was entered, Campbell fired Oliver and refused to pay him. Oliver sought to recover the reasonable value of the services he had rendered to Campbell during trial, $10,000.

Issue: May an attorney recover the reasonable value of his services under quantum meruit when he is replaced after trial but before judgment?

Rule: When a contract has in effect been fully performed, an attorney may recover only upon the contract, not under quantum meruit. His recovery is limited to the amount specified in the contract.

Fracasse v. Brent (1972)

Facts: Brent retained Fracasse to represent her in a personal injury suit, based upon a contingency fee agreement. Before any recovery was obtained, Brent discharged Fracasse. Fracasse filed this action alleging discharge without cause.

Issue: May an attorney who has been discharged without cause recover the full fee specified in the employment contract, regardless of the reasonable value of the services performed at the time of his termination?

Rule: A client may discharge his attorney at any time, with or without cause. Upon being discharged without cause, an attorney's recovery is limited to the reasonable value of his services under quantum meruit. The recovery, however, is contingent upon the success of a client's suit.

Rosenberg v. Levin (1982)

Facts: Levin hired Rosenberg to render legal services for a fixed fee of $10,000, plus a contingent fee equal to 50 percent of all amounts recovered in excess of $600,000. Levin discharged Rosenberg without cause and subsequently settled the matter for $500,000. Rosenberg sued for compensation.

Issue: What is the proper basis for compensating an attorney discharged without cause by a client after substantial legal services have been rendered?

Rule: An attorney discharged without cause is entitled to the reasonable value of his services on the basis of quantum meruit. The recovery is limited to the maximum fee set forth in the contract.

Vitex Mfg. Corp. v. Caribtex Corp. (1967)

Facts: Pursuant to its contract to process wool for Caribtex, Vitex reopened a closed factory, bought chemicals, and hired workers. Caribtex breached and did not supply any wool. Vitex sued and recovered its gains prevented minus losses avoided. Losses avoided including operating costs. Caribtex claimed that Vitex's overhead should have been included in costs avoided and thus deducted to calculate damages.

Issue: Is overhead included in costs when calculating lost profits?

Rule: In a claim for lost profits, overhead is not deducted from gross profits as part of the seller's costs. On the contrary, overhead should be considered a loss caused by breach and be added to gains prevented in the calculation of damages.

Note: Overhead includes salaries, property taxes, general administrative expenses, and other costs that are incurred irrespective of any particular contract.

Fera v. Village Plaza, Inc. (1976)

Facts: Fera leased space in the Fairborn-Village Plaza with the intention of opening a store. Fera sued for lost profits and the deposit after Village Plaza breached the lease by renting to another party. Testimony concerning profitability of stores in the same area or trade was introduced into evidence.

Issue: Are damages for loss of anticipated profits awarded to a new business?

Rule: A new business may recover lost profits if they are established with reasonable certainty.

Wasserman's Inc. v. Township of Middletown (1994)

Facts: Wasserman's entered into a commercial lease for a tract of property owned by the Township. The lease contained a provision that provided that if the Township canceled the lease, it would pay costs and damages of

25 percent of the lessee's average gross receipts for one year. The Township canceled the lease but refused to pay the agreed damages.

Issue: When will a court enforce a liquidated damages clause?

Rule: A liquidated damages clause is enforceable if the amount set is a reasonable forecast of the harm caused by the breach, and the harm is impossible or very difficult to estimate accurately. Liquidated damages clauses are presumptively reasonable, and the party challenging the clause bears the burden of proving its unreasonableness. Gross receipts in general do not reflect actual losses incurred. The court remanded, directing the trial court to take into account the reasoning of the parties, the effect of mitigation of damages, and the market value of other available space.

United States Naval Institute v. Charter Communications, Inc. (1991)

Facts: Naval entered into an agreement granting the defendant, Berkley, exclusive license to publish the paperback edition of *The Hunt for Red October* after a specified date. Berkley shipped the books to retailers before that date, and Naval claimed that this caused lost profits on its hardcover edition. Naval sued for actual damages and Berkley's profits from the sale.

Issue: What should the measure of damages be when a breaching party earns profits from the breach, the plaintiff's loss or the defendant's profit?

Rule: The court should calculate the measure of damages from the non-breaching party's loss, not from the breaching party's gain. The purpose of damages for breach of contract is to compensate the injured party for its actual loss from the breach. An award for the breaching party's profits would tend to be punitive.

Klein v. Pepsico (1988)

Facts: Klein contracted, through a third party, to buy a corporate jet from Pepsico. Pepsico breached the contract and Klein sought specific performance.

Issue: When will specific performance be granted?

Rule: Specific performance will only be granted if the goods sought are unique, or if there are other circumstances that make specific performance equitable. Specific performance is inappropriate where money damages are adequate and recoverable. Here, several other jets of the same model were available on the market.

Walgreen Co. v. Sara Creek Property Co. (1992)

Facts: Walgreen leased space for a pharmacy in a mall owned by Sara Creek. The contract prevented Sara Creek from leasing space to another pharmacy in the same mall. Sara Creek informed Walgreen it was going to lease space to another pharmacy in the mall. Walgreen sued for an injunction.

Issue: When is it appropriate to grant an injunction instead of monetary damages?

Rule: A court may grant an injunction after properly balancing the costs and benefits of the injunction as opposed to monetary damages. If the costs of setting damages through litigation exceed the costs of an injunction, the court should grant the injunction, even if damages would be an adequate remedy.

Note: Judge Posner applies economic analysis to reach this result.

Callano v. Oakwood Park Homes Corp. (1966)

Facts: Pendergast contracted with Oakwood to buy a house and with Callano to plant shrubs on the lot. Pendergast died and his estate did not go through with the purchase. Pendergast did not pay Callano. Oakwood sold the property as enhanced by the shrubs to another buyer. Callano sued Oakwood for unjust enrichment.

Issue: Is there quasi-contractual liability for services or goods received from a party with whom the receiver did not have a direct relationship?

Rule: Recovery based on quasi-contract is only allowed when a direct relationship exists between the parties or there is a mistake on the part of the party conferring the benefit. Callano's remedy is against Pendergast's estate.

In Re Certified Question (Bankey v. Storer Broadcasting Co.) (1989)

Facts: Bankey was fired from Storer in March of 1981 after 13 years of employment. Bankey's employment was originally governed by an employee handbook stating employees could only be discharged for cause. However, in January of 1981, Storer had unilaterally changed its handbook to allow the termination of employees without cause.

Issue: May an employer unilaterally alter an existing employment relationship in the absence of an express reservation of such a right?

Rule: An employer may unilaterally change its existing employment policy, provided employees are given reasonable notice of the policy change. Written employment policies are not required, but are instituted to benefit the employer, and are thus revocable.

Locke v. United States (1960)

Facts: The United States made a contract to buy its requirements for certain goods from several sellers, including Locke, but without cause canceled only Locke's contract.

Issue: May a seller obtain damages if the buyer breaches a requirements contract?

Rule: Yes. Even though a requirements contract does not guarantee the seller any profit, courts may value the loss of the seller's opportunity caused by the buyer's breach. Here, Locke as low bidder is entitled to damages based on a proportionate share of the sales he could not make.

McCallister v. Patton (1948)

Facts: McCallister contracted to buy a car from Patton; he was number 37 on Patton's list of buyers to be sold cars in that order. Patton sold more than 37 cars but didn't sell one to McCallister, who sued for specific performance.

Issue: May a buyer of an automobile obtain specific performance if the seller breaches?

Rule: A court may grant a buyer specific performance of a sale of personal property if it is unusual, unique, or if it has special sentimental value to the buyer, making damages an inadequate remedy. Here, ordinary new cars of this make and model had no such quality and damages could compensate the buyer for the seller's breach.

Walters v. Marathon Oil Co. (1981)

Facts: Walters bought a gas station on strength of Marathon's promise of a dealership. Walters prepared the station site. Marathon did not give him a dealership. Walters sued. The court found Marathon liable under promissory estoppel, and awarded Walters damages, including one year's profit on the station.

Issue: May lost profits be awarded as damages when Plaintiff sues in promissory estoppel?

Rule: Yes. A court may include lost profits in a promissory estoppel case if the promisor induces the promisee to make reliance expenditures with the idea of future profits.

Note: The decision is unusual. Courts more often grant reliance damages (e.g., out-of-pocket expenditures) in promissory estoppel cases.

Kenford v. Erie County (1986)

Facts: County made a contract with Kenford and DSI to build and operate a domed sports and entertainment stadium. The County promised DSI a contract to operate the stadium for 20 years. County breached by not going forward with the project and DSI sued for lost profits. County appealed a verdict for DSI on damages.

Issue: May plaintiff recover lost profits for breach when the project that would have generated the profits was a new one and nearly unique?

Rule: No. There was no proof that the parties contemplated 20 years of lost profits as potential damages when the contract was signed. And the expert predictions of future success here were speculative and not certain enough to support an award of damages for lost profits.

Sparks v. Gustafson (1988)

Facts: Gustafson gratuitously managed a building for Sparks' father. Sparks' father died and Sparks became executor of his father's estate. Gustafson continued to manage the building for two years and sought compensation from the estate based on unjust enrichment.

Issue: May a provider of services who could have demanded payment sue for compensation on a theory of unjust enrichment?

Rule: Yes. If the plaintiff does not intend to provide services gratuitously, and it would be inequitable for the party to whom services were provided to retain their value without compensating the plaintiff, a court may grant the plaintiff compensation.

Della Penna v. Toyota Motor Sales USA Inc. (1995)

Facts: Toyota's American distributor required its dealers by contract to sell a certain model (Lexus) only to customers in the United States and not "for resale outside" the United States. Toyota sought to keep the model in the United States and out of Japan, where it had not yet established distribution of the model. Della Penna wanted to buy that model at retail in the United States made by Toyota and resell the vehicles wholesale in Japan. He sued Toyota for interference with prospective economic relations — the purchase contracts he could not make with U.S. retailers. The trial court instructed the jury that Della Penna had to plead and prove that Toyota's actions were wrongful, and the jury found for Toyota.

Issue: Must plaintiff in an action for interference with prospective economic relations plead that defendant's acts are independently wrongful, or only that defendant is interfering with plaintiff's prospective contracts?

Rule: A plaintiff seeking to recover for interference with prospective economic relations must show that the defendant intentionally interfered with the plaintiff's expected benefit, and must also show that the defendant's interference was wrongful in some way other than the interference itself.

Fertico Belgium S.A. v. Phosphate Chemicals Export Ass'n (1987)

Facts: Phosphate promised to sell and to deliver two large shipments of fertilizer on two specific dates to Fertico. Phosphate told Fertico both shipments would be late. Fertico itself had contracted to deliver those two shipments to a third party and so covered by buying fertilizer for $700,000 more than the price of its purchase from Phosphate. Fertico canceled the second shipment from Phosphate but the first was already en route and paid for. When this extra fertilizer arrived, Fertico resold it, but actually made a profit of $454,000 on this resale to a fourth party. Fertico sued Phosphate for damages of $700,000; Phosphate claimed the $454,000 profit should be deducted from any award to Fertico.

Issue: When a seller breaches by making a late delivery, may a buyer entitled to damages for cover keep any profit made on resale of product that arrives late from the seller?

Rule: When a seller breaches its obligation to deliver a fungible commodity on time, the buyer is entitled to cover in the market and the seller is liable for the buyer's increased cost to obtain that commodity at the time needed. When the commodity finally does arrive, the buyer is entitled to resell it; if the buyer earns a profit on the resale, this does not reduce his award of damages for cover, because this last sale is separate from the other sale.

Note: A dissent argued that this is a double recovery for Fertico.

Jungmann & Co., Inc. v. Atterbury Bros. Inc. (1928)

Facts: Seller agreed to sell and ship 30 tons of casein to Buyer in a written contract. Seller promised to notify Buyer "by cable" as soon as the goods were shipped. Seller shipped 15 tons on June 9 and did not notify Buyer, who refused the goods on June 20. Seller shipped the balance of the order, notifying Buyer of the pending shipment but not by cable immediately after the goods had shipped. Buyer again refused delivery. Seller sued for breach.

Issue: May a contract party recover damages if it has failed to perform as promised?

Rule: No damages may be awarded to a party who has failed to perform as the contract required, when that performance is a condition precedent to the obligations of the other party.

Protectors Insurance Service, Inc. v. United States Fidelity & Guaranty Co. (1998)

Facts: USF&G terminated a line of business that it used to conduct through Protectors, and that formed a large portion of Protectors' business. Protectors alleged the termination was wrongful and in breach of contract. The jury found for Protectors.

Issue: May an award of damages include compensation for both lost profits and for the loss of a going concern?

Rule: Damages for breach of contract may be awarded either for lost future profits or the loss of the value of a going concern. To award damages for both creates a double recovery.

Chronister Oil Co. v. Unocal Refining and Marketing (1994)

Facts: Chronister contracted to sell and deliver 25,000 barrels of oil to Unocal for 60.4 cents per gallon. Chronister discovered that the shipment it intended to deliver was contaminated with water and promised Unocal a later delivery. Unocal refused the later delivery and made up the shortfall from its own storage.

Issue: When a seller fails to deliver a fungible product, is a buyer that uses its own supply of that product entitled to damages from the seller in breach based on cover?

Rule: In order to obtain damages based on cover, the buyer must in fact purchase substitute product in the market. Here, because the buyer actually saved money because of the breach, the buyer is entitled to nominal damages only.

Council of Unit Owners of Sea Colony East v. Carl M. Freeman Associates (1989)

Facts: Freeman and Sea Colony built a multi-story condominium complex. The Council sued them for defects needing repair.

Issue: Is the measure of damages for faulty construction the cost to repair or the diminution in market value caused by the defects?

Rule: Cost of repair is the proper measure of damages for faulty construction unless such cost is clearly disproportionate to the diminution in value caused by the defects.

Note: The court cites Restatement (Second) §348(2)(b).

Humetrix, Inc. v. Gemplus S.C.A. (2001)

Facts: Humetrix contracted with Gemplus to provide electronic patient data storage as Gemplus' partner. Gemplus breached.

Issue: Are lost profits available as damages in a new venture?

Rule: Plaintiff may recover lost profits based on proof showing they are not speculative but are based on expert testimony weighed by the jury. Even if a particular venture is new, the plaintiff's profit experience in similar ventures is relevant and admissible, especially if that experience is what interested the defendant in the plaintiff's participation to begin with.

AM/PM Franchise Ass'n v. Atlantic Richfield Co. (1990)

Facts: An association of 150 franchisees alleged that gasoline sold by ARCO did not meet the seller's warranty, causing engine problems for consumers and a drop in sales and lost profits.

Issue: Is a seller of a product that does not meet the seller's warranty to a buyer who ordinarily resells the product to consumers liable for the buyer's lost profits?

Rule: Lost profits consist of three types: lost primary profits, lost secondary profits, and lost good will. A buyer may recover all three types on sufficient proof. Loss of sales of the product itself that does not meet warranty (the gasoline) to consumers created lost primary profits. Loss of sales of other products that consumers buy when they buy gasoline is secondary lost profits. Loss of good will is the most difficult to prove, but plaintiff may try to do so before the fact finder.

Schurtz v. BMW of North America (1991)

Facts: BMW's warranty was limited to repair or replacement of defective parts, and disclaimed incidental and consequential damages. Schurtz bought a car that could not be repaired.

Issue: May a seller disclaim consequential damages if the warranty fails of its essential purpose?

Rule: A product seller may disclaim consequential damages even if the warranty fails of its essential purpose, so long as the exclusion of consequential damages is not unconscionable. UCC §2-719(3).

Teradyne, Inc. v. Teledyne Industries (1982)

Facts: Seller Teradyne contracted to sell Buyer Teledyne a transistor testing product. Buyer canceled. Seller resold the product to another buyer for a higher price.

Issue: Upon Buyer's breach, is a seller who resells for a higher price entitled to damages?

Rule: If the seller would have made both the first sale to first buyer, but for the breach, and the second sale, the seller is entitled to damages as a lost volume seller.

Note: UCC §2-708(2) appears not to support the lost volume result. The same section as amended in 2003 attempts to fix this. See Comments 1(e) and 5.

City Centre One Associates v. Teachers Ins. & Annuity Ass'n of America (1987)

Facts: City Centre contracted to borrow funds from Teachers Insurance to construct a building. Both sides claimed breach.

Issue: May a lender enforce a promise to borrow specifically?

Rule: Specific performance is not appropriate when a party's damages are readily calculable, as they are in a loan, where the lender's damages are based largely on the lost payment of interest.

Rego v. Decker (1971)

Facts: Decker had an option to buy a service station from Rego, with payment to occur over 50 years. Decker exercised the option, and the trial court enforced it specifically.

Issue: May a court order specific performance against one party without assuring that the party obtaining performance will perform his side of the contract?

Rule: A court may withhold specific performance until the party obtaining that remedy himself provides assurance that he will also perform.

Illinois Central R.R. Co. v. Crail (1930)

Facts: Seller sold Buyer 88,900 pounds of coal at the wholesale price, which arrived 5,500 pounds short. Buyer sought damages for breach based on the retail price at the time and place of delivery.

Issue: Where a seller delivers less than all of a commodity, may the buyer get damages based on the cost to replace the shortage at the time and place of delivery?

Rule: A buyer's damages for the seller's shortage in delivery are not the cost to make up the shortage at the time and place of delivery, that is, the retail price, if the buyer in fact makes up the shortage with wholesale purchases and without any other disruption to the buyer's business, such as an inability to deliver the goods if the buyer had resold them himself.

MindGames, Inc. v. Western Publishing Co. (2000)

Facts: MindGames owned a game and licensed its marketing and distribution to Western. The game sold well at first but poorly later. MindGames alleged that Western had marketed the game ineffectively and sought lost profits as damages.

Issue: Is a plaintiff unable to recover lost profits as damages for breach simply because the plaintiff's business is new?

Rule: A plaintiff is not unable to recover merely because its business is new, but it must prove lost profits are not speculative on the facts. The fact that the plaintiff's business is new is merely a factor in deciding whether an award of lost profits would be speculative. Here, the plaintiff's lost future revenue from the game was just as likely due to waning desire for the game among consumers as to a failure of Western to market the game effectively.

Muldoon v. Lynch (1885)

Facts: A widow contracted for a marble monument for the grave of her husband. The contractor agreed to "forfeit" against the contract price $10 for each day the completion of the monument was late. Shipment of the four large blocks of marble from Italy delayed completion by almost two years.

Issue: If the contract calls a sum to be deducted from the contractor's price a "forfeiture," is it unenforceable as a penalty?

Rule: If the sum stipulated in the contract has the effect of a penalty, it is unenforceable. A sum that is not connected to any injury of the other party cannot be compensatory in nature and is a penalty. Here, the widow failed to show any damages from the delay and the contractor recovered the full price of the job.

Samson Sales, Inc. v. Honeywell, Inc. (1984)

Facts: Samson Sales was a pawn shop that had a contract for burglar alarm services from Honeywell. The contract provided that Honeywell's liability for breach was limited to $50 "as liquidated damages and not as a penalty." A burglary occurred but Honeywell did not alert the police as required by the contract.

Issue: May a contract limit liability to a specific dollar amount as liquidated damages?

Rule: If parties expressly agree on liquidated damages, the amount will not be treated as a penalty if (1) damages would be difficult to prove and uncertain in amount, (2) the contract represents the true intention of the parties and is not unconscionable, and (3) the parties believed that damages in the amount stipulated would result from breach. Here, damages were not difficult to prove or uncertain and Samson could not have believed that an injury worth $50 would result from Honeywell's breach.

Coppola Enterprises, Inc. v. Alfone (1988)

Facts: Coppola Enterprises contracted to build and sell a house with a residential lot to Alfone. Upon notice by Coppola Enterprises the buyer was obligated to have his financing in place to close the sale. The contract provided that time was of the essence. A first closing date was set but the seller put off the closing because of delays in construction. When Coppola Enterprises rescheduled the closing and gave the ten-day notice, Alfone was unable to get financing in time. Coppola Enterprises sold the house and lot to another buyer for a higher price. Alfone sued for the difference between his price and the resale price.

Issue: Is the buyer of a residence entitled to the economic benefit of his bargain if the seller breaches?

Rule: A buyer is entitled to damages upon the seller's breach for the loss of the benefit of the bargain he made. Here, the seller breached because it had waived the stipulation that time was of the essence by delaying the closing when that was in its interest and it could not insist on that condition against the interest of the buyer.

Egerer v. CSR West, LLC (2003)

Facts: CSR was working on a highway construction project and promised to sell "all shoulder excavation" from that project to Egerer for $.50 per cubic yard. CSR breached and stopped delivering shoulder excavation. The identical product was not available in the market, although other material could be used and was available. The low price for "pit run" was $8.25 per cubic yard when CSR breached, but Egerer thought that price was too high for his job. Many months later Egerer bought and used "slide material" for $6.39 per cubic yard. Egerer sued CSR for breach, and sought damages for the difference between the pit run price of $8.25 at the time of breach and the contract price of $.50.

Issue: Upon the seller's failure to deliver, may the buyer claim damages based on the difference between the contract price and the price of substitute goods in the market at the time of breach?

Rule: Even if the buyer does not in fact make a covering purchase upon the seller's failure to deliver, the buyer's damages are the difference between the contract price and the price of substitute goods in the market at the time of breach. UCC §2-712.

Note: This case shows that the buyer not in dire need of the product the seller has failed to deliver may be able to use the UCC's damages formula to his advantage.

Delchi Carrer SpA v. Rotorex Corp. (1995)

Facts: Delchi bought a compressor from Rotorex after Rotorex sent Delchi a sample compressor and performance specifications for efficiency. The compressors that Rotorex delivered did not conform to those criteria because they cooled less and consumed more energy. Rotorex eventually refused to deliver conforming compressors. Delchi sought damages under the Convention on the International Sale of Goods.

Issue: Upon the seller's delivery of nonconforming goods, is the buyer entitled to seek lost profits?

Rule: A buyer is entitled to lost profits as damages. Particular costs connected with the nonconforming goods are subtracted in calculating lost profits, but a share of fixed costs is not.

Note: The CISG recognizes lost profits as damages under Article 74, but does not detail whether fixed as well as variable costs, i.e., those attributable to the breach, can be recovered.

KGM Harvesting Co. v. Fresh Network (1995)

Facts: KGM promised to deliver a fixed amount of lettuce weekly for a set price to Fresh Network, a lettuce broker. When Fresh Network resold to buyers it added a flat amount to its cost. The price of lettuce soared, KGM breached, and Fresh Network covered for a higher price. Fresh Network was awarded damages of the cover price minus the contract price.
Issue: Is a buyer entitled to damages of the cover price less the contract price when the seller breaches by failing to deliver?
Rule: The buyer's damages for a seller's breach are the cover price less the contract price even when the buyer would have resold the goods marking up the price by a fixed amount.
Note: See UCC §2-712 on the buyer's damages in comparison with §2-713, which may limit the buyer's damages to his actual loss in some cases.

Kutzin v. Pirnie (1991)

Facts: The Pirnies contracted to buy the Kutzins' house and put a deposit in escrow. The contract did not state what would happen to the deposit if the buyers breached. The Pirnies did breach.
Issue: May a seller of real estate keep the whole deposit if a buyer breaches a contract to buy real estate?
Rule: If a contract to buy real estate has no liquidated damages clause, a buyer who breaches may prove that the deposit exceeds the seller's true damages and recover that excess.
Note: The rule at common law permitted the seller to keep the deposit if the buyer breached, even at the risk of overcompensating the seller. The modern view, which the Restatement adopts, is consistent with this case.

Commerce Partnership 8098 Ltd. Partnership v. Equity Contracting Co. (1997)

Facts: The general contractor did not pay Equity Contracting, a subcontractor, for surface work on Commerce Partnership's building.
Issue: May an unpaid subcontractor recover directly against the owner on a theory of unjust enrichment?
Rule: A subcontractor may only recover against the owner if the owner has not paid the general contractor and the subcontractor has exhausted its remedies against the general contractor.
Note: Not all courts follow this result.

Florafax Int'l, Inc. v. GTE Market Resources, Inc. (1997)

Facts: Florafax sold flowers by wire and contracted with GTE for telemarketing. GTE provided too few telemarketing sales persons to handle Mother's Day orders, resulting in lost sales and other losses.
Issue: May a product seller recover lost profits from a telemarketer who breaches?
Rule: Lost profits may be recovered as damages if they are certain enough that a preponderance of the evidence could support a reasonable belief that they had been incurred, with the jury to decide the amount based upon the evidence.

Jetz Service Co. v. Salina Properties (1993)

Facts: Jetz leased space in an apartment for its coin-operated laundry machines. Salina bought the building and breached the lease.
Issue: If lessor breaches a lease, forcing a lessee to remove profitable machines from the premises, may the lessee recover lost profits if the lessee places the machines profitably in another location?
Rule: If lessee would have been able to place machines in the new locations regardless of lessor's breach, then the lessee is treated as a lost volume plaintiff who will recover lost profits from the lessor in breach.

Walser v. Toyota Motor Sales, U.S.A., Inc. (1994)

Facts: Toyota told Walser that it had approved a formal letter of intent to give him a Lexus dealership, but this wasn't true.
Issue: May a jury be instructed on a promissory estoppel claim to limit the type of damages it may award?
Rule: A jury may be instructed to limit its damage award on a promissory estoppel claim to the promisee's out-of-pocket expenditures made in reliance on the promise.

Reier Broadcasting Co., Inc. v. Kramer (2003)

Facts: A state statute (Montana) provided that if a contract may not be specifically enforced then a court may not issue an injunction to prevent its breach. Kramer, the head football coach for the University, contracted to broadcast only for Reier, which had an exclusive contract to broadcast sports events for the University. Reier's contract with the University ended while its contract with Kramer remained in effect. The University gave the new broadcasting contract to Clear Channel, and that contract required Clear Channel to use Kramer for its broadcasts, which would violate Kramer's contract with Reier.

Issue: If a promisor promises to provide certain services exclusively for a promisee, may the promisee obtain an injunction to prohibit the promisor's providing those services to a particular third party?

Rule: Where state statute prohibits issuing an injunction to prevent breach of a contract that may not be specifically enforced, an injunction enforcing a negative covenant would have the same effect as specific enforcement of the promise to provide those services directly. Hence the negative injunction may not be granted.

Westhaven Associates, Ltd. v. C.C. of Madison, Inc. (2002)

Facts: A shopping center lease provided for remedies upon lessee's breach.

Issue 1: Is lessor entitled to attorneys' fees in a suit for breach of lease if the lease provides for such attorneys' fees rising from the lessor's efforts to "relet" the premises?

Rule 1: Attorneys' fees related to suit for breach may not be recovered based on a clause providing for attorneys' fees connected with reletting premises.

Issue 2: Are stipulated damages recoverable on breach of lease?

Rule 2: Stipulated damages are recoverable on breach of a lease if the parties intend such damages to compensate the lessor and not as a penalty to lessee, and if the amount is a reasonable estimate of the harm caused by a potential breach made as of the time of contracting, when that harm is in fact difficult to estimate with accuracy.

Inchaustegui v. 666 5th Avenue Limited Partnership (2000)

Facts: Sub-tenant in its sub-lease promised to get liability insurance naming Sub-lessor and Landlord as additional insured, but did not do so.

Issue: When a promisor is contractually bound to name a plaintiff as an additional insured but fails to do so, are damages limited to what the plaintiff would have paid to buy its own insurance?

Rule: When a landlord must pay personal injury damages to a third party because a sub-tenant neglected to name the landlord as an additional insured, the landlord is entitled to recover damages from the sub-tenant as consequential damages.

Rivers v. Deane (1994)

Facts: Rivers contracted to build an addition to Deane's home but built it very poorly.

Issue: What is the proper measure of damages for defective construction of a house?

Rule: For seriously defective construction, damages are measured by the cost to repair the defects. If construction defects are small, the cost to repair is not the proper measure if it greatly exceeds the diminution in value of the property.

Hydraform Products Corp. v. American Steel & Aluminum Corp. (1985)

Facts: American Steel promised to sell Hydraform Products enough steel to make 400 wood stoves. American Steel only sold enough to make 250 wood stoves.

Issue: Is a seller who breaches liable for the buyer's lost profits?

Rule: To recover consequential damages from a seller of goods who breaches, a buyer must prove such damages were foreseeable, certain, and unavoidable. For such damages to be foreseeable, the seller must know how the buyer would use the goods, as the seller did here. To be certain, such damages must be the reasonable consequence of the breach. Loss in value of the business and loss of profits on stoves beyond the 400 are not the reasonable consequence of the breach and were not recoverable as consequential damages. Finally, the buyer must be unable to avoid the loss through cover, and he was unable to do so here.

Douthwright v. Northeast Corridor Foundations (2002)

Facts: Northeast owed Douthwright a judgment of $1.5 million plus statutory interest. Northeast gave Douthwright a check for $1.5 million as full satisfaction of its debt.

Issue: May a check for part payment of liquidated and undisputed debt discharge the whole debt?

Rule: No. For accord and satisfaction to occur, which extinguishes the debt, there must be a true dispute or an unliquidated claim. The debt here, however, was undisputed and liquidated as to both principal and interest.

DeValk Lincoln Mercury, Inc. v. Ford Motor Co. (1987)

Facts: DeValk in its dealership contract with Ford Motor agreed to arbitrate disputes, and the contract contained a clause preventing waiver of arbitration by conduct of a party.

Issue: May conduct of a party to an agreement to arbitrate impliedly waive the right to seek arbitration?

Rule: No. A contract may require an express waiver of an arbitration clause and prevent the effect of conduct that might reasonably be understood as an implied waiver of the right to seek arbitration.

Postal Instant Press, Inc. v. Sealy (1996)

Facts: Franchisor Postal sued franchisee Sealy for breach due to failure to pay royalties on time. As damages Postal got an award of both past due and future royalties. The contract designated failure to pay royalties on time as a material breach.

Issue: May a franchisor terminate a franchise contract for failure to pay royalties when due and get an award of damages based on future royalties?

Rule: No. A franchisor may not recover future royalties as damages when the franchisor's act of termination prevents the earning of future royalties. Moreover, the disparity in bargaining power between franchisor and franchisee makes damages based on future royalties oppressive.

Mears v. Nationwide Mutual Ins. Co. (1996)

Facts: Mears was an employee of Nationwide, which announced a contest with several prizes. Mears entered the contest and later quit Nationwide. Still later, his entry won the contest and he was told his prize was two automobiles. Nationwide refused to give him the prize because he had quit and because it claimed the contest was a joke.

Issue: May the offer of a contest prize be enforced against the offeror?

Rule: An offer of a prize may be enforced against the offeror as a contract if its terms are definite enough that a court may give a proper remedy. Here, the offeror did not specify which model car made by a particular manufacturer would be the prize; the jury's decision to base damages on the least expensive model rendered damages reasonably certain.

Decker v. Browning-Ferris Industries of Colorado, Inc. (1997)

Facts: Browning-Ferris employees who were fired claimed that their employer had violated the covenant of good faith and fair dealing and sued in tort.

Issue: Does an employer commit a tort by violating the covenant of good faith and fair dealing to an employee?

Rule: No. State law does not recognize a tort action in the employment context for violating the covenant of good faith and fair dealing. (Colorado.)

Bayliner Marine Corp. v. Crow (1999)

Facts: Crow wanted a fishing boat that would go 30 mph. He spoke with an agent for Bayliner's exclusive dealer. He gave Crow information from the manufacturer, which included maximum speed, with a disclaimer that the information was "for comparative purposes only." He bought a model with the desired maximum speed listed. Despite repairs and modifications, it rarely exceeded 20 mph.

Issue: What must a buyer prove to prevail on a claim of breach of implied warranties of merchantability and fitness for ordinary purposes?

Rule: For a merchantability claim, a buyer must have evidence that the goods would not pass without objection in the relevant market. Here, Crow provided no evidence of that standard for the offshore fishing boat market. For a claim based on fitness for its ordinary purpose, Crow himself proved that it could be used so as to satisfy that standard.

Citizens for Preservation of Waterman Lake v. Davis (1980)

Facts: The town contracted with Davis to operate a commercial dump. Davis operated the dump so as to violate the state Fresh Water Wetlands Act. A citizens group and the town sought to enjoin Davis's dumping in wetlands.

Issue: May a court issue an injunction to prevent violation of state law as part of a contract action?

Rule: If a state penal statute does not create a private cause of action, a contract cannot create such a private cause of action as an implied term of the contract.

CHAPTER 5

Interpreting Contracts

I. PAROL EVIDENCE RULE

The parol evidence rule is substantive law that renders preliminary negotiations, written documents, conversations, and verbal agreements inadmissible at trial because they are merged into and superseded by the subsequent written contract. Even if a court allows such evidence, its veracity still has to be proved to the jury. The rule controls only what type of evidence is allowed, not whether such evidence is credible.

A. Integration

A writing is integrated if it is adopted by the parties as "a final expression of one or more of the terms of an agreement." (Rest. 2d §209(1).)

1. A writing is partially integrated if the parties did not intend for it to include all the terms of the agreement.

2. A writing is completely integrated if the parties intended it to include all the terms of the agreement.

(Rest. 2d §210(1).)

B. When Parol Evidence Is Admissible

1. Evidence of prior agreements or negotiations may supplement a partially integrated agreement, provided this evidence does not contradict a term of the writing.

2. When an agreement is completely integrated, not even evidence of a consistent additional term is admissible to explain or supplement it. (Rest. 2d §216.)

3. Some courts treat contemporaneous oral agreements as prior oral agreements. Others assert that the existence of a contemporaneous oral agreement automatically proves that the writing is only partially integrated.

4. Parol testimony is admissible to prove a condition precedent to the legal effectiveness of a written contract if the condition does not contradict the express terms of such written agreement.

  5. Even if the writing is a complete integration, parol evidence is admissible to show fraud, mistake, or duress in the inducement of the contract. Most courts hold that a merger clause should not be held a bar to actions for fraud.
  6. Evidence of subsequent oral agreements will not be barred by the parol evidence rule. The rule only applies to agreements made prior to the final contract.
     a. To avoid the admission of this type of evidence, some parties insert no-oral-modification clauses that find statutory support from UCC §2-209(2).
     b. An attempted oral modification of a contract that contains a no-oral-modification clause is effective as a waiver only if it is reasonably relied upon.
C. The UCC Version
  1. A writing intended to be a final expression of an agreement may not be contradicted by evidence of a prior written or oral agreement or of a contemporaneous oral agreement. (UCC §2-202.)
  2. The writing may be explained or supplemented by course of dealing or usage of trade even if it is a complete integration, unless the course of dealing or trade usage is carefully canceled by the contract's terms. (UCC §2-202(1).)
  3. The writing may be explained or supplemented by evidence of consistent additional terms unless the court finds the writing to be complete and exclusive. (UCC §2-202(2).)
D. Judge and Jury
  Whether the parol evidence rule renders extrinsic evidence inadmissible is a question for the judge. (Rest. 2d §209(2).) The concern is that juries would be too sympathetic to oral testimony and not realize that written evidence is more reliable.
  1. Partial vs. Complete Integration
     a. The strict view asserts that this question should be answered through an examination of the writing only (four-corners approach).
        i. According to this view, a clause that states that the writing represents the complete agreement between the parties (merger clause) will usually lead to a determination that the writing is a complete integration, unless it is obviously clear that it is not.
        ii. If a writing is seemingly complete on its face, evidence of a prior oral agreement is admissible only if it is one that the parties would not ordinarily be expected to embody in the writing.
     b. A more permissive approach looks to extrinsic circumstances along with the face of the writing.

      i. The important consideration is the intent of the parties.

      ii. A general merger clause is merely evidence of intent.

    c. UCC §2-202, Comment 3

    Parol evidence of additional terms is not admissible as above unless "the additional terms are such that, if agreed upon, they would certainly have been included in the document."

2. Judges decide whether or not the writing is an integration (i.e., a final expression of accord). Some courts look to the writing; others look to the parties' intent.

3. Judges also determine if the oral additional terms are contradictory or consistent with the writing. The judge must evaluate the oral testimony.

II. INTERPRETING CONTRACT LANGUAGE

In addition to disputes as to whether a term is actually part of a contract, parties may also disagree as to the meaning of those terms that are part of the contract. Difficulties may arise because the parties do not speak the same language or because certain words may have a special "trade meaning" of which one of the parties is not aware.

A. Role of Judge and Jury

1. Although the meaning of language is a question of fact, it has frequently been removed from the jury by calling it a question of law because of a distrust of unsophisticated jurors and a desire for uniformity in interpretation.

2. The test of admissibility of extrinsic evidence to explain the meaning of a written instrument is not whether the instrument appears to be plain and unambiguous on its face, but whether the offered evidence is relevant to prove a meaning to which the language of the instrument is reasonably susceptible.

B. The party that seeks to have a contract term interpreted in a narrower sense that is more favorable to him bears a substantial burden of proof.

C. Objective and Subjective Theories of Interpretation

1. Objectivists and subjectivists agree that where the parties have in fact attached different significance to their language, the objective standard should be used in determining the meaning of the language.

2. Objectivists also argue that even where parties have attached the same meaning to their language, an objective standard should determine the meaning, even if it is different from that which the parties intended.

3. In reality, courts allow parol evidence to help them determine the intended meaning of ambiguous words in a written contract.

D. Restatement (Second) §201
   1. Where all parties have attached the same meaning to an agreement or a term, it is interpreted in accordance with that meaning.
   2. Where the parties have attached different meanings to an agreement, it is interpreted in accordance with the meaning attached by one of them if at the time the agreement was made that party did not know or have reason to know of any different meaning attached by the other, and the other knew or had reason to know the meaning attached by the first party.
   3. There is no binding contract if the parties unknowingly assign different subjective meanings to an important contract term because there was no meeting of the minds. (Rest. 2d §20.)
E. Rules in Aid of Interpretation
   1. Words and conduct are interpreted in light of all the surrounding circumstances. The principal purpose of the contract is given great weight if it is ascertainable in light of all the circumstances. (Rest. 2d §202(1).)
   2. Maxims, such as "the term is to be strictly construed against the draftsman," can be used.
   3. Contracts will be construed to serve the public interest.
      a. An interpretation that gives a reasonable, lawful, and effective meaning to all the terms is preferred to an interpretation that leaves a part of the contract unreasonable, unlawful, or of no effect. (Rest. 2d §203(a).)
      b. Contracts that restrain trade or land use are narrowly construed.
   4. Specific terms and separately negotiated terms are given greater weight than general language and standardized terms, respectively. (Rest. 2d §203(c)-(d).)
   5. Interpret terms with the aid of any relevant course of performance, course of dealing and usage of trade. (Rest. 2d §202(5); UCC §§1-205, 2-208.)
F. Hierarchy of Extrinsic Aids (Rest 2d. §203(b); UCC §2-208(2))
   1. Express Terms
      Look at the contract terms themselves.
   2. Course of Performance
      If the contract has been partially performed, the court will consider how the ambiguous terms were treated.
   3. Course of Dealing
      If the parties have made other contracts in the past, the court will consider whether similarly ambiguous terms were used and how they were interpreted by the parties.
   4. Trade Usage

Whether the ambiguous or disputed terms have a common interpretation in the specific industry or trade in which the parties are engaged will be considered.

5. These standards are inapplicable if the contract specifically bars their use.

III. OMITTED TERMS

How the courts deal with problems that are not addressed by the parties:

A. When the parties to a bargain sufficiently defined to be a contract have not agreed with respect to a term that is essential to a determination of their rights and duties, a term that is reasonable in the circumstances is supplied by the court. (Rest. 2d §204.)

1. The reasonable omitted term may be supplied even if the writing is completely integrated (see parol evidence rule).

2. Although extrinsic evidence may be inadmissible to supply the omitted term (e.g., the writing is completely integrated), it may be used to determine what is "reasonable."

B. There are many instances where a court will supply omitted terms (see Chapters 7 and 8 for court-implied conditions and extraordinary events that make performance impracticable):

1. Obligation of Good Faith
   a. Every contract or duty imposes an obligation of good faith in its performance and enforcement. (UCC §1-203; Rest. 2d §205.)
   b. Requirements and Output Contracts
      There is an obligation of good faith when demanding or tendering requirements or outputs pursuant to the agreement. (UCC §2-306(1).)
      i. This obligation is satisfied if the buyer's demands are in accordance with established course of performance and dealing between the parties and the established usage of trade. (See *Eastern Air Lines, Inc. v. Gulf Oil Corp.*)
      ii. A requirements or output contract usually does not include an implied obligation to continue the business.

2. Best Efforts
   a. A lawful agreement for exclusive dealing, unless otherwise agreed, imposes a return obligation to use best efforts to promote the product. (UCC §2-306(2).)
   b. A clause requiring "best efforts to maintain a high volume of sales" is violated by the philosophy that profit motivation should override sales volume in the absence of consideration.

    c. A promise to publish implies a good faith effort to promote the book, including a first printing and advertising budget adequate to give the book a reasonable chance of achieving success. However, while publishers must perform honestly, there is no requirement to perform skillfully.

3. Percentage Lease
    Rent is fixed as a stated percentage of the lessee's receipts or profits.
    a. If based on gross receipts, a conflict is created. The lessor wants the lessee to maximize gross receipts, while the lessee wants to maximize net profits.
    b. When no minimum rent is reserved, a percentage lease must be construed as including an implied covenant to continue the business.
    c. Such an obligation is not implied if the lessor is protected by a substantial minimum rental provision.

4. Agreements Without End
    a. Employment Contracts
    The majority of states have not implied a duty to terminate employment contracts in good faith.
    b. Franchise Agreements
    There is a three-way division among courts:
      i. Franchisors cannot terminate without cause.
      ii. Franchisors must give reasonable notice of termination.
      iii. Franchisors must allow the franchisee a reasonable opportunity to avail himself of the primary efforts and expenditures incurred in setting up the franchise.

5. Course of Performance, Course of Dealing and Trade Usage
    Extrinsic evidence relating to the usage of trade and the parties' course of dealing is admissible to supplement an unambiguous and complete written contract as long as it does not contradict the written agreement's express terms. (UCC §2-202.)

6. UCC Gap-Fillers
    If it has not been agreed upon, courts determine:
    a. Reasonable price terms. (UCC §2-305(a).)
    b. Place for delivery. (UCC §2-308.)
    c. Date payment is due. (UCC §2-310.)

CASE CLIPS

Mitchill v. Lath (1928)

Facts: The Laths orally promised to remove an icehouse in exchange for Mitchill's written agreement to buy land. The written agreement excluded the Laths' earlier promise. Mitchill sought to introduce evidence of the promise for its enforcement.

Issue: Will a written contract be modified by evidence of a prior oral agreement that addresses and modifies the same issues and obligations?

Rule: An oral agreement is allowed to be in variance of the written contract if the agreement is collateral, it does not contradict express or implied provisions of the written contract, and the parties would *not* ordinarily be expected to embody it in the writing.

Hatley v. Stafford (1978)

Facts: Stafford leased farmland to Hatley with the option that Stafford could buy out Hatley at a figure not to exceed $70 per acre. Six months into the lease, Stafford tried to buy out Hatley but Hatley refused to sell, claiming that the parties had made a contemporaneous oral agreement stipulating that the buy-out option would be effective from 30 to 60 days only. The lease was negotiated without the use of lawyers.

Issue: Will parol evidence be admitted to prove the existence of an oral agreement if it is not inconsistent with the express terms of a written contract that was formed by unsophisticated parties?

Rule: Parol evidence to prove the existence of an oral agreement will be admitted by the court if the oral agreement is not inconsistent with the express terms of the written agreement, and if it is such an agreement that would naturally be made as a separate agreement by the parties situated in their specific circumstances.

Long Island Trust Co. v. International Inst. for Packaging Educ., Ltd. (1976)

Facts: When International failed to repay the recently renewed loan, the Long Island Trust sued four of the five guarantors and International. The guarantors tried to introduce parol evidence of a contemporaneous oral agreement that the endorsement of all the guarantors was required for renewal of the loan. Only four endorsed.

Issue: May a party use parol evidence to attempt to prove the existence of an oral condition that would bar the enforcement of the written agreement if not performed?

Rule: An oral condition precedent may be proved by parol evidence if it in no way contradicts the express terms of the written agreement.

Lipsit v. Leonard (1974)

Facts: Leonard's contemporaneous oral promises to give Lipsit a share of the business induced Lipsit into entering a series of one-year employment contracts. Lipsit sued for fraud and breach of contract after he was fired.
Issue: Can an action in tort based on a fraudulent oral promise be maintained if the promise itself cannot be enforced because proof of its existence is barred by the parol evidence rule?
Rule: Even if a party cannot establish the existence of an oral promise because it falls under the parol evidence rule, an action in fraud based on the oral promise may be sustained. The measure of damages for fraud is limited to out-of-pocket expenses.

LaFazia v. Howe (1990)

Facts: The Howes entered into negotiations to purchase a delicatessen from the LaFazias. After receiving and reviewing the LaFazias' tax returns, the Howes decided against the purchase. The Howes were eventually persuaded to purchase by the LaFazias' representations that the tax returns did not reflect the true value of the business. The Howes purchased the business under a signed contract containing a disclaimer, which stated, "The Buyers rely on their own judgment as to . . . profits . . . and does [sic] not rely on any representations of the seller." The Howes were subsequently forced to sell the delicatessen after a lack of business made it impossible to complete payment of the contract price. The LaFazias instituted suit for recovery of the remaining contract price, and the Howes counterclaimed, asserting misrepresentation.
Issue: Can a written disclaimer be used to uphold a contract that may otherwise be voidable for fraud?
Rule: A specific disclaimer provision that is read and understood by the party asserting fraud estops all allegations made by the complainant that are contrary to the disclaimer, unless the provision itself was procured by fraud.
Note: This rule allows contracting parties to agree that one is not relying on the representations of the other, a form of freedom of contract.

Hoffman v. Chapman (1943)

Facts: A draftsman, who was acting as an agent for both parties, made a mistake in writing the deed, which resulted in the conveyance of more land to the Hoffmans than agreed upon. When the mistake was detected, the Hoffmans refused to reconvey the unsold land.

Issue: Will a court reform a written agreement to reflect the real intention of the parties?

Rule: A written instrument will be reformed to conform to the real intention of the parties if there is clear and convincing evidence of a mutual mistake.

Pacific Gas & Elec. Co. v. G.W. Drayage & Rigging Co. (1968)

Facts: The contract to repair Pacific's steam turbine contained an indemnity clause requiring Drayage to pay for all property damage arising out of performance of the contract. When Drayage damaged the exposed rotor of a turbine, Pacific sued. Drayage sought to introduce extrinsic evidence to show that the indemnity clause only held it liable for damages to the property of third parties, not to that of Pacific.

Issue: Is evidence of the parties' intention admissible to help explain the meaning of a written instrument?

Rule: Extrinsic evidence of the parties' intention is admissible when relevant to prove a meaning to which the language of a written instrument is reasonably susceptible. Even when the meaning of the instrument appears plain and unambiguous on its face, extrinsic evidence having the above effect is admissible.

Thompson v. Libby (1885)

Facts: Thompson brought an action for the purchase price of logs sold. Libby offered oral testimony to prove the existence of a warranty of the quality of the logs.

Issue: May a party use parol evidence to prove the existence of a warranty allegedly made at the time of sale?

Rule: A warranty is an item and term of the contract of sale, not a separate and independent collateral contract, and therefore cannot be added to a complete written agreement by oral testimony.

Zell v. American Seating Co. (2d Cir. 1943)

Facts: Zell orally agreed to procure government contracts for American Seating during the war, in exchange for a flat fee and commissions. A written contract followed omitting the commissions because of government disfavor toward such arrangements. The parties orally agreed, however, that the first oral agreement was the actual contract. American Seating later refused to pay commissions.

Issue: Will the parol evidence rule bar a party from submitting proof of an oral agreement that renders a writing, complete on its face, not binding?
Rule: A purported written agreement, which the parties design as a mere sham, lacks legal efficacy, and extrinsic parol or other written evidence will always be received on the issue.

American Seating Co. v. Zell (S. Ct. 1944)

Facts: See preceding case.
Issue: See preceding case.
Rule: (per curiam) If a written agreement is complete and unambiguous on its face, the parol evidence rule will bar all evidence that is inconsistent with its terms.

Lee v. Joseph E. Seagram & Sons, Inc. (1977)

Facts: The Lees claimed that there was a contemporaneous oral agreement that if they sold their liquor distributorship to Seagram under a written contract, Seagram would relocate Lee's sons in another distributorship. Lee, who had enjoyed a good friendship with Seagram, brought suit when Seagram refused to execute its oral promise. An integration clause was not included in the written contract.
Issue: Does the parol evidence rule bar proof of an oral agreement that does not contradict the written contract if the writing contained no integration clause?
Rule: Proof of an oral collateral agreement that is not contradictory to any terms of a written contract will not be barred by the parol evidence rule if the parties would not be expected to incorporate the oral agreement into the written contract.

Hunt Foods & Indus., Inc. v. Doliner (1966)

Facts: When Hunt sought to enforce a written option contract to purchase stock at a certain price, Doliner attempted to introduce evidence of a contemporaneous oral agreement that the option would only be exercised if Doliner tried to solicit a higher offer elsewhere.
Issue: Is proof of prior or contemporaneous oral agreements admissible if it is consistent with the written contract and would not be expected to be included within its terms?
Rule: Proof of an oral agreement that is consistent with the terms of the written contract is not barred by the parol evidence rule if it would not be expected to be included in the written agreement.

Steuart v. McChesney (1982)

Facts: The Steuarts granted the McChesneys a right of first refusal, or right to make a bid if the Steuarts found a purchaser for a parcel of farmland. The property was appraised at $50,000, and the defendants received offers of over $30,000. However, the McChesneys sought to exercise their right for $7,820, twice the value listed on the tax rolls maintained in the county. The contract provided that county records were to be the source of the McChesneys' offer.

Issue: When an agreement's meaning is clear and unambiguous and yet produces an inequitable result, can extrinsic evidence be introduced to supply another meaning?

Rule: The plain meaning of an unambiguous contract will be enforced despite inequitable results. Plain meaning cannot be distorted to produce ambiguity simply because fairness might warrant a different outcome.

Masterson v. Sine (1968)

Facts: Masterson sold a ranch to Sine (his sister) with an option reserved to repurchase the property. Masterson's trustee in bankruptcy sought to utilize the option, but Sine attempted to prove that there was a prior oral agreement barring assignment of the option to anyone outside of the family.

Issue: When is parol evidence of an oral collateral agreement admissible?

Rule: Evidence of oral collateral agreements is excluded only when the fact finder is likely to be misled. If it appears that the oral collateral agreement might naturally be made as a separate agreement, proof of the collateral agreement is permitted, but if the additional agreed upon terms logically would have been included in the document, the evidence must be excluded. (UCC §2-202.)

Nanakuli Paving & Rock Co. v. Shell Oil Co., Inc. (1981)

Facts: Nanakuli entered into a long-term contract to buy asphalt from Shell. Although not explicitly required to do so, Shell gave Nanakuli price protection for five years in accordance with industry-wide custom in Hawaii. Due to rising costs, Shell raised its prices.

Issue: Will trade usage that is reinforced by the course of dealings between the parties be incorporated into an agreement?

Rule: A course of dealings that complies with a prevalent trade usage of which the parties are or should be aware will be incorporated into an agreement provided it is consistent with the express terms of the contract.

Alaska Northern Development, Inc. v. Alyeska Pipeline Serv. Co. (1983)

Facts: Alaska Northern Development (AND) sent Alyeska a proposal to purchase Alyeska's entire inventory of Caterpillar parts. No price was mentioned. Alyeska responded with its own letter of intent, also without a price term, which included the words "subject to the final approval of the owner committee." AND claimed the language referred only to the price term but Alyeska contended it referred to the whole deal. The lower court found that the contract was partially integrated.

Issue: What definition of inconsistency is to be applied to determine whether parol evidence should be admitted to interpret a partially integrated contract?

Rule: Inconsistency, for purposes of admitting parol evidence, means the absence of reasonable harmony in terms of the language and respective obligations of the party.

Note: Other jurisdictions hold that to be inconsistent, a term must actually contradict or negate a term of the writing.

Luther Williams, Jr., Inc. v. Johnson (1967)

Facts: The defendants testified that they signed the contract for improvements to their home believing it was merely an estimate and not an obligation until they procured the financing. The contract had a merger clause.

Issue: Is parol evidence admissible to prove the existence of an oral agreement that acts as a condition precedent to a written contract?

Rule: Parol evidence is admissible to prove the existence of an oral agreement that acts as a condition precedent to a written contract if the parol condition does not contradict the terms of the writing. The merger clause is an indication, not conclusive, of the intent of the parties with regard to the completeness of their agreement.

Kemp Fisheries, Inc. v. Castle & Cooke, Inc. (1988)

Facts: Kemp contracted with a subsidiary of Castle & Cooke to charter a commercial fishing vessel for the season. The contract provided that (1) the subsidiary would deliver the vessel in good, inspected condition, (2) acceptance is conclusive evidence that Kemp deemed the vessel seaworthy and suitable for its intended use, and (3) delivery would constitute full performance by the subsidiary. The freezing system broke down during the season, forcing Kemp to sell his fish at reduced rates. The trial judge admitted parol evidence to find that the subsidiary had orally warranted that the freezing system would meet Kemp's requirements.

Issue: When should extrinsic evidence be admitted to interpret the language of a contract?

Rule: The parol evidence rule requires that courts consider extrinsic evidence to determine whether a contract is ambiguous, but if the evidence leads to an interpretation that is contrary to a reasonable interpretation of the contract language, the evidence is not admissible.

Frigaliment Import Co. v. B.N.S. Int'l Sales Corp. (1960)

Facts: Frigaliment rejected International's delivery of "stewing chickens" because it said that the contract called for "young chickens." International defended that the contract allowed for it to deliver "any bird of that genus," and that its prices were too low to suggest that it was selling "broilers."

Issue: How does the court determine the meaning of an ambiguous contract term?

Rule: The party who seeks to have a contract term interpreted in a narrower sense that is more favorable to it bears the substantial burden of persuading the court. In order to determine the meaning of an ambiguous term, the court looks to the contract language, prevalence and actual knowledge of the trade usage and the dealings between the parties.

Paymaster Oil Mill Co. v. Mitchell (1975)

Facts: Paymaster contracted with Mitchell to buy 4,000 bushels of soybeans at a set price. This oral agreement was later corroborated in writing. A severe drought damaged Mitchell's crop preventing full delivery.

Issue: Is parol evidence concerning a written contract admissible if it does not conflict with the written contract?

Rule: Parol evidence may be used to further explain or supplement the terms of a written contract so long as it is not contradictory to the terms of a written agreement intended as the final expression of a contract.

Note: Parol evidence may not be used if there has been an adjudication that the writing was intended as the exclusive statement of the agreement.

Trident Center v. Connecticut General Life Insurance Co. (1988)

Facts: Trident Center obtained a $56.5 million commercial loan from Connecticut General at an interest rate of 12.25 percent. The agreement provided that Trident not prepay the loan during the first 12 years. A few years later, interest rates greatly decreased and Trident sought to refinance, but Connecticut General refused to allow it to prepay. Trident claimed that extrinsic evidence could be introduced to show that the agreement struck was actually different from the written language of the contract.

Issue: Under California law, may parol evidence be introduced even when the written contract is clear and unambiguous?

Rule: Even when the terms of a contract are clear, a party must always have the opportunity to introduce parol evidence because language has no objective meaning.

Note: Under traditional contract principles, extrinsic evidence is usually inadmissible to interpret, vary or add to the terms of an unambiguous, integrated written instrument. California law is an exception to the normal rule.

Raffles v. Wichelhaus (1864)

Facts: The contract stated that the plaintiff was to deliver the goods on the ship *Peerless*. Unknown to both parties there were two different ships bearing the same name but sailing at different times. The defendant refused the plaintiff's goods because he expected the delivery to be made on the *Peerless* that sailed earlier.

Issue: Is there a contract if each party gives a different meaning to a material ambiguity in the contract?

Rule: There is no binding contract if the parties unknowingly assign different meanings to an important contract term. Parol evidence may be given to prove that the parties attributed different meanings to a term.

Leibel v. Raynor Manufacturing Co. (1978)

Facts: Raynor and Leibel made an oral distributorship agreement. Raynor agreed to sell its goods to Leibel at the factory distributor price if Leibel agreed to sell, install and service Raynor products exclusively. After two years of decreasing sales, Raynor informed Leibel that their relationship was terminated, effective immediately. Leibel agreed that the relationship was terminable at will, but claimed that reasonable notice of termination was required.

Issue: Under the UCC, may an oral distributorship agreement be terminated without reasonable notice?

Rule: UCC §2-309 requires reasonable notice before an oral distributorship agreement may be terminated. Reasonable notice is required to assure the dealer an adequate opportunity to sell its existing inventory.

Joyner v. Adams (1987)

Facts: Adams entered into a lease with Joyder that required Adams to completely subdivide and "develop" the leased property by a certain date. The lease required Adams to pay a flat rate rent. However, if Adams failed to subdivide and "develop" all of the leased property by the specified date, Adams was required to pay back rent in the amount that would have been due under a higher rent formula. On the specified date, Adams had completely developed and subdivided all the land, with the exception of a single lot, which had been subdivided and prepared, but upon which no buildings had yet been erected. The parties disagreed as to whether the word "develop" required Adams to complete construction of all buildings or to develop the property to the point that building construction could begin.

Issue: If the parties to a contract attribute different meanings to an ambiguous term, which interpretation should apply?

Rule: If A knows or has reason to know the meaning that B attaches to a term, and B does not know or does not have reason to know the meaning that A attaches to that term, the court will interpret the term in accordance with B's interpretation.

Berg v. Hudesman (1990)

Facts: The landlord of a 99-year ground lease claimed that the tenant had not paid him the proper amount due under the lease for several years. The terms of the contract were ambiguous as to how the rent should be calculated.

Issue: What is the proper way to interpret an ambiguous contract term?

Rule: Extrinsic evidence is admissible as to the entire circumstances under which a contract was made, as an aid to ascertain the parties' intent as to the meaning of particular contract terms. Subsequent conduct of the contracting parties, as well as the reasonableness of the parties' respective interpretations, may also be a factor in the determination of an ambiguous term.

Eskimo Pie Corp. v. Whitelawn Dairies Co. (1968)

Facts: Eskimo Pie was involved in a contract with Whitelawn and Supermarket Advisory Sales (SAS), under which Whitelawn had the right to manufacture ice cream products bearing the "Eskimo" name, and SAS had the right to purchase the products. SAS was given "non-exclusive" purchasing rights, and Eskimo subsequently entered into agreements with other parties. SAS brought suit for breach, and proposed to bring in parol evidence to prove the "non-exclusive" clause neither allowed Eskimo to grant licenses to independent companies, nor to compete with SAS in the sale of Eskimo ice cream products.

Issue: Should parol evidence be admitted to ascertain the intended meaning of a contract term?

Rule: The admission of parol evidence is determined by the ambiguity of the contractual language. The admission of parol evidence concerning unambiguous contract language hinges on whether the language might objectively be recognized by a reasonably intelligent person acquainted with the general usage, customs and surrounding circumstances as having special meaning. Where language is ambiguous, a party may use surrounding circumstances, common usage and custom as to the meaning attributed to the language, and the subsequent conduct of the parties, but evidence of subjective understanding will not be admissible.

Gianni v. R. Russell & Co. (1924)

Facts: Gianni claimed that, before renewing his lease, he reached an oral agreement to have the exclusive right to sell soft drinks in lieu of the sale of tobacco in R. Russell's building. Gianni sued for breach when another store was permitted to sell soft drinks.

Issue: Is parol evidence allegedly proving the existence of a prior oral agreement admissible to alter the terms of a written agreement?

Rule: If the subject of the alleged oral agreement is embraced by the written contract, the scope of the oral agreement is taken to be covered by the writing, and the written contract is determined to be the entire agreement between the parties.

Oswald v. Allen (1969)

Facts: Oswald, a Swiss coin collector, offered to buy a collection of Swiss coins from Allen. Allen understood him to mean he wished to buy her "Swiss Coin Collection," which did not include certain Swiss coins in her possession. Oswald, believing he had bought all her Swiss coins, sued for specific performance when she refused to deliver them.

Issue: Does a contract exist when two parties materially differ in their understanding of the object of the contract?

Rule: When terms used to express an agreement are ambivalent, and the parties understand them in different ways, no contract exists unless one party should have been aware of the other's understanding. Such an agreement provides "no sensible basis for choosing between conflicting understandings."

Market Street Associates v. Frey (1991)

Facts: J.C. Penney entered into an agreement with a trust company in which it sold its property to the trust in exchange for financing. The trust was then required to lease the property back to J.C. Penney, but a provision in the contract allowed J.C. Penney to buy back the property for a price below market value if the trust company unreasonably refused a financing request. Years later, Market Street, a successor under one of J.C. Penney's original leases, wanted to buy back the property from the trust, and asked for financing while purposefully keeping silent as to the buy-back provision. When the financing was denied, Market Street attempted to exercise the provision, and sued for specific performance.

Issue: Does a contracting party have a good faith duty to make another party aware of an important clause in a contract?

Rule: Although a contractual relationship does not create a fiduciary duty between the parties to a contract, it is considered bad faith for a party to take deliberate advantage of an oversight by the other party concerning contractual rights.

Dickey v. Philadelphia Minit-Man Corp. (1954)

Facts: Dickey leased land to Minit-Man for washing, simonizing and polishing cars "and for no other purpose." The lease required the defendant to pay a percentage of gross sales in addition to a minimum rent. Dickey sued to recover possession after Minit-Man discontinued only the car washing aspect of the business.

Issue: When the amount of rent to be paid is based upon the lessee's gross sales, is there an implied obligation to continue the business on the premises to the fullest extent reasonably possible?

Rule: There is no implied obligation in a percentage sales lease to continue business to the fullest extent because such an implication is vague, uncertain, and generally impracticable. The basis for rejecting an implied obligation is strengthened if the lessor is guaranteed a substantial minimum rent.

Bak-A-Lum Corp. of America v. ALCOA Bldg. Prod. Inc. (1976)

Facts: ALCOA terminated an exclusive distributorship with BAL, having instigated a major expansion of BAL's facilities at substantial cost.

Issue: Must a franchisor disclose its intention to terminate an agreement when it knows the franchisee will incur substantial costs in fulfillment of the agreement?

Rule: There is an implied covenant of good faith and fair dealing in franchise agreements requiring reasonable notice of termination, reasonableness to be considered under all the circumstances, so as not to impair the right of the franchisee to the fruits of the contract.

Zilg v. Prentice-Hall, Inc. (1983)

Facts: P-H, a publisher, was given contractual discretion in marketing its publication of Zilg's book. After deciding that Zilg's Marxist-leaning book would have limited popularity, P-H revised its initial marketing budget figures downward. Zilg sued, claiming P-H did not use its best efforts to promote his book.

Issue: To what extent does discretion to tailor promotion efforts to a product's likely market limit the implied responsibility to use best efforts to promote a product?

Rule: A promise to promote implies a good faith effort to do so, including an initial production and advertising budget adequate to give the product a reasonable chance of achieving success. Once this initial obligation is fulfilled, only good faith business judgment is required if the contract contains a clause giving the producer/promoter discretion over marketing efforts.

WWW & Assocs. v. Giaconteri (1990)

Facts: Seller owned land that it contracted to sell to Buyer, a developer. The parties included in the contract a clause that permitted either Buyer or Seller to cancel the contract if litigation involving the property had not ended by a date certain. The litigation did not end and Seller canceled. Buyer alleged that the cancellation was for his benefit only and therefore he could waive it, which he wished to do. Buyer sued for specific performance.

Issue: Can the clear language of the contract granting both parties a right to cancel be interpreted to benefit only one of them?

Rule: No. Clear contract language cannot be made ambiguous through the use of extrinsic evidence that the mutual cancellation clause was inserted in the contract only to benefit one party.

Interform Co. v. Mitchell (1978)

Facts: Interform owned forms for the molding of concrete used in construction. Mitchell wanted to use them and submitted a purchase order to Interform. Interform sent documents to Mitchell casting the transaction as one in which Mitchell would rent, not buy, the forms. Mitchell used the forms once, which the lease permitted, and then used them again, Mitchell claiming ownership of the forms. Interform sued for return of the forms and compensation for the second use of them. Mitchell claimed that only the purchase order was admissible as evidence of the contract.

Issue: If the parties to a contract disagree on whether it is a sale or a lease, is extrinsic evidence admissible to prove their intent?

Rule: Extrinsic evidence is admissible to prove whether the parties intended a sale or a lease. It was held that the transaction was a lease.

Note: The appellate court awarded attorneys' fees to Interform, indicating that it believed Mitchell's claims were not made in good faith.

Nelson v. Elway (1995)

Facts: Nelson agreed to sell two automobile dealerships to Elway. Nelson claimed that he and Elway entered a service agreement in which Elway promised to pay as part of the price for the dealerships $50 for every car he sold from the dealerships for seven years. The final closing documents for the transaction did not include the commitment to pay the $50 per car sold, and included a merger clause that prevented enforcement of any agreements or promises that preceded the closing but were not reflected in the closing documents. Nelson sued Elway for breach of the service agreement.

Issue: Does the merger clause render extrinsic evidence of side agreements inadmissible?

Rule: When a merger clause is plain and unambiguous, it makes extrinsic evidence of agreements or promises outside the final document inadmissible.

Brinderson-Newberg Joint Venture v. Pacific Erectors, Inc. (1993)

Facts: Brinderson had a Navy contract to build a power plant. Pacific wanted a subcontract to erect support steel but the signed subcontract contained the phrase "erect complete," which might require Pacific to erect a complete structure. The subcontract stated that it was the whole agreement of the parties.

Issue: Is parol evidence admissible to prove that the meaning of a contract term is that of the subjective understanding of one of the parties?

Rule: Where the parties disagree on the meaning of a contract term, parol evidence is admissible to clarify the correct meaning, provided the term is reasonably susceptible to the asserted meaning on an objective standard. Here, the objective meaning of the term "erect complete" in the industry was inconsistent with the meaning that Pacific claimed for it. And Pacific's claim to have assigned that limited meaning to the phrase in an oral understanding with Brinderson before the subcontract was signed was inadmissible under the subcontract clause that stated it was the whole agreement of the parties, the integration clause.

George v. Davoli (1977)

Facts: George bought jewelry from Davoli for $500. The contract was in writing and permitted George to return it for $440, but it did not state how long George had to return it. Davoli alleged an oral agreement that the jewelry had to be returned by a certain date.

Issue: May a party to a sale testify how long the other party has a right to return goods sold for a refund of a portion of the price?

Rule: The parol evidence rule does not block testimony needed to supplement the written contract so long as the testimony is not inconsistent with the written contract.

Note: The UCC requires that such returns be done "seasonably." UCC §§2-326 & 2-327. See also UCC §2-202, the parol evidence rule.

Beanstalk Group, Inc. v. AM General Corp. (2002)

Facts: AM General owned the Hummer trademark and contracted with Beanstalk to market it as AM General's agent; AM General would receive 65 percent gross receipts from marketing the trademark, and Beanstalk would receive a 35 percent commission. AM General entered a joint venture with General Motors, under which General Motors would acquire 40 percent of AM General's stock, would provide funds for a new manufacturing facility, would design and engineer a new vehicle, and would acquire the Hummer trademark. General Motors assumed none of AM General's obligations, did not assume in particular its obligations to Beanstalk, and would market the trademark itself under the joint venture.

Issue: Does an agency agreement to market a trademark apply to the conveyance of the entire trademark to another company as part of a corporate reorganization?

Rule: A trademark owner's agreement to pay a percentage to an agent for marketing and licensing a trademark does not apply to and does not follow the conveyance of the trademark itself to another company. Licenses under the agency contract are entirely distinct from the conveyance of the trademark itself as part of the transfer of the entire ongoing business.

Betaco, Inc. v. Cessna Aircraft Co. (1994)

Facts: Betaco contracted to buy an airplane from Cessna, signed a purchase agreement, and paid a deposit. Betaco claimed that the airplane did not have the range asserted in Cessna's cover letter that accompanied the purchase agreement, and Betaco canceled the sale. Cessna kept the deposit.

Issue: May Buyer claim breach of an express warranty in a document that accompanies the contract?

Rule: When a contract document fully integrates all the terms of the parties' agreement, the buyer may not claim an express warranty in a separate document. Unless the contract is ambiguous the contract's face shows the intent of the parties.

Luria Bros. & Co. v. Pielet Bros. Scrap Iron (1978)

Facts: Seller promised in writing to sell Buyer scrap iron. Seller breached.
Issue: May Seller introduce evidence that his promise to sell was conditioned on his obtaining goods to meet his obligation?
Rule: Testimony is not admissible to prove an unconditional sale of goods was conditional. This would violate the parol evidence rule.

Pym v. Campbell (1856)

Facts: Pym invented a device he offered to sell to Campbell, who agreed to buy it, provided his two engineers approved. One engineer approved, the other was absent. Campbell signed an agreement to buy the device, with an unwritten understanding that Campbell's second engineer must also approve. He didn't. Pym sued.
Issue: May parol evidence be admitted to show that the parties did not intend to be bound by a written contract unless an unwritten condition occurred?
Rule: Parol evidence does not bar proof that the parties did not intend to be bound by a writing at all unless an oral condition was satisfied first.
Note: Compare Restatement (Second) §217.

Eichengreen v. Rollins, Inc. (2001)

Facts: Rollins installed a security system in Eichengreen's house. The parties' understanding of their contract was in a letter by Rollins on which Eichengreen made notations but did not sign. A fire started outside the house that Eichengreen claimed was Rollins' responsibility.
Issue: Is parol evidence admissible when the parties' understanding is in a single writing?
Rule: A party may not introduce extrinsic evidence to vary the meaning of an unambiguous contract under the parol evidence rule.

Richardson v. Union Carbide Indus. Gases, Inc. (2002)

Facts: Rage manufactured furnace parts, which Hoeganaes bought. Rage's forms and Hoeganaes' purchase orders contained clauses requiring the other to indemnify it for liability, including injury of employees. Hoeganaes' employee Richardson was injured by an exploding furnace. He sued Rage, who sought indemnity, based on its form's indemnity provision, from Hoeganaes, which urged its purchase order indemnity clause applied against Rage.
Issue: Where the forms used by contract parties conflict on an issue, does the contract contain the provision in the last form sent?

Rule: If the seller's form and the buyer's form do not agree, neither party's term controls. Conflicting terms drop out of the contract and any gap is filled by default gap-filling rules of the UCC. UCC §2-207(3).

Tribe v. Petersen (1998)

Facts: Tribe bought a horse from Petersen. Petersen stated the horse was gentle and calm. It bucked when Tribe rode it, injuring him.
Issue: Is the statement by the seller that a horse is gentle and will not buck an express warranty?
Rule: The seller's opinion is not an express warranty. The seller's statement that the horse was gentle and would not buck was an opinion. Even if the statement were held to be an express warranty, there was no proof of breach because even a gentle horse may react to a new environment or new rider by temporarily not behaving gently.

Dore v. Arnold Worldwide, Inc. (2006)

Facts: Dore was promoted to a new position by his employer, Arnold. The letter offering him the new position stated it could be terminated at any time by either Arnold or Dore. Arnold did terminate him. Dore sued, claiming that the at-will clause did not clearly state he could be terminated without cause.
Issue: If an explanation of at-will employment does not expressly state that it means employment is terminable without cause, is the explanation unclear or ambiguous?
Rule: An explanation of at-will employment that states either party may terminate employment at any time is clear. It does not need to state that termination may be without cause to be unambiguous.

Mayol v. Weiner Companies, Ltd.

Facts: Mayol contracted to buy real estate "subject to tenant's rights" and made a deposit. Under the tenant's lease, which Mayol did not see until after signing the purchase contract, the tenant had an option to purchase the property.
Issue: If a buyer agrees to buy property subject to the rights of a third party to that property, is the buyer bound no matter what the particular rights of the third party are?
Rule: If a term of a contract is ambiguous, it is not interpreted against a party not at fault for the ambiguity. Here, the term "subject to tenant's rights" to the buyer meant the tenant's rights to possess and use the property for length of the lease and the seller had no reason to believe that the buyer knew of the special right of this tenant to buy the property

under an option. Thus, the buyer and seller had a misunderstanding as to a material element of the contract. No contract was formed and the buyer recovers the deposit.

Foxco Industries, Ltd. v. Fabric World, Inc. (1979)

Facts: Fabric World contracted to buy "first quality" textiles from Foxco, a manufacturer. The contract did not define "first quality." Fabric World later wanted to cancel the order, but Foxco threatened to claim damages for breach. Fabric World stated a single flaw in the textiles would justify rejecting the whole as nonconforming. Foxco believed it could not meet such a standard and resold the order. Foxco sued for breach. The trial court admitted evidence of the meaning of "first quality goods" under the standards of the Knitted Textile Association.

Issue: Is extrinsic evidence of the meaning in the industry of a particular term admissible to show the meaning of the term?

Rule: Trade usage of an ambiguous term is admissible, even if the source of the trade usage is an association to which the party who gives a different meaning to the term does not belong, and even if there is no evidence that party does not know of the meaning given the term by the trade association. Here, Fabric World was not a member of the Knitted Textile Association and there was no evidence that Fabric World was aware of the Knitted Textile Association standards.

Note: UCC §2-202 makes terms defined by trade usage part of the contract unless a party makes sure they are excluded.

Sherrodd, Inc. v. Morrison-Knudsen Co. (1991)

Facts: Morrison-Knudsen subcontracted earth moving work to Sherrodd. Sherrodd claimed that Morrison-Knudsen's agent stated the work was to move 25,000 cubic yards of earth for the price. The later, written contract that Morrison-Knudsen provided did not state a quantity of earth to move, but Sherrodd signed it anyway. Sherrodd had to move much more than 25,000 cubic yards and sued, alleging fraud, to set aside the contract price and to recover in quantum meruit.

Issue: May a contract party knowingly sign a contract that is missing a key term and later sue to set aside the contract because it is missing that key term?

Rule: A party who orally promises to do a certain amount of work for a price but who signs a contract that does not state the amount of work may not later allege the oral contract over the written one. A written contract may only be amended by a later written contract or an oral agreement that the parties perform.

CHAPTER 6

Policing the Bargain

I. CAPACITY TO CONTRACT

Certain classes of individuals lack full capacity to contract. Contracts they form are often voidable at their option.

A. Minors

Minors can disaffirm any contract, except for necessities, during minority and within a reasonable time after reaching majority. (Rest. 2d §14.)

1. Exceptions are statutory or involve contracts that deal with duties imposed by law (e.g., marriage contract, agreement to support an illegitimate child).

2. Upon a minor's disaffirmance, the non-infant party is limited to restitution, and only if the minor still possesses the goods.

3. A minor can ratify after a contract coming of age, expressly or by conduct that causes reliance by the other party.

B. Mental Incompetents

Mentally incompetent parties can disaffirm a contract if, by reason of mental illness or defect:

1. They are unable to understand in a reasonable manner the nature and consequences of the transaction, or

2. They are unable to act in a reasonable manner in relation to the transaction, and

3. The other party has reason to know of the condition. (Rest. 2d §15.)

C. An intoxicated party can also avoid contractual duties if he does not understand the transaction (majority rule).

II. REVISIONS OF CONTRACTUAL DUTY

A. Pre-existing Duty Rule

If one party promises another that he will do what he is already legally obligated to do, the promise is not a detriment sufficient to satisfy the requirement of consideration. (Rest. 2d §73.)

1. Courts have held that modifications of rents and wages are invalid because of a pre-existing duty.
2. *Foakes v. Beer* Rule
   An agreement to accept payment of a lesser sum on or after the due date of a money debt is not binding for lack of consideration.
   a. This rule is severely criticized because it discourages settlements. It has been overruled in some jurisdictions.
   b. Most jurisdictions follow it, but hold that sufficient detriment exists if payment of a lesser sum is accompanied by some additional act of the debtor.
3. Pre-existing Duty Rule Not Applicable:
   a. Original contract is rescinded and a new contract is executed, with the mutual promises serving again as consideration.
   b. Contract modification is a partial rescission and therefore supported by consideration (*Watkins & Sons v. Carrig*).
   c. Some new detriment can be found for consideration.
   d. Rest. 2d §89(a) allows a modification to be binding if compelled by unforeseen circumstances.
   e. Under promissory estoppel, a modification is binding to the extent that justice requires enforcement because of reliance on the modification.
   f. Some state statutes allow modifications without consideration as long as written and signed.
   g. UCC §2-209(1) repudiated the rate by providing that a modification requires no consideration to be binding.
   h. Dropping an invalid claim serves in most courts as consideration for modification if the party has a genuine and reasonable subjective belief that the surrendered claim is valid.
4. Third-party Situations
   If C, an outsider to the contract, promises compensation to a party to fulfill a contract with another:
   a. Majority holds that the agreement with C is invalid since the party is merely promising to perform his legal obligation.
   b. Minority, which includes the Restatement, holds that a valid contract with C is formed.
B. Economic Duress
   1. Rule
      A contract is voidable if a party was forced to agree to it by use of a wrongful threat precluding his exercise of free will.
   2. Proof
      A party must show that immediate possession of needful goods is threatened and that the goods could not be obtained from another source.

3. The remedy is usually restitution.
4. Exercise of a legal right, such as the right to dispute the value of services, is not economic duress.

C. Check Tendered as Payment in Full
1. Common Law Rule
   If there is a good faith dispute over the amount of a debt and the debtor tenders a check for a lesser amount than creditor's claim, cashing the check, even "under protest," discharges the debt.
   a. A debtor's intention that the check be full satisfaction of the debt must be clearly indicated to the creditor.
   b. Partial payment by a fiduciary (an agent who holds the assets of another) will not result in an accord and satisfaction.
2. UCC §1-207
   a. A creditor can cash a check tendered as "payment in full" and still reserve the right to sue for the balance of the debt by writing words of protest on the check.
   b. This rule protects creditors.
   c. Some jurisdictions ignore this rule because it makes settlement of claims difficult.

III. OVERREACHING IN THE BARGAINING PROCESS

A. Concealment
1. In the absence of a fiduciary relationship, there is no liability for bare nondisclosure of known latent defects.
2. However, half-truths are actionable as whole lies and constitute grounds for contract rescission.

B. Misrepresentation
1. Innocent misrepresentations (i.e., negligent, unintentional) are actionable.
2. The misrepresentation must be a material factor in the contract.
3. The complainant must show justifiable reliance.
4. The misrepresentation must be of facts, not opinions or law.
   a. Opinion is actionable if a fiduciary relationship exists.
   b. Restrictions on relief from misrepresentations of law and opinion are increasingly being relaxed. There is a disposition to treat the nature of the statement (fact or opinion) as only one part of the broader issue of whether reliance was justified.

C. Confidential Relation
   A confidential relation is grounds for avoiding a contract if it is used to contravene the bargaining process.

1. Exemplary relationships include guardian and ward, principal and agent, doctor and patient, etc.
2. A confidential relation is deemed to exist whenever the relative positions of the parties gives one the power and means to take advantage or exert undue influence over the other.
3. Factors that determine such a relation are disparities in age, education, or business experience.
4. If the claimant in an action is the party in whom confidence was placed, he must prove that the bargain was fair and at arm's length (without a confidential relation, however, fraud is not presumed).

D. Relief from Mistake (Rest. 2d §152)
1. Mutual Mistake
   a. The mistake under which both parties are acting must have a material effect on the agreed exchange.
      i. Proof that one would not have entered the contract but for the mistake is not sufficient.
      ii. It must be unfair to require performance.
      iii. Availability of other remedies may lead a court to decide that the mistake's effect is not "material."
   b. The mistake must involve a basic assumption.
      i. Determinative factors are the magnitude of the mistake, the degree of certainty in the minds of the parties and the attitude toward the type of transaction involved.
      ii. Belief that the thing bargained for in the contract actually exists is considered to be a basic assumption.
      iii. Courts are divided as to whether the quality of the agreement's subject matter is a basic assumption (see *Sherwood v. Walker, Wood v. Boynton*).
   c. The adversely affected party must not "bear the risk of the mistake." (Rest. 2d §§152, 154.)
      i. Risk can be allocated by the contract terms.
      ii. Risk is allocated to a party if he enters a contract despite having doubts about the facts to which the mistake relates.
      iii. Risk can be allocated by the court if it is reasonable to do so.
      iv. Negligent failure of a party to know or discover facts as to which both parties are under a mistake does not preclude rescission (see *Beachcomber Coins, Inc. v. Boskett*).
   d. Remedy:
      Usually, rescission of the contract.
2. Unilateral Mistake (Rest. 2d §153)

       a. Courts are less willing to grant rescission in cases where only one party is mistaken because the remedy deprives the non-mistaken party of the benefit of the bargain.

       b. Elements:

          i. Unilateral mistake requires the same three elements that are needed for mutual mistake: basic assumption, material effect on the exchange, and the risk must not have been allocated to the adversely affected party, *and*

          ii. Either the enforcement of the agreement would be unconscionable, or the other party had reason to know of the mistake or actually caused it.

       c. Courts are more likely to grant rescission for a clerical error than a mistake in judgment (see *Elsinore Union Elementary Sch. Dist. v. Kastorff*).

   3. Warranty

       a. Parties that try to avoid a contract by pleading concealment or mistake sometimes have the option of claiming breach of warranty (implied or express).

       b. Warranty analysis is used mostly in sale-of-goods cases.

          i. Look to UCC §2-312.

          ii. The risk of mistake is placed on the seller unless the warranty is excluded in the contract pursuant to the code's provisions.

       c. Implied warranties were recently extended to personal injury claims and to transactions involving the sale of houses.

IV. INEQUALITY OF EXCHANGE

  A. An unequal exchange will not usually void a contract in an action *at law,* especially if the parties deal at arm's length.

  B. Courts will deny equitable relief (i.e., specific performance) to protect a party that refuses to perform its part of a highly disproportionate exchange. (See *Campbell Soup v. Wentz.*)

  C. The adequacy of consideration is judged as of the time of the transaction. **Example:** In an arm's-length agreement, A promises to sell ten law guides to B in exchange for $100. The goods are to be delivered and paid for in 30 days. To the surprise of both parties, the fair market value of law guides increases to $1,000 each by the date of the actual exchange. Although the consideration is vastly disproportionate at the time of the actual exchange, it was adequate at the time the contract was made.

V. UNCONSCIONABILITY AND ADHESION CONTRACTS

A. Unconscionability

The doctrine of unconscionability is used to avoid oppression and unfair surprise, but not to disturb the allocation of risk in contract formation. (UCC §2-302, Comment 1.)

1. UCC §2-302:
   a. Judges decide the issue of unconscionability as a matter of law.
   b. Unconscionability is determined by circumstances at the time the contract was made.
   c. Parties are entitled to a reasonable opportunity to present evidence of the circumstances ("commercial setting, purpose and effect") to aid the court in making its decision.
   d. The doctrine is used mostly in consumer cases, but there are occasional business applications (see *Gianni Sport Ltd. v. Gantos, Inc.*).
   e. Rest. 2d §208, using similar language as UCC §2-302, allows a court to refuse to enforce all or part of an unconscionable agreement.
2. Types of Unconscionability
   a. Procedural
      Unfairness in the bargaining process. Courts usually require some kind of procedural unconscionability before refusing to enforce a contract.
   b. Substantive
      Unfairness in the bargaining outcome. Substantive unconscionability is criticized for interfering with the private right to contract at arm's length.
      i. Unconscionability has been recognized to include an absence of meaningful choice on the part of one of the parties, together with contract terms that are unreasonably favorable to the other party. (See *Williams v. Walker-Thomas Furniture Co.*)
      ii. Courts have used price unconscionability, a type of substantive unconscionability, to invalidate agreements. (See *Jones v. Star Credit Corp.*)
   c. Waivers of defenses and cross-collateral clauses have been found unconscionable.
3. Remedies
   If the agreement, or part of it, is unconscionable, the court may:
   a. Refuse to enforce the whole contract,
   b. Refuse to enforce the unconscionable part of the contract, or

    c. Limit the application of an unconscionable clause to avoid an unconscionable result.

    d. When Remedies Are Limited:

        i. UCC §2-719(2). When a limited remedy "fails of its essential purpose" because of the circumstances, "remedy may be had as provided in this Act." The Comment states that this section is to be applied when the limitation of the remedy works in an "unconscionable manner." (See *Wilson Trading, Corp. v. David Ferguson, Ltd.*)

        ii. UCC §2-719(3). Consequential damages may be limited or excluded, unless the limitation or exclusion is unconscionable. Limitation of consequential damages for personal injury in a consumer-goods case is *prima facie* unconscionable.

B. Standard Form Contracts (Contracts of Adhesion)

  1. Primary Advantages:

    a. Save time and reduce uncertainty.

    b. Allow parties to control risks.

  2. Courts will void provisions in form contracts that were not actually understood and agreed to by the party not writing (see *Henningsen v. Bloomfield Motors*).

  3. Unconscionability will invalidate a form-contract provision if a stronger party uses superior bargaining power to introduce contract provisions that cause the lesser party great hardship.

  4. Nondrafters usually do not realize that printed slips and tickets are contracts to limit the liability of the issuer.

    a. Rest. 2d §212 deals with this difficulty, providing that a paper binds a party only if he "signs or otherwise manifests assent."

    b. If the issuer has reason to believe that the party manifesting assent would not do so if he knew that the writing contained a particular term, the term is not part of the agreement. (Rest. 2d §211(3).)

  5. Measures for Reducing the Problems of Adhesion

    a. Legislation, which is usually aimed at correcting imbalances of bargaining power:

        i. Statutes require contracts to be written in "plain language" and regulations to control the terms of the exchange and remedies.

        ii. The main problem with such statutes is inflexibility.

    b. Judicial Control

    Judicial control is more flexible, but incapable of revising underlying patterns of market relationships.

    c. Administrative Control

    Administrative control creates quasi-judicial responsibility and power within a limited jurisdiction (i.e., to investigate charges against common carriers and to exercise control over contract terms in insurance contracts). Administrative control is fairly flexible because administrative decisions carry less precedential value than judicial decisions.

C. Home-solicitation Sales

1. State statutes provide a cooling-off period, during which a buyer can cancel his purchase.

2. Uniform Consumer Credit Code allows the buyer to cancel "until midnight of the third business day" after a home-solicitation sale.

VI. ILLEGALITY

A. Courts will also void agreements that are valid from the perspective of contract law, but are otherwise in violation of public policy (illegal contracts).

B. Criminal sanctions are a more effective way to handle illegal agreements.

C. Claims for restitution are usually precluded, but sometimes allowed if:

1. The claimant is not *in pari delicto* (equally blameworthy) with the defendant, or

2. The claimant is *in locus poenitentiae* (withdrew before consummation of the illegal bargain).

D. Remitter's Liability

A mere agent or depository of the proceeds of an illegal transaction is not permitted to assert the defense of illegality in an action to recover the proceeds by a party to the illegal transaction.

E. Types of Illegal Contracts and Effects of Illegality:

1. Covenants Not to Compete

Unless made in bad faith, courts enforce such covenants up to the point that is reasonably necessary to protect the employer's interest without imposing undue hardship on the employee.

2. Inducing Official Action

a. Contingent fee arrangements for services in securing the passage of legislation are strictly scrutinized.

b. Contingent fees for lawyers are permissible because they ensure the most humble citizen equal justice under the law.

3. Bribery

a. A contract in which an employee is bribed to take official action is illegal and unenforceable. Most courts will not enforce such a contract even if one party was unjustly enriched.

b. If a party bribes a third party in order to help him perform his obligations under a contract, the contract will not be enforced if public policy is strongly frustrated.

4. Licensing

If the purpose of a licensing requirement is protection of the public, the want of a license will render the contract for the unlicensed services unenforceable (e.g., uncertified doctor, lawyer, etc.).

5. Usury

Loan agreements that charge interest rates in excess of the legal limit are unenforceable.

6. Wagering

Although courts are unwilling to enforce private gambling contracts, they will grant restitution if

a. The claimant is not *in pari delicto* with the defendant, or

b. The claimant was *in locus poenitentiae*.

CASE CLIPS

Mundy v. Lumberman's Mut. Cas. Co. (1986)

Facts: Mundy, an assistant district attorney, was robbed of silverware from his home. The insurance policy in effect at the time of the robbery limited recovery for the loss of silverware to $1,000, although an earlier edition of the policy had contained no such limit. A copy of the new insurance policy, which had been sent to Mundy, contained multiple references to changes made from the old policy, including a one-page summary of the changes, each identified in a separate paragraph and set off from the others by added space and black dots. Mundy argued that the insurance company's notice was inadequate, and thus entitled him to full recovery.

Issue: How should a court decide whether changes made to an insurance policy are binding upon the insured?

Rule: Where a casual reading of the material would give a party notice of changes in an insurance policy (e.g., written in large print or bold type), the insured is bound by limits of the new policy upon receipt, regardless of whether actual notice is effected.

Henningsen v. Bloomfield Motors, Inc. (1960)

Facts: Henningsen purchased a new car from Bloomfield Motors. His wife was injured when the steering failed ten days after the car was delivered. All implied warranties of merchantability were disclaimed by a clause buried in the fine print on the back of the contract.

Issue: In an adhesion contract, can a manufacturer or dealer disclaim all warranties of merchantability?

Rule: When there is vastly unequal bargaining power between the parties to a contract, contract clauses that disclaim the implied warranty of merchantability are void as against public policy.

Broemmer v. Abortion Services of Phoenix (1992)

Facts: Broemmer desired to receive an abortion from the defendant clinic. Upon her arrival at the clinic, Broemmer was directed to complete three forms, one of which contained an agreement to arbitrate any dispute arising between the parties as a result of the procedure. The clinic made no attempt to explain the agreement, nor did it provide copies of the form, and Broemmer could not recall signing the agreement. Broemmer was injured by the procedure, and attempted to bring suit in state court.

Issue 1: What is an adhesion contract?

Rule 1: An adhesion contract is a standardized form offered on a "take it or leave it" basis, where the offeror does not afford the consumer a realistic opportunity to bargain, and refuses service to the consumer unless the contract is agreed to.

Issue 2: When is a provision contained in an adhesion contract enforceable?

Rule 2: An adhesion contract is fully enforceable according to its terms, unless the contract falls outside the reasonable expectations of the adhering party, or the contract is unconscionable. Since the provision in this case was neither negotiated for nor explained, it would be unreasonable to enforce.

Halbman v. Lemke (1980)

Facts: Lemke sold a car to Halbman, a minor. Halbman took the car to a garage for repairs but refused to pay the bill. Halbman later disaffirmed the purchase contract, and the garage sold parts of the car to recover its money. The car was also vandalized. Halbman sued to recover the purchase price.

Issue: Is a minor who disaffirms a contract for an item that is not a necessity and tenders the property to the seller liable for damage to the property prior to the disaffirmance?

Rule: Absent misrepresentation or tortious damage to the property, a minor who disaffirms a contract for the purchase of an item that is not a necessity may recover his purchase price without liability for use, depreciation, damage, or other diminution in value.

Odorizzi v. Bloomfield School Dist. (1966)

Facts: Odorizzi, a teacher, was arrested for alleged homosexual activity. Immediately after he was released on bail, Bloomfield school district officials came to his home and made him sign a resignation, promising that if he did so, his "crime" would be kept quiet. Odorizzi was later acquitted of the charges and sued to rescind the resignation on grounds of undue influence by the school district.

Issue: Can a weak and vulnerable party rescind a contract that it assented to because of excessive pressure used by a dominant party?

Rule: A contract can be rescinded for undue influence if circumstances show that the agreement was reached through use of excessive persuasion by a dominant party against a weak and vulnerable one. Factors used to determine if excessive force was used are discussion or consummation of the transaction at an unusual place or time, insistent demands to get the business done at once, use of multiple persuaders against a single servient party and absence of and dissuasion of the need for third-party advisers to the servient party.

Austin Instrument, Inc. v. Loral Corp. (1971)

Facts: Loral had a contract to produce radar sets for the Navy. The sets had 40 component parts, of which Austin, a subcontractor, produced 23. When Loral received a second contract from the Navy, Austin bid on all 40 parts, threatening to stop delivery of all parts on the first contract if it did not receive a price increase and the subcontract for all 40 parts of the second contract. After unsuccessfully checking with all the other subcontractors on its approved list, Loral agreed to Austin's demands so as to avoid breaching its contract with the Navy.

Issue: Is a contract modification enforceable if it was agreed to by a party who was deprived of free will under circumstances amounting to economic duress?

Rule: A contract is voidable if the party claiming duress was forced to agree by means of a wrongful threat precluding the exercise of his free will. The existence of economic duress is demonstrated by proof that immediate possession of needed goods is threatened and that the goods could not be obtained from another source.

Alaska Packer's Assoc. v. Domenico (1902)

Facts: Sailors contracted to work for Alaska Packer's as fishermen in Alaska, at a rate of $60 for the season plus two cents for each fish caught. Upon arrival in Alaska, the sailors refused to work unless they received higher wages. Alaska Packer's agreed, due to the unavailability of alternative fishermen. Alaska Packer's subsequently refused to pay the higher wages.

Issue: Is an agreement to increase compensation for services that the promisee is already contractually obligated to perform enforceable?

Rule: A new promise to increase the compensation of one already contractually obligated to perform is invalid (pre-existing duty rule).

Brian Constr. & Dev. Co. Inc. v. Brighenti (1978)

Facts: The plaintiff, a contractor, hired the defendant, a subcontractor, to excavate, grade and landscape a foundation for a building. Unanticipated difficulties arose when the defendant unexpectedly discovered rubble from another building on the site, which made the work much more costly. The plaintiff orally promised to pay more after the defendant refused to continue. The defendant returned to work but quit after a week. He claimed he did not breach the contract because he did not give new consideration for the plaintiff's oral promise.

Issue: If unanticipated events make the required performance excessively burdensome, and the parties agree to adjust the compensation, does a valid new contract exist?

Rule: Where a subsequent agreement imposes upon the one seeking greater compensation an additional obligation or burden not previously assumed, the agreement is supported by consideration and is valid and binding upon the parties.

Note: This case illustrates the "unforeseen circumstances" exception to the pre-existing duty rule.

Universal Builders, Inc. v. Moon Motor Lodge, Inc. (1968)

Facts: Universal's construction contract with Moon provided in part that all requests for building modifications had to be written and signed by Moon or its architect. Moon's agent orally requested modifications and promised to pay. Although the agent watched the work being done, Moon refused to pay.

Issue: Is an unwritten contract modification that was agreed upon by both parties valid if a contract requires that modifications must be in writing?

Rule: The effectiveness of a non-written modification, in spite of a contract condition that modifications must be in writing, depends upon whether enforcement of the condition is or is not barred by equitable considerations. When one party materially changes its position in reliance on the other party's waiver of a contract condition that modifications must be in writing, the condition will not be enforced.

Hackley v. Headley (1881)

Facts: Hackley hired Headley to cut logs. Hackley disputed Headley's bill at the end of the job and tendered a smaller sum, which Headley was forced to accept due to financial difficulties. Headley signed a release accepting Hackley's payment as full satisfaction of the debt. Headley sought to rescind the release, claiming it was obtained through economic duress.

Issue: Is it economic duress to merely refuse to pay a debt?

Rule: The exercise of a legal right, such as the right to honestly dispute the value of services, does not constitute economic duress.

Headley v. Hackley (1883)

Facts: To settle a disputed debt he owed Headley, Hackley tendered a smaller sum, which was accepted. Headley claimed the settlement was void because Hackley manufactured a dispute in bad faith to extort a compromise.

Issue: Is a compromise agreement binding if a party negotiates in bad faith to obtain favorable terms?

Rule: A compromise agreement is unenforceable if one party obtained favorable terms by acting unfairly or oppressively and asserting claims that it knew to be void of right.

Marton Remodeling v. Jensen (1985)

Facts: Jensen hired Marton to do remodeling work on his home. The parties disagreed over the amount of the bill. Jensen sent a check for a smaller sum with the condition that endorsement of the check on the back by Marton would constitute full satisfaction. Marton cashed the check after writing "not full payment" on it and sued for the balance owed.
Issue: Has an accord and satisfaction occurred if a check marked "payment in full" is cashed with express protest?
Rule: An accord and satisfaction occurs even if a "payment in full" check is cashed under protest.
Note: UCC §1-207 does not displace the common law rule of accord and satisfaction.

Denney v. Reppert (1968)

Facts: In response to a reward offered by a bank, Denney and many other bank employees gave information that led to the conviction of bank robbers. The reward was given to Reppert, a policeman from another jurisdiction, who assisted in the conviction. Denney sued to receive part of the reward.
Issue: Can a reward offered to the general public be claimed by employees or public officials who acted within the scope of their employment or official duties?
Rule: If a party is already under a legal obligation to perform an act being rewarded, he has not provided consideration for the reward. A policeman is not legally obligated to assist in law enforcement outside of his jurisdiction, and such actions can therefore constitute consideration for a reward.

Jackson v. Seymour (1952)

Facts: Jackson, in need of money, sold a tract of land to her brother, Seymour, for $275. Unknown to both, the land contained valuable timber, on which Seymour made a profit of $2,300. Jackson wished to rescind her sale.
Issue: Can a contract be annulled because the consideration furnished by a party substantially exceeded the value of the consideration it received?
Rule: Generally, inadequate consideration is not grounds for rescinding an agreement. However, if the inadequacy is such as to shock the sensitivities, an agreement can be annulled on grounds of constructive (not actual) fraud. Factors to be considered are the relationship of the parties, the

inadequacy of the price, the parties' financial positions and the relative knowledge of the parties.

Note: The court granted Jackson rescission of the sale on the basis of these factors.

Sherwood v. Walker (1887)

Facts: Both parties believed that the cow Sherwood was buying from Walker was barren. Just before Walker delivered the cow he realized it was impregnated and, therefore, worth about ten times as much. Walker tried to rescind the contract.

Issue: Can a contract be rescinded if both parties are mistaken as to a material fact about the substance of the transaction?

Rule: No contract exists if the parties act under a mutual mistake of fact that is central to the "very nature" of the contract. Mistakes relating to "mere quality" are not grounds for rescission.

Laidlaw v. Organ (S. Ct. 1817)

Facts: Organ was negotiating to buy tobacco from Laidlaw. Organ heard news of the Treaty of Ghent, which ended the War of 1812 and the British blockage of New Orleans, and would cause an increase in the price of tobacco. When Laidlaw asked Organ if he had heard any news that would raise the price of the tobacco, Organ said that he did not. Subsequently, Organ bought the tobacco, but Laidlaw retrieved it after he heard of the Treaty and the resulting increase in the price of tobacco. Organ sued to recover the tobacco, and Laidlaw argued that Organ committed fraud by not disclosing news of the peace treaty.

Issue: Does a vendee have a duty to disclose information exclusively in his possession that is relevant to the price of a commodity?

Rule: (Marshall, C.J.) A vendee has no duty to disclose information exclusively in his possession that is relevant to the price of a commodity. It would be difficult to fashion a rule that compels disclosure when the methods of obtaining information are equally accessible to both parties.

Elsinore Union Elementary School District v. Kastorff (1960)

Facts: Kastorff, a contractor, submitted an erroneous bid for work that was being contracted out by the school district. Kastorff had told the school district that the figures were correct because he did not know of the error. He notified the school district upon learning of the error, which was caused by a clerical mistake. The school district "accepted" the bid despite knowing of the error. Kastorff refused to do the work.

Issue: Is a party relieved of its obligation to perform because its offering price was erroneously calculated?

Rule: A party may be relieved of the obligation to perform according to its offer if the party to whom the offer was made knew, or had reason to know, of a material error in calculation of the price.

Note: Although courts grant relief for clerical errors, this is not the case with errors of judgment, i.e., if a contractor underestimates his costs.

Hinson v. Jefferson (1975)

Facts: The defendants sold land to the plaintiff that was restricted by its deed to residential use only. The plaintiff had to build a septic tank to handle sewage. Before beginning work on the septic tank, the plaintiff was informed that she would have to spend several hundred thousand dollars to prepare the land for the tank because of a nearby marsh. The defendants did not know of the problem when they sold the land.

Issue: Is rescission appropriate if there is a mutual mistake at the time of contract as to the suitability of land for its intended use?

Rule: Although the doctrine of mutual mistake is not applicable in this jurisdiction (North Carolina), a contract may be rescinded where a deed contains restrictive covenants, and subsequent discoveries, which were unknown and not reasonably discoverable by the seller at the time of contract, show that the property cannot be put to the limited use permitted.

Johnson v. Healy (1978)

Facts: Johnson bought a house built by Healy, relying on Healy's assertions that the house was made of the best material and was without defects. After purchase, the house began to settle in such a way as to cause major displacements in foundation walls, and damage to sewer lines. Healy had no knowledge of the faulty construction when he sold the house.

Issue 1: What is the scope of liability for innocent misrepresentation (e.g., misleading statements made without knowledge or intent to deceive)?

Rule 1: Under Connecticut law, strict liability is imposed for innocent misrepresentation, as long as the statements can be reasonably understood as an assertion that the vendor has sufficient factual knowledge of the product, and could reasonably induce reliance by the purchaser.

Issue 2: What is the proper measure of damages for breach of warranty by a vendor?

Rule 2: Damage awards for breach of warranty should serve to place a party in the same position as they would have enjoyed had the good been as warranted.

Cushman v. Kirby (1987)

Facts: Plaintiffs purchased a home from Mr. and Mrs. Kirby. During an inspection of the premises, the plaintiffs asked about the quality of the water on the lot, to which Mrs. Kirby answered, "It's good. It's fine. It's a little hard, but the system downstairs will take care of it." Mr. Kirby, who was present, remained silent. Upon moving into the home, the plaintiffs discovered the water was actually sulfur water, which, due to its foul smell and taste, required treatment to become "tolerable." Instead of using the water on the lot, the plaintiffs chose to hook up to the city water supply and sue for misrepresentation.

Issue 1: What is the legal standard to be applied to determine the occurrence of an intentional misrepresentation?

Rule 1: When a vendor asserts that she has full information, and discloses only part of the information with the intent to deceive, she is guilty of fraud if the statements are relied upon by the purchaser.

Issue 2: When does a vendor's silence rise to the level of misrepresentation?

Rule 2: Silence alone is insufficient to constitute fraud, unless there is a duty to speak. A duty to speak is created where material facts are accessible to the vendor only, and he knows they are not available to the purchaser.

Williams v. Walker-Thomas Furniture Co. (1965)

Facts: Walker-Thomas sold a number of household items to Williams, on an installment plan. The sales contract had an "add on" clause, which stated that all of Williams' purchases were consolidated into a single debt, and that any payment would be credited equally, among all the items. The effect of the clause was that Williams would only own an item after she had paid for *all* of them. In case of default, the furniture was to be repossessed. Walker-Thomas sued to replevy the items, and Williams contested the contract.

Issue: Can a court refuse to enforce an unconscionable contract?

Rule: Where the element of unconscionability is present at the time the contract is made, the contract should not be enforced. Unconscionability has generally been recognized to include an absence of meaningful choice on the part of one of the parties in conjunction with contract terms unreasonably favorable to the other party. (UCC §2-302.)

Jones v. Star Credit Corp. (1969)

Facts: The Joneses, welfare recipients, were to pay $1,234.80 (including tax, finance charges, and insurance) for a freezer that ordinarily retailed for less than $300. UCC §2-302 provided that a court may refuse to enforce a contract or excise an objectionable clause if it finds that the contract or clause was unconscionable at the time it was made.

Issue: Can a contract be void for unconscionability because the price term is excessive?

Rule: A court may refuse to enforce an excessive price term on the grounds of unconscionability.

Kugler v. Romain (1971)

Facts: Romain sold educational books at two and one-half times the retail maximum price using a form contract. Romain's sales solicitations, consciously directed toward consumers of limited education and economic means, represented the exorbitant price as a competitive market rate. Pursuant to a state statute, Attorney General Kugler sued claiming fraud and misrepresentation.

Issue: Is a contract unenforceable if its price is unconscionable in relation to the cost to the seller and the value to the buyer?

Rule: A sales contract is invalid if a price, unilaterally fixed and not open to negotiation, is unconscionable in relation to the cost to the seller and the value to the consumers.

Stilk v. Myrick (1809)

Facts: After two sailors jumped ship, the defendant captain offered to divide their pay among the rest of the crew if they would finish the voyage shorthanded. Upon the captain's refusal to pay the extra wages a member of the crew sued.

Issue: Is an agreement for higher wages brought about as a result of an emergency situation enforceable?

Rule: Adjustments of an employment contract that are prompted by emergency situations are void for want of consideration under the pre-existing duty rule.

Lingenfelder v. Wainwright Brewery Co. (1891)

Facts: Wainwright hired an architect to design and supervise the construction of its brewery. The architect walked off the job after Wainwright awarded a different job to his competitor. Pressed for time, Wainwright promised to pay the architect extra compensation if he resumed work. Wainwright claimed it received no consideration for its promise. The architect's executor sought to enforce the modification.

Issue: Does the resumption of work one was contractually obligated to perform constitute sufficient consideration for a promise that induced the return to work?

Rule: A new contract that was signed to prevent one party from breaching an earlier agreement will fail for lack of consideration.

Note: This is the "pre-existing duty" rule.

Goebel v. Linn (1882)

Facts: The plaintiff, an ice supplier, informed the defendants, brewers, that it could not supply the contractually required amount because of a shortage in the ice crop. The beer brewers needed the ice and agreed to pay more. The ice company sued after the brewers defaulted on the payments.

Issue: Is an agreement for a party to receive additional compensation for contractual duties enforceable?

Rule: Absent a showing of duress, an agreement for a party to receive additional payment for pre-existing contractual duties is enforceable.

Schwartzreich v. Bauman-Basch, Inc. (1921)

Facts: Schwartzreich contracted to work for Bauman-Basch for one year at $90 a week. Before beginning work, Schwartzreich was offered $115 a week by another employer. Bauman-Basch offered to raise his weekly salary to $100, and Schwartzreich accepted. Another contract was made, reflecting the new salary provision, and the old one was simultaneously torn up. Bauman-Basch fired him before the year passed, claiming the second contract was unenforceable for lack of consideration.

Issue: Is a new contract that replaces a prior contract with terms that are similar but more favorable to one party enforceable?

Rule: When an existing contract is terminated by mutual consent and a new one is executed in its place, the mutual promises of the parties constitute consideration. Any changes to an existing contract must have new consideration to support it.

Foakes v. Beer (1884)

Facts: Beer, Foakes' creditor, agreed to forgive all the interest on Foakes' loan if he paid a quarter of the principal at once and the rest in installments. After Foakes completed the installments, Beer sued for the interest.

Issue: Will an agreement to forgo the interest due on a loan in exchange for payment of the principal fail for lack of consideration?

Rule: A creditor's agreement to forgo interest on a debt in exchange for repayment of principal fails for lack of consideration because the debtor only agreed to do that which he was already obligated to perform (pre-existing duty rule).

Consolidated Edison Co. of New York, Inc. v. Arroll (1971)

Facts: After disputing the amount of his electric bills, the defendant arbitrarily selected the amount he thought the bills should have been and sent checks that bore the legend "this check is in full payment and satisfaction." Con. Edison cashed the checks and sued to recover what it felt was still owed.

Issue: Does writing the phrase "full payment and satisfaction" on a check that is tendered for less than the disputed amount of a debt result in a full accord and satisfaction?

Rule: When an amount due is in bona fide dispute, and the debtor sends a check for less than the amount claimed and clearly expresses his intention that the check has been sent as payment in full, cashing or retention of the check by the creditor is deemed an acceptance by the creditor of the conditions stated and operates as an accord and satisfaction of the claim.

Note: Under UCC §1-107, a creditor can reserve his rights to the outstanding debt.

Petterson v. Pattberg (1928)

Facts: Pattberg held a mortgage on Petterson's property and offered to reduce it if Petterson paid off the mortgage by a certain time. Petterson tendered payment according to the terms of the offer, but Pattberg had already sold the mortgage to another party. The plaintiff was the executrix of Petterson's estate.

Issue: Is an offer to enter into a unilateral contract revocable before the other party performs the act requested?

Rule: An offer to enter into a unilateral contract is revocable at any time before the other party performs the requested act.

Goldbard v. Empire State Mutual Life Ins. Co. (1958)

Facts: Goldbard, a barber, filed for insurance benefits after he was infected by a fungus. The insurer disputed the claim, and Goldbard filed a complaint with the State Insurance Department. The insurer offered to settle the claim for a lesser amount. Goldbard telephoned the department representative and, without any discussion of precise terms, accepted the insurer's offer to settle the claim. But when the insurer sent a release form to execute the settlement, Goldbard ignored it and sued for the entire claim.

Issue: When does a subsequent agreement substitute for an existing contract?

Rule: For a subsequent agreement to supersede an existing contract, the parties must objectively manifest such an intent and all the requirements for an enforceable contract must be satisfied (such as a writing where compelled by statute).

Raffles v. Wichelhaus (1864)

Facts: The contract stated that the plaintiff was to deliver the goods on the ship *Peerless*. Unknown to both parties there were two different ships bearing the same name but sailing at different times. The defendant refused the plaintiff's goods because he expected the delivery to be made on the *Peerless* that sailed earlier.

Issue: Is there a contract if each party gives a different meaning to a material ambiguity in the contract?

Rule: There is no binding contract if the parties unknowingly assign different meanings to an important contract term. Parol evidence may be given to prove that the parties attributed different meanings to a term.

Wood v. Boynton (1885)

Facts: Wood sued for rescission when she learned that a stone she sold to Boynton for $1 was worth $700.

Issue: Can a seller rescind a sale if both parties were mistaken as to the value of the product sold?

Rule: If there is no evidence of fraud, a mutual mistake as to the value of the product sold is not grounds for rescission of the sale.

Swinton v. Whitinsville Sav. Bank (1942)

Facts: The Whitinsville Bank knew the house that Swinton was purchasing from it was infested with termites but it did not disclose this information to Swinton.

Issue: Is a party to a contract obligated to reveal known latent defects to the other party?

Rule: There is no liability for bare nondisclosure when parties deal at arm's length, provided a false representation or attempt to conceal the condition was not made.

Sardo v. Fidelity & Deposit Co. (1926)

Facts: Sardo wished to obtain theft insurance for jewelry in his store. The defendant issued an insurance policy that covered securities instead of jewelry, even though there were no securities in Sardo's store. Sardo did not read the policy and mistakenly assumed that it covered jewelry. Sardo's store was robbed, and the defendant refused coverage. Sardo brought suit and had the policy reformed to include jewelry.

Issue: In the absence of fraud, when may a contract be reformed?
Rule: A contract may be reformed, in the absence of fraud, when after the parties have come to a "meeting of the minds," a mutual mistake is made in drafting the contract such that the writing does not reflect the actual intent of the parties. An assumption by one party made without reading a contract does not amount to mutual mistake.

Weaver v. American Oil Co. (1971)

Facts: Unknown to Weaver, a clause in his standardized lease compelled him to indemnify American Oil, the lessor, for any damages or loss incurred as a result of American Oil's own negligence. The clause, which was never explained to Weaver, was written in small print and contained no title heading. Weaver claimed the clause was unconscionable after one of American's employees negligently injured Weaver and an assistant on the leased premises.
Issue: Is a contract clause obtained by the abuse of a party's superior bargaining position unconscionable?
Rule: The doctrine of unconscionability will invalidate a contract provision if, unknown to the lesser party, a stronger party uses his superior bargaining power to his advantage in instituting a contract provision that causes the lesser party great hardship (e.g., by unknowingly waiving valuable rights).

Toker v. Westerman (1970)

Facts: Westerman argued that he paid an "unconscionable" price for a refrigerator. Westerman was charged $1,229.76 for an appliance with a fair market value of between $350 and $400. Toker, the assignee of the seller, sued when Westerman refused to make full payment.
Issue: Can a contract be voided because its terms are "unconscionable"?
Rule: A contract can be voided because the price was unconscionable. (UCC §2-302.)

Griffith v. Brymer (1903)

Facts: Griffith contracted to rent a room from Brymer for the purpose of viewing a coronation procession. Neither party was aware that the coronation had been canceled prior to the formation of the contract.
Issue: Is a contract void if there is a mutual mistake as to facts central to the purpose of the agreement?
Rule: A contract is void where both parties are under a misconception with regard to the existing state of facts about which they were contracting.

Lenawee County Bd. of Health v. Messerly (1982)

Facts: Unknown to the Messerlys, a previous owner of the land had installed an illegal underground septic tank. The Messerlys then sold the property, which included a three-unit apartment building, to Pickles. The contract had an "as is" clause, which shifted the risk of unknown defects to Pickles. Six days after the sale, sewage from the tank oozed up to the surface of the property, and the county condemned the property until the sewage system could conform to the sanitation code.

Issue: Is a hidden defect sufficient grounds for rescission of a contract on the basis of mutual mistake?

Rule: A rescission on the grounds of mutual mistake may be granted when the mistake relates to a basic assumption of the parties upon which the contract is made, and which materially affects the agreed performances of the parties. However, where both parties are equally innocent and have agreed to allocate the risk of loss, rescission will not be granted.

Note: Courts are divided on the effectiveness of "as is" clauses. (Rest. 2d §124.)

1. Travelers Ins. Co. v. Bailey (1964)

Facts: Travelers Insurance printed Bailey's correct descriptive information on the wrong life insurance policy form, giving Bailey more extensive coverage than he paid for. Bailey refused to accept Travelers' attempt to amend the policy so as to correct its mistake.

Issue: Is a party entitled to reformation of a contract where it is penalized by its own erroneous rendition of the agreement?

Rule: Where it is established beyond a reasonable doubt that a contractual agreement between parties was erroneously executed, the party penalized by the error is entitled to reformation, provided there has been no prejudicial change of position by the party benefiting from the mistake.

Bowling v. Sperry (1962)

Facts: Bowling sought to disaffirm a contract for the purchase of an automobile on the grounds that he was a minor. Sperry alleged the defenses that Bowling was accompanied by adults when he made the purchase, that Bowling damaged the car and that the car was a necessity.

Issue: Is a contract of a minor voidable if he was accompanied by an adult at the time of purchase?

Rule: Contracts of minors, except for necessities, are voidable even if the minor is accompanied by an adult at the time of purchase and/or the seller is not returned to the status quo.

Heights Realty, Ltd. v. Phillips (1988)

Facts: Gholson (the original defendant), an aged woman, signed a contract with Heights Realty, under which it listed Gholson's property for sale and found a buyer. Heights Realty was to receive a commission on the sale. The buyer offered an amount greater than the asking price, but Phillips, the conservator of her estate, refused to sell. Heights Realty sought its commission, and the defendant claimed mental incapacity as a defense. Significant but inconclusive evidence was presented to establish Gholson's incompetency and the trial court found for her.

Issue: May a party succeed with a defense of mental incompetence if there is conflicting evidence that indicates she understood the general purpose of the contract and possibly understood the specific terms?

Rule: There is a presumption of mental competency that can only be overcome by clear and convincing evidence. However, where a trial court has weighed all evidence and concluded that a party was mentally incompetent to contract, the presence of conflicting evidence is insufficient to overturn the decision on appeal.

Vokes v. Arthur Murray, Inc. (1968)

Facts: Vokes was unwittingly influenced by a constant and continuous barrage of flattery, false praise, and excessive compliments from Arthur Murray's employees to purchase thousands of hours of dancing lessons at the dance studio.

Issue: Are misrepresentations of opinion by a party possessing superior knowledge actionable?

Rule: A statement of a party having superior knowledge is regarded as a statement of fact, which is actionable if false, even though it would be deemed as opinion if the parties were dealing on equal terms.

Hill v. Jones (1986)

Facts: The Hills sued to rescind an agreement to purchase a house from the Joneses, alleging that the Joneses had made misrepresentations concerning termite damage to the house, and had failed to disclose the existence of the damage and the history of termite infestation.

Issue: Does a seller of residential property have a duty to disclose defects?

Rule: Where the seller of a home knows of facts materially affecting the value of the property, which are not readily observable and are not known to the buyer, the seller is under a duty to disclose them to the buyer. The instant case was remanded for a jury determination of whether the termite damage was material and whether it was readily observable.

Machinery Hauling, Inc. v. Steel of W. Virginia (1989)

Facts: Machinery Hauling was hired to deliver 17 loads of steel for Steel. When all but three were delivered, Steel informed Machinery Hauling that the buyer had rejected the product. Steel directed Machinery Hauling to return the last three loads. Steel then instructed the plaintiff to pay it the price of the last three loads ($31,000) "or else it would cease to do business with plaintiff." The potential loss of business was over $1 million per year. Machinery Hauling sought monetary damages for Steel's "extortionate demands."

Issue: Does the threat to discontinue business relations constitute economic duress?

Rule: Economic duress occurs where a party is forced into a transaction as a result of unlawful threats by another party that leaves it with no reasonable alternative but to acquiesce. Economic duress was not found in this case because the plaintiff did not accede to the defendant's demand and pay over the money, and the expectancy of future business prospects (as opposed to present contractual obligations) is not a right on which a claim of economic duress may be anchored.

Zapatha v. Dairy Mart, Inc. (1980)

Facts: The Zapathas contracted to operate a franchise for Dairy Mart, whereby Dairy Mart provided the store and equipment and paid the utility bills in exchange for a percentage of gross profits. The contract was terminable without cause on 90 days' notice provided Dairy Mart bought back 80 percent of the inventory. Dairy Mart terminated.

Issue: Is a contract clause that permits termination without cause unconscionable?

Rule: A contract provision that provides for termination without cause is not unconscionable if at the time of the execution of the agreement the provision could not result in unfair surprise, was not oppressive, and was not instituted in bad faith toward the allegedly disadvantaged party.

Sinnar v. Le Roy (1954)

Facts: The plaintiff gave a bribe in return for the defendant's promise to help the plaintiff obtain a liquor license. The defendant reneged, and the plaintiff sued to recover the bribe.

Issue: Is an illegal bargain enforceable?

Rule: Courts will not enforce an illegal bargain but will leave the parties where it finds them. Because these bargains violate public policy to a great degree, relief is denied on the basis of illegality if the issue appears in the evidence. A defendant cannot waive the defense if he wishes to do so.

Pearsall v. Alexander (1990)

Facts: Pearsall and Alexander regularly purchased D.C. lottery tickets together, reinvesting their small returns in more tickets. One lucky day, a ticket purchased and scratched by Alexander was a $20,000 winner. Alexander did not want to share the bounty. The Statute of Anne provided that "a thing in action . . . or conveyance made and executed be a person in which any part of the consideration is for money . . . won by playing any game whatsoever . . . or for the reimbursement or payment of any money knowingly lent or advanced [to place a bet] is void. . . ."

Issue: Is a claim to a share of lottery winnings enforceable?

Rule: A claim to a share of legal gambling winnings is enforceable where each man gives consideration for a share in the proceeds. The Statute of Anne does not bar such claims, because such consideration does not derive from one man besting the other in a game of chance or from any sort of a loan.

Homami v. Iranzadi (1989)

Facts: Iranzadi repaid Homami $40,000 on a $125,000 note that stated, "This note shall bear no interest." Homami claimed that the parties had orally agreed that there would be interest and had included the no-interest provision for the purpose of evading income taxes. The trial court concluded that the payment did indeed constitute interest, not principal and ruled that Homami was entitled to the full amount of the note.

Issue: Can a collateral agreement to pay interest on a note that explicitly states that it does not bear interest be enforced?

Rule: Where a note has no stated interest for the purpose of facilitating tax evasion, a collateral interest agreement will not be enforced because illegal contracts are never enforceable.

Data Management, Inc. v. Greene (1985)

Facts: The defendants, former employees of Data, had signed a covenant not to compete with Data in Alaska for five years after termination. Shortly after the defendants' termination, Data sought an injunction to enjoin the defendants from rendering computing services to various named individuals.

Issue: Should courts enforce overly broad covenants not to compete?

Rule: Whenever possible, overly broad covenants not to compete should be reasonably altered by courts to render them enforceable, unless they were not drafted in good faith. The factors comprising reasonableness are the absence or presence of limitations as to time and space, whether the employee represents the sole contract with the customer, whether the employee is possessed with confidential information or trade secrets, whether the covenant seeks to eliminate unfair competition or ordinary competition, whether the covenant seeks to stifle the inherent skill and experience of the employee, whether the benefit to the employer is disproportionate to the detriment to the employee, whether the covenant operates to bar the employee's sole means of support, whether the talents the employer seeks to suppress were developed during the period of employment and whether the forbidden employment is merely incidental to the main employment.

Watts v. Watts (1987)

Facts: The plaintiff and defendant lived together out of wedlock for 12 years in a relationship that produced 2 children. They shared bank accounts, made joint income tax returns, and were listed as husband and wife on other legal documents.

Issue: Does public policy preclude an unmarried cohabitant from asserting contract and property claims against the other party to the cohabitation?

Rule: Public policy does not necessarily preclude an unmarried cohabitant from asserting a contract claim against the other party to the cohabitation so long as the claim exists independently of the sexual relationship (i.e., is founded in breach of implied or express contract, quantum meruit, etc.) and is supported by separate consideration.

Angel v. Murray (1974)

Facts: After he signed a five-year garbage collection contract, Maher requested increased remuneration because an unanticipated construction boom substantially increased the number of homes from which he had to collect garbage. The city council agreed to pay more. Several years later, taxpayers, including the plaintiff Angel, brought suit against Murray, the director of finance for the city, claiming that no consideration was given for the promise to pay more.

Issue: Can a contract be modified because of unanticipated difficulties?

Rule: The pre-existing duty rule, voiding modification of a contract already in effect if no new consideration is given, will not apply, if a party to a contract encounters unanticipated difficulties and the other party, not influenced by coercion or duress, voluntarily agrees to pay additional compensation for work already required to be performed under the contract.

Roth Steel Prod. v. Sharon Steel Corp. (1983)

Facts: Sharon threatened to breach its contract to supply steel if Roth did not agree to price increases. Although Sharon's motive was due to rising costs, it did not offer this explanation until the case came to trial.

Issue: Is an attempted contract modification to compensate for rising costs ineffective if the party did not act in good faith?

Rule: Contract modification must be obtained in good faith by conduct that is both consistent with "reasonable commercial standards of fair dealing in the trade" and "honesty in fact," to be enforceable. (UCC §2-103(1)(b).)

Pettit v. Liston (1920)

Facts: A minor purchased a motorcycle from Liston for $325 of which he paid $125 down, the balance to be paid in $25 monthly installments. After a month, the minor returned the machine and demanded his money back. Liston claimed he had damaged the machine in excess of $150.

Issue: May a minor, who has purchased and taken possession of an article, return it to the vendor and recover his money without paying for any damage?

Rule: When there has been no fraud or undue influence and the contract is fair and reasonable, a minor who has actually paid money on the purchase price and taken and used the article cannot recover the amount of money paid without allowing the vendor reasonable compensation for the use and depreciation of the article while in his hands.

Note: "The privilege of infancy is to be used as a shield and not as a sword."

Ortelere v. Teachers' Retirement Bd. (1969)

Facts: Ortelere's wife, a teacher, built up a reserve of $70,925 in the public retirement system. Ortelere quit his job to care for his wife when she suffered a nervous breakdown. Two months before she died, while suffering from mental illness, Ortelere's wife exercised an irrevocable option to take maximum retirement benefits, depriving him of any right to the remaining portion of her retirement fund at her death.

Issue: Is a contract voidable if a contracting party cannot act reasonably due to mental incapacity?

Rule: A person incurs only voidable contractual duties by entering into a transaction if, by reason of mental illness or defect, she is unable to act in a reasonable manner in relation to the transaction and the other party has reason to know of her condition.

Gallon v. Lloyd-Thomas Co. (1959)

Facts: Gallon claimed that he was coerced into signing an unfavorable employment contract with his employers. In any event, he abided by the terms of the contract for the remaining time he was employed and did not bring legal action for nearly a year.

Issue 1: When is a contract voidable on the grounds of duress?
Rule 1: The contract is voidable when the threats of the person claiming the benefit of the contract eliminated the quality of mind in the victim essential to the making of the contract.
Issue 2: Is a contract entered into as a result of duress ratified after the duress is removed if no claim is made within a reasonable amount of time?
Rule 2: Ratification of a duress-induced contract results if the party who executed the contract under duress accepts the benefits flowing from it or remains silent for any considerable length of time after the opportunity is afforded to render it void.

Francois v. Francois (1979)

Facts: Victor Francois signed a financially disastrous "Property Settlement and Separation Agreement" with his wife because she and her attorney persuaded him that it was the only way to save their marriage. Victor sought rescission of the agreement and reconveyance of all properties transferred to his wife.
Issue: When does the doctrine of undue influence permit the rescission of a contract?
Rule: A contract may be rescinded when a party's assent to an agreement is obtained through the subversion of that party's free will contrary to his own best interests.

Methodist Mission Home of Texas v. N. A. B. (1970)

Facts: Methodist Mission operated as a maternity home and licensed adoption agency to provide care to pregnant unwed women. In addition to board, lodging, and medical care, Methodist Mission provided counseling by trained social workers who strongly encouraged putting the children up for adoption. The lower court held that Methodist Mission used "undue influence" to get N. A. B. to consent to the adoption of her soon-to-be born son.
Issue: When does the "undue influence" doctrine apply?
Rule: Not all influence is "undue" merely because it is persuasive and effective. The finding of "undue influence" is justified only where the actor's free agency and will have been destroyed or subverted to the extent that her act does not express her own will but instead reflects that of the person exerting the influence.

Cousineau v. Walker (1980)

Facts: Cousineau purchased a 9.1 acre lot from Walker after seeing a listing that it contained a large quantity of gravel and 580 feet in highway frontage. However, there was no mention of the amount of gravel or highway frontage in the purchasing agreement. After signing the agreement, Cousineau discovered there was only 415 feet of highway frontage and a small quantity of gravel. He stopped making payments and sought rescission of the contract.

Issue: Is innocent misrepresentation a basis for the rescission of a contract?

Rule: A party is entitled to rescission of a land purchase contract on the basis of misrepresentation if it in fact relied on the statement, the statement concerned a material fact that a reasonable person might be expected to consider important in making a decision, and the reliance was justifiable.

Note: The court also held that caveat emptor did not apply to a purchaser of land and that the purchaser would only be barred from recovery if his actions in failing to discover the defects were irrational or in bad faith.

White v. Berenda Mesa Water Dist. (1970)

Facts: White submitted a bid to build a reservoir for the District. He underestimated the amount of hard rock to be excavated and consequently his bid was too low. White rescinded his bid but the District had voted to accept it and sought to keep White's bid bond.

Issue: When will rescission be allowed for a unilateral mistake containing elements of fact and judgment?

Rule: While traditionally it is only mistakes of fact that permit a grant of relief, it is the facts surrounding the mistake, not a label of "fact" or "judgment" that should control. The law does require, however, that the mistake has not resulted from a party's neglect of a legal duty.

Bollinger v. Cent. Pennsylvania Quarry Stripping & Constr. Co. (1967)

Facts: A written agreement allowed Pennsylvania Quarry to deposit waste on the Bollingers' property. The Bollingers averred that there was a mutual understanding mistakenly not included in the document that Pennsylvania Quarry would cover the waste with topsoil. Pennsylvania Quarry covered the waste at first, but later stopped.

Issue: Will a contract be reformed if part of the agreement was omitted by mutual mistake?

Rule: A court in equity has the power to reform the written evidence of a contract and make it correspond to the understanding of the parties if the omission was caused by mutual mistake. The fact that one of the parties denies that a mistake was made does not prevent a finding of mutual mistake.

K.D. v. Educational Testing Service (1976)

Facts: While registering to take the LSAT, K.D. signed a stipulation stating that the Educational Testing Service (ETS) "reserve[d] the right to cancel any test score if ... there is adequate reason to question its validity." Finding a suspiciously high correlation between K.D. and a nearby student, ETS offered a free retest as an alternative to canceling K.D.'s score. In seeking to enjoin the ETS from canceling his score (he refused the retest), K.D. claimed that he was not bound because it was a contract of adhesion, as he was unable to negotiate its terms or contract elsewhere.

Issue: When may a contract be voided on the grounds that it was an adhesion contract?

Rule: An offending clause of a contract of adhesion may be voided if it is found to be unfair and unreasonable. Here, the court found that ETS had taken a reasonable measure to protect its reputation for accurate aptitude forecasting.

Hewitt v. Hewitt (1974)

Facts: The plaintiff and defendant agreed to live together and share assets and earnings as a husband and wife would. The plaintiff worked hard to support the defendant's education, business and social interests. Although the parties held themselves out as husband and wife, they were not formally married. Common law marriage was not recognized in their jurisdiction. The plaintiff sued to recover half the assets at separation.

Issue: Can two unmarried persons be required to share equally in income and assets if they agreed to such a plan, even though both were aware they were not legally married?

Rule: Courts can determine that the conduct of unmarried persons living together demonstrates an implied contract or an agreement of partnership or joint venture. A nonmarital partner can recover in quantum meruit for the reasonable value of services rendered, less the reasonable value of support received, if s/he can show that services were rendered with the expectation of monetary reward.

Troutman v. Southern Railway Co. (1971)

Facts: The Interstate Commerce Commission issued an order that Southern Railway feared would have a detrimental effect on it and the entire Southern economy. The railway turned to Troutman, a personal friend and ally of President John Kennedy, to persuade the President and Department of Justice to enter the case on the side of Southern. Troutman was successful, and the Justice Department helped Southern win in court against the I.C.C. Troutman demanded compensation for his services.

Issue: Is a contract to exert political and personal influence to gain access to an elected official enforceable?

Rule: Although a contract to use political and personal influence on a public official in the exercise of his duties is illegal and unenforceable, a contract is enforceable when it merely calls for a party to use personal and political influence to gain access and appeal to the judgment of a political official on the merits of the case.

Note: The burden of proving the illegality of the contract is on the party asserting the defense.

Northern Indiana Pub. Serv. Co. v. Carbon County Coal Co. (1986)

Facts: NIPSCO, a public utility, entered into a long-term fixed-price contract to buy coal from Carbon County. Over time, this became a very expensive contract for NIPSCO. It sought to escape it on the grounds, among others, that Carbon County's coal sales were in violation of the Federal Mineral Land Leasing Act of 1920 due to an attenuated affiliation it enjoys with a railroad.

Issue: Will the court enforce a contract that contains elements of illegality?

Rule: The court will weigh the relative benefits of under-deterrence and over-deterrence of illegal behavior. If the illegal act is relatively minor, and it has injured neither the party with which it is contracting nor others, the contract will be enforced.

Bateman Eichler, Hill Richards, Inc. v. Berner (1985)

Facts: A registered securities broker employed by Bateman Eichler induced the plaintiffs to invest in over-the-counter stock by divulging false and materially incomplete information about a company on the pretext it was accurate inside information. The investors purchased the stock, which initially increased dramatically but ultimately declined below the purchase price.

Issue: May a party assert the *in pari delicto* defense barring recovery when both parties are equal wrongdoers in private actions for damages based on federal securities law?

Rule: The *in pari delicto* defense is not permitted except where, as a direct result of his own actions, the plaintiff bears at least substantially equal responsibility for the violations he seeks to redress, and preclusions of suit would not significantly interfere with the effective enforcement of the securities laws and protection of the investing public.

Singleton v. Foreman (1970)

Facts: Singleton employed Foreman to represent her in a divorce action. The parties signed a contract that contained provisions for retainer and contingency fees. Foreman was so verbally abusive and threatening in his behavior toward Singleton that she sought rescission and restitution of her retainer. Contracts for a contingency fee in divorce cases were void and unenforceable under Florida law.

Issue: May the court aid a party to an illegal contract?

Rule: If a party cannot be considered *in pari delicto*, the court may aid a party to the extent of returning the consideration that was tendered in performance of its part of the invalid contract.

Cochran v. Dellfava (1987)

Facts: Cochran sought to recover from Dellfava for the money she lost in the so-called airplane game. This enterprise was a chain distribution game that was prohibited by statute. Knowing it was illegal, Cochran agreed to play. After she had invested money in the scheme, she attempted to withdraw.

Issue: Are there exceptions to the general rule that the court will leave the parties to an illegal contract where their own acts have left them?

Rule: The court will aid a party when the conduct was prohibited by statute rather than by the nature of the conduct, the parties were not *in pari delicto*, and the plaintiff acted under duress, undue influence or out of good will.

Note: Cochran's claim failed because she intentionally promoted the game by entering it.

Copeland Process Corp. v. Nalews, Inc. (1973)

Facts: Due to a delay in progress on two town projects and an upcoming meeting to account for such delay, Copeland, the contractor, terminated its subcontract with Nalews for labor, materials, and services. The letter of termination was a writing of an oral agreement between Nalews and Copeland stating that Nalews would be compensated for cost under the contract thus far and that otherwise the contract was mutually canceled "without prejudice." The language suggested that Nalews was not responsible for future costs incurred by Copeland in the project's completion.

Issue: What effect does mutual rescission of a contract have on the past and future obligations of the parties?

Rule: The obligations of parties following mutual rescission of a contract are to be determined by the intent of the parties as reflected in circumstances surrounding the contract and rescission.

Dodson v. Shrader (1992)

Facts: Dodson bought a truck from the Shraders when he was 16 years old. Nine months later, the truck began to develop engine trouble. Although Dodson was warned by a mechanic that repairs were probably necessary, Dodson ignored the advice and continued to drive the truck. One month later, the truck "blew up" and became inoperable. The truck was damaged further just before the trial, when it was struck by a hit-and-run driver while parked in Dodson's front yard. Dodson told the Shraders he wanted to return the truck, rescind the contract, and obtain a full refund.

Issue: If a party to a sales contract was a minor at the time the contract was made, can the party freely rescind the contract, return the goods, and obtain a full refund?

Rule: If a sales contract to which a minor is a party is freely and fairly formed in good faith, the minor may rescind the contract and obtain a refund, but must allow the vendor reasonable compensation for the depreciation of the goods while they were in the minor's possession.

Totem Marine Tug & Barge, Inc. v. Alyeska Pipeline Service Co. (1978)

Facts: Totem agreed to transport materials from Texas to Alaska for Alyeska Pipeline. Totem encountered many unforeseen difficulties that delayed delivery and increased the transportation costs. After Alyeska promised to pay the increased costs, Totem took out short-term loans to finance its performance. However, Alyeska ordered Totem to dock at Long Beach, California, off-loaded the materials, and terminated the contract without explanation. Totem pressed Alyeska to pay for the transport from Texas to California, but Alyeska resisted. In desperate need of cash to pay off its short-term loans, Totem agreed to release Alyeska from all claims by Totem in exchange for one-third of the amount due. After receiving the settlement payment and paying its immediate debts, Totem sued to have the settlement agreement rescinded on grounds of economic duress.

Issue: When may a party to a contract rescind on grounds of economic duress?

Rule: A party may rescind a contract on grounds of economic duress if the party seeking rescission involuntarily agreed to the transaction due to the wrongful acts and threats of the other party and circumstances were such that the party had no reasonable alternative but to agree to the terms or face serious financial hardship.

Note: This rule embraces several competing policies: the court's desire to correct inequitable or unequal exchanges between parties of unequal bargaining power, the court's reluctance to interfere with the freedom to contract, and the court's desire to encourage private settlement of disputes.

Syester v. Banta (1965)

Facts: The defendants owned a dance studio. Over the course of a year, the defendants sold Syester, a widow in her late 60s, over 3,000 hours of dance lessons at a cost of over $29,000. The defendants employed a wide variety of representations to persuade Syester to purchase the lessons, including promises that the lessons would make her a "professional dancer." The defendant's also exploited Syester's affection for one of the young dance instructors to effect the sales. Syester sued the defendants, but the defendants employed similar tactics to persuade Syester to dismiss the suit and sign two settlement agreements. Shortly afterwards, Syester sued again, alleging fraud and misrepresentation in the defendant's sales and settlement negotiations.

Issue: When may a contract be voided for fraud and misrepresentation?

Rule: A contract may be voided for fraud or misrepresentation when a party is damaged because she relied on false representations of a material matter intentionally and knowingly made by the other party. The court found that the plaintiff in this case had fallen victim to a calculated course of intentional misrepresentations on the part of the defendants.

Wil-Fred's, Inc. v. Metropolitan Sanitary District (1978)

Facts: Wil-Fred's submitted a closed bid and security deposit for a District project. Wil-Fred's was the lowest bidder and was awarded the contract. Because of a mistake by a subcontractor, Wil-Fred's could not perform the contract at its bid price and requested rescission of the bid and return of its deposit.

Issue: Can a contract be rescinded because of a unilateral mistake?

Rule: Rescission of a contract for a unilateral mistake is granted if clear and positive evidence shows that the mistake occurred notwithstanding the exercise of reasonable care; that it is of such grave consequence that enforcement of the contract would be unconscionable; and that the other party can be restored to its original position.

United States ex rel. Crane Co. v. Progressive Enterprises, Inc. (1976)

Facts: Crane contracted to sell a machine to Progressive. Later, Crane sought to raise the machine's price and Progressive acquiesced to the higher price without objection. After delivery of the machine, Progressive refused to pay the new price claiming that the modification was not freely entered into.

Issue: When are modifications to sales agreements unenforceable because they were entered into involuntarily?

Rule: Modification of sales agreements are permitted so long as they are executed in good faith. If the buyer is opposed to a modification he must display some protest against it in order to put the seller on notice. This allows the parties to rely on objective, unequivocal manifestations of assent to modifications.

Bovard v. American Horse Enterprises, Inc. (1988)

Facts: Bovard sued to recover on promissory notes executed in connection with another party's purchase of American Horse Enterprises, which manufactured illegal drug paraphernalia.

Issue: Under what circumstances is a contract illegal and void as contrary to public policy?

Rule: A contract that is contrary to the policy of the express law is illegal and void. Factors that should be considered in determining whether a contract violates public policy include the nature of the conduct, the extent of public harm that may be involved, and the moral quality of the conduct of the parties in light of the prevailing standards of the community.

Williams v. Patton (1991)

Facts: Williams failed to pay child support for eight years. Patton filed a motion for contempt for failure to pay, as well as a motion to modify child support. While the suit was pending, Williams and Patton entered a settlement agreement. The court, however, would not release Williams from his obligation to pay the support in arrears.

Issue: Is a settlement between parents concerning child support payments made before the amount due has been reduced to a final judgment void as against public policy?

Rule: Child support settlements may not be entered into before the unpaid support amount has been reduced to a final judgment. The purpose of this rule is to protect the best interests of the child by encouraging payment of child support, and to protect custodial parents by putting them in a more equal position with non-custodial parents.

Ellis v. Mullen (1977)

Facts: Ellis, who was illiterate, sought to recover damages for personal injuries he suffered when his car was hit by Mullen. Mullen alleged contributory negligence and pled that his insurance company had issued four settlement drafts, totaling $900, two of which were signed by Ellis, stating that the Ellis' endorsements would constitute "full and complete settlement to all claims."

Issue: Is the endorsement of a written release by an illiterate plaintiff enforceable?

Rule: Illiterate persons who are ignorant of the contents of contracts signed by them may be relieved of their obligations under the contract if it is proven that the other party took unfair advantage of their disability.

S.P. Dunham and Co. v. Kudra (1957)

Facts: Dunham, a department store owner, leased its fur department to Hurwitz, a third party. Kudra cleaned and stored furs for Hurwitz, a service for which Kudra was owed a large sum of money. Hurwitz went bankrupt, and Dunham, wishing to fill Hurwitz's back orders, asked Kudra for Hurwitz's stored furs. Kudra refused delivery unless Dunham would cover Hurwitz's debt. Dunham complied for fear of losing valuable customers. Dunham brought an action in restitution, alleging its payments had been made under "business compulsion."

Issue: What constitutes "business compulsion" for which a plaintiff is entitled to restitution?

Rule: A plaintiff is entitled to judgment for "business compulsion," a type of duress, when a defendant's actions induce compliance with improper demands, and the plaintiff lacked a complete and adequate remedy in the courts to resist the demands.

Selmer Co. v. Blakeslee-Midwest Co. (1983)

Facts: Selmer was a subcontractor on a construction project for Blakeslee. Blakeslee failed to fulfill its contractual obligations entitling Selmer to terminate the contract. Instead, Selmer orally agreed to complete the work, provided that it would be paid for the extra costs of completion. Selmer demanded its payment, but Blakeslee offered to settle for little more than one-half the amount due. Selmer accepted the settlement because it was strapped for cash.

Issue: When is economic duress a legitimate defense to invalidate the settlement of a contract dispute?

Rule: Economic duress occurs when a party is forced to accept a contract modification, or else incur costs for which no adequate legal remedy would be available. Since the threatening party's conduct is the primary concern, financial difficulty on the part of the party claiming duress is not enough by itself to justify setting aside a settlement.

Perdue v. Crocker National Bank (1985)

Facts: Each of Crocker's depositors signed a signature card stating that all deposits were subject to the bank's rules, regulations, and charges. No charges or rules were expressly identified on the cards themselves. Perdue filed a class action that challenged the validity of charges imposed by the bank for the processing of checks drawn on accounts with insufficient funds.

Issue 1: Does a signature card create a contract between a bank and its depositors authorizing charges for handling checks written by those who had insufficient funds?

Rule 1: A signature card is a contract between a depositor and a bank that authorizes a bank to impose charges, such as that for the processing of checks drawn from insufficient funds, subject to a bank's duty of good faith and fair dealing in setting or varying such charges.

Issue 2: How does a court determine whether a price term is unconscionable?

Rule 2: A price term may be found unconscionable by looking at the market price, the cost of the good or service to the seller, the inconvenience imposed on the seller, and the true value of the product or service. Further, the absence of meaningful choice, the lack of sophistication of the buyer and the presence of deceptive practices by the seller may also indicate that a term is unconscionable

Stambovsky v. Ackley (1991)

Facts: The Stambovskys, after contracting to purchase a house, discovered that it was widely reputed to be possessed by poltergeists.

Issue: Does the doctrine of caveat emptor apply in situations where it would be unlikely for the buyer to discover any undisclosed details concerning the home he has contracted to purchase?

Rule: Where a condition that has been created by the seller materially impairs the value of the contract and is undiscoverable by or unlikely to be within the scope of knowledge of a purchaser exercising due care, non-disclosure constitutes a basis for rescission as a matter of equity.

National and Int'l Brotherhood of Street Racers, Inc. v. Superior Ct. (1989)

Facts: A race car driver, who suffered crippling injuries during a race, sued the race organizer (Brotherhood of Street Racers) and the track owner. The defendants claimed that the driver had signed a release form discharging them from all claims and liability.

Issue: What is required for a party to ensure that a release will effectively discharge it from liability?

Rule: A release will be effective if it is clear, unambiguous and explicit, and if it expresses an agreement not to hold the released party liable for negligence.

LaFleur v. C.C. Pierce Co., Inc. (1986)

Facts: LaFleur entered into a settlement agreement with an insurance company in the amount of $4,000, after injuring his foot in a work-related accident. LaFleur sought to have the agreement rescinded after learning that the accident had caused him to contract a disease that required him to have his legs amputated. The agreement was originally made under the mistaken assumption that the wound was not serious.

Issue: May a settlement agreement be set aside on the ground of mutual mistake when the parties were unaware at the time of the agreement that the injured party suffered from a serious and unknown injury?

Rule: The "unknown injury rule" states that a release of claims for personal injuries may be avoided on the ground of mutual mistake if the parties were mistaken as to the existence of an injury when the agreement was signed.

Stare v. Tate (1971)

Facts: Defendant, former wife of the plaintiff, proposed a settlement agreement that computed the value of the husband's property, but contained a serious accounting error that undervalued the property. A counteroffer was submitted by the husband that merely rounded off the errant settlement term, and did not call attention to the error. The settlement was agreed to, and the wife later brought action to reform the contract.

Issue: May a written contract be revised when one party makes a mistake of which the other party is aware?

Rule: When one party knows that a writing is erroneous and fails to inform the mistaken party, an agreement may be reformed.

Watkins & Son, Inc. v. Carrig (1941)

Facts: Watkins & Son contracted to excavate a cellar for Carrig. After work began, Watkins & Son encountered solid rock and Carrig orally agreed to pay nine times the original excavation price. Carrig later reneged, claiming his promise was unenforceable due to lack of consideration (i.e., there was a pre-existing duty to do the work anyway).

Issue: Is a modification of an agreement unenforceable because of a lack of consideration?

Rule: Modification involves a partial rescission of the prior contract and therefore the promise to do the original work is new consideration.

Note: After classifying modification as a "partial rescission" of the original contract, the court used same analysis as seen above in *Schwartzreich v. Bauman-Basch, Inc.*

Kiefer v. Fred Howe Motors, Inc. (1968)

Facts: Kiefer, a married man with a young child, bought a car when he was just under 21 years old. He later became dissatisfied with the car and sought to rescind the contract.

Issue: May one rescind a contract on the grounds that it was made while he was still a minor?

Rule: A contract made by a minor, other than for necessities, is either void or voidable at his option because minors require some protection from the pitfalls of the marketplace.

Cundick v. Broadbent (1967)

Facts: Cundick sold ranch lands and other property to Broadbent, for less than half its market value. The contract was later amended to pay an additional sum that was still less than full value. When the sale had almost been completed, Cundick's wife sued to rescind the contract. Three years prior to entering into the contract, Cundick had received psychiatric treatment but nothing further had been said or done about any mental condition until the suit was commenced.

Issue: Is mere weakness of mind sufficient mental incompetency to render a contract voidable?

Rule: Mental capacity to contract depends upon whether the allegedly disabled person possessed sufficient reason to enable him to understand the nature and effect of the act in issue. Average intelligence is not essential to a valid bargain.

McKinnon v. Benedict (1968)

Facts: McKinnon loaned Benedict $5,000, interest free, to buy a resort adjoining McKinnon's property in return for Benedict's promise not to make new improvements on the land between the resort and his property for 25 years. After Benedict repaid the loan, he decided to build a trailer park and tent camp because he was losing money on the property. McKinnon sued in equity to enjoin this activity. The camping facilities were not visible from McKinnon's house during the summer months when McKinnon actually lived there.

Issue: Is a contract that exchanges substantial restrictions for relatively minimal consideration enforceable in equity?

Rule: Inadequacy of consideration, minimal benefit to the party imposing the restrictions, and the oppressive nature of restrictions can combine to make a contract unreasonable and unenforceable in equity.

Tuckwiller v. Tuckwiller (1967)

Facts: Tuckwiller agreed to care for an ailing 73-year-old woman who had promised to bequeath her house and farm to her. The woman died soon afterward without changing her will and before Tuckwiller had provided her with much care. She did, however, have the ambulance attendants witness a paper that contained her promise. Tuckwiller sued the executor of the estate for specific performance of the promise.

Issue: Should the court measure the adequacy of consideration at the time the contract was made or at the time of the alleged breach?

Rule: In determining whether a contract is so unfair, inequitable, or unconscionable as to warrant denial of specific performance, the transaction must be viewed prospectively, not retrospectively. Viewed in this light, prior services and the past relations of the parties may properly be considered in connection with the fairness of the contract and adequacy of the consideration. In the instant case the fact that the woman tried to change her will revealed her satisfaction with the bargain.

Black Indus. Inc. v. Bush (1953)

Facts: Bush contracted to produce and sell mechanical parts to Black Industries, who resold them at a large profit. The assembled parts were ultimately sold to the government. Bush refused to perform, claiming that Black Industries was receiving excessive profits in violation of public policy since the government was the ultimate purchaser.

Issue: Is a contract void as being against public policy if there is no evidence of fraud?

Rule: A contract that is made freely and without evidence of fraud is not void as against public policy unless it violates recognized legal principles. The validity of the contract is not affected by the relative values of the consideration in a contract between businessmen dealing at arm's length.

Kannavos v. Annino (1969)

Facts: Annino converted her single family home into a multi-family apartment building and then sold it to Kannavos without telling him its use violated city zoning laws. Kannavos sued to rescind the contract after the city moved to abate the use of the building.

Issue: Can a sales contract be rescinded when a seller knowingly concealed material facts, if the buyer could have discovered the truth by examining public records?

Rule: If a seller speaks with reference to a given subject, voluntarily or at the buyer's request, and knowingly conceals material facts bearing on that subject, the buyer can rescind the contract, even though he did not check the public records where the truth could have been ascertained.

O'Callaghan v. Waller and Beckwith Realty Co. (1958)

Facts: O'Callaghan was injured due to her landlord's negligence in maintaining and operating the apartment building. A clause in the lease exculpated the landlord from liability for his own negligence.

Issue: Is a contract with an exculpatory clause that relieves a party from the consequences of its own negligence void as against public policy?

Rule: Contracts with exculpatory clauses are generally enforced unless it is against settled public policy or there is something in the social relationship of the parties that militates against upholding the agreement.

Note: The court held that this exculpatory clause was enforceable but current law generally does not allow such clauses in landlord-tenant agreements.

Carnival Cruise Lines, Inc. v. Shute (S. Ct. 1991)

Facts: The Shutes purchased cruise tickets from Carnival that contained a nonnegotiable clause naming Florida as the forum state for all disputes arising from the cruise. During the cruise, Ms. Shute slipped and fell on a deck mat. The Shutes sued Carnival in Washington for negligence, but Carnival argued that the forum selection clause required the Shutes to bring their suit in Florida.

Issue: Is a nonnegotiable forum selection clause in a form contract binding?

Rule: (Blackmun, J.) Forum selection clauses in form contracts are subject to judicial scrutiny for fundamental fairness. A nonnegotiated clause may be permissible if (1) the forum is chosen without a bad faith motive to discourage litigation, (2) the provision is instituted without fraud or undue influence, and (3) the party to be bound has adequate opportunity to reject the contract. Where a forum selection clause establishes a remote forum for resolution of conflicts, the party claiming unfairness bears a heavy burden of proof in showing the provision is inconvenient.

Dissent: (Stevens, J.) Forum selection clauses in passenger tickets are unenforceable because the parties do not have equal bargaining power.

Hopper v. All Pet Animal Clinic (1993)

Facts: Hopper entered into an employment contract with All Pet that contained a noncompetition clause extending for a three-year period from the date of termination. Upon being terminated by All Pet, Hopper started a different clinic in the area, in violation of the clause.

Issue: When is a noncompetition covenant valid and enforceable?

Rule: The enforceability of a covenant not to compete is determined by the specific facts of the case and depends upon a finding that the proper balance exists between the competing interests of the employer and the employee. A valid and enforceable covenant must be (1) in writing, (2) part of the employment contract, (3) based on reasonable consideration, (4) reasonable in duration and geographical limitation, and (5) not against public policy. In this case a one-year limit would have been reasonable under the circumstances.

McConnell v. Commonwealth Pictures Corp. (1960)

Facts: Commonwealth Pictures contracted to pay McConnell $10,000 and a percentage of the profits if he succeeded in getting the distribution rights to a film for Commonwealth. He succeeded and was paid $10,000. Commonwealth, however, refused to pay the percentage of profits, claiming that he used bribery to get the distribution rights.

Issue: Is a legal contract enforceable if performed in an illegal manner?

Rule: A party is denied recovery, even on a contract that is valid on its face, if it appears that gravely immoral and illegal conduct was used to accomplish its performance. There must be a direct connection between the illegal conduct and the obligation sued upon.

X.L.O. Concrete Corp. v. Rivergate Corp. (1994)

Facts: XLO, a concrete construction company, was subcontracted by Rivergate to perform work on a building in Manhattan. XLO was involved in an elaborate scheme, set up by the Mafia, through which the Mafia chose which concrete companies would get certain jobs and took a 2 percent commission of the contract price. The Mafia enforced compliance through threatened or actual labor unrest or violence. Rivergate negotiated the contract with full knowledge of the arrangement, and XLO completed the scheduled work, but Rivergate refused to pay the contract price, arguing that the contract was procured through bribery and extortion in violation of antitrust laws.

Issue: Can the interposition of an antitrust illegality defense prevent enforcement of an otherwise valid contract?

Rule: A contract that is legal on its face is not voidable simply because it resulted from an antitrust conspiracy. A court must decide whether the contract is so related to the illegal arrangement that its enforcement would result in enforcement of the exact conduct made unlawful by the antitrust laws, by analyzing (1) the fairness of the contract price resulting from the arrangement, (2) the relative equality of the parties in the bargaining process, and (3) the public policy concerns.

Brower v. Gateway 2000, Inc. (1998)

Facts: Computer seller Gateway marketed computers directly to buyers, accepting orders by mail or telephone. Gateway delivered computers with a written "agreement" that set out terms and conditions and that stated the buyer would be contractually bound by that document if the buyer kept the computer for 30 days. The agreement contained a clause providing for mandatory arbitration of any dispute between the buyer and Gateway.
Issue: Is an arbitration clause delivered with an item sold via direct marketing unconscionable and therefore unenforceable?
Rule: An arbitration clause that requires a buyer to pay a fee to the entity managing the arbitration that would exceed his recovery of the price of the item bought is substantively unconscionable. A clause need not be both substantively and procedurally unconscionable for a court to grant relief. Terms and conditions that are delivered with the item sold may become part of the contract.
Note: Compare *Hill v. Gateway 2000, Specht v. Netscape Communications Corp.*, and *ProCD v. Zeidenberg* in Chapter 2.

In re Baby M. (1988)

Facts: Whitehead agreed to artificial insemination using Stern's sperm and promised to give up her rights as mother of the child altogether upon its birth. Whitehead became pregnant and gave birth but refused to a termination of her rights as mother of the child. Stern sued for specific performance of her promise.
Issue: May a promise to serve as a surrogate mother be enforced as a contract?
Rule: Surrogate motherhood contracts are unenforceable because they violate the public policy that conflicting claims of custody by the two natural parents must be decided based on the best interests of the child and not in advance by contract. Custody of the child to Stern was confirmed based on the child's best interest, not because of the contract, with possible visitation rights for Whitehead.

Maxwell v. Fidelity Financial Services (1995)

Facts: Maxwell bought a solar water heater for $6,512 at 19.5 percent interest, borrowing the price from Fidelity, which took a security interest in the heater and mortgage on Maxwell's home to secure its claim against her. The heater was never installed. After making payments on the loan for several years, Maxwell brought an action against Fidelity seeking a declaratory judgment that the loan contract was unconscionable and therefore unenforceable. The trial court ruled against her.

Issue: Must a promisor show that a contract is both procedurally and substantively unconscionable in order to defeat its enforcement?

Rule: No. Proof of substantive unconscionability is enough. Here the disparity in the price and security terms was sufficiently great to create a question for the jury, and the court remanded for trial. The concurrence would have found substantive unconscionability as a matter of law and ruled for Maxwell immediately.

Austin Instrument, Inc. v. Loral Corp. (1971)

Facts: The Navy contracted with Loral for radar sets. That contract contained substantial penalties for late performance. Loral contracted with Austin for precision parts for the sets. Austin demanded an increase in price for its performance close enough to the time for delivery of the sets that Loral could not substitute another vendor for Austin without breaching its contract with the Navy. Loral paid the higher price demanded by Austin, performed the contract with the Navy, and then sued to recover from Austin the excess paid over the contract price.

Issue: Must a claim of economic duress be based on proof of a total deprivation of choice and loss of free will?

Rule: A claim of economic duress is made out if the claimant shows that resisting the promisor's demand for a price increase and suing the promisor for breach would have provided a remedy so inadequate that the claimant truly had no choice but to give in.

Toker v. Westerman (1970)

Facts: Consumer bought a refrigerator from a door-to-door salesman.

Issue: Is an excessive price enough to prove unconscionability?

Rule: A grossly excessive price is enough to prove unconscionability. This fact demonstrates unjustifiable inequality.

Washington Mutual Finance Group v. Bailey (2004)

Facts: Bailey and other plaintiffs bought insurance or borrowed money from defendants. The plaintiffs were illiterate. The contracts of insurance and the loans all contained agreements to arbitrate disputes.

Issue: Is an agreement to arbitrate unconscionable if one of the parties to the agreement is illiterate?

Rule: Agreements to arbitrate are not unconscionable without more. The inability to read does not bar the effectiveness of contract terms a party agrees to any more than does a failure to read the contract. Nor is it the duty of the other party to assure that one agreeing to a contract understands all of its terms. (Mississippi law.)

Knapp v. American General Finance, Inc. (2000)

Facts: The Knapps wanted to borrow $1,000 from AGF; the total loan became $1,353, including $315 for insurance. The interest rate was 30.99 percent. Mr. Knapp, who had an eighth-grade education, could not read without his glasses and did not have them. Mrs. Knapp was illiterate. The Knapps claimed they were told they had to buy the insurance, though the forms said they did not. They also claimed that they signed a blank sheet that purported to grant a security interest, on which AGF later added several items, only one of which the Knapps happened to own.

Issue: Does a lender become the fiduciary of an unsophisticated borrower?

Rule: A lender is not the fiduciary of an unsophisticated borrower unless circumstances show that the lender subordinated its interest to the borrower's. A loan may be unconscionable due to gross inequality in bargaining power, as shown by the contract's terms, which the fact finder evaluates. While a borrower ordinarily must read a contract and is bound even if he does not read it, the borrower may prove deception by the lender, permitting the borrower to avoid the contract. A lender is bound also by the covenant of good faith and fair dealing, which AGF violated by filling in the list of security a year after the loan and backdating its signature.

BDO Seidman v. Hirshberg (1999)

Facts: Hirshberg was an employee of BDO. BDO promoted him, conditioned on his agreement to reimburse the firm 1.5 times of the fees the firm had earned in the prior year from any BDO client that Hirshberg might represent within 18 months after leaving the firm.

Issue: Is a promise of an employee who quits to reimburse an employer for work he does for the employer's former clients enforceable?

Rule: Such a promise is enforceable if the employer does not abuse its dominant position and seeks to protect its legitimate business interests. Requiring reimbursement if Hirshberg should come to represent former clients of BDO with which he had no relationship while a BDO employee is unenforceable.

Valencia v. White (1982)

Facts: A minor with a hauling business contracted with White, who replaced the engine in a truck. The minor did not wish to pay for the work.
Issue: May a minor disaffirm a contract and avoid any payment for services and benefits received that are not necessaries?
Rule: Such a minor may be liable for the value of the benefits he in fact received, though not necessaries.
Note: A majority of courts still apply the minority-incapacity rule; this case is in the minority that doesn't.

Williams v. Glash (1990)

Facts: Williams and Glash had an automobile accident. Williams settled her car's damage claim with Glash's insurer, who gave her a check with a blanket release on the back, including personal injury, though the parties never discussed this. Later her personal injuries came to light.
Issue: May a party who signs a general release bring up a new claim unknown to her at the time of the release?
Rule: If both parties to a contract are mistaken about a basic assumption they both have, the contract may be avoided for mutual mistake. Whether the party making the release took the risk that she was mistaken about a basic assumption is a question of fact.
Note: See Restatement (Second) §152.

Bailey v. Ewing (1983)

Facts: The Ehrhardt estate sold one tract of land to Bailey and another to Ewing. Bailey and Ewing disputed the boundary between the tracts.
Issue: May a conveyance be reformed for mutual mistake by the seller and buyer about the placement of the boundary?
Rule: If the seller and buyer both believe the boundary of the lot they are dealing with falls within another lot the seller has sold, their sale may be reformed to reflect their true intents according to the correct boundary.

First Baptist Church of Moultrie v. Barber Contracting Co. (1989)

Facts: Barber submitted a bid to the Church for construction work and realized it had made a miscalculation.
Issue: May a party who miscalculates the price of his work withdraw from the contract?
Rule: A party who makes a unilateral mistake may withdraw if the mistake is material and unintentional. If the unilateral mistake was made through

negligence the party may withdraw if the other party would not be prejudiced by the withdrawal. Loss of the contract based upon the mistake is not prejudice.

Note: See Restatement (Second) §153.

Beynon Bldg. Corp. v. Nat'l Guardian Life Ins. Co. (1983)

Facts: Mortgagor Beynon made final payment on a mortgage note. Then Mortgagee Guardian discovered that the monthly payment amount on the promissory note ($649) was incorrect (should have been $694).

Issue: May a writing that does not reflect the contract of the parties be reformed according to their true intent?

Rule: Reformation is proper where the documentation of the contract contains a mutual mistake. Strong evidence is needed for proof, and the parol evidence rule is not a bar.

Richards v. Richards (1994)

Facts: Husband was a trucker. His wife signed a form that authorized her to accompany him as a passenger. While he was driving a truck owned by Monkem Co., she was injured. Monkem denied liability for her injuries because the form she signed relieved Monkem of any liability to her for harm.

Issue: Does a clause that exculpates a truck owner of all liability for injury to a person violate public policy?

Rule: An exculpatory clause is unenforceable where the public policy against relieving someone of liability who imposes an unreasonable risk of harm on others outweighs the public policy supporting freedom of contract.

Renner v. Kehl (1986)

Facts: Renner bought land to cultivate jojoba. After purchase, Renner drilled test wells and learned it would not produce enough water for his purpose.

Issue: In a case of mutual mistake, is the plaintiff entitled to damages?

Rule: Where both the seller and buyer are mistaken about a basic assumption, the buyer may rescind the contract based on mutual mistake. This entitles both parties to return to their position before the contract occurred after restitution of any benefit conferred through the contract. Here, the buyer is not entitled to damages for expenditures in developing the land.

Selland Pontiac-GMC, Inc. v. King (1986)

Facts: Seller King contracted to sell four bus bodies, to be made by Superior Manufacturing, to Selland. Selland bought four bus chassis in reliance on King's contract. Superior Manufacturing went bankrupt and never made the bus bodies.

Issue: Does the failure of a seller's source of supply beyond his control excuse his performance?

Rule: A seller generally bears the risk that his source of supply will fail. But here both the buyer and seller assumed that the manufacturer would make and supply the goods. Moreover, the buyer acquiesced in delay of delivery knowing that the manufacturer was insolvent. Thus the trial court's holding that the seller did not breach is correct.

Darner Motor Sales, Inc. v. Universal Underwriters Ins. Co. (1984)

Facts: Darner was in the business of leasing cars. It bought liability insurance from Universal to cover its lessees' liability. Darner represented to its lessees that their liability coverage through Universal was $100,000 for a single injury when the coverage was in fact $15,000. Universal's agent stated that the higher number was correct, because Darner's umbrella policy provided the higher coverage for lessees' liability, but this was not the case. Darner received a thick policy document, which it never read. One of Darner's lessees injured a pedestrian in an accident.

Issue: Does the parol evidence rule render extrinsic evidence of the content of a contract inadmissible?

Rule: Parol evidence is admissible to prove the true contract when the contract document is a standardized form contract. The terms of such a standardized form contract are construed against its drafter. The court retains the power to enforce the overriding obligation of good faith and to refuse to enforce an unconscionable contract.

Note: This decision reversed the courts below that had applied the parol evidence to exclude extrinsic evidence of the contract and granted summary judgment to Universal.

Donovan v. RRL Corp. (2001)

Facts: RRL was a car dealer that placed an advertisement for the sale of a used Jaguar for a stated price. The price was about one-third less than RRL intended, but neither the newspaper editors not RRL spotted it. Donovan, however, read and responded to the advertisement by coming to RRL with the price in hand. RRL refused to sell at that price.

Issue: If a seller makes a unilateral error in advertising a price of a single item, is it bound if a buyer arrives ready to buy at that price?

Rule: A contract may be rescinded for a unilateral, material mistake of fact that is honestly made and if enforcement would be unconscionable.

Here, RRL's mistake was unilateral, material, honestly made, and enforcing the contract as advertised would be unconscionable.

Hauer v. Union State Bank of Wautoma (1995)

Facts: Hauer was in a motorcycle accident that injured her brain severely enough that a guardian was appointed for her. After the guardianship ended, she borrowed money from Union State, using an $80,000 mutual fund as collateral. She sued the bank, and the jury voided the loan and returned her collateral.

Issue: If a lender has notice that the borrower is not mentally competent, is their contract voidable by the borrower?

Rule: If a contract party has notice of the mental state of the other party that would cause a reasonably prudent person to inquire into the other person's competence, the other party may void the contract.

Park 100 Investors, Inc. v. Kartes (1995)

Facts: A business entity leased space from Park 100. Park 100 presented a document to Kartes, owner of the business entity, which was in fact a personal guaranty but which was called a "lease agreement." Kartes signed it.

Issue: May a promisee enforce a contract that is induced by fraud?

Rule: A creditor cannot enforce a guaranty against the guarantor who was induced to enter the contract by a fraudulent misrepresentation.

Higgins v. Superior Court of Los Angeles County (2006)

Facts: The Higginses, five recently orphaned siblings (several under 21), were living with the Leomitises. The producer of a television show negotiated with the Leomitises to film an episode in their home. The Leomitises presented the producer's long contract form to the Higginses to sign. They did.

Issue: Is a contract that requires only one party to arbitrate disputes unconscionable?

Rule: A contract that requires one party to arbitrate any dispute, but permits the other to arbitrate or to use ordinary courts is substantively unconscionable.

Note: The contract here was also procedurally unconscionable because of surprise and of disparity of bargaining power.

Adler v. Fred Lind Manor (2004)

Facts: The new owner of Fred Lind Manor required all employees to sign an agreement to arbitrate all disputes. Fred Lind Manor fired Adler, who sued for discrimination and other claims in court. Fred Lind Manor moved to compel arbitration.

Issue: In order to void a contract for unconscionability, are both substantive and procedural unconscionability required?

Rule: The substantive unconscionability of an arbitration agreement is enough. A distinct element of an arbitration agreement may be unconscionable without voiding the whole if it clearly benefits the employer or not unconscionable if it treats employer and employee evenhandedly. Procedural unconscionability must be proved factually; merely because a contract is adhesive does not make it procedurally unconscionable.

Valley Medical Specialists v. Farber (1999)

Facts: Farber was a physician specializing in pulmonology. He signed an agreement not to compete as part of an employment agreement with a corporation of which he was a director and shareholder. When he quit his position, the corporation sought to enjoin his practice of medicine in violation of his agreement not to compete.

Issue: Is an agreement not to compete by a physician treated like an agreement not to compete in an ordinary business setting?

Rule: Public policy demands that agreements not to compete by physicians be construed strictly to favor the ability of the physician to practice medicine, beyond the law's reluctance to enforce anti-competitive contracts in ordinary business.

R. R. v. M. H. (1998)

Facts: M. H. agreed to be a surrogate mother for R. R. and his wife, who could not have a child. M. H. became pregnant but decided while still pregnant not to surrender the child to R. R. and terminated the surrogacy contract.

Issue: Is a surrogacy contract enforceable (in Massachusetts)?

Rule: A surrogacy contract is unenforceable. Enforcing a surrogacy contract forces a judge to decide the custody of a child. Because judge must make that decision in the best interests of the child, no private agreement can preempt that decision.

Andreini v. Hultgren (1993)

Facts: Surgeon presented Patient with a form to sign while being prepared for surgery in which Patient released Surgeon from liability.

Issue: Is a promise to release another from liability enforceable if made under duress?

Rule: No. A contract may be voided for duress if the promisor has no reasonable choice other than to make the promise. Here, a patient who needed the corrective surgery for a deteriorating condition and who was moments away from having the surgery had no other reasonable choice than to sign the release.

Olsen v. Breeze (1996)

Facts: Breeze serviced Olsen's skis and bindings. Breeze required Olsen to sign a document releasing Breeze from liability for negligence, among other types of liability, before Breeze would return Olsen's property. Olsen refused.
Issue: Is an agreement that releases a party of future liability, including for negligence, void as against public policy?
Rule: No. Parties are free to allocate risk between themselves as they see fit. The public interest is not infringed by the release from liability here.

Leon v. Family Fitness Center (1998)

Facts: Family Fitness presented Leon with a Club Membership Agreement, which provided that Family Fitness would have no liability for any claim arising from his use of the facilities. A bench in the sauna collapsed, and he injured his head.
Issue: Is an exculpatory clause enforceable?
Rule: An exculpatory clause may only be enforced if the parties understand the effect of the clause. If the clause is hidden in the document and the document does not otherwise bring the exculpatory clause to the attention of the reader, or if the exculpatory clause is ambiguous, it will not be enforced.

Kelsey-Hayes Co. v. Galtaco Redlaw Castings Corp. (1990)

Facts: In 1987, Galtaco agreed to sell castings for brakes to Kelsey-Hayes. Galtaco told the buyer that it would go out of business unless it could raise the price. Buyer agreed to the price increase because it could find no other supplier for the castings. Later, Galtaco demanded another price increase for the same reason. Kelsey-Hayes sued for breach of the 1987 contract.
Issue: If a party has agreed to a contract modification, may it later sue for breach of the contract as it existed before the modification occurred?
Rule: If a contract modification is agreed to under economic duress, the party who agrees to the modification may later assert breach of the original contract. Here, the existence of economic duress is question of fact for the jury.

CHAPTER 7

Impossibility, Impracticability and Frustration of Purpose

After a valid contract has been made by the parties, unforeseen developments may make performance of the contract impossible or of no value to one of the parties. In such situations, courts may excuse nonperformance of a party's contractual duties on the grounds of impossibility, impracticability or frustration. These doctrines can be used as defenses by a party who seemingly breaches or refuses to perform.

I. IMPOSSIBILITY GENERALLY

A. Effect
   Contractual duties are discharged if their performance becomes impossible.
   1. Temporary impossibility does not completely discharge performance but suspends it until the impossibility ends.
   2. If performance is partially impossible, contractual duties are only discharged to the extent that the impossibility applies.
B. Allocation of Risk
   If the parties have expressly allocated the risk of the occurrence of the impossibility, or surrounding circumstances or the conduct of the parties suggest that one party should bear the risk (implied allocation), then the excuse of impossibility is unavailable. In other words, if the contingency is sufficiently foreseeable, it will be included among the parties' contractual risks.

C. Timing

The impossibility must arise after the contract has been formed. Impossibility that results from circumstances existing at the time of the contract (i.e., one of the parties knows that performance of the other's duties will be impossible, but makes the contract anyhow) is treated as fraud or mistake.

D. Objective Test

Courts usually require that performance must be objectively impossible. It must be impossible for anyone to perform, not just the defendant. Exceptions:

1. Where a party cannot perform due to insolvency, it does not matter that a solvent party could have performed.

2. In contracts for personal services, the death of the party required to render the services will dissolve the contract.

E. If performance of a collateral provision is impossible, courts are less likely to excuse nonperformance than if an essential element was involved.

1. Courts require that a party must utilize an alternative mode of performance to satisfy the collateral provision.

2. UCC §2-614 provides for use of reasonable alternative methods of delivery or payment if those provided for in the contract become impossible to perform.

II. WHEN IMPOSSIBILITY DISCHARGES PERFORMANCE

A. Traditional View

Prior to the nineteenth century, courts did not recognize impossibility as an excuse for nonperformance. The rationale was that a contingency could always have been provided for in the contract.

B. Modern View

If subject matter essential to the performance of the contract is destroyed through no fault of the parties, the contract will be discharged.

1. Construction

If a party contracts to construct a building, he is not ordinarily excused from performance if the building is destroyed through no fault of his own. The builder is said to have assumed the risk of any construction problems.

2. Repair

A party that contracts to repair an existing structure is discharged if the structure is destroyed. The structure to have been repaired is considered to be the "essential subject matter of the agreement," and its existence was a "basic assumption" on which the contract was made.

3. Sale of Goods Contracts (UCC)

   If the contract involves specifically identified goods that are destroyed or damaged through no fault of either party, and the buyer has not assumed the risk of such damage, the contract is discharged if the loss is total. In cases of partial damage, the buyer can choose to either void the entire contract or accept the goods with due reduction from the contract price for the damaged goods. (UCC §2-613.)

   a. It is essential that the goods be specifically described in the contract and be unique in some way; otherwise, impossibility will not apply because substitutes are available.

   b. If an agreed source of supply is destroyed, nonperformance is excused.

   c. Goods Not Identified

      If the contract requires the seller to provide goods from his inventory without specifying the goods and the goods are destroyed, the seller is excused if their existence was a basic assumption of the contract. (UCC §2-615.)

   d. If the shipping terms are "free on board seller's plant," the risk of destruction of the goods is shifted from the seller to the buyer once the goods are placed with the carrier. If seller makes a destination contract ("free on board buyer's business"), risk is shifted only after the buyer receives the goods.

C. Supervening Illegality

   A contract that was valid when entered into may be rendered illegal by a subsequent change in the law. This "supervening illegality" is frequently treated as a form of impossibility that discharges performance.

D. Defective Specifications

   1. If a buyer/owner prepares defective contract specifications, the manufacturer/contractor is usually excused from performance.

   2. If the manufacturer/contractor prepares defective specifications, he is not excused from performance.

E. Third Party's Failure to Perform

   1. If a third party's performance or a particular source of supply is either contractually required or assumed to be part of the agreement, performance is discharged if the third party or source of supply cannot perform.

   2. The nonperforming party must employ all due measures to try to assure himself that the third party or source of supply will not fail. (UCC §2-615, Comment 4.)

3. If a third party's performance or a particular source of supply is not contractually required and not assumed to be part of the agreement, performance is not discharged.

III. IMPRACTICABILITY

Modern courts will discharge duties that are commercially impracticable to perform, even though they may be possible.

A. Test to Determine Impracticability
   1. An extreme and unreasonable obstacle hinders performance, and
   2. The obstacle was unforeseen at the time the contract was made.

B. Performance Is Discharged If:
   1. It is rendered impracticable, without fault of one of the parties, by the occurrence of an event,
   2. The nonoccurrence of the event was a "basic assumption" on which the contract was made, and
   3. The party did not expressly or impliedly assume the risk of the occurrence. (Rest. 2d §261.)

C. Sale of Goods Context
   Nondelivery or delay in delivery by a seller is not a breach if:
   1. Performance as agreed has been made impracticable by the occurrence of a contingency,
   2. The nonoccurrence of that contingency was a basic assumption on which the contract was made, and
   3. The seller did not assume a "greater obligation" (i.e., did not assume the risk of unforeseen developments).

D. Increased Costs
   1. Increased costs are not usually grounds for impracticability unless the cost increase is extreme, and the nonperforming party did not assume the risk of its occurrence.
   2. Comment 4 to UCC §2-615
      Increased cost alone does not excuse performance unless the rise in cost is due to some unforeseen contingency that alters the essential nature of the performance.
      a. Severe shortage of supplies due to war, embargo, local crop failure or unforeseen shutdown of sources of supply usually warrants nonperformance.
      b. Neither a rise nor collapse in market prices is in itself a justification.
      c. Entire-enterprise Test
         In determining whether the negative impact of a price increase is sufficient to render performance impracticable, some courts look to the overall profitability of the

organization, including earnings from contracts with other parties.

IV. FRUSTRATION OF PURPOSE

If the essential purpose of a contract is frustrated, each party's duty of performance is discharged, even if performance is not impossible.

A. Elements (Rest. 2d §265)
1. A party's principal reason for making the contract is substantially frustrated by a supervening event.
2. Nonoccurrence of the event was a basic assumption upon which the contract was made.
3. The party did not expressly or impliedly assume the risk of the occurrence.

B. Sale of Goods
Frustration of purpose is included under the UCC §2-615 provisions (see commercial impracticability, above).

V. REMEDIES

(Apply to All Three Doctrines.)

A. Restitution and reliance recovery are allowed for part performance prior to discharge of contractual duties. (Rest. 2d §377.) The party receives the contract rate or the reasonable value of the part performance.

B. Generally, there is no recovery for reliance that has not conferred a benefit on the other party. However, Restatement (Second) §272(2) opposes the general rule and allows relief "as justice requires," including protection of the parties' reliance interests.

C. Reformation
Instead of dissolving a contract whose principal purpose has become frustrated, impossible, or impracticable, some courts will reform the problematic provisions and make the contract performable.

CASE CLIPS

Taylor v. Caldwell (1863)

Facts: The plaintiff contracted to rent the defendant's concert hall. The defendant was unable to convey the hall because it had burned down through no fault of his own. The plaintiff claimed that the defendant breached the contract and brought suit to recover advertising expenses.
Issue: Are both parties excused from performance if that which was essential to their performance ceased to exist?
Rule: In contracts in which performance depends on the continued existence of a given person or thing, there is an implied condition that impossibility of performance arising from the destruction of the person or thing excuses performance.

Tompkins v. Dudley (1862)

Facts: The defendants guaranteed the performance of a contractor to construct a schoolhouse. The schoolhouse burned down before it had been completed. The plaintiff sued for the money advanced by them under the contract.
Issue: If a party expressly and unconditionally agrees to erect a building, will his nonperformance be excused if a fire destroys the building before completion?
Rule: Where a party expressly creates a duty upon himself to perform an act, an accident will not excuse nonperformance because the party could have provided against such a contingency in the contract.

Carroll v. Bowersock (1917)

Facts: The plaintiff agreed to construct a reinforced concrete floor in the defendant's warehouse. When fire destroyed the warehouse, the plaintiff sued to recover for work done prior to the fire.
Issue: May a party under contract to do repair work be compensated for work done before the structure was destroyed?
Rule: When a party's obligation to do repair work is excused on the basis of impracticability, the party can receive compensation for work completed under the contract that the owner would have received the benefit of in the absence of the casualty. Preparatory work (work that does not inure directly to the owner) is not recoverable.

Bunge Corp. v. Recker (1975)

Facts: Recker agreed to supply the Bunge Corp. with soybeans. Recker claimed that he was excused from performance because severe winter weather destroyed a large part of his crop. The contract, however, did not indicate that the soybeans had to be produced on the Recker's lands.

Issue: Will an act of God that destroys goods to be delivered under a sales contract relieve the seller of his performance if the goods were only specified in the contract by kind and amount?

Rule: An act of God that destroys goods to be delivered under a sales contract will not excuse nonperformance if the seller could have obtained substitute goods from another source.

American Trading & Prod. Corp. v. Shell Int'l Marine, Ltd. (1972)

Facts: American Trading, under contract to transport lube oil for Shell, incurred almost 30 percent higher costs because the Suez Canal was closed due to a political crisis. Although the canal route was mentioned in the contract, it was not considered to be the exclusive route. Also, American Trading's ship had sailed to Suez knowing that potential problems could arise.

Issue: Does an increase in cost render performance impracticable?

Rule: Although extreme or unreasonable difficulty, expense, injury, or loss renders performance impracticable, mere increase in cost alone is not a sufficient excuse for nonperformance. The court found that an increase of less than one-third over the contract price was not sufficient to constitute commercial impracticability. (See *Transatlantic Financing Corp. v. United States.*)

Krell v. Henry (1903)

Facts: Henry placed a deposit on a room to be rented to watch the king's coronation. When the coronation was canceled, he refused to pay the balance owed for the rental of the room.

Issue: Are duties under a contract discharged if the essential purpose of the contract is frustrated?

Rule: If the essential purpose for contracting is frustrated, each party's duty of performance is discharged, even if performance is not impossible (i.e., the defendant can still rent the room).

Lloyd v. Murphy (1944)

Facts: Shortly before World War II, the defendant leased land from the plaintiff with the restriction that it be used only for selling gasoline and new cars. During the war, new-car sales were restricted and the defendant broke the lease claiming frustration of purpose, although the plaintiff waived the land-use restrictions. Prior to the outbreak of war, there had been much public anticipation that future car sales would be limited.

Issue: If a lessee leases land subject to restrictions on its use and subsequent regulations that limited its profitability were foreseeable, is the lessee excused from performance?

Rule: The doctrine of frustration of purpose will only excuse a party from performance if the risk of the frustrating event was not foreseeable and the value of counterperformance is totally or nearly totally destroyed.

Chase Precast Corp. v. John J. Paonessa Co. (1991)

Facts: Paonessa entered into a contract with the Commonwealth of Massachusetts for a highway reconstruction project. Paonessa hired Chase under a subcontract to provide concrete barriers to be used in replacing the grass median strip on the highway. A group of citizens filed suit to stop the installation of the barriers and negotiated a settlement terminating the installation. Paonessa had earlier notified Chase of the impending difficulties and advised it to stop producing the barriers. Paonessa canceled the remaining portion of the contract, although it had paid Chase for the amount of barriers it already had produced. Chase sued to recover the anticipated profits lost from cancellation of the contract.

Issue: May a party be held liable for damages that result from the cancellation of a contract for reasons beyond the party's control?

Rule: The doctrine of frustration of purpose may be used as a defense when an event unforeseeable by either party, the risk of which was not allocated by contract, destroys the object or purpose of the contract. When this occurs, the parties are excused from any further performance under the contract.

Note: Frustration of purpose is nearly identical to UCC §2-615, commonly referred to as commercial impracticability.

Woollums v. Horsley (1892)

Facts: Horsley, an experienced businessman, contracted to buy the mineral, gas, and oil rights to Woollum's land for 40 cents an acre. Woollums, an uneducated and ill man, refused to convey a deed when he learned that his land was worth much more (about $15 an acre). Horsley sued for specific performance.

Issue: Can a party who was misled or acted under a gross misapprehension avoid specific performance of a contract?

Rule: Courts of equity will not grant specific performance where the contract is founded in fraud, imposition, mistake, undue advantage or gross misapprehension.

Waters v. Min Ltd. (1992)

Facts: Waters entered into a contract to assign her annuity policy, which had a cash value of $189,000, to the defendants in exchange for $50,000.

One of the defendants, Beauchamin, who had been romantically involved with Waters, represented her in the negotiations. Beauchamin acted in his own self-interest during the negotiations, causing himself to be named as the beneficiary of the annuity and having some of his debts forgiven by other defendants. Waters brought suit to rescind the contract, and the defendants counterclaimed for specific performance.

Issue: May a court refuse to enforce a contract that would result in oppression or gross disparity of consideration?

Rule: The defense of unconscionability may be used to avoid a contract where a gross disparity of consideration, oppression, or unfair surprise indicates that the agreement was improperly obtained.

State v. Avco Fin. Service of New York, Inc. (1980)

Facts: Avco's loan agreement forms included a clause that stated that the loan was secured by all the property the borrower owned at the time of the agreement. The New York Attorney General, acting on a consumer complaint, sued to declare the clause unconscionable and void without providing any factual support for the claim.

Issue: Can a court find a contract clause unconscionable without support from factual evidence?

Rule: A determination of unconscionability requires factual evidence presented by the parties to show that the clause involved is so one-sided as to be unconscionable under the circumstances existing at the time of the making of the contract.

Paradine v. Jane (1647)

Facts: The lessee (the defendant) claimed that he did not have to pay rent because the land was occupied by an invading army, which prevented him from obtaining any profits.

Issue: If the purpose for contracting is frustrated, will a party be bound to the contractual duties he agreed to?

Rule: A party must fulfill a duty he contractually imposes upon himself, notwithstanding any inevitable intervention, because he could have provided against contingencies in his contract.

Savile v. Savile (1721)

Facts: The plaintiff sued the defendant for the balance of the purchase price of a house the defendant agreed to buy, after the defendant had decided to withdraw and forfeit his deposit because the price he had offered later seemed unreasonable.

Issue: When a deposit is thought to be a sufficient pledge, will forfeiture of the deposit be punishment enough for the buyer if he withdraws from the contract?

Rule: When a deposit is thought to be a sufficient pledge, forfeiture of the deposit is punishment enough for the buyer if he withdraws before completing the contract.

Hall v. Wright (1859)

Facts: Wright claimed he was incapable of performing his contract to marry the plaintiff because he had acquired a dangerous bodily disease.
Issue: Does the impossibility of specifically performing a contract relieve a party from paying damages for the breach?
Rule: The impossibility of performing a contract does not relieve the contractor from paying damages for the breach.

School Trustees of Trenton v. Bennett (1859)

Facts: When the schoolhouse Evenham and Hill agreed to build collapsed due to the latent softness of the soil, they refused to complete their obligations under the contract. The School Trustees sued Bennett, who was the guarantor for Evenham and Hill.
Issue: Must an agreement be performed if performance is not absolutely impossible, and the contingency was not expressly provided against in the contract's terms?
Rule: An agreement must be performed, no matter what the cost, so long as performance is not absolutely impossible and the contingency complained of was not expressly provided against in the contract's terms.

Canadian Indus. Alcohol v. Dunbar Molasses Co. (1932)

Facts: Dunbar, a middleman, contracted to supply Canadian Industries with 1,500,000 gallons of molasses. Dunbar could only deliver 344,000 gallons because the refinery both parties relied on had to cut back production. Dunbar did not have a contract with the refinery to guarantee him a minimum supply.
Issue: Is a middleman excused from delivering contracted-for goods if it failed to make a contract with the supplier to assure itself of a sufficient supply?
Rule: A party's nonperformance will not be excused if he impliedly bears the risk of the performance becoming difficult.

Kel Kim Corp. v. Central Mkts., Inc. (1987)

Facts: Kel Kim leased a vacant supermarket from Central Markets to be used as a roller rink, under the condition that Kel Kim obtain a public liability insurance policy. For several months no insurer would extend the requisite coverage to Kel Kim, who asked to be relieved of the condition, either because performance was impossible or because the inability to procure insurance was within the lease's *force majeure* clause.

Issue: May a condition requiring a lessee to carry insurance be waived on the grounds of impossibility if no insurer is willing to provide coverage?

Rule: Because an insurance requirement is a bargained-for economic protection, and inability to obtain coverage is foreseeable, such a condition may not be excused on the basis of impossibility.

Transatlantic Fin. Corp. v. United States (1956)

Facts: Transatlantic was forced to sail 3,000 additional miles to deliver U.S. wheat because the Suez Canal was closed due to war. After receiving only the contract price, Transatlantic sued in quantum meruit (i.e., for what it deserved) for the extra expense.

Issue: Will added expense excuse performance of a contract under the doctrine of impossibility?

Rule: Increased cost will not render performance of a contract legally impossible. The impossibility requires that an unexpected contingency occurred, the risk of the occurrence was not allocated, either by agreement or custom, and the occurrence of the contingency rendered performance commercially impracticable, or possible only by excessive and unreasonable cost.

Note: In the instant case, the plaintiff claimed that the closure of the canal made the agreement impossible to perform, and that use of the new route required a new contract. However, the court ruled that there was no contractual requirement to use the Suez Canal.

Stees v. Leonard (1874)

Facts: Leonard, following all of the plans and specifications in the contract, tried unsuccessfully twice to construct a building. Leonard sought to be excused from performance because the land was composed of quicksand.

Issue: If confronted with an unforeseen impediment, is a contractor excused from performing his obligations?

Rule: If a party binds himself, by a positive, express contract, to do an act in itself possible, performance is required unless is it rendered impossible by an act of God, the law or the other party to the contract.

Albre Marble & Tile Co. v. John Bowen Co. (1959)

Facts: John Bowen Company's general contract with the state was declared invalid because of its improper bidding procedures. The subcontractor, Albre Marble, sued to recover expenditures incurred in preparation of its duties under the subcontract.

Issue: May a party recover reliance damages if the other party's nonperformance has been excused on the basis of impossibility?

Rule: A party may recover the fair value of acts done in conformity with a specific request of the contract if the other party has been relieved of performance on the ground of impossibility. A contributing factor in allowing the plaintiff to recover in this case was that the event that rendered the defendant's performance impossible was partly caused by the defendant.

Missouri Pub. Serv. v. Peabody Coal Co. (1979)

Facts: Missouri Public Service contracted to buy coal from Peabody at a fixed price. Peabody, faced with escalating costs due to global economic events and increased government regulation, later sought to renegotiate the price and said it would discontinue shipments if a better agreement was not reached.

Issue: Does an unforeseen increase in costs caused by extrinsic events excuse a party from performance due to impracticability?

Rule: A bad bargain not caused by the failure of a basic assumption or the essential nature of the performance does not constitute commercial impracticability.

Mineral Park Land Co. v. Howard (1916)

Facts: Howard agreed to take all of its gravel requirements for a bridge-building contract from Mineral's land. Howard removed all of the gravel that was above water level but refused to remove any gravel from below water level because to do so would have been very expensive.

Issue: May nonperformance be excused if the cost of performance is extremely high?

Rule: Performance of a contract premised on the assumption that goods are available may be excused for impracticability where the cost is so great that the effect is to make the goods unavailable.

United States v. Wegematic Corp. (1966)

Facts: After contracting to provide the United States with a "revolutionary" computer, Wegematic requested discharge of its duties because it could not manufacture the machine.

Issue: Is a manufacturer excused from performance if it does not possess the technology to manufacture a contracted-for product after representing that production was possible?

Rule: In the absence of exculpatory language, a manufacturer is not excused from performance on the basis of impossibility if it does not possess the technology to produce a good that it agreed to produce.

Dills v. Town of Enfield (1989)

Facts: The Town of Enfield wished to have a private developer construct an industrial park on town property. Dills contracted to purchase the land to be developed, putting $100,000 down toward the purchase price. Because Dills was unable to obtain necessary mortgage financing, he was unable to submit final construction plans as required by the contract. Enfield voted to terminate the agreement, as permitted by the contract, and kept the deposit as liquidated damages. Dills claimed that his duty to provide the plans was excused on the grounds of impracticability.

Issue: Does the failure to obtain financing excuse performance of a construction contract as impracticable?

Rule: In order for financial burdens to warrant the discharge of a contract on the grounds of impracticability, the burdens must be highly exceptional and unforeseen at the time of the contract. Failure to obtain financing for a business venture is far less exceptional than other situations in which duties have not been excused (e.g., unexpected war), and is also a highly foreseeable event that was within the contemplation of the parties at the time of contracting.

Louisiana Power & Light v. Allegheny Ludlum Indus. (1981)

Facts: Allegheny stopped delivery of steel tubing because of an increase in the cost of performance, which would have deprived it of anticipated profit.

Issue: Is the fact that performance under a contract will cause a party losses sufficient to show commercial impracticability?

Rule: A party seeking to excuse his duties by reason of a cost increase must show both that he can perform only at a loss and that the loss will be especially severe and unreasonable.

Note: This case was appealed on the issue of summary judgment and was therefore remanded for a factual application.

Kaiser-Francis Oil Co. v. Producer's Gas Co. (1989)

Facts: Kaiser-Francis and Producer's Gas had a contract under which Producer's Gas was required to pay for certain minimum quantities of gas from Kaiser-Francis' wells. The contract also contained a provision relieving the parties of liability if their failure to perform was due to *force majeure*. Producer's Gas claimed that this provision relieved it of the duty to take or buy when market demand resulted in a resale price below the contract price.

Issue: Does a *force majeure* clause relieve a take-or-pay vendee of its obligation to take or pay when market forces make the contract unprofitable?

Rule: A *force majeure* provision does not relieve a buyer from a take-or-pay provision when market changes make the contract unprofitable because this would unfairly reallocate bargained-for risks to the seller.

Washington State Hop Producers, Inc. v. Goschie Farms, Inc. (1989)

Facts: Washington State Hop Producers rented hop allotments, which were scarce farming commodities created by the Department of Agriculture (USDA). Goschie Farms submitted bids and was awarded a contract to purchase hop allotments from the plaintiff. Shortly after the contract was formed, the USDA unexpectedly made hop allotments much easier to purchase, reducing the rental value of some allotments by over 90 percent and rendering other allotments worthless. Goschie Farms and other buyers refused to perform and claimed frustration of purpose as a defense.

Issue: Can a party be excused from performance on the basis of frustration of purpose caused by unforeseen economic changes?

Rule: Unforeseeability and decline in market price are not grounds for rescission of a contract, but they are often evidence that the purpose of the contract was substantially frustrated.

Opera Co. of Boston, Inc. v. Wolf Trap Found. for the Performing Arts (1987)

Facts: The Opera Company contracted to perform four operas in the Wolf Trap National Park. Wolf Trap canceled the last performance claiming that an electrical storm had terminated power to the pavilion rendering performance impossible.

Issue: When does the doctrine of impossibility excuse a party from performance?

Rule: A party may rely on a defense of impossibility of performance when there is an unexpected occurrence of an intervening act, such occurrence is of a character that its nonoccurrence is a basic assumption of the agreement, and it makes performance impracticable.

Note: The court accepted §265 of the Restatement (Second) as the proper statement of the doctrine of impossibility.

Northern Corp. v. Chugach Electric Assoc. (1974)

Facts: Northern was under contract to transport rock across a frozen river in order to repair a dam. Two half-filled trucks crashed through the ice, killing the drivers, before Northern terminated the contract for impossibility.

Issue: Does the doctrine of impossibility excuse performance if the contract could be completed using means other than those specified in the contract?

Rule: A party is discharged from its contractual obligations, even if it is technically possible to perform them, if the cost of performance would be so disproportionate to that reasonably contemplated by the parties as to make the contract commercially impracticable.

Eastern Airlines, Inc. v. McDonnell Douglas Corp. (1976)

Facts: McDonnell Douglas breached a series of contracts to build planes for Eastern by delivering late. It blamed these delays on informal government requests to give priority to military orders needed for the Vietnam War but was not allowed to introduce evidence that these requests were the cause of the delay. The informal requests contained an implied threat of formal sanctions to compel placing priority on military orders. The contract contained an excusable delay clause that included, but was not limited to, delay due to government priorities.

Issue 1: Does UCC §2-615 prohibit parties from contracting to expand or limit the excuses available to a promisor for nonperformance?

Rule 1: Parties may contract to narrow or broaden excuses available to a promisor.

Issue 2: Does UCC §2-615, which excuses delay when agreed upon performances have been rendered commercially "impracticable," require that an event be unforeseeable at the time the agreement was executed?

Rule 2: Section 2-615 may apply even when the superseding event is foreseeable if the circumstances causing the breach have made performance so different from what was anticipated that the contract cannot reasonably govern.

407 East 61st Garage Inc. v. Savoy Fifth Avenue Corp. (1968)

Facts: The Savoy Hilton Hotel had a five-year contract with a local garage in which it referred its guests to the garage for car services and in return received 10 percent of the parking revenues derived from these guests. The hotel closed prior to the expiration of the contract.

Issue: May a party be excused from performance under the impossibility doctrine because of financial difficulty?

Rule: A party may not unilaterally abrogate a contract merely because it would be financially disadvantageous to perform.

J.J. Brooksbank Co. v. Budget Rent-A-Car Corp. (1983)

Facts: For nearly ten years, Budget provided Brooksbank, pursuant to their franchise agreement, with one-third of its reservations for cars free of charge. Technological advancements allowed Budget to centralize the system. Following these advances, Budget attempted to charge Brooksbank for all reservations.

Issue: May a party be excused from performance on the basis of impracticability due to technological change if such was not expressly accounted for in the contract?

Rule: If a substantial change occurs in a relationship, the agreement may be adapted to the new realities of their arrangement consistent with the original contract, but a party will not be excused from its obligations as a result of technological change.

Note: The court ruled that Budget is obligated to continue to provide Brooksbank with a discount of one-third off reservation costs.

Karl Wendt Farm Equipment Co. v. International Harvester Co. (1991)

Facts: International Harvester entered into a franchise agreement with Wendt. Due to a dramatic downturn in the farm equipment market, International Harvester sold its farm equipment division, and Wendt lost his franchise. Wendt claimed breach of the franchise contract. International Harvester claimed that it could not perform the contract because of economic hardship.

Issue: Do the doctrines of impracticability or frustration excuse failure of performance because of economic loss or hardship?

Rule: Economic loss or hardship caused by a dramatic downturn in a market does not excuse performance under the doctrines of impracticability or frustration.

International Mineral and Chemical Corp. v. Llano, Inc. (1985)

Facts: Llano sold natural gas to IMC under a contract requiring IMC to purchase a minimum amount of gas each month. A government regulation caused IMC to shut down its operation, which used most of the natural gas purchased from Llano. IMC claimed that the regulation made it pointless to purchase the minimum amount of gas under the contract.

Issue: Is a buyer excused from performance if a government regulation makes performance impracticable?

Rule: A buyer is excused from performance if compliance with a government regulation makes performance impracticable, even if the buyer voluntarily complies with the regulation. Performance is impracticable if the regulation creates an unanticipated circumstance that renders performance fundamentally different from what reasonably should have been within the contemplation of both parties when they entered into the contract, or if the regulation makes performance unreasonably costly.

Swift Canadian Co. v. Banet (1955)

Facts: Banet contracted to buy lamb pelts from Swift, but later notified Swift that he would not accept any additional shipments because new federal regulations prevented the importation of pelts into the United States. The contract provided that neither party was liable for acts of the government and that the goods were sold "F.O.B. seller's plant."
Issue: Can a party recover for breach of contract if the other party refuses to perform due to frustration of profitability?
Rule: A party ready to perform its part of a bargain is entitled to the value of the contract if the other party, which refuses to perform because profitability has been frustrated, bears the risk of loss.
Note: Here, the court found that the risk of loss shifted to the buyer when the seller became ready to perform.

Young v. City of Chicopee (1904)

Facts: Young was hired to repair a bridge, which was subsequently destroyed by fire without fault of either party. Young sued to recover for work completed and unused materials destroyed in the fire.
Issue: Is an owner liable for work completed and materials bought in preparation for future work if the object of the contract is destroyed without fault of either party?
Rule: If a structure upon which work is to be done is destroyed absent either party's fault, the owner is liable for work that has been completed but not for unused materials.

Western Properties v. Southern Utah Aviation, Inc. (1989)

Facts: Cedar City leased vacant land to Western, and Western subleased it to Southern for 15 years. The sublease bound Southern to construct a building on the land, which would become Western's at the end of the sublease. Southern applied for city approval of the project, which the city denied. Southern stopped paying rent and left the premises.
Issue: When does an unforeseen event render a contract party's performance impossible so as to excuse it?
Rule: Where both parties assume an event will not occur, its occurrence discharges the obligation of the promisor. Here, both parties assumed the

city would approve the construction project and construction could not go forward without it.

Nissho-Iwai Co. v. Occidental Crude Sales (1984)

Facts: Occidental contracted to sell oil produced in Libya to Nissho. Occidental owed money to Libya, which it refused to pay. Libya retaliated with an embargo of oil exports.

Issue: May a seller rely on a *force majeure* clause that includes government acts if the seller provokes the government to take action that interferes with its sales contract?

Rule: For *force majeure* to excuse performance, the cause that interrupts performance must be outside the reasonable control of the party obligated to perform.

Sunflower Electric Cooperative, Inc. v. Tomlinson Oil Co. (1981)

Facts: Tomlinson contracted to sell natural gas from a certain field to Sunflower. Tomlinson could not deliver because the field had much less gas than he believed.

Issue: May a seller plead impossibility when there is much less product to sell than he believed?

Rule: When a seller contracts to sell product from a source not yet fully proven, he may not plead impossibility as a defense to the buyer's action for breach. Such a seller implicitly assumes the risk that the field will be less productive than he hoped.

Mel Frank Tool & Supply, Inc. v. Di-Chem Co. (1998)

Facts: Di-Chem leased a storage and distribution facility from Mel Frank Tool to use for chemicals. Di-Chem wanted to store and distribute some hazardous chemicals on the leased premises but did not inform Mel Frank Tool of that. A new city ordinance prohibited storage of such chemicals within the city's jurisdiction, which included the leased premises. Di-Chem moved out. The lessor sued for breach.

Issue: Is a tenant still bound by a lease if a new government regulation makes the tenant's intended use of the premises illegal?

Rule: The tenant's obligation to pay rent under a lease continues even if a new regulation makes its planned use of the premises illegal, if there is still some legal use for the premises consistent with the contract of lease.

CHAPTER 8

Conditions

A condition is an *event*, not certain to occur, which must occur, unless its nonoccurrence is excused, before performance under a contract becomes due (Rest. 2d §224). Failure to perform a condition discharges the other party's duty to perform. **Example:** B promises to pay A on the condition that A delivers the goods by a certain date. B does not have to pay if A does not make delivery in time: the condition fails.

I. CATEGORIZATION OF CONDITIONS ACCORDING TO TIME

A. Condition Concurrent

The parties are bound to perform at the same time so that the performance of each one is dependent on the simultaneous performance of the other. **Example:** B hands cash to C with one hand and takes goods with the other.

B. Condition Precedent

An event, other than a lapse of time, must occur before the other party has an absolute duty of performance. **Example:** A must deliver the goods before B has a duty to pay.

C. Condition Subsequent

An event discharges an already existing absolute duty of performance (very rare).

D. Precedent vs. Subsequent

1. No Substantive Difference

2. Procedural Difference

a. The party to whom the duty is owed must prove that a condition precedent has occurred.

b. The party who owes the duty must prove that the condition subsequent has occurred.

3. The Restatement (Second) does not distinguish between conditions subsequent and precedent.

II. EXPRESS CONDITIONS

Parties can expressly agree that some event must occur before a party's duty to perform arises. Usually, all of the requirements of the express condition must be met before a duty to render the dependent performance arises. For example, if a contract for the sale of a car requires that a down payment be made by a specific date as a condition of delivery, late payment discharges the duty to deliver.

A. Courts try to avoid forfeiture and may excuse the nonoccurrence of a condition if it is not a material part of the exchange. (Rest. 2d §229.)

B. Courts may not strictly enforce a condition if substantial performance can be proved.

C. To determine whether a contract contains an express condition, courts look at:

   1. Language

      Words such as "provided that," "when," "as soon as," and "after" all suggest that a condition exists.

   2. Intent of the Parties

      Intent of the parties is determined by looking at the contract, circumstances surrounding its formation, and the parties' conduct subsequent to its formation.

   3. Control

      If occurrence of the event is within the control of one of the parties, it is more likely to be a condition.

D. Conditions of Satisfaction

   An agreement can make a party's performance conditional upon his satisfaction with the other party's performance.

   1. Objective standard of reasonableness is used where the condition calls for satisfaction as to commercial value or quality, operative fitness, or mechanical utility.

   2. Subjective satisfaction is required where the condition involves fancy, taste, or judgment (dissatisfaction can be unreasonable as long as it is in good faith).

   3. Satisfaction of an Independent Party

      a. **Example:** A party's duty to pay can be conditioned upon an architect's subjective approval of the builder's performance.

      b. Majority Rule

         To suspend a third party's approval as a condition, it must be demonstrated that the refusal was made in bad faith, not that approval was unreasonably or unfairly withheld.

      c. Minority Rule

         An unreasonable refusal is sufficient to excuse a third party's approval as a condition to payment.

III. CONSTRUCTIVE CONDITIONS

In the interest of fairness a court will sometimes imply certain events (performances) to be conditions that must be fulfilled prior to the rendering of future performance. That is the case, for example, when the parties have agreed to what duties are expected of each other but have not provided a sequence of performance for those duties. **Example:** A agrees to pay B and B agrees to build A's house, but there is no payment schedule.

A. A party's performance is a constructive condition to the performance of the other party's stated subsequent duties.

B. Order of Performance Not Agreed Upon

    1. If exchange of performances can be rendered simultaneously, then courts view the performances as constructive concurrent conditions, i.e., conditions precedent to each other, and both must be performed simultaneously. (Rest. 2d §234(1).)

    2. If the performance of one party requires a longer period of time, his performance is usually due first and is a constructive condition precedent to the other's performance. (Rest. 2d §234(2).)

    3. Where a contract is made to perform work and no agreement is made as to time of payment, the work must be substantially performed before payment can be demanded.

C. Bilateral Contracts

The modern rule is that there is a presumption that mutual promises in a contract are dependent and are to be so regarded whenever possible.

IV. WHEN CONDITIONS ARE EXCUSED

If a condition to a party's performance has not been satisfied, that party is discharged from having to perform, unless the nonoccurrence is legally excused.

A. Nonmaterial Breach

The constructive condition that full performance must be rendered before the other party is required to perform is excused where the party rendering incomplete performance has only committed a nonmaterial breach. **Example:** A paid B $499. The contract price was $500. The "injured" party has to perform, but can recover any damages caused by the breach.

B. Material Breach

If there is a material breach, the breaching party has failed to fulfill the constructive condition of full performance. The "injured" party's duties do not arise, and he is discharged from having to perform. He has the option to repudiate the contract.

1. Factors Determining Materiality of Breach (Rest. 2d §241)
   a. The extent to which the injured party will be deprived of benefit expected.
   b. The adequacy of damages.
   c. The extent to which the breaching party would suffer forfeiture.
   d. The likelihood failure will be cured.
   e. Whether the breaching party's behavior comported with good faith and fair dealing.
2. If a party repudiates a contract, claiming failure of a condition, which is later excused, he will have materially breached.
   a. As a caution, an injured party can request an assurance of due performance if there are reasonable grounds for insecurity. (UCC §2-609; Rest. 2d §251.)
   b. Although a party has no right to refuse performance of one contract because the other party has breached a separate contract between them, such a situation may give rise to reasonable grounds for insecurity.

C. Doctrine of Substantial Performance
   Primarily applied to building contracts, this excuses the condition of complete performance if the work is substantially performed.
   1. The test is whether the breach was material or not (see above for factors).
   2. If a breach was minor, and there was substantial performance, the injured party has a claim for damages but must perform its obligations.
   3. The rule prevents forfeiture where a breach is minor.
   4. It is applied mostly to constructive conditions.
   5. UCC §2-601
      Under the UCC, if the goods in a sale-of-goods contract are defective "in any respect," the buyer is entitled to reject the entire shipment, reject only the defective goods, or accept the whole. Courts have often applied the doctrine of substantial performance to limit a buyer's right to rejection.
      a. The parties can "otherwise agree," i.e., provide an arrangement other than rejection for defective goods.
      b. The buyer cannot reject goods under an installment contract unless the flaw substantially impairs the value of that installment or of the whole contract. (UCC §2-612.)
      c. Rejection by the buyer must take place "within a reasonable time." (UCC §2-602(1).)
      d. After the buyer has accepted under UCC §2-606:
         i. There is no right of rejection.
         ii. Revocation of the acceptance is valid only if the nonconformity substantially impairs the value of the goods to him and takes place within a reasonable time. (UCC §2-608.)

      e. If the goods were rejected, and the time for performance has not expired, the seller may cure the defect. (UCC §2-508.)

D. Promise vs. Condition

    1. The performance of a party can be construed as either a condition, which must be fulfilled before the other has to perform, or as an absolute obligation (promise), which is not a condition to future performance. Due to the harshness of forfeiture, courts sometimes interpret express conditions to be promises in cases where a nonmaterial deviation from the required performance occurs. **Example:** B contracts to design C's home and to secure the city's approval of the plans. B does the work, but the city does not grant approval. To avoid forfeiture, courts may rule that B's obligation to secure the city's approval was a promise and not a condition for payment. Of course, C is entitled to damages for breach.

    2. Courts look to the intent of the parties to determine if the contract language is a promise or a condition.

    3. The language of the contract will be interpreted as a promise to avoid forfeiture in some cases. (See *Jacob & Young v. Kent.*)

    4. Conditions with an Implied Promise

    A contract term may be both a condition and a promise for one party.

       a. A condition within control of the party may carry an implied promise of "best efforts" to perform the condition. **Example:** B promises to buy C's home, if he can obtain financing. B must make "best efforts" to obtain financing. Where a conditional promise is not performed, the other party is entitled to suspend performance and sue for damages.

       b. Order of Preferences

       The order of preference in interpreting nonperformance is first as a promise, then as a condition, and if the other two are not possible, as a promissory condition. (Rest. 2d §227.)

E. Divisible Contracts

It is not a condition precedent to the other party's performance that all segments of a divisible contract be performed.

    1. If the part to be performed by one party consists of several distinct items, and the price to be paid by the other is apportioned to each item to be performed, such contract will generally be held to be divisible.

    2. If a party performs a segment of a divisible contract, he is entitled to the other party's equivalent performance for the completed segment. (Rest. 2d §240.)

F. Anticipatory Repudiation

An anticipatory repudiation occurs when a party clearly indicates that it will not render future performance when it becomes due.

Example: A contracts to sell wheat to B in November. In July, A informs B that he will not deliver the wheat. There is a requirement that the threatened future breach be total or material for the nonrepudiating party to be excused from rendering performance.

1. The nonrepudiating party is, therefore, excused from performing the constructive condition of manifesting a prospective ability and willingness to perform.

2. The nonrepudiating party is entitled not only to suspend his performance, but also to cancel the contract and immediately sue for damages. (Rest. 2d §253; UCC §2-610.)

3. The doctrine of anticipatory breach has not ordinarily been extended to unilateral contracts. Even if the party repudiates an installment contract, each delinquent installment must be sued upon after it becomes due.

4. Repudiation may be retracted prior to any material change of position by the other party in reliance on the repudiation. (Rest. 2d §256(1); UCC §2-611.)

5. If a party's conduct indicates an inability to perform, the non-repudiating party may suspend performance and request an adequate assurance of performance. Failure to give assurance within 30 days (UCC) or within a reasonable time may be treated as a repudiation. (Rest. 2d §251; UCC §2-609(1).)

6. UCC Damages for Seller's Repudiation:
   a. UCC §2-713(1) states that damages are measured from the time the buyer learns of breach by the seller.
   b. This section is modified by §2-610(a), which states that the nonrepudiating party may await performance for a commercially reasonable time.

G. Prevention of Performance

The nonoccurrence of a condition will be excused if the conduct of the party benefiting from the condition prevents the occurrence of the condition.

1. The test is whether the party being prevented from performing the condition assumed the risk of the preventing party's conduct.

2. Making performance more difficult, but not impossible, will not necessarily excuse the condition.

3. In every contract, there is a constructive condition of cooperation. (Rest. 2d §205.)

H. Waiver of a Condition

1. Which Conditions May Be Waived
   a. A party may waive performance of a condition inserted for his benefit.

      b. A party cannot, by waiver of a condition precedent to his own liability, create an obligation where none previously existed, unless consideration is given for the waiver.

      c. Material conditions cannot be waived.

  2. Types of Waiver

      a. Estoppel Waiver

      Estoppel waiver is binding if manifestation of waiver of a condition, before it was to happen, is materially relied upon by the other party. However, a waiver can be retracted if no reliance occurred.

      b. Election Waiver

      Election waiver is binding if a party decides to continue under the contract after a condition has not been performed.

  3. After waiving a condition, a party still has a right to damages.

CASE CLIPS

Howard v. Fed. Crop Ins. Corp. (1976)

Facts: Howard, a farmer, informed Fed. Crop Insurance that his tobacco crop was damaged. Howard replanted the field before an adjuster could inspect the damage. Fed. Crop Insurance claimed the inspection was a condition precedent to payment of the claim and refused to pay.

Issue: Are words that are ambiguous as to whether they create a promise or a condition construed as creating a condition precedent?

Rule: The provisions of a contract will not be construed as conditions precedent in the absence of language plainly requiring such conditions.

Gray v. Gardner (1821)

Facts: Gray sold Gardner a certain amount of whale oil, for which Gardner agreed to pay $5,198.87. The contract specified that if a greater quantity of oil arrived this year than last, the agreement was void.

Issue: Which party has the burden of proving the occurrence of a condition subsequent?

Rule: The party that wishes to avoid its obligation under a contract has the burden of proving the occurrence of a condition subsequent.

Parsons v. Bristol Dev. Co. (1965)

Facts: Parsons' construction contract provided that he be paid 25 percent of the money at the start of work and that Bristol would be obligated to pay the rest only on condition of obtaining a loan, which it failed to do. Parsons sued for the value of the work done. The trial court ruled that Bristol was not obligated to pay because the condition was not met.

Issue: Is an appellate court compelled to accept any reasonable interpretation of a written instrument adopted by a trial court?

Rule: Where there is no conflict in the evidence, or a determination has been made upon incompetent evidence, an appellate court is not bound by a construction of the contract based solely upon the terms of the written instrument without the aid of extrinsic evidence.

Thomas J. Dyer Co. v. Bishop Int'l Engineering Co. (1962)

Facts: Dyer, a subcontractor, worked for Bishop, a general contractor, under a contract that provided that Dyer would be paid five days after the owner paid Bishop. The owner paid Bishop a partial amount of the total due, and Bishop likewise reduced payment to Dyer.

Issue: Can a contractor shift the risk of nonpayment by the owner onto the subcontractor by making payment by the owner a condition to payment to the subcontractor?

Rule: If not clearly stated in the contract, payment by the owner will not act as a condition precedent to receipt of payment by the subcontractor. The contractor must pay, regardless of whether he is paid, unless there is a clear and definite contractual provision to the contrary.

Royal-Globe Ins. Co. v. Craven (1992)

Facts: Craven was involved in a hit-and-run accident and was taken to the hospital where she remained in intensive care for 23 days. Craven's insurance policy required her to notify Royal-Globe of the accident within 24 hours of its occurrence as a condition to coverage. Craven waited for more than three months after her release from the hospital before notifying Royal-Globe of her accident. Royal-Globe sought a declaratory judgment on its potential liability.

Issue: May a disability serve to excuse performance of an express condition?

Rule: A disability may only serve to delay performance of an express condition until the disability is removed. The obligation is reinstated once the party burdened by the condition is able to fulfill its requirements.

Gilbert v. Globe & Rutgers Fire Ins. Co. (1919)

Facts: Gilbert did not file a claim within 12 months after his cottage burned down, because the insurance company's adjuster promised he would be paid anyway. A year later the insurance company informed Gilbert that it would contest the claim, but he still waited close to three years before suing for damages.

Issue: Is an insurer, previously estopped from asserting that a condition was not met, allowed to make such an assertion if the reason for not bringing suit is no longer applicable and the insured is notified?

Rule: An insurer's promise that induces an insured party to not bring suit within the time limitation estops the insurer from pleading that the contractual condition has not been met. If the reason for not bringing suit is no longer effective, and the insured is notified, the insured must commence his action within a reasonable time.

Porter v. Harrington (1928)

Facts: A contract provided that if payment default continued for a period of 31 days, the agreement would become void without notice, and all previous payments would be kept by the defendant as liquidated damages.

After constantly accepting overdue payments for years, Harrington sought to cancel the contract without notifying Porter. The contract also provided that waiver of a breach was not a waiver of a subsequent breach of the same condition.

Issue: After constantly waiving a condition, can a party insist upon strict performance of a contract provision without notice if it would lead to a forfeiture by the other party?

Rule: When a party, without objection, has constantly waived a condition, an order of business has been established that supersedes the strict terms of the agreement. A party cannot then insist on strict compliance without giving notice, if doing so would cause forfeiture to the other party.

Clark v. West (1908)

Facts: West, a publisher of law books, promised to pay Clark $6 per page for an acceptable manuscript if Clark did not drink and $2 per page if he did. West discovered that Clark was drinking alcohol during the term of the contract but told Clark not to worry. When the book was finished, West offered to pay only $2 per page. Clark claimed that the alcohol provision was a condition to the contract, which was expressly waived by West. West claimed abstinence was consideration for the contract.

Issue: May a condition to a contract be waived?

Rule: While a condition to a contract can be expressly waived, merely accepting a party's performance (West took the finished book) does not constitute waiver.

Inman v. Clyde Hall Drilling Co. (1962)

Facts: Inman's employment contract provided that, in case of any claim against the company, Inman had to send written notice within 30 days after the claim arose and bring suit 6 months after giving notice and not later than one year thereafter. Inman sued 12 days after being wrongfully discharged, without giving notice.

Issue: Must a party fulfill an express notice of claim requirement before filing a suit for breach of contract?

Rule: A notice of claim requirement, which was made an express condition precedent to recovery on the contract, must be fulfilled before suit is filed for breach of contract.

Grenier v. Compratt Constr. Co. (1983)

Facts: Grenier contracted to perform various construction work for Compratt, agreeing to provisions conditioning payment upon the acquisition and delivery of a letter from the city engineer, warranting that a certificate of occupancy could be obtained by Compratt for any of its lots upon which Grenier worked. Although Grenier substantially completed its work within the required time, it was unable to promptly procure the letter because the city engineer did not ordinarily write such letters. More than a week later, Grenier acquired a comparable letter from the assistant city attorney.

Issue: If satisfaction of a condition is impracticable, may the condition be excused?

Rule: Enforcement of a condition is subject to the principles of impracticability. If the occurrence of a condition is not a material part of the exchange, the condition may be excused, provided it was not in the contemplation of the parties when they entered into the contract that the condition would be impracticable and a forfeiture would result from its enforcement.

Nolan v. Whitney (1882)

Facts: Nolan had substantially completed work due under the contract but was unable to secure the architect's certificate, which was required for payment of the last installment, because of minor defects.

Issue: If a party has substantially complied with the terms of the contract, may an architect refuse approval necessary for payment, if the performance involves only trivial defects?

Rule: Refusal to give an architect's certificate, because of trivial defects, to a party who has substantially performed his contractual duties is unreasonable, and dispenses with the approval requirement.

Fursmidt v. Hotel Abbey Holding Corp. (1960)

Facts: Fursmidt's employment at Hotel Abbey was subject to the hotel's satisfaction with Fursmidt's performance. Hotel Abbey dismissed Fursmidt, claiming dissatisfaction.

Issue: What standard is used to determine if a party properly exercised its right to accept or reject a party's performance?

Rule: In contracts containing satisfaction clauses, the jury must look to see if the party is honestly dissatisfied before that party may terminate the contract. There is no requirement of reasonableness.

Nichols v. Raynbred (1615)

Facts: Nichols promised to deliver a cow, while Raynbred promised to pay him 50 shillings.

Issue: Must a party assert that he performed his part of a bilateral contract in order to bring suit against the other party?

Rule: In a bilateral contract, a party may bring a lawsuit without asserting that he performed his part of the bargain.

Note: This case illustrates the older view that promises were independent of each other and that they were not constructive conditions for each other.

Kingston v. Preston (1773)

Facts: Preston promised to sell his business to Kingston, and Kingston promised to post a bond as security guaranteeing his payment. When he did not give security, Preston refused to sell. Kingston sued for breach, claiming that his promise was not a condition to the defendant's duty to sell.
Issue: When each party to a contract makes an interdependent promise to the other, may a party sue for breach without having substantially performed on its promise?
Rule: When parties exchange promises that are not independent, each party's substantial performance of its promise is a constructive condition to the other party's performance of any subsequent duties.

Price v. Van Lint (1941)

Facts: Van Lint agreed to lend Price money to build a house. The contract required Price to take out a mortgage to secure Van Lint's loan, but both parties realized that due to some difficulties the mortgage would only be taken out after the loan was made. Van Lint was unable to make the loan on time and claimed he was excused from doing so because Price could not meet the condition precedent to making the loan.
Issue: Are mutual promises independent if the parties were aware that the performance of one promise may arrive sooner than the other?
Rule: Where a contract contains mutual promises to pay money or perform some other act, and the time for performance by one party does, or may, arrive before the time for performance by the other, the latter's promise is an independent obligation. Therefore, although the party that is required to perform first is entitled to sue for breach, he must still render performance or else be sued for breach himself.

Ziehen v. Smith (1896)

Facts: The defendant contracted to sell property to the plaintiff, who was unaware that the property was encumbered by an outstanding mortgage placed by the previous owner. An action to foreclose the mortgage was brought before the date on which the defendant was to transfer the property to the plaintiff, and a sale to a third party resulted. The plaintiff sued to recover his deposit and other expenses.
Issue: Is a formal tender of performance by the vendee necessary to maintain an action if performance by the vendor is impossible?

Rule: If the vendor of real estate under an executory contract is unable to perform on his part, a formal tender by the vendee is not required to maintain an action to recover the money paid on the contract or for damages.

Note: "Tender of performance" means that the party demanded performance by the other.

Cohen v. Kranz (1963)

Facts: Cohen refused to buy Kranz's land after he discovered that the fence extended beyond the property, there was no certificate for use of the pool, and use of the land was restricted (by a covenant that could be removed). Cohen sued for his deposit.

Issue: Is a vendee required to tender performance and demand title in order to place a vendor with curable title defects in default?

Rule: Although a vendor with incurable title defects is automatically in default, a vendor with curable title defects must be placed in default by a vendee's tender of performance and demand for a good title deed.

Stewart v. Newbury (1917)

Facts: Although a contract for excavation work did not specify the terms and conditions regarding time or manner of payment, Stewart alleged that payment was to be made in "the usual manner" (85 percent every 30 days). After Newbury refused to pay, Stewart asserted he was excused from completely performing the contract.

Issue: May a party discontinue performance and demand payment without having substantially performed?

Rule: Where a contract is made to perform work, and no agreement is made as to time of payment, the work must be substantially performed before payment can be demanded.

Tipton v. Feitner (1859)

Facts: In one contract, Tipton agreed to sell Feitner an amount of dressed hogs for a certain price and an amount of live hogs for a different price on different delivery dates. The dressed hogs were delivered but not paid for, and the live hogs were never delivered. Feitner claimed that delivery of the live hogs was a condition precedent to payment of both contracts.

Issue: Is a contract severable if it includes two transactions that differ in subject matter, price, and delivery date?

Rule: A contract may be severable if it includes two transactions that differ in subject matter, price, and delivery date. Performance of either transaction cannot act as a condition precedent for the other independent transaction.

In each individual transaction, however, delivery and payment are each conditions of the other, and neither party can sue for breach without having offered performance on his part.

Bartus v. Riccardi (1967)

Facts: Bartus supplied Riccardi with a Model A-665 hearing aid, an updated version of the Model A-660 that Riccardi had ordered. When Riccardi, who was dissatisfied, returned the hearing aid, Bartus immediately informed him that he would either replace the model that had been delivered or would obtain the Model A-660 for him. Riccardi refused the offer.
Issue: May a seller cure a nonconforming tender?
Rule: Where the buyer rejects a nonconforming tender that the seller had reasonable grounds to believe would be acceptable, the seller is given a reasonable period of time in which to make a conforming tender if he gives the buyer seasonable notice. (UCC §2-508(2).)

Plante v. Jacobs (1960)

Facts: Plante contracted to build a home for Jacobs who later refused to continue payment because of defects in the construction. Plante did not complete the house and sued for the unpaid balance. Jacobs claimed that Plante failed to substantially perform. The market value of the house was not significantly affected by the defects.
Issue: Is a contractor liable for failure to substantially perform if there are construction defects that do not significantly affect market value?
Rule: The test for substantial performance is whether the performance meets the essential purpose of the contract. As applied to construction of a house, substantial performance does not mean that every detail must be in strict compliance with the specifications and the plans. Contract recovery will be determined by the *cost of replacement rule* for small defects or by the *diminished value rule* to avoid unreasonable economic waste for defects, correction of which is expensive but adds little or nothing to the value.

Worcester Heritage Society, Inc. v. Trussell (1991)

Facts: Worcester sold an historically significant building to Trussell. Under the agreement, Trussell was to perform a complete historic restoration of the property. The exterior portion of the restoration was to be completed within one year. If Trussell failed to complete the restoration within the year, Worcester could hire its own workers, at Trussell's expense, to complete the restoration. Although Trussell attempted to complete the project, work went much slower than expected, and five years later the exterior was only 75 percent complete. Worcester brought suit for rescission of the contract.

Issue: Is a court required to grant rescission for breach of a contract term?

Rule: In the absence of an express agreement to the contrary, a court has discretion to refuse to grant rescission as a remedy for breach, if the nonperformance of the contract term is not material enough to go to the "essence" of the contract and other legal remedies are available.

K & G Construction Co. v. Harris (1960)

Facts: K & G Construction, a contractor, hired Harris, a subcontractor, pursuant to a contract that required Harris to perform in a "workmanlike manner." Harris breached this requirement by negligently demolishing a wall, and the company refused to pay him. K & G Construction sued for its loss after it had to pay another subcontractor an additional sum to finish the work.

Issue: Are mutual promises dependent or independent promises?

Rule: Covenants are construed as dependent or independent according to the intention of the parties and the good sense of the case. The failure of a contractor (subcontractor) to perform in a workmanlike manner may justify an owner's (contractor's) refusal to make a progress payment.

Note: The modern rule holds there is a presumption that mutual promises in a contract are dependent and are to be so regarded, whenever possible.

Hathaway v. Sabin (1891)

Facts: The defendant hired the plaintiff to perform a concert. Defendant was required to rent a hall and to pay the plaintiff's salary but decided not to rent the hall when a snowstorm made it almost impossible for the musicians to come from a nearby town.

Issue: Will a reasonable belief that the other party will not be able to perform his part of the bargain excuse a party's failure to perform his own contractual obligations?

Rule: A party's reasonable belief that the other party will be prevented from performing does not excuse a failure on his part to perform his contractual duties.

Greguhn v. Mutual of Omaha Ins. Co. (1969)

Facts: Greguhn was covered for his permanent disability under an insurance policy that his two insurance companies, the defendants, repudiated. The trial court awarded Greguhn a lump-sum judgment for all future payments.

Issue: Does repudiation of an installment due under a unilateral contract amount to an anticipatory breach of the rest of the installments not yet due?

Rule: The doctrine of anticipatory breach has not ordinarily been extended to unilateral contracts. Even if the party repudiates the installment contract, each delinquent installment must be sued upon separately after it becomes due.

Britton v. Turner (1834)

Facts: Britton breached a 12-month employment contact without reason after completing 9½ months.

Issue: Is a party who voluntarily breaches an employment contract entitled to recover anything for the labor actually performed?

Rule: Although not entitled to recover on the contract itself, a defaulting plaintiff may receive the reasonable value of his services less the damages incurred by the other party. In determining the reasonable value of services, the contract price cannot be exceeded.

Jacob & Youngs v. Kent (1921)

Facts: Jacob & Youngs, a contractor hired to build a home for Kent, inadvertently installed a different brand of pipes than that specified in the contract. The pipes used were of comparable price and quality to those specified. Kent refused to pay Jacob & Youngs unless the pipes were replaced.

Issue: When will the inadvertent breach of a condition invoke damages rather than forfeiture?

Rule: When a party inadvertently breaches a contract in a nonmaterial manner the measure of damages will be the difference in value between the specified and the actual performances rather than the cost to correct.

In Re Carter's Claim (1957)

Facts: The plaintiff's contract to buy the defendant's business included a warranty that the financial condition of the company had not materially changed since the inception of negotiations and a condition that the plaintiff could refuse to buy if the company's financial condition was less favorable than at the time of negotiations. The plaintiff bought the company but later claimed breach of warranty because the financial condition was not as favorable.

Issue: May the failure of an express condition precedent be handled as a breach of warranty action for damages?

Rule: A failure of an express condition precedent may not be handled as a breach of warranty. If the condition is not fulfilled, the injured party has the right to refuse consummation of the sale or can waive the condition by completing the transaction (which the plaintiff did in this case).

Note: This case revolves around the interpretation of a provision, i.e., is it a condition or warranty/promise?

Vanadium Corp. v. Fidelity & Deposit Co. (1947)

Facts: Vanadium Corp. acquired Redington's interest in two leases for $13,000, subject to approval by the Secretary of the Interior. After being denied, Vanadium made no further efforts to secure approval and actually urged the Secretary not to reconsider his position. Redington had obtained a bond from Fidelity binding himself and the surety to return all of the money in the event of the Secretary's disapproval.

Issue: If both parties are required to make a good faith effort to secure a contract condition, can one act to hinder its occurrence?

Rule: Wherever the cooperation of the promisee is necessary for the performance of the promise, there is a condition implied in fact that cooperation and a good faith effort will be given.

Morin Building Prod. Co. v. Baystone Constr., Inc. (1983)

Facts: General Motors hired Baystone as general contractor for a construction project. Baystone subcontracted the siding to Morin. Morin installed siding, but a General Motors representative rejected it because of an aesthetic defect. Baystone hired another subcontractor to redo the job and refused to pay Morin.

Issue: Is a contract for the installation of siding on a commercial building judged by a subjective standard?

Rule: An objective standard governs the acceptability of the performance in a commercial setting, not individual taste. A subcontractor in a commercial contract should not be presumed to risk the price of substantial work on the whim of the other party, but may take that risk expressly in its contract.

Mattei v. Hopper (1958)

Facts: Mattei agreed to buy Hopper's shopping center. The agreement called for a $1,000 down payment and the balance to be paid within 120 days subject to Mattei obtaining satisfactory leases. Hopper refused to complete the sale, claiming Mattei's promise was illusory because he was not actually bound: Hopper was obligated to sell, but Mattei only had to buy if he was satisfied with the leases.

Issue: Does a contract lack consideration if the assent of one party to the agreement is conditioned by a satisfaction clause?

Rule: An agreement that contains a satisfaction clause is not illusory (lacking consideration or mutuality of obligation) if performance of the condition can be judged by a reasonable person standard or the party subject to the satisfaction clause acts in good faith.

J.N.A. Realty Corp. v. Cross Bay Chelsea, Inc. (1977)

Facts: Cross Bay Chelsea, through inadvertence, did not renew its lease with J.N.A. Realty within the time allotted. J.N.A. Realty sought to recover possession of the premises, and Cross Bay Chelsea asked the court to relieve it from a forfeiture.

Issue: Does a tenant suffer forfeiture when, through its own negligence, it forgets to renew its lease within the allotted time, and the landlord wishes to recover possession of the property?

Rule: An option to renew does not itself create any interest in property, and thus its loss is not a forfeiture, unless the tenant has invested substantially in improving the property for its use. Also, the court cannot rule, without a careful examination of the facts, whether negligence should be cause for the denial of equitable relief.

Kanavos v. Hancock Bank & Trust Co. (1985)

Facts: Kanavos contracted to acquire the right of first refusal to buy stock from Hancock Bank. The bank later sold the stock to a third party without giving Kanavos an opportunity to exercise his right.

Issue: In a contract that calls for concurrent performances, when is a repudiating party liable for its breach?

Rule: For a repudiating party to be liable for breach of a contract that calls for concurrent performances, the nonrepudiating party must prove that it had the capability to satisfy its contractual obligations.

Walker & Co. v. Harrison (1957)

Facts: Harrison rented a neon sign from Walker. The contract provided that Walker was to maintain the sign. Harrison repudiated the agreement after the company failed to clean graffiti and tomatoes from it.

Issue: May a party repudiate his contractual duties if the other party has committed only a minor breach of his obligations?

Rule: A party must prove that the other party committed a material breach of the contract before the contract can be repudiated. Repudiation is "fraught with peril," for should the court not find that the other party materially breached the contract, the repudiator himself will have been guilty of material breach.

Hochster v. De La Tour (1853)

Facts: De La Tour repudiated an employment contract before the contract was to commence. Hochster, the employee, immediately brought suit for breach of contract.

Issue: May a repudiating party be sued before his performance is due under the contract?

Rule: Renunciation of a contract to do a future act may be treated as a breach of contract, and the repudiating party can be sued before his performance is due under the contract.

Taylor v. Johnston (1975)

Facts: Taylor contracted to use the Johnston's stallion as a breeding stud for Taylor's mares. The contract provided that if the encounter was unsuccessful, Taylor would be entitled to another chance the following year. The Johnstons sold their stallion and informed Taylor that the contract was canceled, but agreed to let Taylor's mares breed, upon threat of suit. The stallion was constantly "booked" by its new owners and unavailable for Taylor's mares. Taylor bred his mares with another stud before the year was up, but had to abort the foals. (Taylor sued for breach, but the court decided that only an anticipatory breach could have occurred, because the year was not over.)
Issue: What are the remedies available to a party who disregards a repudiation that is later retracted prior to the time of performance?
Rule: Anticipatory breach occurs when a party to a bilateral contract expressly or impliedly repudiates the contract prior to the time set for performance. If the second party disregards the repudiation, and it is later retracted prior to the time of performance, then the repudiation is nullified, and the injured party is left with his remedies, if any, invocable at the time of performance.

Oloffson v. Coomer (1973)

Facts: Oloffson refused to accept Coomer's repudiation of a contract to buy corn. Although "cover" was immediately and easily available, Oloffson covered at high prices on the date when the corn should have been delivered.
Issue: If "cover" is immediately available, may a buyer refuse to accept a seller's anticipatory repudiation until the date when the goods should have been delivered?
Rule: If cover is immediately and easily accessible to the buyer, it is not "commercially reasonable" to await performance by the repudiating seller (UCC §2-610(a)) as the buyer should "cover . . . without unreasonable delay" (UCC §2-712(1)) or sue for damages at the time he learned of repudiation. (UCC §2-713(1).)

Pittsburgh-Des Moines Steel Co. v. Brookhaven Manor Water Co. (1976)

Facts: Pittsburgh-Des Moines Steel (PDM) contracted to build a water tank for Brookhaven. Although Brookhaven was not required to pay until the work was completed, PDM requested that the money be placed in escrow or that its president would personally guarantee the payment, after it heard incorrect rumors that Brookhaven was in financial difficulties. When Brookhaven refused to do either, PDM sued for anticipatory breach.

Issue: Are rumors of financial difficulties sufficient grounds for insecurity with respect to the other party's ability to perform its obligations?

Rule: UCC §2-609 allows a party to ask for adequate assurance of due performance and suspend its own performance until it receives such assurance only when reasonable grounds for insecurity arise with respect to the other party's performance. Rumors do not constitute reasonable grounds for insecurity.

AMF, Inc. v. McDonald's Corp. (1976)

Facts: AMF contracted to sell 22 computerized cash registers to McDonald's. McDonald's canceled the contract after AMF's prototype performed unsatisfactorily, projected delivery of the units was delayed, AMF's plant was incapable of assembling the units, and AMF failed to provide adequate performance standards.

Issue: Can a party repudiate a contract if it has "reasonable grounds for insecurity"?

Rule: A contract can be repudiated if a party has reasonable grounds to believe the other party will not perform and no adequate assurances of performance are given. (UCC §2-610.)

T.W. Oil, Inc. v. Consolidated Edison Co. (1982)

Facts: T.W. Oil tendered defective merchandise to Con Ed, which properly refused it.

Issue: If a seller, acting in good faith and without knowledge of any defect, tenders nonconforming goods to a buyer who properly rejects them, does the seller have a right to cure?

Rule: If the seller meets commercial standards of fair dealing such that he acted in good faith when tendering the nonconforming goods, he has the right to cure.

Patterson v. Meyerhofer (1912)

Facts: Patterson agreed to sell four houses to Meyerhofer. Both were aware that Patterson did not own the homes but intended to buy them at a foreclosure sale. Before the foreclosure occurred, Meyerhofer repudiated the contract and outbid Patterson for each house during the sale. Meyerhofer also bought a fifth house, which both parties had orally agreed Patterson would keep. In defense of Patterson's suit for damages, Meyerhofer claimed Patterson breached the contract because he never conveyed the properties to her.

Issue: Can a party who causes the other party not to perform their contract raise such nonperformance as a defense to damages?

Rule: Every contract contains an implied promise by each party not to intentionally and purposely prevent the other party from carrying out the agreement. One who causes the breach of an agreement is precluded from recovering damages for nonperformance or from interposing it as a defense to an action on the contract.

Iron Trade Products Co. v. Wilkoff Co. (1922)

Facts: Wilkoff Co. was to supply Iron Trade Products with rails. Since there were only a few rail suppliers, Iron Trade Products' substantial purchases from parties with whom Wilkoff had been negotiating reduced the supply and drove up the price, which caused it to refuse to perform.

Issue: May a party refuse to perform if the performance of his contractual obligations has been made more difficult by the actions of the other party?

Rule: Mere difficulty of performance will not excuse a breach of contract. A seller's duty to supply goods is not excused if the buyer's additional purchases of the goods elsewhere makes them scarce and difficult to obtain.

Parev Products Co. v. I. Rokeach & Sons (1941)

Facts: In exchange for the exclusive right to produce Parev's cooking oil. Rokeach promised to pay Parev royalties. Rokeach also promised not to market products that would compete with Parev's (and thus reduce Parev's royalties). Rokeach was forced to introduce a new, cheaper cooking oil because of increasing competition.

Issue: Does an exclusive right to sell a product imply a covenant not to compete?

Rule: Although a party who acquires an exclusive right to sell is entitled to sell a competing product, it must compensate the product's owner for loss of sales caused by the sale of the second product.

Wood v. Lucy, Lady Duff-Gordon (1917)

Facts: Lady Duff-Gordon, a famous designer, gave Wood exclusive agency to place her endorsements on clothing designs, to place her designs on sale and to license others to market them. In exchange, Wood promised to keep the books and to split the profits evenly with Duff-Gordon. Duff-Gordon breached by endorsing designs herself and keeping the profits. In defense, she claimed that Wood's promise was illusory, as she had granted him exclusive agency, but he was not obligated to find designs or to sell her labels.

Issue: Is a contract void for lack of mutuality because one party did not promise to use reasonable efforts to perform his duties?

Rule: A promise to use reasonable efforts can be implied from a contract and, therefore, a contract does not fail for lack of mutuality because it does not contain explicit clauses requiring good faith efforts. (UCC §2-306(2).)

Feld v. Henry S. Levy & Sons, Inc. (1975)

Facts: The defendant agreed to sell to the plaintiff the entire output of bread crumbs from its factory for a one-year period. Each party had the right to cancel upon six months' notice. The defendant stopped production because its obsolete equipment was uneconomical, and offered to resume production at a higher price.

Issue: Must a seller who signs an output contract continue to produce goods for the term of the contract?

Rule: A party to an output contract is obligated to act in good faith and may cease production as long as it is acting in good faith. Whether a party acted in good faith is a jury question. (The case was remanded for further proceedings.)

Bloor v. Falstaff Brewing Corp. (1979)

Facts: Falstaff bought Bloor's brewing labels, trademarks, etc., for a set price plus a royalty for each barrel of Ballantine beer sold. Falstaff allowed sales of Ballantine beer to fall in the interest of increasing profits. A clause in their contract required Falstaff to use its "best efforts to promote and maintain a high volume of sales under Bloor's rights."

Issue: Is a "high volume of sales" clause breached by an emphasis on profits without regard to the effect on sales volume?

Rule: Although a party is not required to spend itself into bankruptcy, a clause requiring "best efforts to maintain a high volume of sales" for a specified product is violated by a philosophy that emphasizes profit without fair consideration of the effect on the sales volume.

Grouse v. Group Health Plan, Inc. (1981)

Facts: Grouse resigned from his job because he received an employment offer from Group Health. The offer was later revoked.

Issue: Are damages resulting from revocation of an at-will employment offer recoverable?

Rule: Under the doctrine of promissory estoppel, a promise that the promisor should reasonably expect to induce action or forbearance on the part of the promisee, and that does induce such action, is binding if nonenforcement would result in injustice.

Dove v. Rose Acre Farms, Inc. (1982)

Facts: Rose Acre offered Dove a bonus if certain construction work was completed, provided that Dove worked five days a week for ten weeks. Dove missed two days in the last week because he had strep throat, and he refused to make up the work on the weekend. Dove sued for the bonus although he was fully aware of the strict policies concerning absenteeism.
Issue: Is a party entitled to recovery on a contract if it does not perform all of the conditions of the contract?
Rule: A party must perform all conditions knowingly assented to before performance by the other party is due.

Wai-Noon Corp. v. Hill (1975)

Facts: The lessees, Wai-Noon, replaced their roof without notifying the lessors, and then sued the lessors for the cost of replacing the roof in accordance with the lessors' express covenant to repair and maintain the roof.
Issue: Is the lessor's performance under an express covenant to repair conditional upon notice from the lessee even if not expressly required by the contract?
Rule: Unless explicitly excluded therein, notice from the lessee is a condition precedent to the lessor's performance under an express covenant to repair.

International-Rotterdam, Inc. v. River Brand Rice Mills, Inc. (1958)

Facts: A contract for the sale of rice required shipment by the end of December with at least two weeks' notice to the shipper, River Brand Rice. The shipper canceled the contract after International-Rotterdam failed to give notice by December 17. The buyer's letters of credit only guaranteed payment for a December delivery.
Issue: May a party cancel a contract upon the nonoccurrence of a condition precedent in a sale of goods contract?
Rule: If a provision "goes to the essence" of a sale of goods contract, it can serve as a condition precedent to delivery, the nonoccurrence of which entitles the seller to rescind the contract even if the buyer later performs.

North American Graphite Corp. v. Allan (1950)

Facts: North American Graphite hired Allan, an engineer, to design plans for the rehabilitation of a mine. The contract provided that $4,000 of his salary would be paid "as soon as the plant is in successful operation." North American Graphite later abandoned the project and wrongfully discharged

Allan, but claimed it was not liable for paying the money because the condition precedent to payment, i.e., successful operation, had not occurred.
Issue: Will the courts make payment of a debt contingent upon the occurrence of a condition if the parties have neglected to expressly provide for such an arrangement?
Rule: Courts will imply a condition precedent to payment of a debt if it is consistent with the intentions of the parties as gathered from the language used, the situation of the parties, and the subject matter of the contract as presented by the evidence.

Universal Builders, Inc. v. Moon Motor Lodge, Inc. (1968)

Facts: Universal Builders' construction contract with Moon provided in part that all requests for building modifications had to be written and signed by Moon or its architect. Moon's agent orally requested modifications and promised to pay. Although the agent watched the work being done, Moon refused to pay.
Issue: Is an unwritten contract modification that was agreed upon by both parties valid if a contract requires that modifications must be in writing?
Rule: The effectiveness of a non-written modification, in spite of a contract condition that modifications must be in writing, depends upon whether enforcement of the condition is or is not barred by equitable considerations. When one party materially changes its position in reliance on the other party's waiver of a contract condition that modifications must be in writing, the condition will not be enforced.

Aetna Casualty and Surety Co. v. Murphy (1988)

Facts: Murphy allegedly damaged a building that Aetna insured. When Aetna sued Murphy, Murphy impleaded his insurer, Chubb, as a third-party defendant. The insurance contract between Murphy and Chubb stated that; "If claim is made or suit is brought against the insured, the insured shall immediately forward to [Chubb] every demand, notice, summons, or other process. . . ." Chubb denied coverage because Murphy did not notify it of the suit for two years.
Issue: When is a party entitled to relief from disproportionate forfeiture due to breach of an express condition of an adhesion contract?
Rule: A party may be excused from the consequences of failing to comply with a contract condition if he can demonstrate that the noncompliance did not materially prejudice the other party.
Note: In the instant case, Chubb was allowed to deny coverage because Murphy did not show that his failure to comply with the notice requirement was not detrimental to Chubb's legitimate purpose of guaranteeing itself an opportunity to investigate accidents.

Goodison v. Nunn (1792)

Facts: The plaintiff never tendered the estate he agreed to convey but sued for breach of contract when the defendant did not pay the purchase money.

Issue: If a party has not tendered performance of his contractual duties, is the other party in breach if it does not perform?

Rule: A party is not guilty of breach of contract for nonperformance if the other party has not tendered performance of his reciprocal contract duties.

Palmer v. Fox (1936)

Facts: The plaintiff's assignor, Louis G. Palmer & Company, contracted to sell a parcel of land to the defendant on an installment plan. As part of the contract, Palmer & Company was to make improvements on the land, such as installing a sewer system, water pipes, etc. Palmer & Company was to convey the land when full payment was made. Fox ceased payment after the plaintiff failed to make an improvement, and the plaintiff sued for damages, claiming that Fox's duty to pay was not dependent on the plaintiff's performance.

Issue: Will a party's nonperformance be excused if the other party materially breached a dependent covenant?

Rule: A party's material breach of a dependent covenant excuses the other party's counterperformance. Covenants are to be construed to be independent or dependent according to the "intentions of the parties and the good sense of the case." Given that both performances were to run concurrently, that the contract does not expressly state that the covenants are independent and that the agreed consideration was to be paid when the improvements were completed, it is reasonable to imply that the covenants are dependent.

O.W. Grun Roofing and Constr. Co. v. Cope (1975)

Facts: The plaintiff, Cope, hired Grun Roofing, a contractor, to install a new roof of uniform color. The roof installed had "streaky" shingles on three sides, but was durable.

Issue: Has a contractor substantially performed if his work was defective in a material way and cannot be remedied short of completely replacing the roof?

Rule: Substantial performance permits only such deviations that are inadvertent and unintentional, not caused by bad faith, do not impair the structure as a whole, and are remediable without doing material damage to other parts of the building in tearing down and reconstruction. In the matter of homes, an owner's taste or fancy may be controlling so that variations that would otherwise be considered trifling may bar a finding of substantial performance.

Lowy v. United Pacific Ins. Co. (1967)

Facts: Wolpin, a contractor, was hired to do excavating and grading of a street together with street improvement work. Payment for each type of work was listed separately, and Wolpin gave a different surety bond for each phase of the work. Wolpin performed 98 percent of the grading work before a dispute arose and he stopped performance. The plaintiffs hired another contractor to do the paving work. The plaintiffs claimed Wolpin should not be paid because performance of both phases was a condition to payment.

Issue: Can a contractor recover if it has substantially performed one phase of a severable contract and was prevented from completing the other phase by the other party's hiring of another contractor?

Rule: A contractor may recover under a contract for work it has completed if it has substantially performed one phase of a severable contract and was prevented from completing the other phase by the other party. (Rest. 2d §240.)

Centronics Corp. v. Genicom Corp. (1989)

Facts: Genicom had agreed to purchase business assets from Centronics. The contract provided that any dispute about the value of property transferred would go to arbitration. An escrow account was set up to provide compensation if a party was overpaid or underpaid. The contract provided that the "only way funds can be released is upon final determination of the purchase price." A dispute over the purchase price arose and release of the funds was withheld, pending resolution. Centronics asserted that Genicom's refusal to release funds was meant to pressure the plaintiff into conceding the disputed item.

Issue: May a contract provision be modified on the grounds that it is being utilized in bad faith?

Rule: A claim for relief from a violation of the implied covenant of good faith only applies where there is a promise that allows a party such a degree of discretion that its practical benefit can be withheld. Since the defendant in this case had no control over the amount of time that funds would be withheld, and whether the funds would be withheld was a bargained-for provision available to both parties, summary judgment was granted in favor of Genicom.

Omni Group, Inc. v. Seattle-First Nat'l Bank (1982)

Facts: Omni contracted to buy land from the Clarks subject to the requirement that Omni would be satisfied with a feasibility report made by its engineers and architects. The Clarks refused to sell, claiming lack of consideration because Omni's promise was illusory.

Issue: Does a condition precedent involving the satisfaction of a party render the said party's promise to perform illusory?

Rule: A condition precedent that requires a party's subjective satisfaction does not render a contract unenforceable, because it imposes a duty of good faith upon the said party in exercising good judgment.

Neumiller Farms, Inc. v. Cornett (1979)

Facts: A contractual provision permitted Neumiller Farms, a vegetable broker, to refuse to accept delivery of Cornett's potatoes if it was not satisfied with them. After market prices fell, Neumiller Farms claimed it was not satisfied with subsequent shipments, which experts later found to be suitable.

Issue: Must a rejection of goods based on a claim of dissatisfaction be made in good faith?

Rule: A claim of dissatisfaction by a merchant or buyer must be made in good faith, meaning both "honesty in fact and the observance of reasonable commercial standards of fair dealing in the trade." A rejection in bad faith is ineffectual and constitutes breach of contract.

Michael-Curry Co. v. Knutson Shareholders (1989)

Facts: A contract contained a clause that provided "any controversy arising out of or relating to . . . the making [of this agreement] shall be settled by arbitration."

Issue: Is an arbitration clause applicable to controversies concerning allegations of fraud?

Rule: Whether issues of fraud are subject to arbitration depends on the intent of the parties, as manifested by the language of the arbitration clause. Issues of fraud are subject to arbitration if the language specifically shows that the parties intended to arbitrate fraud, or is sufficiently broad to comprehend that the issue of fraudulent inducement be arbitrated.

McCloskey & Co. v. Minweld Steel Co. (1955)

Facts: Minweld Steel contracted to supply and erect steel for the construction of hospitals. Due to the outbreak of the Korean War, Minweld Steel was unable to obtain the steel and asked for assistance from McCloskey & Co., the plaintiffs. Although Minweld Steel stated that they "were anxious . . . that there be no delay in the final completion of the buildings," McCloskey sued for anticipatory breach.

Issue: Does a request for help in fulfilling contractual obligations amount to an anticipatory breach absent a positive statement of unwillingness to perform?

Rule: To give rise to a renunciation amounting to a breach of contract, there must be an absolute and unequivocal refusal to perform or a distinct and positive statement of an inability to do so. The court also stated that failure to take preparatory action before the time for performance is not an anticipatory breach.

Audette v. L'Union St. Joseph (1901)

Facts: The decedent, Audette, received medical attention from a doctor who refused to give him a sworn certificate necessary in order to receive benefits from L'Union St. Joseph. His administratrix sued to compel the defendant to pay for Audette's medical care.
Issue: Is the refusal of a third party to aid compliance with the terms of a contract grounds for excusing a party from complying with those terms?
Rule: A party to a contract is not excused from the performance of some term by the uninfluenced refusal of a third party to aid in its fulfillment.

General Credit Corp. v. Imperial Casualty and Indemnity Co. (1959)

Facts: General Credit financed the leasing of two cars to Service Trucking, which had the cars insured by Imperial. The insurance agreement stated that General Credit's interest in the cars was covered under the policy "provided, also, that in case the Lessee . . . shall neglect to pay the premium due under such policy the Lienholder [General Credit] shall, on demand, pay the same." After the lessee fell behind on insurance payments and crashed both cars, General Credit brought this action against Imperial for $1,839.20 in damages to the cars. Imperial counterclaimed that General Credit was responsible for $1786.86 in insurance premiums owed by the lessee.
Issue: Do clauses in a unilateral contract act on a promisee as conditions or promises?
Rule: While unilateral contracts bind promisors to their promises, they impose only conditions on promisees.
Note: Insurance policies are typical of unilateral contracts in which only one party makes a promise. Only the insurance company is bound to its promises upon the condition of premium payment by the beneficiary. As a matter of construction, these agreements will be read to operate most strongly against the interests of the authoring party.

Monroe Street Properties, Inc. v. Carpenter (1969)

Facts: Western Equities, Inc., represented by Carpenter, offered to buy ten insured first mortgages and notes with $1 million of Western stock from Monroe Street Properties. Monroe promptly accepted the offer complete with Western's condition that the stock would not be redistributed but held as an investment for three years. Monroe then deposited ten uninsured, heavily encumbered mortgages in the escrow account that had been created and demanded that Western deliver the stock. Seeing that the mortgages did not meet the contract specifications, Western did not comply.

Issue: What constitutes an adequate tender of performance?

Rule: Tender of performance means the ability and willingness to execute performance concurrently with the other party, plus notice of that ability.

Note: A party must tender its own performance before declaring the other party in breach. In this case, Monroe never made an adequate tender because the mortgages were unfit for the transaction.

A.B. Parker v. Bell Ford, Inc. (1973)

Facts: Parker purchased a Ford truck from Bell Ford with defective wheel casements. Parker complained to Bell Ford that the defects caused excessive tire wear, prompting an unsuccessful attempt by the dealer to repair the vehicle. Without further contact with Bell Ford or any contact with Ford Motor Co., Parker sued on warranty and contract theories.

Issue: What is a buyer's obligation upon learning of a defect in goods before action for recovery may be brought?

Rule: UCC §2-607(3)(a) provides that a buyer must provide notice to the seller of any breach in order to open the way for negotiation, settlement and remedy without the need for litigation.

Martin v. Schoenberger (1845)

Facts: Not stated.

Issue: Is recovery available to a party who has only partially performed?

Rule: No recovery is permitted for a party who has failed to perform the entire agreement.

Note: This is the common law rule based on the idea that a party should not benefit from its own wrong. This has been modified in favor of the rule adopted in the Restatement (Second) of Contracts, which allows limited restitution in order to prevent the nonbreaching party from obtaining a windfall.

Lancellotti v. Thomas (1985)

Facts: Thomas agreed to sell his business to Lancellotti for $25,000 and to lease the land it occupied with the stipulations that only Lancellotti would own and operate the business and that he would erect an additional building within a year. After a dispute arose over the additional building, Lancellotti breached and sued to recover the $25,000.

Issue: Can a breaching party recover for any loss incurred in the attempt to perform?

Rule: The Restatement (Second) of Contracts §374 provides that a party in breach is entitled to restitution for any benefit conferred upon the other party in excess of the loss caused by the breach.

Swartz v. War Memorial Commission of Rochester (1966)

Facts: A contract that gave the exclusive concession for the sale of food, beverages and souvenirs to Swartz provided that Swartz obtain all necessary licenses and share a certain percentage of the profits with the War Memorial Commission. When the prohibition on the sale of alcoholic beverages at the War Memorial was lifted, Swartz refused to apply for the necessary license. The Commission terminated his concession, and he brought this action.

Issue: What duty is imposed upon a party to a contract with regard to the goal of the agreement?

Rule: A party to a contract is required to use reasonable efforts to carry out the mutual intent of the agreement. Here, the mutual intent was to earn a profit, and Swartz's failure to attempt to obtain the license constituted a default on his obligation.

Stop & Shop, Inc. v. Ganem (1964)

Facts: Stop & Shop, Inc. leased a lot with a supermarket to Ganem for a substantial rent with the provision that the lessors would also receive a percentage of gross sales over a certain amount. Ganem operated the space as a market for several years, opened two competing markets and decided to close down the lot in question.

Issue: When a contract provides for contingency payments, is there an implied covenant that the party to pay will attempt to operate so as to produce those payments?

Rule: Covenants will not be found by implication unless the implication is clear and undoubted according to justice, common sense and the probable intention of the parties.

Note: In this case, the substantiality of the rent being paid weighed against an inference that the percentage rent clause included a covenant to continue operations.

Sharp v. Holthusen (1980)

Facts: The Sharps entered into a contract for the sale of land to the Holthusens that stipulated that the Holthusens would make monthly payments to the Sharps, assume the Sharps' outstanding loan, and satisfy both in full within a year. Three months after the due date for the entire payoff, the Holthusens attempted to tender payment but were stalled by the need to correct a water supply problem. Shortly thereafter, full tender including attorneys' fees incurred by the delay was made to the Sharps. The Sharps rejected the tender and brought this action for forfeiture.

Issue: Is there any relief from forfeiture for a party in default?

Rule: The court provides relief from forfeiture to parties who make full compensation to the other party within a reasonable time period and who have made good faith efforts to avoid default.

Burger King Corp. v. Family Dining, Inc. (1977)

Facts: Burger King granted Family Dining Buck and Montgomery Counties in Pennsylvania as their "exclusive territory" subject to the condition subsequent that one Burger King restaurant be opened and maintained each year for the first 10 years and that these 10 be maintained for the remaining 80 years of the agreement. When Family Dining fell behind on the fourth and fifth restaurant, Burger King allowed it an extension. When it fell behind on the ninth and tenth, Burger King terminated the "exclusive territory" agreement.

Issue: When may a condition subsequent be excused?

Rule: A condition may be excused if its requirement will impose extreme forfeiture and its occurrence forms no essential part of the exchange.

Note: Here, Burger King had previously waived the condition and provided no notice that it had been reimposed as an essential element of the contract.

C & J Fertilizer, Inc. v. Allied Mutual Ins. Co. (1975)

Facts: C & J bought an insurance policy from an agent of Allied to cover their loss in case of burglary. The policy was purchased before it was produced for C & J to read. During negotiation, C & J was led to believe that the only exception to the coverage was a burglary by an "insider" of the corporation. In fact, the burglary definition required that there be visible damage to the exterior of the building. When approximately $10,000 in chemicals were stolen, C & J was denied coverage because the evidence of force was on the interior of the building.

Issue: On what bases will a court refuse to enforce an adhesion contract?

Rule: A contract containing a few negotiated terms and a number of obscure ones will be read to comport with the reasonable expectations of the promisee, to satisfy an implied warranty of fitness for the purpose intended, and to avoid any outcomes that reflect an absence of assent on the part of the promisee, unfair surprise, failure of notice, disparity of bargaining power or substantive unfairness.

Western Hills, Oregon, Ltd. v. Pfau (1973)

Facts: Pfau and his partner contracted to buy a tract of land from Western Hills, subject to the condition that a development plan satisfactory to both parties was approved by the city planning commission. The commission's reaction to the initial plans was favorable. Pfau tried to back out of the contract, having pursued approval no further on the ground that the city sewer arrangements were unsatisfactory. Pfau was aware of the sewer arrangements at the time of contracting.

Issue 1: May a party rely on the absence of a condition to withdraw from a contract if the party itself failed to pursue that condition?

Rule 1: Where a contract contains a provision for a condition to be met by a party, that party must make a reasonable effort to meet the condition.

Issue 2: When may a party to a contract with a condition of satisfaction not use personal dissatisfaction to escape obligations imposed by the contract?

Rule 2: If a party anticipates or is aware of circumstances before contracting, it cannot claim dissatisfaction with such circumstances to avoid its obligations under the contract. Any such claim must be made in good faith.

Van Iderstine Co., Inc. v. Barnet Leather Co., Inc. (1926)

Facts: The sales by Van Iderstine to Barnet of 15,000 veal skins in August and 6,000 in September were subject to the approval of the quality of the skins by an impartial expert, Jules Star. Jules Star rejected 3,500 of the first batch and all 6,000 of the second as inferior. When Van Iderstine later tendered completion of the first order, Barnet refused to purchase the skins regardless of approval by Jules Star.

Issue: What constitutes a waiver as a matter of law of a condition precedent to an exchange?

Rule: If a party refuses to accept a tender of performance regardless of whether the condition was satisfied or interferes in bad faith with the fulfillment of a condition, that party has waived the condition as a matter of law.

Note: Barnet breached by failing to accept the remainder of the first order regardless of approval, but was justified in refusing tender of the inferior second order, which was rejected by Jules Star.

Daniels v. Newton (1874)

Facts: The defendants had 60 days to perform their agreement to purchase land but breached the agreement before the end of the 60 days.

Issue: Can suit be brought against a party who renounced a contract before the time for performance has arrived?

Rule: One can only recover for actual injuries. Therefore, a party cannot recover for anticipated injuries when the other party announces his intention not to render a future performance. Suit can only be brought after the time for performance has passed.

Jones Associates, Inc. v. Eastside Properties, Inc. (1985)

Facts: Jones, an engineering and surveying firm, contracted with Eastside to supply a number of studies and maps concerning Eastside's 180-acre land parcel. A contract term provided that Jones was "responsible for obtaining King County approval for all platting." Jones was unable to obtain the county plat approval. Eastside withheld payment, claiming that Jones' inability to obtain the approval was a failure of a condition precedent to payment, and thus excused performance.

Issue: How should a court decide whether or not a contract provision is a condition precedent, failure of which would excuse performance, or a mere promise, failure of which leads to damage liability?

Rule: A contract provision will be construed to create a condition precedent if, after examining the contract in light of the surrounding circumstances, the court finds the parties clearly intended to create a condition precedent. If the intent of the parties is unclear, the provision will be interpreted as a promise, since the law disfavors forfeitures.

Sackett v. Spindler (1967)

Facts: Spindler owned and operated a newspaper. Sackett agreed to pay $85,000 in a series of three installments in exchange for 6,316 shares of stock in the newspaper. Sackett paid the first two installments on time. Sackett paid Spindler the final installment by check, but the bank returned the check for insufficient funds. Spindler granted Sackett a number of extensions in the payment deadline, but after two months, Spindler informed Sackett that Sackett had breached the contract and that Spindler would not sell Sackett the stock.

Issue: When does a failure to perform by one party constitute a breach such that the other party's duty to perform is discharged?

Rule: Whether a party's duty to perform under a contract is discharged depends upon whether the failing party's performance constitutes a material breach. Factors considered in determining the materiality of a failure include whether the injured party will substantially obtain the benefits of the contract; whether damages will adequately compensate the injured party; partial performance by the failing party; the hardship on the failing party if the contract is terminated; the failing party's willfulness, negligence, or innocence; and the certainty or uncertainty of completed performance by the failing party.

Merritt Hill Vineyards Inc. v. Windy Heights Vineyard, Inc. (1984)

Facts: Merritt Hill agreed to purchase a majority stock interest in one of Windy Heights' vineyards and tendered a $15,000 deposit. The agreement provided "conditions precedent" to be satisfied before the deal went through. Merritt refused to close when it learned that Windy Heights failed to satisfy a condition.

Issue: What is the difference between a promise and a condition?

Rule: A promise is a manifestation of an intention to act or not act in a manner specified so as to ensure a commitment to the other party (Rest. 2d §2). A condition is an event that must take place, unless excused, before a contractual obligation is to take effect (Rest. 2d §224).

Margolin v. Franklin (1971)

Facts: Franklin entered into an installment contract for the purchase of a car. Franklin asked Margolin if the payment schedule could be modified, and Margolin orally agreed. Franklin paid the monthly installments pursuant to the new schedule, but the car was repossessed.

Issue: May a seller declare a forfeiture after he has orally modified the buyer's written installment payment schedule?

Rule: Forfeiture may occur where a payment clause has been waived only if the vendor gives the purchaser reasonable, definite, and specific notice as to a change of intention to waive.

Oneal v. Colton Consolidated School District No. 306 (1976)

Facts: Oneal, a teacher suffering from failing eyesight, tendered his resignation to the school board conditioned upon his receipt of sick-leave benefits. The school board denied his request for sick-leave benefits and discharged him. Oneal claimed that the school board breached the contract by denying him sick-leave benefits. The school board argued that it could not have breached its contract, because Oneal's failing eyesight made it impossible for him to perform the contract.

Issue: Does a party breach a contract when the contract is impossible to perform?

Rule: Where performance is impossible, a party cannot be charged with breach of contract, because the contractual duty is discharged by law.

Handicapped Children's Education Board of Sheboygan County v. Lukaszewski (1983)

Facts: The Board hired Lukaszewski to serve as a speech and language therapist. Lukaszewski breached her contract by accepting another job, but returned after being threatened with legal action. Lukaszewski then visited her doctor, who diagnosed her as having high blood pressure induced by her job. Lukaszewski resigned and a new therapist was hired.

Issue: Under what circumstances may health problems justify a breach of contract?

Rule: A health danger will excuse nonperformance when the danger is not caused by the breaching party, or if the danger is not foreseeable when the party enters into the contract.

Whitman v. Anglum (1918)

Facts: Whitman contracted to purchase 175 quarts of milk each day for a year from Anglum. Anglum's cows were quarantined, and eventually killed. Anglum claimed he was excused from performance by reason of the quarantine, which made it illegal for him to deliver milk.

Issue: Is a supplier excused from performance when the supplier's source of product is destroyed, but the contract does not specify that the product must come from a particular source?

Rule: When a supplier's source of products need not come from any particular source, the performance of the contract is not excused for impossibility if the supplier's source is destroyed.

Aluminum Co. of America v. Essex Group, Inc. (1980)

Facts: ALCOA agreed to produce aluminum for Essex. The contract tied the price of the aluminum to the Wholesale Price Index-Industrial Commodities (WPI-IC). ALCOA claimed that both parties had intended this formula to serve as an objective measure of increases in ALCOA's non-labor costs of producing the aluminum. However, the WPI-IC formula failed to track the actual cost of production, causing ALCOA to face more than $75 million in losses. ALCOA sued to have the contract modified on the ground of mutual mistake.

Issue: What are the circumstances under which a party may obtain judicial relief through mutual mistake?

Rule: Where both parties make a mistake of fact that relates to a basic assumption of the contract, the law of mutual mistake allows for judicial relief where the lack of equivalence between the parties is severe, so long as the party negatively affected has not assumed the risk. The doctrines of impracticability and frustration of purpose also discharge an obligor from his duty to perform a contract where a failure of a basic assumption of the parties produces an extremely inequitable relationship.

Hope's Architectural Products, Inc. v. Lundy's Construction, Inc. (1991)

Facts: Hope's, a custom window manufacturer, contracted to sell windows to Lundy's. Lundy's allegedly threatened to withhold payment after a delayed delivery by Hope's. Hope's then demanded that Lundy's pay before delivery. Lundy's did not pay and Hope's did not deliver. Lundy's then terminated the contract and obtained an alternate supplier.

Issue: Is a party who suspends performance after demanding assurances and not receiving them entitled to damages if the other party terminates the contract?

Rule: If one party asks for assurances of performance and the other party fails to give them, the party requesting assurance is entitled to suspend performance and may recover damages if the other party subsequently terminates the contract.

National Knitting Co. v. Bouton & Germain Co. (1909)

Facts: Bouton ordered a quantity of gloves from National, a large portion of which was delivered. National, however, failed to deliver the remainder. Bouton did not pay, and National sued to recover for the goods actually delivered.

Issue: How do courts determine whether a contract is severable?

Rule: If a contract is naturally severable (e.g., goods are measured in units and a per-unit price is provided), courts are inclined to hold a contract severable and grant recovery for the goods that were actually delivered. If, however, the express or implied intent of the parties is to condition payment upon delivery of all items, then the court will consider the contract to be non-severable.

Graulich Caterer Inc. v. Hans Holterbosch, Inc. (1968)

Facts: Holterbosch operated a pavilion at the World's Fair and needed food. It arranged to obtain food from Graulich. Graulich's first delivery did not compare favorably with the original samples and was rejected. The second installment was similarly unacceptable.

Issue: May a party cancel a contract when its supplier makes multiple deliveries of nonconforming goods?

Rule: When nonconformity substantially impairs the value of a delivered installment and the nonconformity cannot be cured, a party may reject the installment. When the nonconformity substantially impairs the value of the contract, a buyer may cancel the whole contract. (UCC §2-612.)

Manitowoc Steam Boiler Works v. Manitowoc Glue Co. (1903)

Facts: Plaintiff constructed and connected a steam boiler for Manitowoc Glue. When operated, the boiler failed to meet the specifications of the contract. Both parties tried to increase the efficiency of the boiler, but were unable to do so. When the defendant refused to pay, the plaintiff sued to recover the contract price.

Issue: May a party recover on a contract when his performance does not meet contract specifications?

Rule: A party who makes a contract cannot recover payment until he performs the contract entirely and according to its terms. However, recovery may be allowed when a party, unintentionally and in good faith, completes a structure that substantially accomplishes the purposes for which it was built, and when the cost of bringing the structure up to contract specifications is easily ascertained.

Oak Ridge Construction Co. v. Tolley (1985)

Facts: Oak Ridge contracted to construct a house and drill a water-supply well for the Tolleys. The contract specified that the well should be 150 feet in depth, but provided a formula for calculating an extra charge if a deeper well was required. The completed well was 800 feet deep. Tolley disputed the extra charge for the well. Oak Ridge then claimed breach of contract, terminated the contract, and ceased performance.

Issue 1: When may a party terminate a contract based on the anticipatory breach of the other party?

Rule 1: A party may terminate a contract based on anticipatory breach when the other party acts or uses language in such a way as to constitute a "definite and unconditional repudiation" (UCC §2-610, Comment 2). Mere expression of doubt as to a party's willingness or ability to perform is not enough to constitute repudiation.

Issue 2: How do courts determine whether a failure to perform is a material breach?

Rule 2: In determining whether a failure to perform is a material breach, the courts will consider whether the injured party was deprived of the expected benefits of the contract, whether injured party can be adequately compensated for deprivation of the benefit, whether forfeiture could occur, the likelihood that the nonperforming party will cure its failure, and whether the nonperforming party comported with good faith and fair dealing practices.

Model Vending, Inc. v. Stanisci (1962)

Facts: Model, a lessor of vending machines, entered into an agreement giving it the exclusive privilege of selling merchandise from its machines in Stanisci's bowling alley. One year into a five-year agreement, Stanisci closed down the machines. During the third year, a fire destroyed the premises. Model claimed damages for the loss of profits over the full five-year period.

Issue: If a party breaches a contract, but performance would have been subsequently excused because events occurring after the breach made performance impossible, is the nonbreaching party entitled to damages for the full term of the contract?

Rule: Where performance is excused for impossibility, damages for breach of contract by the promisor are limited to those damages recoverable prior to the occurrence of the impossibility.

Printing Center of Texas, Inc. v. Supermind Publishing Co., Inc. (1954)

Facts: Supermind paid Printing Center to print books. Upon delivery, Supermind found the books to be nonconforming and rejected the delivery. Supermind sued for a refund.

Issue: May a buyer reject goods that fail to conform to a contract?

Rule: A buyer may reject goods in good faith if the evidence establishes nonconformity with the contract.

Moore v. Fellner (1958)

Facts: Moore, an attorney, represented the Fellners at trial on the basis of a contingency fee agreement. When the case was appealed, Moore sent a letter asking for $2,000 plus costs to further represent them. The Fellners obtained substitute counsel to handle the appeal. The trial court's decision was affirmed and Moore sought to recover his contingency fee.

Issue: Does an attorney breach his contract and forfeit his right to recovery of a contingency fee when he asks his client for an additional fee to continue representation on appeal?

Rule: Where a contract is deemed divisible, an attorney has the right to recover reasonable compensation for his services during the duration of the attorney-client relationship, less the expenses incurred by the client in obtaining other counsel.

Gibson v. Cranage (1878)

Facts: Gibson expressly agreed to the condition that Cranage must be personally satisfied with his portrait of Cranage's deceased daughter before being required to pay. Cranage was dissatisfied and refused to pay.

Issue: Is a contract term requiring personal satisfaction an enforceable condition?

Rule: If a contract's express terms provide that a party is to be personally satisfied before having to perform his part of the contract, that party may insist upon his right as given him by the contract. However, the dissatisfaction must be in good faith.

Luttinger v. Rosen (1972)

Facts: Luttinger agreed to buy a home from Rosen subject to the express condition that Luttinger obtain mortgage financing at a stipulated interest rate. Luttinger was only able to get financing at a higher rate and refused to go through with the purchase even though Rosen offered to change the terms of the contract. Luttinger sued for the return of the deposit.

Issue: Is a contract unenforceable if a condition precedent is not fulfilled?

Rule: If a condition precedent is not fulfilled, the contract is not enforceable. Any offer to alter the express condition to enable the parties to comply with its terms may be rejected.

Gill v. Johnstown Lumber Co. (1892)

Facts: As a result of a flood, Gill was only able to drive and deliver part of the four million feet of logs specified in a contract. The contract provided that Gill be paid set prices per thousand feet of logs delivered, depending on the type of log. Johnstown claimed that since not all the logs were delivered, it was not obligated to pay.

Issue: Is there a divisible contract if the work undertaken consists of several items and the consideration to be paid is apportioned among the several items?

Rule: A contract will generally be held severable if the part to be performed by one party consists of several distinct items, and the price to be paid by the other is either apportioned to each item to be performed or left to be implied by law.

Kirkland v. Archbold (1953)

Facts: Kirkland defaulted after only partially completing the repairs and improvements required under a contract to work on Archbold's house.

Issue: Can a breaching party who has bestowed some benefit on the other party recover for the value of his part performance?

Rule: A defaulting contractor who has materially enriched the estate of the other contracting party may receive the reasonable value of the work done, less whatever damage the other party has suffered.

Bill's Coal Co. v. Board of Public Utilities, Etc. (1982)

Facts: The Board of Public Utilities had a contract to purchase coal from Bill's Coal. The contract provided that the Board could terminate the contract if it could find another supplier who charged at least 15 percent less. The contract was unclear on the method for such a price comparison, although the coal company's interpretation was ridiculous.

Issue: Is a bad faith interpretation of a contractual term a repudiation of the contract?

Rule: The bad faith urging of an interpretation of a contractual term is neither a failure to perform contract obligations (breach) nor an indication those obligations will not be performed in the future (repudiation).

Cosden Oil & Chem. Co. v. Karl O. Helm Aktiengesellschaft (1984)

Facts: Cosden Oil anticipatorily breached a contract to sell and deliver polystyrene to Helm. In assessing Helm's damages, the jury ruled that its subsequent purchases did not "cover" for the polystyrene Cosden Oil was to have supplied. Helm was entitled to the difference between market and contract prices.

Issue: If an anticipatory breach occurs, which market price is used to measure damages?

Rule: A buyer's damages after a seller's repudiation are measured at a commercially reasonable time after the buyer learns of the repudiation (UCC §§2-713, 2-610), but before the time for performance arrives.

United States v. Seacoast Gas Co. (1953)

Facts: Seacoast contracted to supply gas to a federal housing project. During performance, Seacoast, anticipating a breach by the government, notified the government that it was repudiating the contract. The government refused to recognize Seacoast's right to cease performance and subsequently notified Seacoast that the government would accept a bid for a replacement contract unless Seacoast retracted its repudiation within three days. Seacoast did not retract within the three days, and the government accepted a bid from Trion. Before the government had signed the contract with Trion, however, Seacoast announced that it was retracting its repudiation.

Issue: When is a repudiating party barred from retracting its repudiation?

Rule: All that is required to bar a repudiator from retracting its repudiation is definite action by the other party indicating that the anticipatory breach has been accepted as final. Final acceptance can be indicated either by the filing of a suit or a firm declaration that unless the breach is repudiated within a fixed time, it will be accepted.

Norcon Power Partners v. Niagara Mohawk Power Corp. (1998)

Facts: Niagara, a public utility, contracted to buy electricity from Norcon, a power producer. Over the 25-year life of the contract, the price could be adjusted due to market conditions so that Norcon might be obligated to refund much of the price that it had received at the end of the contract. Niagara demanded adequate assurance that Norcon could meet these multi-million dollar obligations. Norcon sued Niagara in federal court for a declaratory judgment that under New York common law it did not have an obligation to provide adequate assurance. The federal courts certified the question to the Court of Appeals of New York.

Issue: Under the common law, may a promisee demand adequate assurance of performance when reasonable grounds exist to believe that a solvent promisor will not perform?

Rule: Yes. The court based the result in this case on the close parallel between this contract to sell electricity, not a sale of goods, and sales of goods that produce energy, such as oil. Sales of goods would be governed by UCC §2-609, which recognizes the right to adequate assurance. The court stopped short of recognizing the adequate assurance right for all cases.

Oppenheimer & Co. v. Oppenheim (1995)

Facts: Tenant Oppenheimer agreed to sublease office space to Subtenant Oppenheim. Tenant promised to get the written consent of the principal landlord to the sublease and to physical changes that Subtenant wanted to make. "Unless and until" Tenant got that written consent, the sublease would not take effect, and Tenant didn't get it. When it sued Subtenant for breach, it argued that Tenant had substantially performed its obligations, including the obligation to get written consent. The jury gave a verdict for Tenant.

Issue: May a party assert substantial compliance with an express condition precedent to the enforceability of a contract?

Rule: No. Getting the written consent of the landlord here was an express condition precedent that can only be carried out exactly as agreed by the parties. Moreover, substantial performance is not a question of fact for the jury but one of law for the court.

Wholesale Sand & Gravel v. Decker (1993)

Facts: Wholesale contracted to install a gravel driveway for Decker. The contract had no completion date; payment was due within 90 days of the contract. Because the ground was very wet, which would have increased the cost substantially and made the job unprofitable, Wholesale deferred the work. No work had been done at about 45 days after the contract signing, and Wholesale failed to begin work after repeated requests by Decker, even after Decker threatened to terminate the contract. Decker hired another contractor to do the work, and Wholesale sued for breach.

Issue: Did Wholesale's repeated failure to begin the work as promised constitute an anticipatory repudiation of the contract?

Rule: Yes. After beginning the job, Wholesale removed its equipment from the job site. Despite several promises to return to it, Wholesale never did, even when Decker threatened termination. This was a definite and unequivocal manifestation of intent by the contractor that he would not do the job promised.

Corenswet, Inc. v. Amana Refrigeration, Inc. (1979)

Facts: Amana had a distribution agreement with Corenswet that gave an exclusive territory to Corenswet to sell Amana products wholesale. The distribution agreement permitted either party to terminate the contract for any reason. Amana demanded that Corenswet prove it had a solid credit structure, and Corenswet made changes to do so. Corenswet expanded distribution of Amana products consistently. Nevertheless, Amana terminated the contract.

Issue: Must the decision to terminate a contract be exercised in good faith?

Rule: If a contract permits either party to terminate a contract for any reason, the decision to do so need not be exercised in good faith.

Greer Properties, Inc. v. LaSalle National Bank (1989)

Facts: LaSalle had title to land that Old Orchard had bought. They agreed to sell the land to Greer Properties for $1.25 million, and undertook to clean up environmental waste. If the cleanup became "economically impracticable," they could terminate the agreement to sell. They did elect to terminate the agreement to sell, but only because another buyer offered them $1.455 million.

Issue: May a contract party with a right to terminate for one reason terminate the contract for another?

Rule: The discretion to terminate a contract must be exercised reasonably and in accord with the obligation of good faith and fair dealing. Here, the decision to terminate did not meet that standard.

Fry v. George Elkins Co. (1958)

Facts: Fry agreed to buy a residence, provided he could get a loan of $20,000 for 20 years at 5 percent. He applied for but did not get such a loan at two banks. Western Mortgage, which held the current mortgagee on the house, was willing to finance Fry's loan on the terms he had specified, and tried to contact Fry, who did not respond. Fry declared the condition on his obligation to purchase had not been satisfied, and demanded the return of his deposit.

Issue: Must a contract party act in good faith with respect to a condition precedent?

Rule: A contract party must make a good faith effort to fulfill a condition precedent to his performance. Here, Fry prevented fulfillment of the condition precedent by failing to respond to the invitations of Western Mortgage.

Pannone v. Grandmaison (1990)

Facts: Pannone served in the military, monitoring radiation levels in the air, and was concerned about them. He offered to buy a house, provided a radon inspection met with his approval. The inspector he hired found a level of radon gas in the house at the bottom of readings in the state and well within Environmental Protection Agency standards. He canceled his agreement to purchase and sued to recover his deposit.

Issue: When a condition of a contract is subject to the approval of a party, must the party exercise that approval according to an objective standard of good faith?

Rule: If a contract grants a party discretion to decide whether a condition has been met, he may exercise that discretion in good faith from his subjective point of view when his individual satisfaction is in fact the condition, and need not meet an objective standard. Here, while Pannone's disapproval of the radon inspection might appear in bad faith objectively, it was in good faith from his subjective point of view. He did not arbitrarily apply his own standard for radiation to this transaction alone.

Godburn v. Meserve (1944)

Facts: The Godburns agreed to live as tenants in Wells' home and to provide food and to care for her as long as she lived. Wells promised in return to leave them her property in her will. Wells complained a great deal, and eventually the Godburns moved out, and Wells changed her will. Upon her death they sued her estate for breach of contract.

Issue: Did Wells' difficult behavior permit the Godburns not to perform their part of the contract?

Rule: Because the Godburns knew of Wells' difficult personality when they undertook to care for her, this by itself is not enough to excuse their nonperformance. They are excused only if Wells' behavior violated her duties under the contract, and the court concluded it didn't.

Ramirez v. Autosport (1982)

Facts: The Ramirezes bought a camper from Autosport, trading in a van. When they went to pick it up, it was scratched and missing parts. When they returned, it was still not ready. When they returned again, it was not given to them.

Issue: Is a buyer obligated under a contract of sale to accept goods that possess minor defects?

Rule: A buyer may reject goods that do not fully conform to the contract. Upon rejection it is the seller's right to cure the nonconformity if the time for the seller's performance has not passed. After that time, the seller may still cure defects within a reasonable time. Here, the buyers rejected and the seller did not cure the defects.

Baker v. Ratzlaff (1977)

Facts: Ratzlaff promised to raise popcorn and to sell it to Baker for $4.75 per hundredweight. Baker was to pay on each delivery and Ratzlaff could refuse to deliver any more popcorn until paid. Ratzlaff delivered two truckloads but did not ask for payment. A week later he terminated the contract and resold the popcorn to another buyer for $8.00 per hundredweight. Baker covered and bought popcorn at $10.30 per hundredweight.

Issue: If a contract of sale permits the seller to terminate the contract if payment is not made upon delivery, may the seller in good faith terminate the contract without asking for payment first?

Rule: A seller who has the right to terminate a contract unless paid on delivery must ask for payment before terminating the contract. A seller terminates the contract in bad faith unless he asks for payment first.

Badgett v. Security State Bank (1991)

Facts: The Badgetts had borrowed money from Security. On the Badgetts' request, Security had also in the past given them new terms for their loan. They again requested new terms in order to be eligible for federal support, but Security did not give the new desired terms on their loan or even consider their request.

Issue: Does a lender violate the duty of good faith and fair dealing by not considering the borrower's proposed new terms for loan?

Rule: Failure to consider new terms cannot violate the duty of good faith and fair dealing.

Gruenberg v. Aetna Insurance Co. (1973)

Facts: Fire destroyed Gruenberg's business. He had overinsured it, so his insurers investigated him, suspecting arson, and refused to pay. They also reported him, which provoked a criminal investigation leading to criminal charges. The charges were dismissed.

Issue: Does an insurer violate the duty of good faith by reporting an insured to the authorities?

Rule: Good faith requires an insurer not to take action that will block the ability of the insured to be compensated on the insurance policy. Reporting an insured to the authorities on grounds the insurer knows to be baseless violates that duty of good faith.

Note: Here, the insured's allegation was taken as true for the purposes of review.

Beck v. Farmers Insurance Exchange (1985)

Facts: Beck was in an automobile accident with an uninsured car. He made a documented demand on Farmers, his carrier, for $20,000, his policy limits. Farmers denied the claim and made no counteroffer. Beck later settled with Farmers for $15,000 and reserved his right to pursue a claim for bad faith.

Issue: May an insurer flatly deny a claim without investigation of the facts or negotiation without violating the duty of good faith?

Rule: An insurer that unreasonably fails to investigate a claim or to negotiate with the insured violates its duty of good faith. This claim is contractual in nature, and can support damages like any other breach of contract, such as consequential damages.

New York Bronze Co. v. Benjamin Acquisition Corp. (1998)

Facts: New York Bronze agreed to sell another company to Benjamin Acquisition for $4.5 million and the assumption of that company's debt. Part of the price was included in a nonnegotiable promissory note for $350,000, which New York Bronze had to surrender in order to be paid that sum.

Issue: Is the surrender of a promissory note a condition precedent to its enforcement, so that failure to surrender it extinguishes the obligation of the maker to pay the note?

Rule: When a contract provision may be interpreted either as an express condition or as a promise, the provision should be read as a promise, particularly when the result of an express condition is forfeiture of a right, such as to payment.

Note: See Restatement Second §227(2) & (3).

J. J. Shane, Inc. v. Aetna Cas. & Surety Co. (1998)

Facts: The County contracted a construction project to Recchi as general contractor, and Recchi subcontracted a portion of the work to Shane. The subcontract provided that Shane would be paid provided the County paid Recchi.

Issue: May a general contractor condition its obligation to pay a subcontractor for work done?

Rule: A subcontract may condition the general contractor's obligation to pay the subcontractor on the job owner's payment of the general contractor, provided the condition is stated expressly, thus shifting the risk of nonpayment by the owner to the subcontractor.

Scavenger, Inc. v. GT Interactive Software, Inc. (2000)

Facts: Scavenger contracted to sell four separate electronic games to GT. Each game had its own production and payment schedule. Scavenger delivered two games; GT did not pay. Scavenger sued for payment. GT alleged Scavenger had breached its contract to deliver the final two games.
Issue: May a promisee sue to enforce part of a contract when the promisor breaches part of a contract?
Rule: If a contract is divisible, breach of one part does not make the other parts unenforceable. A contract that provides for distinct payment and performance schedules for distinct items is divisible.

Chodos v. West Publishing Co. (2002)

Facts: Chodos had a contract to write a book, worked on it for several years, consulted with the West's editors, and submitted the final manuscript. West decided not to publish.
Issue: May a publisher reject a manuscript at the end of the editing process?
Rule: A publishing contract that provides the manuscript must be satisfactory as to form and content does not justify a decision not to publish based on a sense of the likelihood of the commercial success of the book.

Gulf Construction Co. v. Self (1984)

Facts: Good Hope Refinery contracted with Gulf as general contractor to construct buildings. Gulf subcontracted part of the work to Self. Good Hope went bankrupt and did not pay Gulf.
Issue: Does a subcontractor suffer a total loss if the subcontract provides that the general contractor is not "obligated" to pay the subcontractor "until" the owner pays the general contractor?
Rule: If the failure of a condition precedent on one interpretation of the contract would cause a forfeiture for one party but on another interpretation would not, then the second interpretation is applied. Here, the pay-when-paid clause may be interpreted not as a forfeiture of the subcontractor's right to payment but merely a covenant on the manner in which payment should occur.
Note: The suit was against Gulf and Gulf's surety.

Shaw v. Mobil (1975)

Facts: Mobil leased a service station to Shaw. Shaw was obligated to pay a rent of 1.4 cents per gallon of gasoline delivered, but no less than a minimum of $470. If 33,572 gallons or more were delivered, Shaw would not owe the minimum rent. Shaw ordered 34,000 gallons, but Mobil delivered about 25,678 because the federal government allocated deliveries among dealers. Mobil demanded the minimum rent.

Issue: If one party's performance depends on the other party's performance, which does not occur but is excused, is the first party's performance excused also?

Rule: Such a performance is excused. Shaw's promise to pay a minimum rent depended upon Mobil's promise to deliver a minimum quantity of gasoline; when Mobil did not deliver its minimum quantity, Shaw did not have to pay his minimum rent.

Carter v. Sherburne (1974)

Facts: Carter made several contracts to perform construction jobs for Sherburne. Sherburne terminated the contracts because of Carter's failure to finish the jobs on time.

Issue: If time is not stated to be of the essence in a construction contract, will failure to finish the work on time end the contract?

Rule: If time is not of the essence, a contractor's late performance does not terminate the contract, although the contractor will be liable for damages due to the late completion. Here, the contractor had substantially completed the work and was entitled to payment.

Capitol Dodge Sales v. Northern Concrete Pipe, Inc. (1983)

Facts: Capitol sold Northern a truck. Northern took possession. The engine overheated and the problem could not be corrected. Northern canceled the purchase.

Issue: Does a buyer accept goods because he possesses and attempts to use them?

Rule: A buyer may possess goods for the purpose of inspecting or testing them without accepting them. The buyer has a reasonable time to inspect them and then indicate acceptance or rejection for nonconformity (or acceptance despite nonconformity).

Colonial Dodge, Inc. v. Miller (1984)

Facts: Miller bought a car with extra wide tires and returned it when he learned it had no spare tire and none could be provided.

Issue: Must a buyer keep a thing if its nonconformity substantially impairs its value to him?

Rule: A buyer may revoke acceptance of a thing if its nonconformity substantially impairs its value to him. Although a missing spare tire may not cause a substantial drop in market value, Miller had particular reasons to have one when he drove.

Sullivan v. Bullock (1993)

Facts: Sullivan hired Bullock to redo her kitchen. When Sullivan was not home, one of his workers climbed through one of her windows to enter. After that, Sullivan refused to let Bullock or his crew work in her home.

Issue: When is a party's failure to perform excused by the behavior of the other party?

Rule: A party's nonperformance is excused if the other party acts in a way inconsistent with the contract or the reasonable expectations of the parties under the contract. Here, denying access to the worksite is sufficient evidence on which a jury might find a basis to excuse a contractor's nonperformance.

Moe v. John Deere Co. (1994)

Facts: Moe bought a tractor from Deere promising to pay the price in five annual installments. Deere accepted the first two payments, which were late. Deere repossessed the tractor when the third payment was late.

Issue: Must a creditor who has accepted late payments notify the debtor that it will enforce strict compliance with contract obligations from then on?

Rule: Such a creditor must notify the debtor that all obligations must be performed as the contract states before the creditor may resort to remedies such as repossession.

Conley v. Pitney Bowes (1994)

Facts: Pitney Bowes' employee benefits plan provided that when the employer notified an employee of a denial of benefits the employer also had to notify the employee of the administrative procedures the employee must use in order to appeal the denial of benefits. The plan also provided that unless the employee exhausted these administrative procedures he could not challenge the denial in court. Conley was a Pitney Bowes employee injured in an accident whom Pitney Bowes notified of a denial of benefits, but that notice did not inform Conley of the procedures for appealing the denial. Conley sued.

Issue: In a bilateral contract, is the performance of the promise of one party a condition precedent to the duty to perform a return promise?

Rule: When one party must perform its promise before the other party must perform a return promise, the performance of the first promise is a constructive condition precedent to the duty of the other party to perform. The failure of the condition precedent must be a material breach.

Note: Here, Pitney Bowes had to perform its promise to notify Conley of what procedures to use to appeal his termination so that he could exhaust his administrative remedies within the company. Performance of that promise was a constructive condition precedent to Conley's duty to exhaust his administrative remedies before beginning litigation against his employer.

Plateq Corp. of North Haven v. Machlett Labs, Inc. (1983)

Facts: Plateq made lead-covered steel tanks according to Machlett's specifications. A Machlett engineer inspected the tanks on Plateq's premises and noted problems, which Plateq promised to fix so as to have the tanks available for Machlett to pick up the next day. The engineer led Plateq to believe that Machlett would send a truck to do so. Machlett canceled the order by telegram several days later and Plateq sued for breach.

Issue: Is a buyer ever bound to accept nonconforming goods?

Rule: A buyer may reject nonconforming goods, and if the buyer does so the seller has a right to cure the nonconformity. A buyer may also accept goods despite their nonconformity if he signifies that he will accept them after a reasonable opportunity to inspect. The buyer is presumed to accept nonconforming goods if he fails to reject them after a reasonable opportunity to inspect has passed.

Note: Here, the contract permitted Plateq to inspect the tanks after delivery to verify that they would contain radiation. By inspecting the tanks before that time, it seems to have lost a contract right that it otherwise could have exercised. UCC §2-508.

Dalton v. Educational Testing Service (1995)

Facts: Dalton took the SAT twice. Because of a 410-point increase in the score, and a difference in the handwriting, ETS canceled his later score.

Issue: Is a testing service that by contract has the final decision on whether to report a score entitled to exercise its discretion freely in making that decision?

Rule: A covenant of good faith and fair dealing binds a contract party not to interfere with the legitimate expectation of the fruits or benefits of a contract for the other party. The court ordered ETS to release the second score.

Alamance County Bd. of Educ. v. Bobby Murray Chevrolet, Inc. (1996)

Facts: Bobby Murray contracted to sell school bus chassis to several school boards. He ordered the chassis from GM. GM warned Bobby Murray the chassis would be late because a component part was delayed.

Issue: Is a seller's failure to deliver excused when its supplier of the goods it contracted to sell cannot deliver or when the goods will not comply with new regulations?

Rule: A seller, not the buyer, bears the risk that its supplier will not perform.

Note: The seller also sought to be excused because the Environmental Protection Agency issued regulations that the chassis would not comply with. The seller's contract with the school boards addressed the contingency of compliance with government regulations and assigned the seller responsibility for this also.

Truman L. Flatt & Sons Co. v. Schupf (1995)

Facts: Buyer Flatt canceled a land purchase contract when rezoning was denied, but then decided to buy the land anyway.

Issue: May an anticipatory repudiation be retracted?

Rule: An anticipatory repudiation of a contract may be retracted if the other party does not rely upon the repudiation to change position or elect to rescind the contract because of the anticipatory repudiation.

Hornell Brewing Co. v. Spry (1997)

Facts: Spry had an exclusive contract to distribute Hornell Brewing's beverages in Canada. Spry failed to pay for shipments as required and Hornell sought a declaratory judgment that Spry had no more rights as distributor.

Issue: Is a party's failure to provide adequate assurance upon demand a breach that allows the other party to terminate the contract?

Rule: Late payments and bad checks justify a request for adequate assurance of performance, and without such assurance the contract may be terminated.

Seidenberg v. Summit State Bank (2002)

Facts: Summit Bank bought Seidenberg's brokerage firm. He was to continue as its executive. His contract of employment obligated employer and employee to collaborate to increase the income of the brokerage, on which Seidenberg's own income depended. Summit fired him.

Issue: May a terminated employee bring a claim of breach of the implied covenant of good faith and fair dealing?

Rule: A terminated employee may make a claim of breach of the implied covenant of good faith and fair dealing by showing the employer has used its discretion under the contract to frustrate the employee's legitimate expectations. The parol evidence rule only blocks evidence that varies the express terms of a written contract. This implied covenant goes not to the making but the interpretation of the performance of the contract.

Locke v. Warner Bros., Inc. (1997)

Facts: Locke abandoned her case against Eastwood in part for Warner's promise to consider producing any moving picture she might develop. She alleged Warner never intended to consider any picture of hers, rejecting them all automatically.

Issue: Must a party given discretion under the contract exercise that discretion in good faith?

Rule: Discretion must be exercised in good faith and according to fair dealing. Rejecting all projects without a good faith evaluation is bad faith. Whether a party acts in bad faith is a question for the jury.

Donahue v. Federal Express Corp. (2000)

Facts: Donahue worked for Federal Express for 18 years. Federal Express terminated his employment after following its internal procedures.

Issue: May an at-will employee who is terminated bring an action for breach of the implied duty of good faith and fair dealing?

Rule: If the underlying claim arises out of the termination of the contract of employment, an at-will employee cannot sue his employer for breach of the implied duty of good faith and fair dealing. An alleged failure of the employer to follow internal guidelines, which the employer is not contractually bound to follow, does not alter the result.

Best v. United States National Bank (1987)

Facts: The Bank raised its fees (from $3 to $5 per check) to process checks its depositors wrote on insufficient funds. The agreement for its accounts stated that the depositors would owe service charges in effect at the time the Bank performed a particular service, such as processing a bad check. Best and others challenged the new fees as set in bad faith.

Issue: Is a bank's fee for checks written against insufficient funds governed by the obligation of good faith?

Rule: A bank is required to set its service fees in good faith, meaning in accordance with the reasonable contractual expectations of the parties. A fee charged for processing checks written on insufficient funds might be so large as to fail the test of good faith as a matter of law or simply large enough that a fact finder might conclude that the fee was not established in good faith. Here, if good faith requires the Bank to set its fees in line with its costs and profits, there was sufficient evidence for a fact finder that the Bank had not met the standard.

CHAPTER 9

Third-Party Beneficiaries

Generally, contracts between two parties only confer benefits on the parties. Sometimes, two parties may make a contract for the benefit of a third party. The overriding issue in these cases is who is entitled to sue in case of breach. **Example:** A pays C to sing for B. If C does not sing, can B, the third-party beneficiary, sue C? Can A sue C?

I. INTENDED VS. INCIDENTAL BENEFICIARIES

Only an intended third-party beneficiary is entitled to sue if the contract made for his benefit is breached.

A. Intended Beneficiary

To conclude that a third party was intended to be the beneficiary, courts must determine that this would effectuate the intentions of the parties, and either:

1. The obligee was to pay money to the beneficiary, or
2. Circumstances indicate that the promisee intended to give the beneficiary the benefit of the promised performance, as indicated by:
   a. Whether the beneficiary is named in the contract.
   b. Whether performance was to be made directly to the beneficiary.
   c. Whether the beneficiary can change the terms of the performance.
   d. Whether the beneficiary could have reasonably relied on the contract.

B. Incidental Beneficiary

Although an incidental beneficiary receives the benefits of a contract made between other parties, he is not entitled to sue if that contract is breached because it was not intended that he receive any benefits. A party is an incidental beneficiary if he does not satisfy the standards of an intended beneficiary.

Example: A contracts with State to build a new exit for the highway. B owns a gas station near the site of the new exit. The new exit will be beneficial to B's business, but he is only an incidental beneficiary of the contract.

II. TYPES OF BENEFICIARIES

Traditionally, there were two types of beneficiaries.
A. Creditor Beneficiary

If a party contracts with a second party to repay the first party's debt to a third party, the third party is called a creditor beneficiary. **Example:** A owes B $100. C owes A $100. To satisfy his debt with A, C promises A that he will pay B (the creditor beneficiary) $100. Note: The creditor (B) always retains the right to sue the original debtor (A).

B. Donee Beneficiary

If a party contracts with a second party to confer a benefit on a third party, the third party is called a donee beneficiary. **Example:** B promises A to give C $1,000 from A's estate at A's death.
Note: The donee beneficiary (C) does not have a right to sue the promisee (A), but may sue the promisor in case of breach.

C. Restatement (Second) §302

The traditional "creditor" and "donee" categories have been eliminated. All beneficiaries are classified as intended or incidental.

III. ENFORCEMENT BY THE BENEFICIARY

Lawsuits arise when the promisor fails to confer the agreed-upon benefit to the intended beneficiary.
A. Intended Beneficiary vs. Promisor
   1. The promisor's defenses include any defenses that could have been raised if the promisor were sued by the promisee (no mutual assent, failure of consideration, etc.).
   2. The promisor cannot raise any claims that the beneficiary and the promisee may have against each other because the promisor's rights and obligations stem only from the contract with the promisee.
   3. Exception: If the promise was qualified, such that the promisor agreed to make payment "only if the promisee was indebted to the beneficiary," then the promisor may prove that there was no debt.
B. Intended Beneficiary vs. Promisee
   1. If the benefit is not conferred onto the beneficiary, that party cannot bring suit against the promisee because it is not involved in a contractual relationship.

    2. Exception: A creditor beneficiary may sue the promisee directly on the original contract lending to the promisee.

C. Promisee vs. Promisor

A promisee may bring suit against a promisor to enforce a promise that would benefit a third-party beneficiary.

IV. MODIFICATION OF A BENEFICIARY'S RIGHTS

A. After a contract has been made for the benefit of a third party, the contracting parties may usually modify or rescind the contract, denying the benefit to the intended third party, unless:

    1. The contract expressly states that it cannot be modified, or

    2. The contract is silent on the issue of modification, and the third party has materially relied on it, brought suit to enforce it or manifested assent to it.

B. The beneficiary is entitled to any consideration the promisee gets from the promisor for an ineffective attempt to modify the contract.

CASE CLIPS

Lawrence v. Fox (1859)

Facts: Holly owed Lawrence $300. Holly loaned Fox $300 on condition that he repay the $300 to Lawrence, in satisfaction of Holly's debt. Fox did not pay.

Issue: Can a third-party creditor beneficiary sue to enforce a contract between two other parties that was made for the benefit of the third party?

Rule: A third party can sue to enforce an agreement between two other parties that was made for the benefit of the third party even though there is no privity with the third party.

Seaver v. Ransom (1918)

Facts: Beman was about to die and wanted to change her will to provide for her niece, Seaver. Because Beman was afraid she would die before a new will could be written, her husband promised that he would provide for their niece at his death if the will was left unchanged. At his death, her husband left nothing to Seaver, who sued his administrator.

Issue: May a third-party donee beneficiary enforce a promise made between two others for its benefit?

Rule: A party may enforce a contract made for its benefit by two other parties. Third-party beneficiaries are an exception to the requirement of privity between contracting parties.

F.O. Bailey Co. v. Ledgewood, Inc. (1992)

Facts: Plaintiff owned a building and occupied a portion of it for the purposes of operating an antique business. A third party eventually obtained property rights to the unoccupied portion of the building, and subsequently entered into a series of contracts with the defendant for the renovation of the building. Some of the work benefited the plaintiff exclusively, while other parts benefited the entire building. Upon completion of the renovation, the plaintiff sued for breach, claiming that the work done under the contract was faulty and incomplete.

Issue: When may a court allow a plaintiff who benefits from a contract to which it is not a party bring suit for breach of the contract?

Rule: In order to bring a successful third-party beneficiary contract claim, a plaintiff must prove a clear and definite intention on the part of the contracting parties to give the plaintiff the benefit of their performance. Otherwise, the plaintiff is merely an incidental beneficiary and may not sue to enforce the contract.

H.R. Moch Co. v. Rensselaer Water Co. (1928)

Facts: Rensselaer contracted with the city to provide it with water. A fire burned down Moch's warehouse because of inadequate water pressure in the city's hydrants, caused by Rensselaer's negligence. Moch sued for damages, claiming to be the third-party beneficiary of Rensselaer's contract with the city.

Issue: Can a member of the general public sue for improper performance of a government contract made on the public's behalf?

Rule: One who indirectly benefits from a contract made between two other parties cannot sue to enforce the contract. To have standing the party must prove an intention to make the defendant liable to the general public.

Heyer v. Flaig (1969)

Facts: Flaig, an attorney, drew up a will for his client, who wished to leave her entire estate to her daughters, the plaintiffs. Flaig neglected to exclude his client's second husband from the will, and the plaintiffs' inheritance was reduced by $50,000 as a result.

Issue: Is an attorney who erred in drafting a will liable to a person named in the instrument?

Rule: A client's intended beneficiaries can sue an attorney for malpractice if he negligently failed to fulfill the testamentary instructions of the client.

Robson v. Robson (1981)

Facts: The defendant and his son signed a contract that provided that the son's wife, the plaintiff, would receive $500 per month for life if the son died. The plaintiff divorced the son before he died and sued to enforce the clause.

Issue: May contracting parties revoke a benefit promised to a third party prior to the vesting of the beneficiary's rights?

Rule: Contracting parties may discharge, rescind or revoke benefits promised to a third party before the rights vest, provided that the beneficiary did not detrimentally rely on the right prior to its vesting.

Rouse v. United States (1954)

Facts: Winston signed a promissory note for construction of a heating system in her house. The United States eventually took assignment of the note. Rouse bought Winston's house agreeing to assume Winston's debt, but failed to make payments. The United States sued to enforce the contract, claiming it was a third-party beneficiary. Rouse defended that

Winston fraudulently misrepresented the condition of the heating plant and that it had not been properly installed and, thus, the United States did not deserve to be paid.

Issue: What defenses can be raised against a third-party beneficiary?

Rule: A party that promises to make a payment to another party's creditor can assert any defense against the creditor that it could have asserted had it been sued by the promisee. If a promisor's agreement is to be interpreted as a promise to discharge whatever liability the promisee is under, the promisor is allowed to show that the promisee was not actually liable (because of improper performance by the third party). However, when the promise was to pay a certain amount of money to the promisee's creditor, it is immaterial to challenge whether the promisee is actually indebted.

Vrooman v. Turner (1877)

Facts: Evans mortgaged his property to Vrooman, the plaintiff. Evans later conveyed the property to Mitchell, who conveyed it to Sanborn. Neither Mitchell nor Sanborn agreed to assume the mortgage as part of the conveyance. Sanborn conveyed to Turner, the defendant, who agreed to assume the duty to pay the mortgage. Vrooman sued to foreclose the mortgage.

Issue: Is a purchaser of property, who agrees to assume the mortgage on it, obligated to repay the mortgage if the seller did not have such an obligation?

Rule: A purchaser of property who agrees to assume a mortgage on it is not liable to the mortgagee if the property is purchased from who was not liable to the mortgagee.

Note: Evans cannot enforce the Sanborn-Turner agreement as a third-party creditor beneficiary because Sanborn had no obligation to Evans. Vrooman can only sue Evans.

Lucas v. Hamm (1961)

Facts: Hamm, an attorney, prepared a will for his client. After the will was probated, a provision was declared invalid because of an error made by Hamm. The plaintiffs sued Hamm because they received $75,000 less than they would have received had the provision been valid.

Issue: May an intended beneficiary of a will sue an attorney for improperly drawing the will?

Rule: When the main purpose and intent of a testator in making his agreement with an attorney is to benefit a third party named in the will, as a matter of policy the intended beneficiaries may recover as third-party beneficiaries in the event of the attorney's breach.

Martinez v. Socoma Companies, Inc. (1974)

Facts: Socoma was paid by the government to retrain "hard-core unemployed" persons. Socoma breached the contract and the plaintiffs, unemployed persons, sued, claiming to be third-party beneficiaries. The contract provided that in case of breach, Socoma would return the money it received to the government.

Issue: May a member of the public sue to enforce a government contract if he lost benefits as a result of its breach?

Rule: Merely being a potential recipient of benefits from a government contract does not by itself confer upon a party the right to enforce the contract. It must be shown that a clear intention existed to benefit the specific party and that, in appropriate cases, a private right of action was created as remedy in case of breach.

Holbrook v. Pitt (1981)

Facts: The government enacted a program to provide housing assistance to low-income families by paying subsidies to landlords (defendants). Tenants were only eligible for assistance after being certified by the landlord, and they were not automatically given "retroactive certification" (i.e., subsidies accruing between the time that a family is eligible for assistance and the time of certification). Tenants (plaintiffs) sued to demand, as third-party beneficiaries, retroactive certification and that unreasonable delays in granting certification be declared a breach. The legislative history, the method used to calculate subsidies, and the language of the act suggested that protection of tenants was its primary goal. The program was also intended to minimize claims on housing insurance funds.

Issue: Must a governmental contract for the protection of third parties have that goal as its sole purpose in order to allow the third parties to claim rights as beneficiaries?

Rule: Where a government program is designed for the specific protection of a class, as evidenced by the legislative history, the purpose of the program, the method used to calculate subsidies, and express language in the contracts embodying the program, members of that class have standing to enforce it in case of breach. The existence of other subsidiary purposes does not defeat the parties' status as protected beneficiaries.

Copeland v. Beard (1928)

Facts: Beard bought land from Copeland's debtor, agreeing to pay the debtor's obligation to Copeland. Before Copeland could agree to the assignment of the debt, Beard resold the property to another party who promised to repay the debts. Copeland sued Beard when he was not paid by the second buyer.

Issue: Does a creditor beneficiary have a cause of action against a promisor who was discharged of the duty to repay the debt before the beneficiary agreed to the assignment?

Rule: When a debtor contracts with another, for a valuable consideration, to assume and pay his debt, the creditor has an option to accept or reject the new party as his debtor. The promisor and promisee, however, can rescind or discharge their duties at any time before the election is made.

Hale v. Groce (1987)

Facts: Groce was to draw up a will and trust for a client who wanted a certain gift left to Hale. After the client died, Hale discovered that Groce had failed to put in a provision declaring Hale a beneficiary.

Issue: May a third-party beneficiary of a contract recover for negligent acts of the parties to the contract?

Rule: A third party may recover for the negligent performance of a party to a contract.

Johnson v. Holmes Tuttle Lincoln-Mercury, Inc. (1958)

Facts: Holmes Tuttle, a car dealer, sold Caldera a car, promising that full insurance coverage would be provided. Although Holmes Tuttle added the cost of premiums to Caldera's monthly payments, it failed to take out a policy, Caldera got into an accident with Johnson, the plaintiff. Johnson sued Holmes Tuttle claiming that it was a third-party beneficiary of the promise to take out insurance.

Issue: May a third-party beneficiary enforce a contract if he was a member of a class that was to obtain a benefit under the contract?

Rule: A third-party beneficiary may enforce a contract made by two other parties, even if he was not identified as an individual, as long as he is a member of the class for whose benefit the contract was made.

Lonsdale v. Chesterfield (1983)

Facts: Chesterfield subdivided and sold parcels of land. Each sales contract contained a clause stating that Chesterfield would install a water system, which was to be paid for by the owners of the parcel. Chesterfield sold its interest to Sansaria. A clause in their contract provided that Sansaria would install the water system, but it did not. Purchasers of the subdivisions sued to enforce the agreement between Sansaria and Chesterfield.

Issue 1: May a party enforce a contract between two other parties if it is to benefit from the contract?

Rule 1: Third parties who benefit from a contract between two others may enforce the contract, provided the parties to the contract intended that one party assume a direct obligation to the third party.

Issue 2: May one avoid liability by delegating duties?

Rule 2: Liability cannot be avoided by delegating a duty. The delegator remains secondarily liable.

Fourth Ocean Putnam Corp. v. Interstate Wrecking Co., Inc. (1985)

Facts: Fourth Ocean owned a hotel that had been destroyed by fire. Believing that the structure was a public nuisance and a fire hazard, the Village hired Interstate Wrecking to tear down the building, to remove all walls and foundations one foot below grade level, and to crush and remove the slab. The Village later recovered the costs from Fourth Ocean. A few years later, Fourth Ocean began new construction on the site and discovered that the walls and foundations had not been removed, and the slab had not been crushed.

Issue: Where two parties contract to satisfy the obligation of a third party, does the third party have rights as a third-party beneficiary?

Rule: Where two parties contract to satisfy the obligation of a third party, the third party does not have rights as a third-party beneficiary if the parties performed the contract for the purpose of satisfying some other party (i.e., the third party's obligee).

Note: Thus, the court found that the contract between Interstate Wrecking and the Village was intended to benefit the villagers by satisfying Fourth Ocean's obligation to remove the hazard.

Zigas v. Superior Court of California (1981)

Facts: In a class action suit, a group of tenants sought damages for landlords' violations of a financing agreement with the federal government that limited the amount of rent landlords could charge tenants.

Issue: Is state law applicable in determining whether tenants have standing to maintain a third-party cause of action to enforce provisions of a financing agreement where the federal government is a party?

Rule: State law is applicable to determine whether tenants have standing to sue as third-party beneficiaries to enforce provisions of a financing agreement between private parties and the federal government, provided the controversy raises no questions regarding liability of the United States.

1. Alexander H. Revell & Co. v. C.H. Morgan Grocery Co. (1919)

Facts: C.H. Morgan contracted to have Lidke install new fixtures in its store. Lidke did a poor job, and the parties made a second contract whereby C.H. Morgan agreed to pay for the materials if Lidke finished the work properly. Lidke did not do the work, and C.H. Morgan refused to pay Alexander H. Revell, a materialman, for supplies.

Issue: Are the rights of a third-party beneficiary dependent on proper performance of the obligations of the contracting parties?

Rule: When a contract is entered into by two parties for the benefit of a third, the third party's rights are subject to the "equities" between the original parties. Any defense that can be asserted against *one* of the contracting parties can also be asserted against the third party.

Tweeddale v. Tweeddale (1903)

Facts: In exchange for consideration, Daniel Tweeddale gave his mother a bond (promise) that he would give her and his brother Edwin Tweeddale a share of the money Daniel would receive from the sale of land. To secure the bond, Daniel gave his mother a mortgage on the property. Daniel later sold the land and settled with his mother (who discharged the mortgage) and revoked his promise to his banker. Edwin only became aware of Daniel's promise after it was rescinded. Edwin sued as a third-party beneficiary of Daniel's contract with their mother.

Issue: May a third party's rights be rescinded before he is aware of them?

Rule: When two parties contract to pay money to a third party in exchange for consideration, the law establishes privity between the promisor and the third person, and the liability is binding, regardless of whether the beneficiary has knowledge of the transaction.

Detroit Bank & Trust Co. v. Chicago Flame Hardening Co., Inc. (1982)

Facts: Three partners made a contract to provide a cash stipend to their spouses in case of their death. The agreement was later rescinded, but one of the spouses challenged the rescission after her husband died.

Issue: May a contract be modified or rescinded to the detriment of a third-party beneficiary?

Rule: A contract may be modified or rescinded to the detriment of a third-party beneficiary at any time before the contract is accepted, adopted or acted upon by the third-party beneficiary.

Western Waterproofing Co. v. Springfield Housing Authority (1987)

Facts: Western Waterproofing was a subcontractor to Bildoc, which had a waterproofing and weatherization contract with Springfield Housing Authority (SHA). The contract required SHA to procure a payment bond from Bildoc, which it did not do. Western contributed labor and materials toward completion of the project but never received its payment of $129,000. After failing to collect on its default judgment against Bildoc, Western resumed proceedings against SHA as a third-party beneficiary.

Issue: May a third-party beneficiary sue a public entity when such entity has failed to secure a surety bond as required by the contract?

Rule: If an element of a contract is intended for the direct benefit of a third party, such third party may sue for breach. Payment bonds, by definition, exist for the protection and direct benefit of third parties.

Erickson v. Grande Ronde Lumber Co. (1939)

Facts: Erickson was a creditor of Grande Ronde. The Stoddard Company assumed the debts of Grande Ronde. Erickson sought judgment against both companies.

Issue: Is a creditor entitled to judgment against both a debtor and the promisor who has assumed its debts?

Rule: Both promisor and debtor are liable for a debt to the credit beneficiary though there can be only one satisfaction of the debt.

Drewen v. Bank of Manhattan Co. (1959)

Facts: As part of a divorce agreement between husband and wife, the husband promised to never reduce their children's interest in his estate as set forth in a will executed on the day of the agreement. Later, after his ex-wife had died, the husband executed a new will that altered the arrangements for the children. The suit was brought by the administrator of the ex-wife's estate against the executor and trustee of husband's will.

Issue: Does a promisee of a contract for the benefit of a third party have a right to sue for damages?

Rule: A promisee of a contract for the benefit of a third party has sufficient interest in the enforcement of the promise to sue for damages.

Note: The ex-wife's right to enforce the contract passed to her estate with her death.

Pierce Associates, Inc. v. The Nemours Foundation (1988)

Facts: Nemours hired a general contractor to complete the interior of its hospital. The general contractor hired Pierce, as subcontractor, to complete the mechanical work on the project. The entire hospital project was plagued by delays and disputes that prompted Nemours to withhold payments due to Gilbane under the general contract. In response, Pierce suspended performance of its subcontract. Nemours hired a new contractor to complete Pierce's work and sued Pierce for damages.

Issue: When is a nonparty considered a third-party beneficiary of a contract?

Rule: A nonparty is considered to be a third-party beneficiary to a contract when the language of the contract expresses an intent to confer third-party beneficiary status to that party.

Septembertide Publishing, B.V. v. Stein & Day, Inc. (1989)

Facts: Stein & Day, a publishing house, agreed to pay Septembertide (representing the author of a book) an advance, and subsequent royalties and sublicensing income in exchange for the exclusive right to license and publish the book within the United States. Stein & Day soon entered into a sublicensing agreement with New Library for the publication of the book in paperback. Stein & Day used advance money obtained from New Library to pay a portion of the advance owed to Septembertide, but subsequently became insolvent and was unable to pay the balance by the due date. Septembertide, suing as a third-party beneficiary to the paperback agreement, sought an injunction against New Library compelling payment to Septembertide of sublicensing income due to Stein & Day.

Issue: When is a party considered a third-party beneficiary to a contract?

Rule: A party is a third-party beneficiary to a contract if recognition of a right to performance in the beneficiary is appropriate to effectuate the intent of the parties and either (1) performance will satisfy the promisee's obligation to pay the beneficiary money or (2) circumstances indicate that the promisee intends to give the beneficiary the benefit of the promised performance.

Hampton v. Federal Express Corp. (1990)

Facts: Hampton, a 13-year old cancer patient, was awaiting a bone marrow transplant at a hospital in Omaha, Nebraska. A transplant operation was scheduled at a hospital in Iowa City, Iowa, where five potential donors had been found. To match Hampton with the most suitable donor, the Omaha hospital sent five samples of the boy's blood via Federal Express to a doctor at the Iowa City hospital. The doctor never received the samples, and the boy died one month later. Federal Express' transport agreement with the hospital included a provision limiting Federal Express' liability for lost shipments to $100. Hampton's parents sued Federal Express.

Issue: What damages may a third-party beneficiary recover for breach of a contract?

Rule: A third-party beneficiary, like any plaintiff, may only recover for a loss that, in the ordinary course of events, would result from the defendant's breach or for a loss that was in the contemplation of the parties at the time the contract was made. In this case, the Omaha hospital did not inform Federal Express of the package contents, or insure the package for a higher value; therefore Federal Express had no reason to anticipate a liability beyond the agreed $100.

Jardel Enterprises, Inc. v. Triconsultants, Inc. (1988)

Facts: Jardel hired Brooks Western Builders to construct a fast-food restaurant. The contract specified a completion date and provided for liquidated damages of $100 for each day performance was delayed. Brooks subcontracted Triconsultants, who made a surveying mistake that resulted in a 65-day delay. Brooks paid Jardel $6,500 in accordance with the general contract. Brooks sued Triconsultants for breach of the subcontract and the parties settled for $25,000. Jardel sued Triconsultants and claimed that the settlement agreement did not bind it.

Issue 1: When is a third-party beneficiary considered a creditor beneficiary?

Rule 1: A third-party beneficiary is a creditor beneficiary if performance of the contract satisfies an actual duty owed by one of the parties to the beneficiary.

Issue 2: What rights may a creditor beneficiary assert against a breaching party?

Rule 2: A creditor beneficiary may assert rights equal to, but not greater than, the rights of the contract promisee, because the creditor beneficiary's right to the contract is purely derivative of the right of the contract promisee. In this case, the plaintiff was a creditor beneficiary, and the general contractor's settlement with the subcontractor was therefore binding on the plaintiff.

Bain v. Gillispie (1984)

Facts: A collegiate athletic conference (the Big Ten) contracted with Bain to referee basketball games. Bain called a foul (on University of Iowa) that permitted the opposing team (Purdue) to win an important game on a foul shot. Gillispie began selling items from his novelty store depicting Bain in a hangman's noose. Bain sued Gillispie to enjoin the sales. Gillispie counterclaimed alleging he was a third-party beneficiary of Bain's contract with the Big Ten, seeking damages on the theory that if Bain had performed his contract properly Gillispie's store would have made profits on the sale of University of Iowa paraphernalia following Iowa's victory over Purdue.

Issue: Is a person who stands to gain from the performance of a contract a third-party beneficiary of that contract?

Rule: The promisee must intend to confer a benefit on a beneficiary for him to make out a claim as third-party beneficiary. Here, Gillispie could show no such intent on the part of the Big Ten conference.

The Cretex Companies, Inc. v. Construction Leaders, Inc. (1984)

Facts: Northland Mortgage contracted with Construction Leaders for work on a project. Travelers Indemnity issued a performance bond to Northland Mortgage guaranteeing Construction Leaders' performance of the work. Construction Leaders bought materials for the work from Cretex, did not pay, and Cretex sought payment as a third-party beneficiary from Travelers Indemnity on the bond.

Issue: Can a materialman recover from the surety of the contractor who bought materials and did not pay for them?

Rule: A third party can recover as a beneficiary on a contract if the parties to that contract intended to benefit the third party. Materialmen are not presumed to be third-party beneficiaries of such performance bonds, so the bond must specifically state that they are.

United States v. Wood (1989)

Facts: Wife and Husband divorced. Wife agreed in their property settlement to use the house to pay Husband's income tax debt to the federal government. She eventually sold the house for much more than the income tax debt but did not pay it. The federal government sued her.

Issue: May a third party enforce a contractual claim based on a divorce settlement?

Rule: If there is consideration moving from promisee to promisor, and the promisee intends to benefit the third party, then the third party may enforce the benefit promised to the third party. Here, Wife is the promisor, Husband is the promisee (she promised to pay his taxes), and the federal government is the intended third-party beneficiary of this promise in their divorce settlement.

Ertel v. Radio Corp. of America (1974)

Facts: Economy Finance lent funds to Delta Engineering, which granted Economy Finance a security interest in its accounts receivable. Ertel, an officer of Delta, also guaranteed the loan to Economy Finance. RCA bought equipment from Delta on credit, and Delta assigned that account to Economy Finance and gave notice to RCA to pay the debt it owed to Delta to Economy Finance instead. Delta defaulted to Economy Finance and Ertel paid the debt. Ertel thus became subrogated to Economy Finance's claim against RCA. RCA, however, claimed a right of set-off against the account, because the equipment Delta had sold it was defective.

Issue: Is one who is subrogated to a creditor's claim against an account debtor subject to a right of set-off by the account debtor against that claim?

Rule: Yes. The subrogee of the creditor takes the claim subject to any defenses that could have been urged against the creditor/subrogor. RCA's right of set-off against Delta survives its assignment and the subrogation of another to the claim against RCA.

Cheney v. Jemmett (1984)

Facts: Cheney as Seller and Jemmett as Buyer signed a purchase agreement for real estate. Jemmett agreed not to assign the purchase agreement without Cheney's consent.
Issue: May the beneficiary of a promise not to assign a contract withhold his consent for any reason whatsoever?
Rule: The seller may withhold his consent to the buyer's assignment of a purchase agreement if he does so in good faith.

Anderson v. Fox Hill Village Homeowners Corp. (1997)

Facts: Fox Hill leased property on which it operated a retirement complex for which it assumed responsibility to maintain. The lease also obligated Fox Hill to remove snow and ice promptly. Anderson, whose employer had space on the premises, slipped on ice in the parking lot.
Issue: May a person injured on premises for which the lessee under its lease has responsibility and has the particular duty to remove ice and snow sue the lessee as a third-party beneficiary of the lease?
Rule: A third party must show that both lessor and lessee intended that the lessee's performance of a duty under the lease would benefit the third party. Such an intent must be clear and definite. Otherwise, the third party is an incidental beneficiary, who cannot recover in contract from the lessee.

Lumley v. Gye (1853)

Facts: Lumley contracted with a singer named Wagner for her exclusive performances at his opera house. Gye induced her to breach that contract by offering her more money to sing at his theater.
Issue: If a third party induces a party to a contract to breach, may the other party sue the third party for damages?
Rule: A third party may be liable for inducing a breach of contract. Such a third party is liable with the party in breach for contract damages, and may be liable in addition for more damages if they are necessary to make the innocent party whole.
Note: The basis of the action against the third party is in tort, now labeled the tort of malicious interference with contract.

J. D. Edwards & Co. v. Podany (1999)

Facts: SNE manufactured windows and hired Edwards to provide software to aid that manufacturing process. Before Edwards had finished its work, SNE became a division of another company, which asked Mercer Management Consulting and its employee Podany to review the decision to use Edwards' software. Podany advised that SNE should breach its contract with Edwards and use other software instead, which happened to be the only software Podany was familiar with. SNE did so.

Issue: May a party to a contract whose contract is breached sue a consultant who in good faith advised the other party to breach?

Rule: A consultant's advice in good faith that a contract should be breached enjoys qualified privilege that protects the consultant from claims by the other party to the contract for intentional interference with contract. The advice must be within the scope of the consultant's contract, and the advice must be honest, that is, not offered for the benefit of the consultant.

Note: Here, there was sufficient evidence to justify the jury verdict for Edwards, because Podany appeared to have manipulated the decision not to use Edwards because he was not able to work with its software and to use another software provider, whose product was in fact the only one he could work with. The jury also knew that the substitute software Podany recommended had failed badly.

Grigerik v. Sharpe (1998)

Facts: Lang contracted to sell land to Grigerik. Lang hired Sharpe to prepare plans for the site. After the sale, Grigerik was unable to obtain a building permit.

Issue: May a foreseeable third-party beneficiary of a contract sue a contract party for damages?

Rule: At least one of the contract parties must intend that the contract benefit the third party. Here, Grigerik did not prove such an intent.

Scarpitti v. Weborg (1992)

Facts: The developer of a subdivision hired Weborg, an architect, to oversee enforcement of deed restrictions on the building of houses within the subdivision. Weborg enforced the restrictions against plaintiffs, who built accordingly. Weborg waived the restrictions for some later construction. The plaintiffs sued Weborg.

Issue: If the parties to a contract do not intend to benefit a particular third party, is that party precluded from suing as a third-party beneficiary to that contract?

Rule: If someone contracts for services that will benefit an entire but defined group, members of that group are intended beneficiaries. Here, the architect's contract with the subdivision owner intended to benefit all buyers of lots through the consistent enforcement of building restrictions.

Vogan v. Hayes Appraisal Associates, Inc. (1999)

Facts: The Vogans borrowed money from MidAmerica Savings Bank to build a house. MidAmerica hired Hayes Appraisal to monitor construction so that MidAmerica could disburse funds to the contractor as the job progressed. Hayes Appraisal's progress reports were inaccurate. The contractor defaulted, causing a loss to the Vogans.

Issue: When may a third party sue a party to a contract for faulty performance of that contract?

Rule: The third party must be the intended beneficiary of the contract, and is an intended beneficiary of the contract if it is apparent that the promisee intended the promisor's performance to benefit the third party. Here, MidAmerica as promisee did intend that Hayes Appraisal's progress reports would benefit the Vogans.

KMART Corp. v. Balfour Beatty, Inc. (1998)

Facts: Balfour Beatty constructed a shopping center under a contract with the owner, Tutu Park, Ltd. KMART was a tenant in the shopping center. Winds damaged the roof. KMART alleged it was a third-party beneficiary of the contract between Balfour Beatty and the owner, which included KMART's construction specifications, required warranties by Balfour Beatty to KMART directly, and required that Balfour Beatty submit design drawings to KMART.

Issue: May a tenant of a shopping center owner recover as third-party beneficiary of a contract between the owner and a contractor constructing the shopping center?

Rule: A shopping center tenant may recover as third-party beneficiary of a contract between the center's owner and a contractor if the tenant is an intended beneficiary of that contract. Here, KMART was clearly an intended beneficiary of the construction contract, and not merely an incidental beneficiary.

Pierce Associates, Inc. v. The Nemours Foundation (1988)

Facts: Gilbane was the general contractor for Nemours on a hospital project and Pierce was a subcontractor. Pierce did not complete its work. Both Nemours and Gilbane recovered damages against Pierce in a jury trial.

Issue: May a job owner recover damages directly against a subcontractor?
Rule: No. Here, the parties used an American Institute of Architects form subcontract that provides the subcontractor's rights and duties are to the general contractor, not the owner. Thus, the owner is not an intended beneficiary of the subcontract and cannot sue the subcontractor as a third-party beneficiary.

CHAPTER 10

Assignment of Rights and Delegation of Duties

Assignment and delegation involve the transfer of contractual rights or duties to a third party. The issues that usually arise involve questions of which rights/duties are transferable, what are the consequences of such transfers for the original parties, and what is the extent of the third party's obligations.

I. DEFINITIONS

A. Assignment
   A party to a contract (assignor) transfers contractual rights to a third person (assignee).
B. Delegation
   A party to a contract (obligor/promisor) transfers contractual duties to a third person (delegatee).
C. Assignment and Delegation vs. Third-Party Beneficiary vs. Novation
   1. Assignment and delegation occur after a contract is executed. There is no requirement that both parties agree to it.
   2. Third-party beneficiaries are created at the time the contract is made.
   3. Novations occur when both parties agree that a third party substitute for one party.

II. ASSIGNMENT

A. An assignment is a present transfer of contractual rights. A promise to transfer contractual rights at a future date is not an assignment. UCC Article 9 now covers most assignments of rights in the commercial context.

B. Rights That May Be Assigned

Generally, all contractual rights are assignable, with the following exceptions:

Mnemonic: **POP FRED**

1. **P**rohibited by Law

   A right cannot be assigned if a statute or public policy prohibits the assignment of that type of right. The most common examples are rights to future alimony payments, torts claims that are assigned to lawyers, and rights to wages.

2. **OP**tions

   a. Unilateral options may be assigned. **Example:** Joe tells Moe, "If you give me $250,000 within 30 days, I will sell you my house." Moe can assign the option to Bo.

   b. Options for bilateral contracts can only be assigned if unaccompanied by an impermissible delegation. **Example:** Joe tells Moe, "I will give you 30 days to promise me that you will buy my house for $250,000 and also play tuba at my wedding as part of the deal." Moe can assign his right (option) to Bo, but Bo's acceptance is only valid if Moe, not Bo, plays the tuba (a duty) at Joe's wedding. Note: See "Delegation" for more on impermissible delegations.

3. **F**uture Rights

   Rights that are expected to arise in the future are not assignable. An attempt to make a present assignment of future rights has the effect of a promise to assign the rights when they do arise. If the assignment is based on an existing contract, however, it is enforceable. **Example:** B, a buyer, assigns the rights to future deliveries he will receive from S, a seller, under their present contract. The assignment would be shaky if B promises to assign future deliveries from a contract he hopes/expects to make with S in a few months.

4. **R**isk to Obligor Substantially Altered

   Assignment is not permitted if the obligor's risk will be materially changed as a result. Risks do not have to be increased, just altered. **Example:** S sells a plane to B and attempts to assign the insurance policy on it. The assignment is ineffective because the policy is based on the age, experience, etc., of the pilot, which varies from person to person.

5. **E**xpress Contractual Clause Not to Assign

   A general clause prohibiting assignment will not usually invalidate an assignment of rights under the contract. Although the assignment is effective, the assignor is held to have breached the contract. The Restatement Second §322 and UCC §2-210 provide that an express contractual clause prohibiting assignment is valid and that subsequent assignments are breaches of the contract. The Restatement provides the following exceptions (rights assignable regardless of contrary clauses):

a. The right to sue for breach of contract by the other party.

b. The right to return performance where the assignor has fully performed his obligations.

c. An anti-assignment clause is waivable by the party for whose benefit it was made.

d. An agreement not to "assign the contract" is construed to bar delegation of duties only, not assignment of rights. However, language that clearly bars assignment will be upheld as barring assignment of rights also (see *Allhusen v. Caristo Construction Corp.*). Note: Under UCC Article 9, which covers commercial financing, any anti-assignment term in a contract that comes within the scope of Article 9 is ineffective.

6. **Duty of Obligor Altered**

   Assignments that materially change an obligor's duties are prohibited.

   a. Personal Service Contracts

      Employers cannot assign rights to receive services if the services are unique or based on a special relationship.

   b. Output Contracts

      At common law, such contracts were not assignable. The UCC allows assignment of output contracts if the output of the assignee will not be unreasonably disproportionate to the assignor's expected production under the original contract.

III. REQUIREMENTS OF AN EFFECTIVE ASSIGNMENT

A. Present Transfer

B. Adequate Description of the Right to Be Assigned

C. Does not have to be in writing, except for the following:

   1. Interest in land
   2. Sale of goods over $500
   3. Chose in action worth more than $5,000
   4. Security interests under UCC Article 9
   5. Wage assignments

D. Consideration is not required. However, a gratuitous assignment is revocable.

   1. Automatic revocation occurs upon:

      a. Death of assignor.
      b. Bankruptcy of assignor.
      c. Subsequent reassignment of the right by assignor to another person.

      d. Notice is given by assignor to assignee that the assignment has been revoked.
  2. Gratuitous assignments can be made irrevocable by:
      a. Delivery to the assignor of a document symbolizing the right that was assigned (stock certificate, bankbook, insurance policy, etc.).
      b. A writing, made by the assignor, providing that the assignment will not be revoked.
      c. Detrimental reliance by the assignee on the assignment.
      d. Obligor rendering the assigned performance.
      e. Giving consideration for the assignment.

IV. RIGHTS OF THE PARTIES AFTER AN ASSIGNMENT

A. Privity of contract is established between the obligor and assignee and erased between obligor and assignor.
B. Rights of the Assignee
The assignee "steps into the shoes" of the assignor and thus can directly enforce the contract.
C. Rights of the Obligor
The obligor may assert any defense against the assignee that would have been available to assert against the assignor. For example, if the assignor did not give consideration or misrepresented a material fact, this defense can be raised against the assignee's right.
D. Rights of Assignee Against Assignor
If the assignee is unable to recover from the obligor, that party may try to recover from the assignor.
  1. Gratuitous Assignment
  Assignee will not recover unless detrimental reliance is shown.
  2. Assignment for Value
  An assignment that is given for consideration contains the following implied warranties:
      a. Assignor will not impair enforcement of the right.
      b. The right assigned is valid and all encumbrances have been disclosed.
      c. Any documents that evidence the transferred right are valid.
      d. The assignor does not warrant the creditworthiness of the obligor unless the assignor expressly agrees to guarantee it.
E. Rights of Sub-assignees
If an assignee assigns the right to yet another party, all of the implied warranties of the original assignor are not automatically transferred unless the original assignor makes an express agreement. However, the sub-assignee is responsible for the transferred duties.

V. MODIFICATION BY THE OBLIGOR AND ASSIGNOR

An obligor and assignor may attempt to modify their agreement in a way that will affect the assignee's rights. The effect of such modification depends on the extent of the obligor's awareness of the assignee:

A. Modification Before Obligor Receives Notice of the Assignment
   The obligor and assignor can modify in good faith. (Rest. 2d §318.)

B. Modification After Obligor Receives Notice of the Assignment
   The assignor and obligor can only make a "good faith" modification if the assignor has not fully performed all duties under the contract.

VI. DELEGATION OF DUTIES

Delegation involves the transfer of contractual duties. Unlike an assignor, whose rights to benefits terminate, a delegator remains liable under the contract should the delegatee improperly perform his duties.

A. Types of Nondelegable Duties
   1. Contracts involving performance requiring special skills. A contract is delegable, despite a personal preference of the obligee that the original obligor perform, if the services do not require a special skill.
   2. "Special trust" relationships (e.g., doctor-patient).
   3. Contract provision expressly prohibiting delegation.

B. Rights and Duties After Delegation
   1. Obligee must accept services that were lawfully delegated.
   2. The delegator remains liable for performance after delegation unless the obligee specifically consented to the delegation, thus forming a novation.
   3. The Delegatee
      a. Delegation
         Delegatee may perform the duties at his option.
      b. Assumption
         Delegatee must perform because he agreed to do so in exchange for consideration. The obligor becomes a third-party beneficiary to delegatee's agreement to perform.
      c. Novation
         Under a novation, all parties must agree to the new arrangement. Delegation and assumption do not have to be approved by the obligee to be valid.

CASE CLIPS

Macke Co. v. Pizza of Gaithersburg, Inc. (1970)

Facts: Pizza of Gaithersburg contracted to have vending machines installed by Virginia Coffee Co. The defendant sought to terminate the contract when Virginia Coffee's assets were purchased by Macke, which assumed Pizza of Gaithersburg's contract as a result.

Issue: Are rights and duties that arise out of an executory bilateral contract assignable?

Rule: Rights are assignable under an executory bilateral contract. A duty is delegable when the services are not of a personal or unique character.

Allhusen v. Caristo Constr. Corp. (1952)

Facts: Caristo Construction contracted with a subcontractor to paint. The subcontractor assigned his right to payment to a third party, who assigned it to Allhusen. A contract clause prohibited assignment of "monies due or to become due" without written permission from Caristo.

Issue: What is the legal effect of a contractual provision prohibiting assignment?

Rule: When clear language is used, parties may limit the freedom of alienation of rights and prohibit an assignment.

Ford Motor Credit Co. v. Morgan (1989)

Facts: Morgan purchased a car at a car dealership from a salesman who gave assurances of the economy and reliability of the car. Morgan financed the acquisition through Ford Motor Credit. Over the next 18 months, Morgan experienced multiple problems with the car, and finally decided to discontinue payments to Ford. Ford took action to recover and sell the vehicle, but found that the car had been vandalized beyond repair. Subsequently, Ford sued to recover the outstanding balance owed by Morgan. Morgan counterclaimed for damages against Ford, claiming that as assignee of the sales contract, Ford was liable for the dealer's fraud in selling the vehicle.

Issue: May the assignee of a contract be held affirmatively liable for the wrongful acts of the assignor?

Rule: An assignee of a contract may not be held affirmatively liable for claims that could be brought against the assignor. The principle that the assignee "stands in the assignor's shoes" means only that a debtor may raise the same defenses against the assignee as could have been raised against the assignor, but does not imply a transfer of liability to the assignee for the assignor's wrongs.

Homer v. Shaw (1912)

Facts: Homer lent money to a subcontractor in exchange for an assignment of half the subcontractor's profits. Shaw, who had hired the subcontractor, agreed to cancel their contract and form a new one when the subcontractor told him that he would not finish the work due to financial difficulties. Homer sued for the assigned profits. Shaw claimed that the new contract nullified the former, assigned one.

Issue: May an assignee's claims be nullified by a rescission and new contract due to the impossibility of performing the original contract?

Rule: When performance of a contract is impossible due to unforeseen circumstances, the parties may rescind the contract and form a new one, even if an assignment is nullified.

Boston Ice Co. v. Potter (1877)

Facts: Citizen's Ice Co. contracted to supply Potter with ice. The Boston Ice Co. bought Citizen's and continued to supply ice to Potter, although it did not inform him of the change in ownership.

Potter refused to pay when he discovered the change a year later. Potter had previously contracted with Boston Ice directly and was extremely dissatisfied with services provided under that contract.

Issue: Does performance by a party who was assigned a contract impose liability on the other party?

Rule: Acceptance of an assignment may not be presumed from the acceptance of goods. Therefore, privity of contract only exists when the purchaser of the goods has been notified of and accepted the assignment.

Evening News Ass'n v. Peterson (1979)

Facts: Peterson, a newscaster at a TV station, contested the assignment of his employment contract when the station was sold.

Issue: May an employment contract be assigned?

Rule: An employment contract is assignable if it was not based on a personal relationship, and the employment was not materially changed by the assignment.

Larese v. Creamland Dairies, Inc. (1985)

Facts: Larese, a franchisee, agreed that it would not sell or lease its interests in the franchise without Creamland Dairies' consent.

Issue: Does a franchisor have an absolute right to refuse to consent to the sale of a franchisee's interest to another prospective franchisee?

Rule: If the franchisor does not specifically bargain for an absolute right of refusal, the right of refusal will be limited to only reasonable refusals.

Fitzroy v. Cave (1905)

Facts: Five creditors assigned to Fitzroy debts owed them by Cave. Fitzroy attempted to force Cave into bankruptcy so that he would be dismissed from his position as a director of Fitzroy's corporation.

Issue: May an otherwise proper assignment be challenged because of the improper motives of the assignee?

Rule: A valid assignment is not affected by the assignee's motive.

Crane Ice Cream Co. v. Terminal Freezing & Heating Co. (1925)

Facts: Mr. Fredrick, an ice cream plant owner, made a requirements contract to buy ice from Terminal. Terminal renewed the contract because he was satisfied with Fredrick's adherence to the contract terms, which included exclusivity, timely payment and good faith efforts to maintain a sufficient volume of purchases. Terminal refused to honor Fredrick's assignment of the contract to Crane Ice Cream.

Issue: Is an assignment invalid if the contract was induced by personal factors?

Rule: A contract may not be assigned if part of its inducement was based on personal factors. A person has the right to the benefit accruing from the character, credit and substance of the other party to the contract.

Note: The court was motivated largely by the fact that because this was a requirements contract, Terminal was in a vulnerable position.

Continental Purchasing Co., Inc. v. Van Raalte Co., Inc. (1937)

Facts: Potter assigned all of her wages to Continental Purchasing as security for an account. Van Raalte, Porter's employer, continued to pay Potter's wages to her, despite notification of the assignment.

Issue: Is one liable for paying his indebtedness to an assignor rather than an assignee?

Rule: If a debtor who has been given notice of an assignment pays an assignor any money that, under the assignment, belongs to the assignee, or if he does anything prejudicial to the rights of the assignee, the debtor is liable to the assignee for any resulting damages.

Sally Beauty Co. v. Nexxus Prods. Co., Inc. (1986)

Facts: Nexxus had entered into a contract under which Best Barber would be the exclusive distributor of Nexxus haircare products throughout most of Texas. Best Barber was acquired and merged into Sally Beauty, which was the subsidiary of another manufacturer of haircare products and a direct competitor of Nexxus. The defendant canceled the contract, claiming that it was not assignable in such a situation.

Issue: May a "best efforts" contract be assigned to a marketplace competitor of the obligee?

Rule: A "best efforts" contract may not be assigned to a marketplace competitor of the obligee without the obligee's approval, because it is reasonable to expect that the performance the obligee will receive will be substantially different from that for which he bargained.

Dissent: Such a contract may be assigned because in businesses, unlike the legal-services industry, there is no fiduciary duty that makes it impossible to sell competing lines of merchandise. In the absence of monopolistic situations, there is no reason to assume that a distributor would unfairly favor its parent's products over other lines, because such action would not be consistent with the main objective of maximizing profit in a competitive market.

Donovan v. Middlebrook (1904)

Facts: Middlebrook employed Toch to sell his real estate in New York City and agreed to give him a commission if he was successful; Toch procured a purchaser with the assistance of Horowitz. In exchange for his help, Toch agreed to pay Horowitz one half of his commission. Horowitz further gave his claim to Donovan who sought to recover from Middlebrook.

Issue: Does the agreement to pay a debt out of a designated fund constitute a valid assignment?

Rule: The agreement to pay a debt out of a designated fund does not operate as an assignment since the assignor retains control over the subject matter.

Seale v. Bates (1961)

Facts: The Seales contracted for 300 hours of dance lessons with Bates Dance Studios. Bates then assigned the contract to Dance Studio of Denver. The Seales continued to take lessons but were very dissatisfied and sought rescission.

Issue: If a party assents to the assignment of a contract, may it later claim that the contract is non-assignable?

Rule: When a party implicitly consents to an assignment, it is in effect a waiver of this possible breach.

Western Oil Sales Corp. v. Bliss & Wetherbee (1927)

Facts: McCamey, Sheerin & Dumis contracted with Western to sell and deliver oil. The contract contained a provision allowing assignment. Western renounced all liability under the contract after assigning all the benefits and obligations to American Oil. Because Western would not recognize its continued liability, McCamey, Sheerin & Dumis refused to continue performance and treated the contract as terminated. They subsequently conveyed all their rights and claims under the contract to Bliss & Wetherbee.

Issue: May a party release itself, by assigning its obligation to another, from liability under a contract without the consent of the other party to the contract?

Rule: When a contract is assignable, a party may assign the benefits and delegate the obligations under the contract, but it remains liable for the proper performance of those obligations unless the other party to the contract consents to the assignment.

Note: By repudiating all liability, Western committed an anticipatory breach enabling the sellers to terminate the contract.

Franklin v. Jordan (1968)

Facts: Ackerman assigned to Franklin an option contract for the exclusive right to purchase a tract of land from Jordan. The contract required that Ackerman sign a note personally promising to pay the balance of the purchase price, due after the initial payment. Franklin sued for specific performance after submitting a promissory note signed only by himself.

Issue: May an option holder assign his obligation to sign a promissory note?

Rule: An option holder in a bilateral contract may assign his rights to receive benefits but not his obligation to make promises when the terms of the agreement prohibit such a delegation.

John Ludwick, Assignee of Jacob Bollinger v. Michael Croll (1799)

Facts: Bollinger claimed the right to 1,152,000 acres of land in Kentucky based upon a pretended survey. He sold the land to Croll and four others and then assigned his right to receive payments to John Ludwick. After realizing he had been swindled, Croll refused to pay John Ludwick.

Issue: May the assignee of a bond collect payment when the obligor, who is responsible for payment, was swindled by the assignor?

Rule: The assignee of a bond takes it at his own peril, subject to every defense that may be used by the obligor against the assignor.

Federal Deposit Insurance Corp. v. Registry Hotel Corp. (1986)

Facts: A bank made a series of loans to Frownfelter Construction. In consideration for the loans, Frownfelter assigned the bank a security interest in a construction contract it had with Registry. Registry accepted the bank as an assignee of the contract. Registry later terminated the contract with Frownfelter, which defaulted on its loans. Registry contracted with another company to do the work, which then subcontracted with Frownfelter. After the bank went into receivership, the FDIC sued Registry.

Issue: Does an assignee of a contract acquire corresponding rights in new contracts that do not closely correspond to the original agreement?

Rule: If the original parties to an assigned contract are not in privity to new contracts made after the breach, the assignee of the original agreement does not acquire corresponding rights in any new contracts undertaken if done so in good faith and in accordance with commercial reasonableness.

Fall River Trust Co. v. B.G. Browdy, Inc. (1964)

Facts: Fall River Trust had an arrangement with a bankrupt company to take assignments of its accounts receivable as security for money advanced. Fall River claimed that Browdy owed it $7,596.93 because of its outstanding account with the bankrupt company. As a defense, Browdy claimed the company owed it at least that amount because of goods the bankrupt company had received from Browdy but never returned.

Issue: If a party has a claim or defense under a contract that has been assigned, may this claim or defense be raised against the assignee?

Rule: A party to the original contract may claim a defense to the rights of an assignee when its claim arises from the contract between itself and the assignor.

First American Commerce Co. v. Washington Mutual Savings Bank (1987)

Facts: First American received a loan from First Security Realty Services, which then assigned its proceeds to Washington Mutual. A portion of the loan was held back pending completion of tenant improvements on a commercial building. Upon completing the improvements, First American requested the release of the withheld funds and was refused by First Security, claiming that its duties under the loan terminated with the assignment to Washington Mutual.

Issue: Does an assignment of benefits by a contracting party also discharge that party's duties under the contract?

Rule: A party retains its duties under a contract unless it substitutes an assignee for itself with a novation. A novation is not created by inference; it must be clear that the parties to the original contract intended to pass responsibility to another by either novation or clear, express language to the same effect.

Old West Enterprises, Inc. v. Reno Escrow Co. (1970)

Facts: Old West received legal services from an attorney. The attorney assigned his rights to payment for the services to Reno in the form of an "account stated" agreement with Old West. Old West disputed the sum it owed to Reno, claiming that the amount stated was excessive.

Issue 1: What is an account stated?

Rule 1: An account stated is an agreement, based upon prior transactions between parties, where the parties agree to a certain sum due from the transactions and a promise is made to pay that sum. Before the sum is agreed upon by both parties, the agreement is an account rendered.

Issue 2: May a party's silence as to objections to the terms of an account rendered serve to create an account stated?

Rule 2: Failure to object to the terms of an account rendered raises only a rebuttable inference that the debtor consents to the account.

Herzog v. Irace (1991)

Facts: Jones told Irace, his attorney, that he was assigning a portion of his proceeds from a pending lawsuit to Dr. Herzog in exchange for medical treatment. Jones directed Irace to pay Herzog directly from the proceeds upon conclusion of the suit. After the lawsuit was settled, Jones told Irace that he had changed his mind and that he would pay Herzog himself. Irace sent the funds to Jones. Jones sent Herzog a check, but Jones' check was returned for insufficient funds. Herzog sued Irace.

Issue 1: May an assignee enforce an assignment against an obligor who has been charged by the assignor with forwarding the assigned fund?

Rule 1: If the assignor notifies an obligor that he is irrevocably assigning his rights in a fund to a third party and directs the obligor to pay that fund directly to the assignee, the obligor thereafter holds the assigned fund in trust for the assignee. If the obligor pays the assigned fund to any party other than the assignee, the assignee may enforce his obligations against the obligor directly.

Issue 2: May a party validly transfer his right to proceeds from pending litigation?

Rule 2: The transfer of a future right to proceeds from pending litigation is a valid and enforceable assignment. The entire future right need not be transferred; a partial assignment is valid.

Julian v. Christopher (1990)

Facts: Julian owned a tavern and restaurant business that was located in a building he rented from Christopher. The lease contained a term prohibiting the tenant from subletting or assigning the property without the consent of the landlord. Julian asked the landlord for permission to sublet an apartment located atop the tavern, but the landlord refused to consent unless the tenants paid additional rent. Nevertheless, Julian sublet the apartment without Christopher's permission. Christopher then sued for repossession of the building.

Issue: Does a clause in a lease stating that the landlord can withhold consent to a sublease or assignment give the landlord the right to withhold consent arbitrarily and unreasonably?

Rule: A landlord cannot withhold his consent arbitrarily or unreasonably if a lease contains a clause providing that the tenant must obtain the landlord's consent in order to assign or sublease.

Note: A landlord may reserve the right to arbitrarily and unreasonably prevent a sublease or assignment by a freely negotiated provision in the lease clearly spelling out his intent.

Klinkoosten v. Mundt (1916)

Facts: Klinkoosten sued Mundt to recover on a $25 promissory note Mundt had given in partial payment for printing machinery. Before the note matured, Mundt had transferred the machinery to a third party who had agreed to execute new notes for the unpaid balance on the machinery. The new notes, however, were never executed.

Issue: What is required to create a valid novation?

Rule: A valid novation requires (1) an express or implied agreement on the part of the creditor to substitute the new debtor in place of the original debtor and (2) an express or implied agreement to release or discharge the original debtor.

Smith, Bell & Hauck, Inc. v. Cullins (1962)

Facts: Plaintiff purchased an insurance agency operated by Cullins' former employer. Plaintiff sought to enforce a prior covenant between Cullins and the former employer that prohibited Cullins from engaging in the insurance business for three years following termination of his employment.

Issue: Is an employee's agreement not to compete assignable?

Rule: A restrictive covenant signed by an employee governs only the relationship between the employee and the employer with whom the covenant was made. Thus, an agreement not to compete with an employer is personal, and is not assignable without the consent of the employee.

Note: Other jurisdictions hold that an employee's covenant not to compete is not personal, but marketable, along with other assets of an employer's business.

Mitchell v. Aldrich (1990)

Facts: Mitchell contracted to buy Comette's herd of cows, but because many of Comette's assets (including the cows) served as security for a mortgage, the approval of Comette's bank was required. The bank sent Aldrich to appraise Comette's cows. Aldrich brought Drew with him. Aldrich told Comette that the bank would never approve Comette's contract with Mitchell and suggested that Comette sell the cows to Drew instead. Comette, believing that Aldrich was acting as the bank's agent, agreed, and sold the cows to Drew. Mitchell sued Aldrich for wrongful interference with contractual relations.

Issue: When may a party be held liable for wrongful interference with contractual relations?

Rule: An interfering party is liable to another party when it knowingly and intentionally intrudes in a contractual relationship with the purpose of disrupting that relationship.

Septembertide Publishing, B.V. v. Stein & Day, Inc. (1989)

Facts: Septembertide, representing the author of a book, agreed to give Stein & Day exclusive licensing rights within the United States in exchange for an advance and two-thirds of all subsequent royalties from sublicensing agreements. Stein & Day subsequently sublicensed the rights to paperback publication to New Library. When Stein & Day failed to pay the required advance, Septembertide sued as a creditor beneficiary for direct payment of amounts due to Stein & Day from New Library. Stein & Day, however, had assigned its rights under the sublicensing agreement to Bookcrafters as security for a loan. Bookcrafters claimed that as Stein & Day's assignee it had priority over Septembertide to the New Library payments.

Issue: Does an assignee have priority over a creditor beneficiary to the proceeds of a contract?

Rule: An assignee "stands in the shoes" of its assignor and takes subject to those liabilities of its assignor that were in existence prior to the assignment. In this case, Stein & Day had already given its rights to two-thirds of the sublicensing income to Septembertide, and therefore only had rights to one-third of the income left to assign to Bookcrafters.

Chemical Bank v. Rinden Professional Ass'n (1985)

Facts: Intertel Co. leased an office phone system to Rinden, which agreed to make monthly payments. Intertel assigned the payment rights to Chemical after Rinden waived all defenses to payment. Rinden stopped payment three years later when the phone system malfunctioned.

Issue: Can a buyer/obligor waive warranty rights against an assignee?
Rule: Under UCC §9-206(1), a waiver of defenses against an assignee, which was made for value, in good faith, and without notice of a claim or defense given to the assignee at the time of waiver, is valid.

Ford Motor Credit Co. v. Morgan (1989)

Facts: Morgan bought a car from a dealer, who assigned the contract to Ford Credit. The assignment stated that Ford Credit was subject to all claims and defenses Morgan could assert against the dealer. Morgan complained of defects and stopped payments on the car and let the insurance lapse. Ford Credit sued Morgan for vandalism damage that could not be reimbursed by the insurance that Morgan had let lapse. Morgan defended by alleging dealer fraud in the sale of the car.
Issue: May an assignee-creditor be liable in damages?
Rule: An assignee-creditor is not liable in damages except in limited cases. Federal Trade Commission regulations require only that a consumer debtor may recover sums paid to the assignee if the thing has not been delivered; these rules do not create a more general remedy.

Seattle-First Nat'l Bank v. Oregon Pacific Industries (1972)

Facts: Buyer Oregon Pacific bought plywood from Seller Centralia Plywood, which assigned the invoice to Assignee Seattle-First. Assignee notified Buyer of the assignment. Buyer refused to pay Assignee because Buyer claimed a right of set-off against Assignee arising out of Seller's failure to fill several of Buyer's orders.
Issue: May the debtor on a claim assigned by a creditor to an assignee assert against the assignee defenses arising out of the debtor's relationship with the creditor/assignor?
Rule: A debtor may not assert defenses against the assignee of a money debt unless they came into being before notice of the assignment occurred. Here, Buyer's claim against Seller for failure to deliver came about after Assignee gave Buyer notice of the assignment.
Note: The court applied UCC §9-318, which changed the law for jurisdictions that permitted debtors to assert such defenses against assignees. (Article 9 of the UCC was revised after this case, effective 2001.)

Bel-Ray Company v. Chemrite (PTY) Ltd.

Facts: Chemrite agreed to distribute Bel-Ray's products in South Africa. Their contracts stated that Chemrite's rights under them were not "assignable" without Bel-Ray's "express prior written consent." Chemrite assigned the contracts to Lubritene, which acquired Chemrite.

Issue: Is a contract's prohibition of assignment of rights under that contract effective?

Rule: Unless the contract provides otherwise, a prohibition of its assignment does not render an assignment ineffective for the assignee, but the assignor may be liable for damages for breach of the agreement not to assign it.

A. C. Associates v. Metropolitan Steel Industries, Inc. (1983)

Facts: Walsh as general contractor agreed to several construction projects for Presbyterian Hospital. Walsh subcontracted metal work to Metropolitan. Walsh defaulted and Presbyterian assigned its contracts to Metropolitan. Metropolitan later sued Presbyterian for work done by Walsh before the assignment.

Issue: Does the assignment of a contract transfer the assignor's existing liabilities under the contract to the assignee?

Rule: Assignment of a contract transfers rights under the contract but not of any liability that might exist to the former contract party that arose prior to the assignment. Thus, the job owner's assignment of the general contract does not transfer any debt of the job owner owing to the former general contractor.

Taylor v. Quality Hyundai, Inc. (1998)

Facts: Taylor bought a car and an extended warranty from a Hyundai dealer. The dealer assigned these contracts to Bank One.

Issue: May an action for violation of the Truth in Lending Act be brought against the assignee of a contract?

Rule: An action under the Truth in Lending Act may be brought against an assignee of a contract if the violation of the Act is apparent on the face of the TILA disclosure statement. The assignee has no duty to inquire under TILA.

Clapp v. Orix Credit Alliance, Inc. (2004)

Facts: Laser Express, a common carrier, bought a highway tractor, giving a promissory note and granting a security interest in the tractor to Orix Credit to secure payment of the price. Laser's agreement with Orix prohibited assignment by Laser of its contract to a third party. It did so, assigning it to Clapp. She made all payments to Orix as called for by the contract until the highway tractor was destroyed in an accident. Clapp notified Orix that she had been assigned the contract, that the tractor was destroyed, and that she was entitled to insurance proceeds above the balance she owed to Orix. Orix paid the excess to Laser. Clapp sued them both.

Issue: Is an anti-assignment clause enforceable against the assignee?

Rule: An anti-assignment clause is not enforceable against an assignee. It may be enforceable against the assignor.

Note: Assignments are dealt with in UCC Article 9. UCC §9-401(2) states that anti-assignment clauses don't prevent assignments from "taking effect."

Owen v. CNA Insurance/Continental Casualty Co. (2001)

Facts: Owen had entered a structured settlement of a personal injury claim. CNA was obligated to make the initial payment and five annual payments thereafter. The settlement agreement included a non-assignment clause, which provided Owen could name a new payee by written notice to CNA and the change would take effect when CNA agreed to it.

Issue: Is a clause that restricts the assignment of structured settlement payments enforceable?

Rule: An agreement not to assign rights to deferred payments under a structured settlement may only be enforced if it is express and if an assignment would materially increase the burden on the debtor obligated to make the payments. Here, the non-assignment clause did not clearly restrict Owen's power to assign her rights to future payments. The state statute here (New Jersey) provides that settlement payments are assignable unless the agreement expressly provides that they are not.

CHAPTER 11

Statute of Frauds

The general rule in contracts is that most oral agreements are valid and enforceable. However, under the Statute of Frauds, which originated in England, certain types of contracts are only enforceable if they are in writing. The main purpose of the Statute is to prevent fraudulent claims by requiring that written evidence of the claims be shown. The Statute of Frauds is only a screening device; a party that has written proof of an agreement does not automatically prevail. Rather, the party must then proceed to prove its case on the merits (i.e., was there a breach? consideration? duress?). Thus, to say that a contract "falls within" the Statute simply means that it will only be enforced if it is in writing, and the plaintiff prevails on the merits. Conversely, a contract that "falls outside" the Statute is one that can be enforced without written documentation if the plaintiff wins on the merits. Moreover, oral contracts that fall within the Statute are enforced on grounds of equity (fairness) in some circumstances.

I. CONTRACTS WITHIN THE STATUTE OF FRAUDS

The following types of contracts fall within the Statute of Frauds:
Mnemonic: **MAD GLO**

A. Contracts Made in Consideration of **M**arriage (Rest. 2d §124)

A promise to give or pay property in exchange for marriage is unenforceable unless written. If no property is involved (e.g., A promises to marry B "in exchange for" B promising to marry A), there is no writing requirement.

B. **A**dministrator or Executor (Rest. 2d §111)

A promise by an administrator or executor of an estate to personally pay the debts of the estate must be in writing to be enforceable.

C. **D**ebt of Another/Suretyship (Rest. 2d §110)

A promise to pay the debts or defaults of another (suretyship agreement) is enforceable only if written. To fall within the Statute a suretyship must have the following elements:

1. Secondary Liability

   The promisor/guarantor must be only secondarily liable for another's debt. **Example:** B tells C to deliver a boat to A. If B intends to pay for the boat in the case that A defaults, then the agreement is a surety and has to be in writing. But if B tells C to charge the purchase price to his account, then there is no suretyship, and an oral promise is enforceable.

2. Promisee's Awareness

   The promisee-creditor must be aware or have reason to know that a suretyship relationship existed between the parties, and the promise must be made to the creditor directly. If the creditor does not know that a suretyship existed, the promises are enforceable, even if they are oral. The reason for this rule is to protect a creditor from being tricked into relying on a party's oral promise, which is actually a surety that requires writing to be enforceable.

3. Novation

   A novation is a promise to pay the debt of a third party that is given in exchange for a promise that the third party will no longer be liable. Novations are outside the Statute of Frauds and are valid if oral.

4. Main-Purpose Rule (Rest. 2d §116)

   In order for a promise of suretyship to fall within the Statute of Frauds, the main purpose of the promisor must have been to benefit the third party whose debts he guarantees. If a promisor acts to further his own interests, such a promise is enforceable even if oral. Usually, the issue of who benefits from the promisor's guarantee can be determined by looking at the consideration that is given in return for it.

D. Sale of **G**oods for More Than $500 (UCC §2-201(a))

   Any contract for the sale of goods (including securities) that is for $500 or more must be in writing. Exceptions: There are sale of goods contracts for $500 or more that are enforceable if unwritten: Mnemonic: **SAG**

1. **S**pecifically Manufactured Goods Not Suitable for Others

   An oral agreement/promise involving unique goods that are specially manufactured is enforceable. (UCC §2-201(3)(a).) Rationale: A seller would not produce these goods if there was no agreement, because there is no market for them.

2. **A**dmission by Party Against Whom Enforcement Is Sought

   If a party admits that an agreement existed, no written memorandum is required. However, the contract is limited to those terms (i.e., quantity) that are admitted. (UCC §2-201(3).)

3. **G**oods Accepted or Paid for by the Buyer

No written evidence is needed with respect to goods that have been paid for or have been received and accepted. (UCC §2-201(3)(c).)

E. Interest in Land (Rest. 2d §125). A contract for the sale or purchase of an interest in land must be in writing to be enforceable.

1. Types of Interests: Mnemonic: **MELT**

a. **M**ortgages

A promise to give a mortgage as security for a loan must be in writing. However, assigning rights of a mortgage is valid if orally done.

b. **E**asements

c. **L**eases

Some states allow oral leases of less than one-year duration.

d. **T**imber

Contracts for sale of timber must be written if buyer will cut wood after title to the land passes to him. Contracts involving minerals, oil, etc., must be in writing if minerals are to be removed.

2. A contract that incidentally involves land (e.g., to build a house or to lend money to buy land) does not fall under this provision.

3. Part Performance

An initially unenforceable oral land contract may become binding if the parties act in reliance upon it.

a. A vendor who conveys land under an oral contract can recover the contract price.

b. A vendee who acts in reliance upon an oral land contract (e.g., improves the land, takes possession, or pays taxes on the land) can have the contract enforced.

F. Performance Takes Longer Than One Year (Rest. 2d §130)

A contract that, by its terms, cannot be performed within one year is unenforceable if it is not written.

1. The one-year period begins to run from the date the contract is formed, not the date set for beginning performance.

2. One-Year Duration

For a contract to fall under this provision of the Statute of Frauds, performance in less than a year must be impossible. This requires more than an expectation that it is highly unlikely that a contract will actually be performed within a year. The basic issue is whether, theoretically, the agreed performance could occur within a year, even if the contract expressly provides a longer duration.

a. Performance vs. Discharge

The fact that a contract could be discharged within a year (by impossibility of performance, death of one of the parties, etc.)

does not mean that the contract is taken out of the one-year provision.

    i. If the contract is prematurely terminated by some event, and its principal purpose has been fulfilled, the performance requirement is met. **Example:** A promises to hire B for the duration of B's life. B could die within a year, so the contract is outside the Statute of Frauds because the main purpose, to hire B for life, has been achieved.

    ii. A premature death will satisfy the performance requirement if the death of a party will not mean that full performance was not rendered. **Example:** A promises to support B, a minor, until B is 18 years old. If B died within a year, A would still be considered to have met his obligation, so the contract is outside the Statute. However, if A hires B to sing in a club for five years, and B dies within a year, his obligation was not met and the contract still falls within the Statute.

  b. Termination

    i. A contract that may not be completed within a year but could be terminated within that time is covered by the Statute and must be written.

    ii. The courts are split as to whether contracts that cannot be performed in one year, but allow either party the right to terminate (so that it could theoretically end within a year), are covered by the Statute of Frauds.

II. ELEMENTS REQUIRED TO SATISFY THE STATUTE OF FRAUDS

  A. A written contract or memorandum must contain the following elements to satisfy the Statute of Frauds (Rest. 2d §131):

    1. Purpose of the contract.

    2. Terms and conditions of the agreement (essential terms).

    3. Parties to the contract.

    4. Consideration.

    5. Signature of the party to be charged. A party's initials or stamped or typed name may also suffice.

  A written memorandum that contains the above elements will satisfy the Statute even if it was not created for that purpose.

  B. UCC §2-201 Requirements

    1. Under the UCC, which applies to sale-of-goods contracts, the requirements of a written memorandum are satisfied if a writing is:

      a. Sufficient to indicate that a contract for sale has been made between the parties, and

      b. Signed by the party against whom enforcement is sought.

2. A writing that omits or erroneously states a term is still valid, but the agreement is only enforceable as to the quantity of goods stated in the memorandum.
3. A memorandum that omits a price term may be enforceable if the parties can introduce collateral evidence as to the agreed-upon price or if the court will imply such a term. (UCC §2-305.)
4. An unsigned, written confirmation of an oral agreement that is sent between merchants will satisfy the Statute if it is received, the party receiving it knows or should know of its contents, and the party does not object to it within ten days. (UCC §2-201(2).)

III. CONTRACTS THAT VIOLATE THE STATUTE OF FRAUDS

A contract that does not satisfy the requirements of the Statute will be either voidable, at the option of the parties, or void, depending on the jurisdiction.

A. If only part of the contract is within the Statute, the entire contract is unenforceable if that part does not satisfy the Statute. This rule does not hold, however, if the portion within the Statute has already been fully performed.

B. Full Performance
   As a general rule, any oral contract that has been fully performed will be enforced. **Example:** A orally promises to work for B for two years and has completed performance. The contract is enforceable. Contracts for the sale of goods are enforceable for the amount of goods that have been accepted or paid for.

C. Alternative Promises
   A party that promises to perform any of several alternative performances, some of which violate the Statute of Frauds, can be bound to perform those that do not.

IV. MODIFICATION AND RESCISSION

A written agreement can be orally rescinded. However, modification of an existing contract will be effective only if it satisfies the requirements of the contract (i.e., if this is a type of contract that has to be written, then the modification must also be written). An invalid oral modification of a contract leaves the original contract in effect without the changes. However, material reliance on an oral modification may make it enforceable to avoid injustice. (Rest. 2d §150.)

V. REMEDIES

A party that has partly performed under a contract that is later invalidated by the Statute of Frauds is entitled to certain remedies.

A. Unjust Enrichment

A party that confers benefits upon another is entitled to restitution for those benefits if the contract is later voided. A plaintiff can recover the market value (as opposed to contract price) of his performance if he can prove it. If the defendant is willing to perform, then there are no restitution damages. Additionally, a party can sometimes recover the value of acts done in reliance upon the contract. **Example:** A moves to New York to fulfill his oral agreement with B. A may be able to recover his moving expenses.

B. Promissory Estoppel

A court will sometimes enforce an "invalid" oral contract on its terms if it was foreseeable that the defendant's conduct would cause the plaintiff to change his position in reliance on the oral contract. Usually, if a defendant has willfully lied by saying that the contract was not subject to the Statute of Frauds or that he would not raise the Statute as an objection, a court will enforce the oral contract. In some cases, if a plaintiff performs his obligations without any fraudulent inducement, a court may enforce the promise so as to avoid injustice. (Rest. 2d §139.)

CASE CLIPS

Boone v. Coe (1913)

Facts: Coe agreed to provide a dwelling for the plaintiffs on the condition that they would move from Kentucky to Texas and cultivate his farm for one year. The agreement violated the Statute of Frauds because it could not be performed within one year from the date of its inception. The plaintiffs sued to recover their traveling expenses.

Issue: Can a party recover the value of expenses incurred in reliance on a contract that is unenforceable under the Statute of Frauds?

Rule: Damages may not be awarded for violation of a contract that is unenforceable under the Statute of Frauds.

Note: Today, such reliance damages would probably be awarded to avoid injustice.

Lawrence v. Anderson (1936)

Facts: After her father was injured in an accident, Anderson orally promised to pay the plaintiff, a doctor who provided emergency care for her father. After the father died, the plaintiff tried unsuccessfully to collect from his estate. He then tried to sue Anderson.

Issue: Is an oral promise to pay for services provided to another enforceable under the Statute of Frauds?

Rule: A promise to pay for services to be provided to a third party makes the promisor a surety. Such an agreement is subject to the Statute of Frauds if it is apparent that the promisee (who provided the services) intended the third party to be the primary debtor and the promisor to be only secondarily liable.

Eastwood v. Kenyon (1840)

Facts: The defendant, for consideration, orally promised to pay the plaintiff's debt to a third party. The defendant refused to pay, claiming the agreement was void as against the Statute of Frauds.

Issue: Does the Statute of Frauds void an oral agreement between a debtor and a party that promised to assume the debtor's debts?

Rule: Promises to pay the debt of a third person are within the Statute of Frauds only if they were made to a creditor. An oral promise made to a debtor, however, is outside the Statute.

Taylor v. Lee (1924)

Facts: Lee orally promised to pay for supplies plaintiff would furnish to a third party during the course of a year (suretyship agreement).

Issue: Does the Statute of Frauds void an oral promise to pay for future goods that will be delivered to a third party?

Rule: The Statute of Frauds does not void an agreement to pay for goods supplied to a third party when credit was granted because of the agreement.

Witschard v. A. Brody & Sons, Inc. (1932)

Facts: Brody orally promised the plaintiff that it would guarantee payment for supplies delivered to a third party if the party defaulted. The plaintiff extended credit to the third party who eventually defaulted. Brody refused to pay, claiming the oral agreement violated the Statute of Frauds.

Issue: Must a promise to pay for the debts of another be written to be enforceable?

Rule: A promise to pay the debts of another must be in writing if the original debtor remains primarily liable (i.e., the promisor only pays in case of default by original debtor).

Colpitts v. L.C. Fisher Co. (1935)

Facts: Fisher, a corporation, was in debt to its creditors and employees, the plaintiffs. It decided to reorganize itself by assigning its assets to its creditors (to prepay that debt). Fisher also orally agreed with its workers that if they forbore from collecting their debt against the old corporation, the reorganized company would employ them and repay the debts of the former corporation to them. Fisher later claimed that its promise to repay the debt of a third party (the former corporation) was void because it was unwritten. The plaintiffs answered that Fisher's main purpose in assuming the debt of the old corporation was to benefit itself by keeping its employees, and thus under the "Main-Purpose" rule, the oral promise was enforceable.

Issue: Is an oral assumption of another's debt enforceable if the promisor's main purpose in making the promise is to further his own interests?

Rule: Under the Main-Purpose rule, a promisor who orally assumes the debt of another for the primary purpose of furthering his own interests is bound to his oral promise, and the Statute of Frauds will not apply.

Note: In this case, the promisor, Fisher, did not act for its own benefit.

Bader v. Hiscox (1919)

Facts: Hiscox's son seduced and impregnated the plaintiff, who brought a civil action for damages and initiated criminal charges against him. Hiscox orally promised to give the plaintiff a tract of land if she dropped the civil action and married his son (a marriage would cause the dismissal of the criminal action). The plaintiff agreed but Hiscox refused to convey the land, claiming that oral promises involving conveyance of land, marriage and assumption of another's debt all violated the Statute of Frauds.

Issue: Can an oral promise, made in consideration of marriage, be enforced if marriage was only incidental to the true purpose of the contract?

Rule: An oral promise given in consideration of marriage does not fall within the Statute of Frauds if the main purpose was not marriage but to escape criminal liability. Furthermore, since the plaintiff had fully performed, Hiscox was estopped from claiming that an oral promise to convey land is void. Finally, Hiscox's obligation was primary and upon his own credit when he acted to dismiss his son's liability for damages from a civil suit.

Doyle v. Dixon (1867)

Facts: The defendant sold his store to the plaintiff and orally promised to refrain from opening another one for five years. The defendant later opened a new store and claimed his promise violated the Statute of Frauds because it could not be performed within one year.

Issue: Is a promise to refrain from competition for five years within the Statute of Frauds?

Rule: An agreement regarding personal services falls outside the Statute of Frauds if it is possible that the agreement would be fully performed if a party died within a year of making the contract.

Note: In the instant case, the promisor's death would not defeat the purpose of the contract, which was to avoid competition.

Harvey v. J.P. Morgan & Co. (1937)

Facts: J.P. Morgan orally promised Harvey a lifetime pension after she sustained injuries while working. J.P. Morgan later reneged, claiming the promise violated the one-year provision of the Statute of Frauds.

Issue: Must a promise of a lifetime pension be in writing to be enforceable?

Rule: A promise of a lifetime pension is outside the Statute of Frauds because the contract could theoretically be completed within a year if the promisee died.

Crabtree v. Elizabeth Arden Sales Corp. (1953)

Facts: Crabtree was hired to work for the Elizabeth Arden cosmetics company. His employment was to last for two years with prearranged pay raises. Although a formal contract was never executed, the terms were listed in several informal writings — welcome memos, payroll change cards and secretary's notes — some of which were signed by Elizabeth Arden.

Issue: Can several writings be used to construct a memorandum that satisfies the Statute of Frauds?

Rule: Several writings can be joined to form a memorandum that satisfies the Statute of Frauds if they all refer to the same transaction or subject matter, are properly signed and describe the terms of the agreement.

Alaska Airlines, Inc. v. Stephenson (1954)

Facts: Stephenson relocated his family after he was promised a written employment contract by Alaska Airlines.

Issue: Can an oral agreement, which is otherwise invalid under the Statute of Frauds, be binding on the theory of estoppel?

Rule: An oral contract that is ordinarily within the Statute of Frauds is valid on the theory of estoppel if the additional factor of a promise to reduce the contract to a writing is present.

North Shore Bottling Co. v. C. Schmidt & Sons, Inc. (1968)

Facts: North Shore orally contracted to be the exclusive distributor of Schmidt's beer in New York "for as long as Schmidt sold beer in the New York metropolitan area." Schmidt later contracted with another distributor and claimed its oral promise was unenforceable because it could not be performed within a year.

Issue: Does an oral contract of indefinite duration violate the Statute of Frauds?

Rule: An agreement that could theoretically terminate within a year does not violate the one-year provision of the Statute of Frauds, even if the parties contemplated a longer duration.

Note: The court reasoned that Schmidt could stop doing business in New York within a year.

Mason v. Anderson (1985)

Facts: By oral agreement, Mason loaned $5,000 to Anderson's decedent, to be repaid in monthly installments of $200. Only $1,100 had been repaid when the borrower died. Mason sued for the remaining amount. Anderson claimed that the loan could not be enforced under the Statute of Frauds because it would have taken over a year to repay.

Issue: Does the Statute of Frauds apply to an agreement that cannot be performed within one year where one party has fully performed?

Rule: Where one party fully performs under an agreement and thereby incurs a detrimental change of position, the one-year provision of the

Statute of Frauds does not prevent that party from proving the existence of a contract by parol evidence.

National Historic Shrines Foundation v. Dali (1967)

Facts: Dali, an artist, orally agreed to paint a picture of the Statue of Liberty during a televised fund raiser and to donate the picture to the Foundation so that it could sell it.

Issue: Is an oral promise to paint and donate a picture worth more than $500 within the Statute of Frauds?

Rule: Painting and donating a picture is not a "sale of goods" and is therefore outside the Statute of Frauds.

Drury v. Young (1882)

Facts: Young orally contracted to buy tomatoes from Drury. Drury later reneged, claiming his promise violated the Statute of Frauds. Young seized Drury's records, in which there was a written memorandum detailing their agreement. The memo was kept in Drury's safe.

Issue: Must a writing that is required by the Statute of Frauds be delivered?

Rule: Delivery is not essential to the validity of a note or memorandum of sale, as long as it is signed by the party to be charged, and other evidence suggests that the party knew of the agreement.

Clark v. Larkin (1952)

Facts: Pursuant to an oral contract, Larkin made a down payment on land he bought from Clark. He wrote the essential terms of the agreement on the back of the check. Larkin later tried to renege, asserting the Statute of Frauds.

Issue: Is the Statute of Frauds satisfied by written notations on the back of a check?

Rule: A check fulfills the writing requirement of the Statute of Frauds if the names of the parties, the terms and conditions of the contract and a description of the property sufficient to render it capable of identification are written on the back.

Azevedo v. Minister (1970)

Facts: Minister orally contracted to sell hay to Azevedo. Minister sent periodic accountings to Azevedo as the hay was delivered that mentioned the quantity of hay bought, among other terms. Azevedo later refused to accept more hay.

Issue: Do periodic accountings that are sent subsequent to an oral agreement to which they refer satisfy the writing requirement of the Statute of Frauds?

Rule: An accounting satisfies the requirement of a writing if the party receiving the accounting of the oral agreement does not object within a reasonable amount of time. (UCC §2-201.)

DF Activities Corp. v. Brown (1988)

Facts: DF asserted and Brown denied that the latter agreed by phone to sell a chair to DF. DF sent a letter of confirmation and a $30,000 check, but Brown returned the letter and the check and wrote that the chair was no longer available. The UCC Statute of Frauds barred the court from hearing the case, unless Brown were to admit in her pleading, testimony or otherwise in court that a contract for sale was made. Brown denied under oath that a contract had been made. DF argued that if it could have deposed Brown, she would have admitted otherwise.

Issue: Is a plaintiff entitled to discovery where a sworn denial by the defendant serves to dismiss the suit under the Statute of Frauds?

Rule: A party in a suit on a contract within the Statute of Frauds may not resist a motion to dismiss, backed by an affidavit that the other party denies the contract was made, by arguing that discovery may prove otherwise. The high unlikelihood that the other party will blurt out an admission in a deposition, since doing so may be an admission of perjury, does not warrant the additional judicial proceedings.

R.S. Bennett & Co. v. Economy Mechanical Indus., Inc. (1979)

Facts: Bennett, a pump supplier, orally reduced the price on its pumps on the condition that if the contractor, Economy, was awarded the job it would buy from Bennett. Economy lowered its bid, using Bennett's lower price and was awarded the job. Economy then bought pumps elsewhere, despite its oral promise.

Issue: Does asserting the Statute of Frauds as a defense preclude recovery on a promissory estoppel theory?

Rule: A successful defense based on the Statute of Frauds does not preclude recovery under promissory estoppel because of the requirement that relief is granted to avoid injustice.

Hopper v. Lennen & Mitchell, Inc. (1944)

Facts: Hopper entered into an oral contract to advertise the products of Lennen & Mitchell for a minimum of 26 weeks and a maximum of five years. The five years consisted of ten equal periods; before the end of each,

Lennen & Mitchell had the option to cancel. Lennen & Mitchell repudiated the contract.

Issue: Does the Statute of Frauds bar enforcement of a contract that may be terminated within one year but that extends for more than one year?

Rule: A contract that may be completed and legally terminated within one year is not rendered unenforceable by the Statute of Frauds.

McIntosh v. Murphy (1970)

Facts: While living in Los Angeles, McIntosh accepted a one-year oral employment contract to be an assistant sales manager at Murphy's car dealership in Hawaii. Two months after accepting the job and relocating, he was fired.

Issue: Is there a remedy for a party who detrimentally relies on an oral contract in violation of the one-year provision of the Statute of Frauds?

Rule: Principles of equity allow a party in detrimental reliance on a promise within the Statute of Frauds to enforce the promise if injustice can be avoided only by enforcement. The court adopted §139 of the Restatement (Second) of Contracts.

Note: A contract falls within the Statute of Frauds if the time from the date of contracting to completion is expected to be greater than one year.

Cohn v. Fisher (1972)

Facts: Fisher wrote a check as a deposit on Cohn's boat stating on the memorandum "Deposit on aux. sloop, D'Arc Wind, full amount $4,650." Unable to have the boat inspected in time, Fisher attempted to postpone the closing date. Cohn refused, sold the boat to someone else at a lower price and sued to recover the difference.

Issue: In order to satisfy the Statute of Frauds, what function must be performed by written evidence of an oral contract for the sale of goods?

Rule: The writing need only afford a basis for believing that the offered oral evidence rests on a real transaction. The writing should state the object of the contract and the quantity term and should be signed by the party to be bound.

Note: Fisher's check satisfied the requirement of a writing. The Statute of Frauds can also be satisfied by the admission of a party bound to the contract or by tender and acceptance of partial payment.

Potter v. Hatter Farms, Inc. (1982)

Facts: After orally contracting with Hatter Farms for the sale of young turkeys, Potter turned down offers from other buyers. Hatter repudiated the contract.

Issue: Is promissory estoppel an exception to the Statute of Frauds?
Rule: If all the elements of promissory estoppel are proven (actual reliance, substantial change in position by the promisee and foreseeability to the promisor), the doctrine bars the assertion of the Statute of Frauds as a defense.

Yarbro v. Neil B. McGinnis Equipment Co. (1966)

Facts: Yarbro made oral promises to pay delinquent payments on a tractor that Russell had purchased from McGinnis. Yarbro had wanted to buy the tractor himself and used it repeatedly after Russell bought it.
Issue: When can oral promises to pay the debt of another (i.e., suretyship) be enforced despite the Statute of Frauds?
Rule: When the "leading object" of the promisor in paying the debt of another is to secure a benefit to himself, his oral promises to pay can be enforced despite the Statute of Frauds' requirement of a writing.

Dienst v. Dienst (1913)

Facts: The husband in a divorce proceeding claimed that his wife made an oral promise to execute a will leaving her estate to him if he should survive her, in exchange for his leaving his employment and moving to her town to marry her.
Issue: Is an oral promise in exchange for agreement to marry enforceable?
Rule: The Statute of Frauds renders void any oral promise made upon consideration of marriage, except the mutual promise to marry.

Shaughnessy v. Eidsmo (1946)

Facts: The Shaughnessys leased a house from Eidsmo for a year with the option to buy it afterwards. At the end of the year, they expressed their intention to buy to which Eidsmo responded positively, stating that he did not have time to execute a contract but that his word was good. One year later they still did not possess the deed, prompting this action for specific performance.
Issue: In order to enforce an oral contract for specific performance of a real property exchange, will partial performance by possession and payments suffice to remove the contract from the Statute of Frauds?
Rule: The acts of taking possession and of making part payment, when they are performed in reliance upon an oral contract so as to be unequivocally referable to a vendor-vendee relationship, are sufficient to remove the contract from the Statute of Frauds without proof of irreparable injury through fraud.

Winternitz v. Summit Hills Joint Venture (1988)

Facts: Winternitz operated a pharmacy under a six-year lease with Summit Hills. Near the end of the lease, Winternitz told Summit Hills that he would like to renew his lease. He also mentioned that he might sell his pharmacy and asked if he would be able to assign the renewed lease. Summit Hills orally agreed to renew the lease and said Winternitz could assign the lease if the new tenant was financially sound. Winternitz found a financially sound tenant who wanted to buy the pharmacy, but Summit Hills refused to renew Winternitz's lease. Summits Hills said it wanted to negotiate a new lease with the buyer on its own.

Issue: Is an oral agreement to renew a lease enforceable under the Statute of Frauds?

Rule: An oral agreement to renew a lease is unenforceable under the Statute of Frauds because a lease conveys an interest in land.

Note: An oral agreement to renew a lease may, however, serve as a basis for a malicious interference with contractual relations claim with respect to a third party.

Bazak International Corp. v. Mast Industries, Inc. (1989)

Facts: Mast offered to sell Bazak certain textiles that Mast was closing out. Bazak agreed to buy the textiles after orally negotiating the terms of the sale. At Mast's request, Bazak faxed five purchase orders outlining the terms of the agreement. None of the purchase orders contained explicit words of confirmation and each of the purchase order forms contained pre-printed language identifying it as "only an offer." Mast received the purchase orders and expressed no objection to any of the terms. However, Mast refused to deliver the textiles.

Issue: Must a writing contain explicit words of confirmation or express references to a prior agreement to satisfy the requirements for confirmatory writings between merchants under UCC §2-201(2)?

Rule: A writing need not contain express references to a prior agreement or explicit words of confirmation to satisfy UCC §2-201(2). A writing satisfies the requirements of the UCC for confirmatory writings between merchants if it affords a basis for believing that it reflects a real transaction between the parties.

Langman v. Alumni Association of the University of Virginia (1994)

Facts: Langman wished to make a gift to the University of Virginia consisting of property she owned. She gave a deed to the Alumni Association, explaining that the property was mortgaged, and providing that the

Association would assume responsibility for the payments of the mortgage. The Association did not sign the deed and made no effort to pay the loan charges. Langman was forced to reimburse the lender for risk of default and she sued the Association to recover the payments. The Association refused to repay Langman, claiming that in the absence of a signed writing, the Statute of Frauds barred enforcement of the mortgage assumption.

Issue: Does the suretyship provision of the Statute of Frauds extend to a mortgage assumption clause?

Rule: A grantee who assumes an existing mortgage is not a surety, because the grantee merely promises the grantor that it will pay the mortgagee, and does not directly promise the mortgagee anything. A mortgage assumption is thus an original undertaking and is not barred from enforcement by the Statute of Frauds.

Monarco v. Lo Greco (1950)

Facts: Lo Greco was orally promised by his mother and stepfather that he would inherit their farm if he remained on the site and managed its operations. He did so and helped raise the value of the farm from about $4,000 to $100,000 over 20 years. However, his stepfather decided to will the farm to a grandson, Monarco. The California Statute of Frauds provided that agreements not to be performed during the life of the promisor are not valid unless written.

Issue: Under the doctrine of promissory estoppel, may a party be estopped from relying upon the defense of the Statute of Frauds?

Rule: A promise that the promisor should reasonably expect to induce action or forbearance on the part of the promisee or a third person, and that does induce the action or forbearance, is enforceable, notwithstanding the Statute of Frauds, if injustice can only be avoided by enforcing the promise.

Chevron U.S.A. Inc. v. Schirmer (1993)

Facts: Schirmer entered into a written option contract with Chevron for the sale of property, but Chevron failed to exercise the option before it expired. Although both parties continued to act as if there was a valid contract, Schirmer refused to convey the property upon Chevron's request. Chevron sued for specific performance of the contract, claiming the written option had been modified, or alternatively, the parties had through their actions entered into a new oral option contract.

Issue 1: May a written option contract be modified after its expiration date?

Rule 1: Exact compliance with an option contract's terms is stringently enforced because an optionor is strictly bound while an optionee may freely accept or reject terms. Therefore, once an option has expired it can no longer be modified.

Issue 2: Does the Statute of Frauds permit a court to uphold an oral option contract for real property for reasons of waiver or part performance?

Rule 2: A party is barred from using a Statute of Frauds defense to defeat an oral option contract if the party admits the specific terms of the alleged contract. Moreover, a party is barred from using a Statute of Frauds defense if the parties conducted business solely in furtherance of the alleged contract. Neither of these two exceptions to the Statute of Frauds was applicable in this case.

Radke v. Brenon (1965)

Facts: Brenon wrote and signed letters to his neighbors offering to sell each an equal share of a parcel of land, naming the price. Radke received one of these letters. When some declined, the size and price of the remaining parcels in the offer were increased, and Radke accepted. Brenon revoked his offer, and Radke sued for specific performance.

Issue: Does the Statute of Frauds permit a letter to serve as a writing sufficient to form a contract?

Rule: A memorandum signed by the seller for the sale of land that names the price satisfies the Statute of Frauds (Minnesota law).

Cloud Corp. v. Hasbro, Inc. (2002)

Facts: Hasbro had a written contract with Cloud, a toy manufacturer, to produce the Wonder World Aquarium. Cloud signed a Hasbro form that obligated Cloud to supply product only as called for by Hasbro's written purchase orders. The parties exchanged various written communications but no new purchase orders. Cloud was able to use the same amount of raw material to produce more toys, and did so, but without authorization in a purchase order. The demand for the Wonder World Aquarium dropped, and Hasbro rejected the toys made in excess of the purchase orders. Cloud sued for breach.

Issue: May informal writings modify a written contract?

Rule: A written contract for the sale of goods for more than $500 may be modified by other informal writings under UCC §§2-201 & 2-209. Under the UCC, such informal writings satisfy the Statute of Frauds. Hasbro also failed to object to production in excess of purchase orders. And Hasbro waived the requirement that modifications be in a formal writing of the parties.

Ehrlich v. Diggs (2001)

Facts: Ehrlich managed the musical group Gravediggaz pursuant to an unwritten contract. Diggs was a member of the group who began to work by himself. Ehrlich alleged that the oral contract with the group gave him the right to commissions on individual work by the group members.
Issue: May an unwritten management contract be enforced?
Rule: The Statute of Frauds requires any contract whose performance must take more than one year to be in writing. If a contract may be terminated at will by either party, it is treated as to be performed within one year and the Statute of Frauds does not block enforcement.
Note: California adopts this rule. New York would apply the Statute of Frauds in such a case, because some of the obligations under the contract, such as the payment of royalties, extend beyond one year.

Satterfield v. Missouri Dental Ass'n (1982)

Facts: Satterfield claimed that Missouri Dental Association made an unwritten promise to continue to employ her until she retired. It did not.
Issue: Is an oral promise of employment until retirement enforceable?
Rule: The Statute of Frauds requires promises not to be performed within one year to be in writing. A promise to continue employment until retirement, and therefore beyond one year, is such a promise. Nor did the employee rely to her detriment on the promise; she simply continued doing the job she was already doing.

Eastern Dental Corp. v. Isaac Masel Co. (1980)

Facts: Manufacturer Eastern alleged a contract by Masel to sell Eastern its requirements of certain products it wanted to resell but not manufacture. The contract was not in writing. Masel made several sales and then stopped.
Issue: Is a requirements contract not in writing enforceable?
Rule: Where the good faith measurement of the buyer's needs for products in a requirements contract exceeds $500, the contract is not enforceable unless in writing under the Statute of Frauds.

Thomson Printing Machinery Co. v. B. F. Goodrich Co. (1983)

Facts: Goodrich as seller and Thomson as buyer agreed orally to the sale of a surplus printer. Thomson sent Goodrich a written memorandum of the transaction, to which Goodrich did not object.
Issue: Is an oral contract to sell goods confirmed by the buyer unenforceable under the Statute of Frauds?

Rule: A merchant who makes an oral contract to sell goods and receives a written confirmation from the buyer and does not object within ten days may not plead the Statute of Frauds as a defense.

Note: This common law merchant exception appears in UCC §2-201(2).

Power Entertainment, Inc. v. Nat'l Football League Properties, Inc. (1998)

Facts: Power Entertainment alleged that NFLP agreed to transfer a license to sell official National Football League cards in return for Power Entertainment's agreement to assume the debt of a third party to the NFLP. The third party was the current licensee that was bankrupt.

Issue: If the secondary purpose of an oral agreement is to pay the debt of another, does the Statute of Frauds block enforcement?

Rule: If the main purpose of an oral agreement is to serve the interest of a promisor and not to pay the debt of another, the Statute of Frauds does not apply. Here, the main purpose of Power Entertainment's agreement with the NFLP was not to pay a third party's debt but to acquire the license that Power Entertainment would receive in return for undertaking to pay the third party's debt.

Johnson Farms v. McEnroe (1997)

Facts: McEnroe orally gave Johnson Farms an option to acquire his farmland, provided McEnroe would receive similar farmland elsewhere in exchange. McEnroe backed out.

Issue: May a court grant specific enforcement of an oral agreement to sell real property if it has been partially performed?

Rule: The Statute of Frauds does not bar the buyer's proof of partial performance consisting of paying the price, taking possession, or making improvements to the real estate.

Buffaloe v. Hart (1994)

Facts: On a handshake, Buffaloe claimed he bought tobacco barns from Hart, paid with a check, and took possession.

Issue: Does the Statute of Frauds prevent enforcement of an oral contract for sale of goods?

Rule: Where Seller delivers and Buyer receives goods, an oral sale is enforceable despite the Statute of Frauds.

Taylor v. State Farm Mutual Automobile Ins. Co. (1993)

Facts: Taylor's automobile insurer was State Farm. After he was in an accident, State Farm paid him $15,000 in uninsured motorist benefits.

His own attorney drafted the release, which settled all "contractual" claims. Others in the accident got verdicts against Taylor for more than the limits of his policy. Taylor sued State Farm for failing in bad faith to settle that case within policy limits.

Issue: Is parol evidence admissible to interpret the meaning of an ambiguity in a release?

Rule: If the release may reasonably be understood as one party asserts, extrinsic evidence, including testimony of a party as to his understanding, is admissible. Thus, the trial court might conclude that the release did not cover the insured's claim of bad faith against the insurer.

Brookside Farms v. Mama Rizzo's, Inc. (1995)

Facts: Buyer Mama Rizzo's agreed to buy its requirements of basil leaves from Brookside in a written contract, which required that any modification of the contract also be in writing. Brookside agreed to remove more of the stem from the leaves if Mama Rizzo's agreed to pay $.50 more per pound: this agreement was not in writing. Mama Rizzo's accepted more shipments under this modified contract and paid for them with a check. The last check bounced.

Issue: Is an oral contract to sell goods enforceable for goods that the buyer has paid for or for goods that have been delivered and accepted by the buyer?

Rule: Receipt and acceptance of goods by the buyer or of their price by the seller is enough to prove the existence of a contract of sale, despite the Statute of Frauds or a no-oral-modification clause.

Note: No-oral-modification clauses were not effective at common law but are effective under UCC §2-209(2).